J

Qualitative Research Methods
in Nursing

Qualitative Research Methods in Nursing

Edited by

Madeleine M. Leininger, R.N., Ph.D., Lh.D., F.A.A.N.

Professor of Nursing and Anthropology
Wayne State University
Detroit, Michigan

Grune & Stratton, Inc.
Harcourt Brace Jovanovich, Publishers

Orlando   New York   San Diego   Boston   London
San Francisco   Tokyo   Sydney   Toronto

Library of Congress Cataloging in Publication Data
Main entry under title:

Qualitative research methods in nursing.

Includes bibliographies and index.
1. Nursing—Research. I. Leininger, Madeleine M.
[DNLM: 1. Nursing. 2. Research—methods—nurses'
instruction. WY 20.5Q15]
RT81.5.Q35   1984   610.73'072   84-9145
ISBN 0-8089-1676-9

Grune & Stratton, Inc.
Orlando, FL 32887

Distributed in the United Kingdom by
Grune & Stratton, Ltd.
24/28 Oval Road, London NW 1

Library of Congress Catalog Number 84-9145
International Standard Book Number 0-8089-1676-9
Printed in the United States of America

85   86   87   10 9 8 7 6 5 4 3 2

Dedication

Because of the tremendous impact of anthropologist James Spradley's work on the intimate knowledge and understanding of people, I dedicate this book to him posthumously. Professor Spradley was my classmate in the Department of Anthropology at the University of Washington, and we shared a common interest in providing fresh breakthroughs from traditional norms in our fields and spearheading new ways of generating knowledge through field research. Spradley was a dynamic and creative ethnographic field worker who was willing to study the unknown yet highly common human lifeways such as those of skid row bums and cocktail waitresses. With similar pioneer zeal, I established the field of transcultural nursing as a new academic field of study and practice, and initiated the systematic study of human care and life patterns to advance nursing knowledge. Realizing the great importance of qualitative research methodologies, we both "dared to be different" and demonstrated the role of qualitative research methods that challenged dependency upon quantitative methodologies.

Today, Spradley's books on methodology are much in use by nurses and other social scientists. It has lead to this book as the next step to advance the use of qualitative methods in nursing research. Thus, this book is dedicated to Spradley in appreciation for his past substantive contributions to field research methods and to prepare readers for this new approach in doing health field research.

This book is also dedicated to graduate nursing students who have been persistent seekers of qualitative research methods.

Contents

Acknowledgments

Any major publication must have stimulation, encouragement, and support from advocates who know what is needed in a field of study or practice. Several nursing colleagues, students, and research associates recognized the need for *Qualitative Research Methods in Nursing* and I acknowledge their active support and interest. The graduate students in transcultural nursing and disillusioned quantitative nurse researchers have been especially encouraging in the completion of this book. They recognized that breaking from traditional norms and practices in nursing requires fortitude and a challenging posture. I accepted such a challenge because there is a critical need for the students and researchers of tomorrow to learn about qualitative research methods in order to know and understand people in an intimate and comprehensive way.

I am most appreciative of and gratefully acknowledge the 18 authors who have contributed to this book. They are outstanding research methodologists who are most knowledgeable about qualitative research methods. They took time from busy schedules to share their expertise and insights so that this comprehensive qualitative research book could become a reality. It was a pleasure to work with them over the several months it took to prepare this book. Their interest, patience, and perceptiveness were much appreciated.

I am thankful for the encouragement and support of the staff of Grune & Stratton. Their continued interest and cooperation have been noteworthy.

I also want to express my appreciation to Julia Fitzgerald, Betty Klink, and Violet Peterson, who assisted with different parts of the manuscript. Their conscientious work is evident in this book.

Finally, I lovingly acknowledge my dear family, who always seem to understand my "busy projects" throughout the years. Their patience and thoughtfulness have always been truly commendable.

Preface

The field of nursing is changing and will continue to change as it becomes a fully recognized profession and discipline. This goal is important, but to achieve it requires some fresh approaches to old problems and new modes of thinking in the field. Most of all, there is a need for exploring and examining new and different types of research and theories to explicate the nature and essential features of nursing.

Some new philosophical and epistemological perspectives are essential to know and understand the sources of nursing knowledge, and to critically examine these sources for an accurate and meaningful portrayal of nursing, especially from a cross-cultural human care viewpoint. Alternative research methods can help nurses to discover the complex holistic, humanistic, and multicultural care dimensions of human thought and action. Even the diversity of ecological and sociocultural contexts in which people are born, live, and die largely awaits our discovery.

Indeed, there is a need to think anew and to keep an open mind for new ways to collect, analyze, and interpret nursing data. The prevailing quantitative type of research used in nursing reflects logical positivism and an emphasis on studying people as reducible and measurable objects independent of historical, cultural, and social contexts. Different philosophies of humankind and different research methods to know the "truths" and nature of humans and their care needs can help challenge the belief that people are mainly statistical figures or data that can be known in finite ways. Indeed, to reduce people and nursing practices to parts, machine-like operations, or sensual empirical data has never been congruent with nursing's traditional values of personalized, intimate, holistic, and human services.

There also prevails a belief that the essential elements of nursing are health, environment, energy, and time. But it is the author's long-standing and firm position that *human care* is the critical and essential element of nursing. Explication and verification of humanistic and scientific components of *care* require quite different research methods and modes of analysis than quantitative methods of data collection and analysis. For to discover the elusive, vague, and still largely unexplored nature of human care necessitates exquisite participant observations, interviews, documentations, and other research skills and techniques mainly associated with qualitative types of research.

This book was prepared to help nurses learn about the nature, purposes, and different kinds of approaches to qualitative research. It is my belief that it is time to use alternative methods of research that can enable nurses and other health research-ers to get close to people, their lifeways, and their human conditions. This refocus should help health researchers to reconsider their present heavy reliance on quanti-tative research as the only true, legitimate, and defensible type of research. Hence, the reader will be exposed in the book to several different kinds of qualitative research methods and modes of analysis that should stimulate further study, interest in, and use of the ideas presented.

Discovering ethnography, ethnonursing, ethnoscience, life histories, world view approach, phenomenology, participant-observation, audiovisual, and many more qualitative types of research that are barely known or used in nursing today can lead to new insights about nursing and health care. Indeed, I predict that data derived from many of these qualitative types of research will revolutionize nursing knowl-edge and research practices. Only time will tell if nurses are willing to systematically develop and use qualitative research methods with the same degree of interest, rigor, and precision they have been giving to quantitative types of research. Nurses are just beginning to discover and value the role, importance, and kinds of qualitative research methods with their potential uses to advance nursing knowledge and clini-cal practices.

This is the first comprehensive qualitative research book developed by and for nurse researchers. However, the book may be used by researchers in other fields, who should also find the ideas and content helpful to them. The book provides a wealth of new ideas, models, and substantive content to help the reader realize the differences between and the consequences of qualitative and quantitative types of research methods. The epistemological and philosophical sources of qualitative research are largely the social sciences and the humanities; however, the clinical and nursing perspectives provide some rich and different ways to study people. Through-out the book, emphasis is given to the importance of the researcher knowing the *what, why,* and *when* of using different types of qualitative research. As nurse research-ers become knowledgeable and skilled in using qualitative research methods, they may cease to feel guilty about relinquishing experimental or quasi-experimental meth-ods for qualitative research. Nurses who understand the differences between the two major types of research and their uses can and should make deliberate choices about these methods. Although the scientific method, with its focus on measurement, control, and objectivity, has a place in knowledge generation and verification, so does qualitative research, which allows the nurse to know and understand people, events, conditions, historical factors, and other human phenomena. These points and the rationale for the methods are emphasized in the book to help the reader become knowledgeable, confident, and competent in using qualitative methods with-out perceiving the method as a second-rate research type.

The purpose of this book is to provide a rationale and a description, with examples, of several qualitative research methods that can be used in nursing and health research. This book can be viewed as essentially a breakthrough in challeng-ing present-day reliance on qualitative methods as the only way to discover, verify, and use nursing knowledge. It reflects a new cultural movement in nursing and other health fields to redress and rethink current dependence upon quantitative research methods for desired purposes and goals. Differences and similiarities between the two types of research are highlighted in several places in the book.

The book contains original articles prepared by qualified nurse researchers who have used or developed qualitative methods over time. The contributors all have a genuine interest in and a deep commitment to qualitative research. My own use of the qualitative method for more than two decades is shared with the reader and reflects some innovative ways to develop, modify, or refine qualitative methods for the study of nursing and health phenomena. The creative work and experiences of the authors in the use of the qualitative method make this book unique and valuable. The conceptual research models, theoretical views, and tools related to qualitative investigations will undoubtedly be useful to both the novice and the experienced qualitative researcher. There are examples of how qualitative research methods may be used alone or in combination, according to the researcher's purposes. The variety of qualitative methods presented in the book—ethnographic, ethnonursing, ethnoscience, life history, historical, phenomenological methods, and a host of others—should encourage the reader to try new ways. The reader will also discover the importance of hermeneutical, subjective, intuitive, inferential, symbolic, and ritual data and their value in explicating nursing and health phenomena. Getting close to people, obtaining information, and grasping their world views, lifestyles, and patterns of behavior will soon become recognized as the unique and distinctive features of futuristic health care research, which is largely derived from the use of qualitative methods. Nurse researchers who have not used qualitative methods often say, "Why wasn't I taught this method earlier? It has helped me to see the informant's world in ways I have never seen by quantitative methods." Other nurses say, "It is a very special and unique privilege to get inside the world of the person one is studying by the use of qualitative methods. It is almost impossible with quantitative methods to get *emic* data."

The first chapters in this book are arranged to help the reader become oriented to the nature, importance of, and differences between qualitative and quantitative research methodologies. The ethnographic and ethnonursing research methods are presented next to offer a broad viewpoint for studying people. These methods are followed by additional methods ranging from simple to complex and different types of qualitative research methods. It must be kept in mind that not all possible qualitative research methods have been presented; rather, those that currently show promise for explicating nursing and health knowledge are most emphasized.

In general, the editor takes the position that qualitative types of research must be given more consideration in the future than today. Qualitative methods have been greatly neglected or devalued in the health field. With greater knowledge and use of qualitative research, it can be predicted that many more nurses and social and health researchers will become attracted to and value these methods. Qualitative methodologies are, indeed, the true and sound way to know the nature of human beings, their lifeways and health conditions.

Contributors

Mary Bailey, R.N., M.S.N. Doctoral Student in Anthropology, University of Michigan, Ann Arbor, Michigan.

Joyceen S. Boyle, R.N., Ph.D. Associate Professor of Nursing, University of Utah, Salt Lake City, Utah.

Michael A. Carter, R.N., D.N.Sc., F.A.A.N. Dean and Professor of Nursing, University of Tennessee, Center for the Heatlh Sciences, Memphis, Tennessee.

Myrna M. Courage, R.N., M.N. Assistant Professor of Nursing, University of Florida, Gainesville, Florida.

Molly C. Dougherty, R.N., Ph.D. Professor of Nursing and Anthropology, University of Florida, Gainesville, Florida.

Veronica Evaneshko, R.N., Ph.D., F.A.A.N. Associate Professor, Arizona State University, Tempe, Arizona.

Delores A. Gaut, R.N., Ph.D. Dean and Professor of Nursing, Seattle University, Seattle, Washington.

Rita A. Kroska, M.P.H., M.S.N., R.N., C.N.M., Ph.D. Distinguished Visiting Sorrell Professor of Nursing, Troy State University, Troy, Alabama.

Marc W. Kruman, Ph.D. Assistant Professor of History, Wayne State University, Detroit, Michigan.

Madeleine M. Leininger, R.N., Ph.D., Lh.D., F.A.A.N. Professor of Nursing and Anthropology, Director of Center for Health Research, Founder and Leader, Transcultural Nursing, Wayne State University, Detroit, Michigan.

Judith Lynch-Sauer, R.N., Ph.D. Assistant Professor, Psychiatric–Mental Health Nursing, University of Michigan, Ann Arbor, Michigan.

Blythe Hudgens Peterson, R.N., M.N. Educator, Scottsdale Memorial Hospital, Scottsdale, Arizona.

Marilyn A. Ray, R.N., Ph.D. Assistant Professor of Nursing, University of Colorado, Denver, Colorado.

Lynne S. Schilling, R.N., Ph.D. Assistant Professor and Chairperson, Pediatric Nursing Program, Yale University School of Nursing, Hartford, Connecticut.

Phyllis Noerager Stern, R.N., D.N.S., F.A.A.N. Professor and Director, School of Nursing, Dalhousie University, Halifax, Nova Scotia, Canada.

Toni Tripp-Reimer, R.N., Ph.D. Associate Professor of Nursing, University of Iowa, Iowa City, Iowa.

Jean Watson, R.N., Ph.D., F.A.A.N. Dean and Professor of Nursing, University of Colorado, Denver, Colorado.

Anna Frances Z. Wenger, R.N., M.S.N. Doctoral Student in Nursing, Wayne State University, Detroit, Michigan.

Qualitative Research Methods
in Nursing

1

Nature, Rationale, and Importance of Qualitative Research Methods in Nursing

Madeleine Leininger

A new cultural movement is occurring in the way humanists and scientists are philosophizing and discovering the nature of knowledge, reality, and human expressions. This movement calls for new ways of conceptualing knowledge and experiences to discover the interrelatedness of diverse phenomena from a broad holistic and changing perspective. Understanding our multicultural world and ways of knowing people in different frames of reference is challenging researchers and calling for new research methods and paradigms.

Capra's recent book helps provide an awareness of this new cultural movement; in addition, it points to the need for a new research approach and conceptual modes to grasp the nature of human phenomena and the universe in which we live. Capra states:

> The new vision of reality we have been talking about is based on awareness of the essential interrelatedness and interdependence of all phenomena—physical, biological, psychological, social, and cultural. It transcends current disciplinary and conceptual boundaries and will be pursued within new institutions. At present there is no well-established framework, either conceptual or institutional, that would accommodate the formulation of the new paradigm, but the outlines of such a framework are already being shaped by many individuals, communities, and networks that are developing new ways of thinking and organizing themselves according to new principles.*

*From Capra, F. *The turning point.* New York: Bantam Books, 1983, p. 265.

This statement clearly challenges scientists and other discoverers of knowledge to develop an interdisciplinary perspective and go beyond past segmented views of phenomena. Discovering the broad holistic life forces influencing human lifeways and realities within different cultural, social, and physical environments is a tremendous challenge that should have far-reaching effects on the study of people. Researchers bound by traditional methods, unidiscipline thought, and narrow conceptualizations of theory will be challenged to pursue creative and different ways to discover human realities and world-wide phenomena.

Until recently, the Western scientific method has been viewed as *the major* and only valid and reliable way to approach knowledge and understand people. This method is now under serious scrutiny and is being questioned as non-Western views of knowledge acquisition become known to Western methodologists. Moreover, the past view that scientific knowledge is the only valid knowledge is clearly being challenged as too narrow and reductionistic. Non-Western philosophical modes of discovering knowledge through a variety of approaches and conceptualizations of reality and truth are beginning to be studied by Western scientists. Even the hard-core physicists are reappraising the scientific method as Capra leads the way with these ideas:

> Scientific theories can never provide a complete and definitive description of reality. They will always be approximations to the true nature of things. To put it bluntly, scientists do not deal with truth; they deal with limited and approximate descriptions of reality. . . . Scientists will not need to be reluctant to adopt a holistic framework, as they often are today, for fear of being unscientific. Modern physics can show them that such a framework is not only scientific but is in agreement with the most advanced scientific theories of physical reality. (Capera, 1983, pp. 48, 49)

This trend toward the discovery of interrelatedness and interdependency in a broad holistic perspective has barely been initiated in medicine and nursing. In these professions, the scientific method prevails as the dominant and desired mode of discovering knowledge. A few nurse researchers have, however, realized the inadequacies and limitations of the scientific method in gaining a better understanding of humans and their health care needs. Most of these nurse researchers have been prepared in anthropology, philosophy, education, and history. They are keenly aware that people are more than a cluster of cells, a body system, or a diagnostic case to be treated or understood from a narrow viewpoint. Nurse anthropologists and nurse philosophers recognize that people are cultural beings with broad and divergent views of life, of living, and of experiencing. Accordingly, health and illness states are embedded in the cultural values, religious views, economic conditions, and social environments of human expressions. Indeed, the real meaning and quality of life, health, and care are best known from a holistic and social structure frame of reference.

For these reasons and others, health researchers must shift to a broad view of understanding human behavior, health, and illness phenomena so that interrelationships of different lifeways can be studied and known. The concept of living and dying within a holistic frame of reference and according to people's beliefs and values is important for developing new research paradigms and theories of health and care. As stated, the scientific method is far too narrow, reductionistic, and controlled to let one know human beings in their totality and help them in times of wellness and illness. Because of this, a cultural movement is slowly taking place in nursing, shifting the focus away from the quantitative research methods and paradigms of the scientific mode to qualitative and other alternative research methods.

This cultural movement could well revolutionize nursing knowledge and practice and provide new directions in nursing. It is possible that some entirely new theories will evolve concerning essential phenomena and components of nursing, such as care, health, contextual environment(s), and illness. It would seem that, on the one hand, the scientific method had yielded only limited substantive knowledge about the nature of nursing. Qualitative research methods, on the other hand, are revealing the broadest conceptualizations of understanding human groups and their care and health needs. Qualitative methods give new hope to the discovery of extremely covert, subtle, and subjective realities and truths about the meaning and expressions of health in individuals both within health institutions and in community settings.

This chapter describes the nature, rationale, and importance of qualitative types of research methods to help nurses conceptualize and use alternative research methods and paradigms to generate nursing knowledge. Contrasts between the qualitative and quantitative types of research are presented, along with their epistemological and philosophical assumptions; these contrasts are offered so that the reader can make informed choices in the conduct of nursing research. This is important as some nurses feel bound to rely on only quantitative types of research methods and the scientific method paradigm. A comparative method perspective is essential to advance nursing knowledge and to become cognizant that different methods can lead to different paradigms and findings. There is also the need to redress the gap in knowledge of qualitative types of research as far too little attention had been given to the use and merits of qualitative types of research in nursing.

Because of past emphasis, assumptions, and trends, some nurses blindly accept and use quantitative research methods as the *sine qua non* for nursing research. The view that quantitative scientific methods are superior and the most legitimate means of discovering nursing phenomena is challenged by the author and others who have used and who value qualitative research methods for discovering insights and meanings about human health conditions and behavior. There is also a growing cadre of graduate nursing students who are eager to learn qualitative research methods and use them in future nursing research. These young nurse researchers find a dearth of courses supporting the use of qualitative research methods in schools of nursing, and few faculty research mentors prepared in qualitative methods.

In general, it is my position that qualitative research methods offer a valuable new and promising alternative means to explain the complex and obscure dimensions of nursing phenomena. As more nurses learn and value qualitative research some of the essential components of nursing, such as care phenomena, will be fully revealed and society will value more than ever nursing's contribution to society and to the world.

GENERAL CONTRASTS BETWEEN QUALITATIVE AND QUANTITATIVE TYPES OF RESEARCH

Over the past three decades, the majority of nurse researchers have been strongly socialized to value and use quantitative types of research as the only legitimate method for "scientific" nursing research. There has been an obvious lack of interest in qualitative methods despite the work of a few nurse researchers who continued to use and support qualitative methods in nursing. Interestingly, nursing students usually get a brief introduction to "descriptive" research, as a broad type of non-scientific research, and it is viewed as "soft' and of limited research value by many faculty. Moreover, research books only tacitly acknowledge the use and value of qualitative types of research, and only a few pages or, at most, one chapter, relating to such methods may be found in current textbooks. Graduate students interested in qualitative types of research are often discouraged from using any qualitative method as a basis for the thesis or doctoral dissertation since "the method will usually not be approved by the faculty." As a consequence, these graduate students have reported that they must use the "numbers method [as they refer to it] as the only research method acceptable to faculty for graduation." But after completion of their graduate program, these students often say they try to find qualitative nurse researchers who are knowledgeable about qualitative methods such as the ethnographic, ethnonursing, phenomenological, and historical methods, in order to pursue their original research interests. Because of such second class views, there are only a few nurse researchers prepared in qualitative research methods. There are approximately 50 research experts prepared today in anthropology, phenomenology, philosophy, and history methods. Accordingly, these qualitative nurse researchers often receive limited support in most schools of nursing and recognition for their research expertise. Thus qualitative nursing research remains limitedly acknowledged and valued in schools of nursing today.

The adequacy of quantitative methods has been questioned, and what constitutes "truth" and accurate interpretations of data relating to people has been challenged by only a small number of nurse researchers. However, it has been difficult to "turn the tide" of thinking because so few nurses have critically examined where qualitative and quantitative methods lead to in knowledge discovery and verification. Current norms of nursing are to follow the "scientific" quantitative method unquestionably.

To get to the characteristics, nature, and essence of nursing knowledge, it is necessary to use qualitative methods, for the epistemological, philosophical, and phenonomological offer rich insights about nursing phenomena. Thus, it is essential to understand the purposes and rationale for the two major research methods in order to discover and know the nature of nursing. To assume that there are no major differences between the methods, or to accept the supremacy of one method over the other in blind conformity to tradition is questionable and may not be in the best interests of advancing nursing knowledge. In-house and public discussions and debates about the values and uses of qualitative and quantitative methods would be enormously helpful to understand and raise questions about the two major types of research. Systematic study of the benefits or virtues of qualitative versus quantitative research methods would be a timely goal for nurse researchers. Without this openness, nursing will fall seriously short in learning about qualitative methods and their role in nursing research. It is also important that nurses become more involved in what philosophers, humanists, and social and physical scientists are saying about the generation of knowledge and of verification modes by qualitative methods. These researchers are actively sharing their thoughts with the public and are openingly reconsidering past trends in research methods. Books and research articles on the qualitative method by several methodologists are opening the door to support and encourage the new cultural movement in qualitative research, among them Cook & Reichardt (1979); Frake (1962); Filstead, (1970); Gaut (1983); Glaser and Strauss (1966); Kalisch & Kalisch (1981); Leininger (1969, 1984); Patton (1980); Pelto (1970); Raggucci (1972); and Van Maanen (1983). Their work and research are turning the tide to help nurses and others reconsider and value qualitative research. With this background in mind, let us turn to some major contrasts and differential characteristics between qualitative and quantitative research methods.

Qualitative Research Methods

The qualitative type of research refers to the methods and techniques of observing, documenting, analyzing and interpreting attributes, patterns, characteristics, and meanings of specific, contextual or gestaltic features of phenomena under study. With this research method, the focus is on identifying the qualitative features, characteristics, or attributes that make the phenomenon what it is. This includes documenting and fully describing the major features of the phenomena such a human events, life situations, experiences, symbols, rituals, and other aspects under study. In the field of nursing research, for example, the researcher is especially directed to document patterns, themes, and attributes of people within particular natural or recurrent life contexts or environments. In addition, the meanings and interpretations of behavior and the use of nonmaterial symbols, rituals, and metaphors are important dimensions of qualitative research methods. Considerable skill is required to identify, document, and validate each aspect of these dimensions.

Essentially, the *goal* of qualitative research is to document and interpret as fully as possible the totality of whatever is being studied in particular contexts from the people's viewpoint or frame of reference. This includes the identification, study, and analysis of subjective and objective data in order to know and understand the internal and external worlds of people. These dimensions of knowing are essential to ascertain quality features of the informant's feelings, views, and patterns of action (or lack of action) and *their* interpretations or explanations. Grasping the essential features of whatever is being studied so that the essence and nature of the person, object, actions, or large domains of study are revealed as of great importance. Attributes and meanings of patterned and nonpatterned behaviors within particular settings can provide qualitative attributes by which phenomenon can be known and understood. In general, qualitative research methods focus on identifying, documenting, and knowing (by interpretation) the world views, values, meanings, beliefs, thoughts, and general characteristics of life events, situations, ceremonies, and specific phenomena under investigation. Verbatim statements, thoughts, and action patterns are studied critically to discover patterns and themes within particular natural life settings. At no time does the qualitative researcher control or manipulate individuals or groups of people for naturalistic and familiar data are valued and sought in order to know people.

Some of the epistemological sources of knowledge, assumptions, premises, and expectations related to qualitative research can be summarized below:

1. The context or natural environment with cultural, physical, social, and historical aspects provides rich and meaningful qualitative data about people.

2. Understanding from the informants how they know their world, life events, and happenings through time and ecological settings is essential to know quality attributes of living, surviving, or dying.

3. *Both* subjective (inward) and objective (outward) life experiences are sources of qualitative knowledge and help reveal the totality of reality, patterns of living, and experiencing.

4. The nature of human beings reflects attributes or characteristics that are generally patterned by themes or gestaltic features, which can generally be identified and understood through the use of qualitative research methods.

5. Language, history, oral and written accounts, religion, philosophy, symbols, myths, and material and nonmaterial goods are but a few of the rich sources by which to gain insight into and understanding of qualitative attributes.

6. People have cognitions that help them to make sense of their world, and the researcher needs to discover and understand these cognitive world views and lifeways of humans.

7. Organizing or ordering data on how people experience their world, live in and relate to others is one essential feature of qualitative research.

8. Discovering the meaning of experiences and the way such experiences are objectively and subjectively interpreted by informants provides rich qualitative sources of data.

9. Entering the individual's world to grasp intimate personalized and firsthand information (primary data) is essential to discover and value humanistic qualitative expressions. (Such an experience should be valued as a privilege and opportunity to know someone, and it carries ethical considerations.)

10. "Contextual stripping" or removing experiences and ideas from situations or environmental sources must be avoided to explicate and preserve features of qualitative research (Mishler, 1979).

11. Substantive qualitative data are derived from the informant's particular lifeways, experiences, situations, and known environmental contexts.

Several of these features and assumptions about qualitative research were discovered, valued, and confirmed by the author with her ethnographic and ethnonursing research of Western and non-Western cultures. For example, the Gadsup people of th Eastern Highlands of New Guinea shared their cognitions and lifeways with me as I actively listened to and observed their unique and very different lifeway in their natural setting. I observed their bathing rituals, their caring for children and the elderly, and their political and social activities. The Gadsup had to interpret their lifeways to me, and I carefully recorded and documented them. Indeed, my nursing and health ways were very different from theirs. I had to enter their world and learn directly from them their interpretations and lifeways. Nor could I have predetermined and controlled selected variables prior to studying the Gadsup people as these variables were not known to me nor other researchers. Qualitative research assumptions guided me to discover these unknown people and their ways. Measurement was not the goal of my study (Leininger, 1978).

Qualitative research is often the initial way to discover phenomenon and to document unknown features of some aspect of people, events, or the life setting of people under study. It is the major research method to discover essences, feelings, attributes, values, meanings, characteristics, and teleological or philosophical aspects of certain individuals or group lifeways. (Pelto, 1970; Spradley, 1979). Grasping the totality of how events, situations, and experiences fit together and form the people's viewpoint and world view is a major feature of qualitative research. Identifying and describing humanistic, holistic, and objective and subjective data require an open mind, attentiveness to details and gestalts, and an ability to discover the actual nature of things and the explanations for (or interpretations) of them. While there are tendencies for the researcher to offer his knowledge of more universal ideas or *etic* knowledge, it is well to hold back on them until the local viewpoints or *emic* knowledge are documented an interpreted by the people. In ethnography and ethnoscience research methods, *etic* refers to the universal or common explanations of behavior, while *emic* refers to the *local* or indigenous interpretations. An *emic* focus is valuable for generating accurate data. Analyzing data as it comes from the people's viewpoint and with detailed and full accounts is essential for qualitative research (Frake, 1962; Garfinkle, 1967; Leininger, 1966, 1969, 1970, 1984). The researcher's goals and theoretical interests are also studied from a qualitative perspective.

Quantitative Research Methods

In contrast, *quantitative research focuses upon the empirical and objective analysis of discrete and preselected variables that have been derived a priori as theoretical statements in order to determine causal and measurable relationships among the variables under study* (Cook & Reichardt, 1979; Filstead, 1970; Patton, 1980; Van Maanen, Dabbs & Faulkner, 1982). Quantitative research is rooted in logical positivism with the goal of generating knowledge that is determinate and empirical with finite relationships between facts and objective reality (Cook & Reichardt, 1979; Morgan & Smircich, 1980).

The quantitative "scientific" method is derived from the natural sciences with the view of controlling and manipulating data; data measured through experimental or quasi-experimental techniques. Quantitative research makes an epistemological assumption that the social world lends itself to objective forms of measurement, and so the researcher tries to determine the causal and lawful relations between the elements to obtain accurate and measurable data abstracted from their life context. Morgan and Smircich (1980) express concern about this practice:

> In manipulating data through sophisticated quantitative approaches, such as multivariate statistical analysis, social scientists are in effect attempting to freeze the social world into structured immobility and to reduce the role of human beings to elements subject to the influence of a more or less deterministic set of forces (p. 498).

This ontological assumption that subjects can be studied selectively and objectively by large-scale empirical surveys or controlled experimental designs poses questions about knowing the full and accurate nature of human beings. This is one of the current issues about the quantitative method. Selecting certain data and stripping the data from their natural context poses questions about the truth and reliability of the findings. Historical changes, contextual information, and the lack of data by which human beings know and interpret ideas in symbolic, metaphoric, or other modes of discourses are usually absent in quantitative types of research.

With quantitative research, the investigator identifies selected variables of interest from an a priori theoretical scheme, and then systematically examines these few variables. There is an assumption of determinism that all phenomena have antecedent events (preceding causes), and natural (random or accidental) events are assumed not to happen (Polit & Hungler, 1978, p. 23). Subjects are generally selected using a randomized and defined procedure. Sampling techniques are followed to minimize intervening variables and to obtain objective, reliable, and valid data. The research design is developed carefully to limit data collection areas and to elicit responses that fit predetermined categories. Carefully controlled experiments and precise measurements of data are generally the major features of quantitative research (Cook & Reichardt, 1979; Patton, 1980) rather than knowing and interpreting data in it's full context.

The purpose of the scientific research is to shed light on causes, determinants, or underlying causal phenomena (Polit & Hungler, 1978, p. 23). The search for objective measurable data is the goal and the researcher must not be influenced by extraneous factors. Measuring data objectively and excluding subjective or personalized facts is important. This scientific method generally includes the use of hypodeductive theories with operationalized statements (hypotheses) to be tested and variables to be manipulated with controls. The data analysis is preplanned, with reliance on deductive logic; standardized instruments that have been pretested are used to examine the variables being tested. Quantitative measures are precise, parsimonious and can be quickly aggregated for computer analysis. Quantitative reports are generally presented with standardized tables and in a succinct and systematic manner.

Returning to qualitative research, this method has largely been derived from the social sciences and humanities, especially philosophy and history. For a long time, anthropology, with its historical and contemporary perspective of human beings and of human nature and its knowledge of evolutionary changes in time, context, and space, has helped to shape qualitative methods (Frake, 1962; Garfinkle, 1967; Malinowski, 1922; Pelto, 1970; and others). The use of anthropological field studies (ethnographies) and an array of ethnomethodological investigations led to development of nature, purpose, and rationale for qualitative methods. During the 18th and 19th centuries, the qualitative method was influenced by German idealists, who challenged Bacon's belief that the world could be understood only through one's senses. The dominant beliefs of the 15th and 16th centuries regarding empirics, realism, reason, and logic to know the world also challenged other modes the thinking. German philosophers put much credence on physical reality and how individuals influenced and created the social world and knowledge. Sharp philosophical and anthropolgical differences between realism and idealism led to qualitative and quantitative dichotomies about the world and ways of knowing and experiencing humans and their world views (Pelto, 1970).

Essentially, qualitative social scientists and philosophers viewed the world as humanistic and preceived the world as dynamic, changing, and evolving with individuals who share diverse lifeways and experiences. In contrast, quantitative philosophers and scientists supported a mechanistic, static conception of the world that could be known by objective knowledge of social and natural phenomena and by the use of logical inquiry, the senses, and similar mechanistic procedures (Sjoberg & Nett, 1966). These two perspectives of the world reveal noticeable differences in conceptual and research methods to study people and things. In the qualitative method emphasis is placed on the importance of accurately knowing, understanding, and interpreting the nature and meanings of past and current events or situations, whereas the quantitative method stresses mechanistic and logical inference to attain objective knowledge and deterministic or causal explanations.

The two philosophical and epistemological lines of inquiry exist today; however, "hard" scientists still hold the view that the scientific method is the only way to discover and verify knowledge. These "hard"scientists tend to view humanistic, subjective, phenomenological, or historical research as "soft." Furthermore, the two methods have often been sex-linked, with qualitative methods reflecting a woman's intuitions, emotions, feelings, and subjective, personalized ways of knowing, and quantitative methods reflecting male ideals of being knowledgeable and definitive about numbers (facts), measurements, and objective reality.

During the past decade, qualitative researchers have stepped forward to challenge the restricted and narrow posture of quantitative researchers and give more credence to the values of qualitative research (Cook & Reichardt, 1979; Leininger, 1978, 1984; Patton, 1980; Reinharz, 1979; Van Maanan, 1982). This shift in emphasis is occurring to give qualitative research importance in research methodologies, in the discovery of truths about people regarding their life experiences and interpretations. Comprehending the totality of human life experiences and understanding people in their familiar and natural life contexts or ecological settings is now gaining interest to health researchers. Comparative historical, phenomenological, ethnographic, symbolic, semantic, subjective, cybernetic and audiovisual methods with specific modes of analysis are some of the new methods of interest to health investigators. What constitutes "scientific," "reliable," and "truthful" valid research is also being questioned. Qualitative researchers believe that there is more to knowing people than what can be seen, sensed, and measured. They believe it is equally important to study and document what people know, experience, and give meaning to, both subjectively (internal reality) and objectively (external reality). Understanding human expressions (including cultural values and beliefs), knowing contextual experiences, and grasping the world view of people open the door to new and more meaningful insights about people.

WESTERN AND NON-WESTERN INFLUENCES ON THE TWO RESEARCH PROTOTYPES

Ontological and telelogical positions or views of human beings from Western and non-Western worlds have had a major impact upon the evolution of the two major types of research. In addition, historical, anthropological, philosophical, and sociological knowledges have influenced ideas about the nature of human beings, world views, and the ways of knowing people. Table 1–1 (developed and used by the author for more than a decade) identifies some major contrasts between Western and non-Western world views that merit consideration to understand qualitative and quantitative types of research (Leininger, 1970). The marked contrasts have influenced research paradigms, and helped change research designs of investigators. Such differences between Western and non-Western world views are related to variations in philosophical, historical, religious, cultural, and social ideologies and processes through time.

All too frequently, nurses and other health researchers are unaware of these philosophical differences in world views that have greatly influenced the use of qualitative or quantitative research methods. Such differences need to be studied in research

Table 1-1 *Contrasts Between Western and Non-Western Philosophical World View Influencing Research Paradigms*

Western Orientation	Non-Western Orientation
1. Focus is on recent human conditions, events, and future developments.	1. Focus is on early historical and prehistorical human conditions or events.
2. Emphasis is on biological, chemical, economical, technological, psychological, and genetic factors to explain human behavior, especially rational thinking modes.	2. Emphasis is on philosophical, historical, epistemological, and esthetical explanations about human behavior. Deal with rational and irrational thought.
3. Use an action and testing focus to "prove" reality and causes.	3. Use a contemplative and reflective focus to know and understand reality or nonreality.
4. Use logical deductions and systematized data base to study and explain phenomena.	4. Use humanistic, cultural, social, experiential, philosophical, historical, and a variety of other means to know and explain circumstances.
5. Focus is primarily on individuals and small groups who are to be studied and explained.	5. Focus is on families, institutions, corporate groups, history, civilizations, and humanistic experiences which are to be explained and understood.
6. Humans are complex, but can be known by a few significant variables of a biophysical, emotional, economical, and social nature. Reduction to uni-causes or a few variables prevails.	6. Human behavior is complex and multifaceted, but it is human conditions, lifeways, and quality of life through time that are important with religion, culture, values, and history providing *multiexplanatory* findings.

Western Orientation	Non-Western Orientation
7. Research largely focused on objective reality to verify phenomena (extrinsic factors important).	7. Research focused on both subjective and objective factors to know the situation or condition (intrinsic factors slightly more important than extrinsic ones).
8. Focus on discrete human behavior, problem solving, and proving reality by testing.	8. Focus on human conditions, symbols, rituals, lifeways, and patterns are important.
9. Emphasis on experimental and quasi-experimental (measurable) research.	9. Emphasis on naturalistic (environmentalist) research.
10. Holds that reality experiences are objective and definable.	10. Focus on spiritualism, magic, healing potential, estheticism, and mysticism to be understood.
11. Time and changes are very important (now and in the near future).	11. Changes within cultural values and within historical, contextual, and environmental factors are important, especially past historical factors.
12. Parts, objects, and selected aspects of life are important. (the "piece-perspective").	12. Totality of life experiences is important (the "wholistic perspective").
13. Objects, things, and relationships are of prime important.	13. Context, people, and historical situations are most important.

and theory courses to help nurses understand the philosophical and epistemological orientation of humans, the nursing profession, and the nurse's own world view of Western and non-Western societies. Without such awareness, the researcher remains blind to his or her own ethnocentric views and to potential problems in planning and conducting research. Hence, Table 1–1 offers essential knowledge to guide researchers to assess and discover his or her own philosophical orientation and to understand comparative research types of world views. Furthermore, I believe that the "degrees of freedom" concept used in research needs to be related to the degrees of freedom in knowing and understanding different philosophical approaches to research typologies.

DIFFERENTIAL FEATURES OF THE TWO RESEARCH PROTOTYPES

Table 1–2 shows some of the major contrasts between qualitative and quantitative types of research. This model has been developed and used by the author for nearly two decades to help graduate students study different research methodologies. Table 1–2 presents some essential attributes, characteristics, and purposes of the two methods along other comparative features. Recently, Cook and Reichardt (1979) and Reinharz (1979) have produced similar contrasts, which support the author's views and research approaches described in this book.

From Table 1–2, it is clear that each type of research method has some noteworthy features that lead to distinct research purposes, paradigms, and outcomes. For example, quantitative studies lead to measurable statistical and objective outcomes that can be generalizable to other populations, but this method usually provides limited information on qualitative features, such as meanings, feelings, characteristics, and subjective data. One student expressed the dilemma by saying: "The number of bones are there [referring to quantitative outcomes] but the flesh is absent [referring to qualitative research]. Qualitative research methods help the researcher to obtain in-depth knowledge of human realities and meanings, participant expressions, relevant contexts, and intrinsic and extrinsic attributes of human experiences. The size of the sample is, of necessity, small because of in-depth study and analysis of data.

The value of in-depth observations, interviews, participant experiences, and the informant's own interpretation or explanation of ideas is a relatively new emphasis in human investigations. Filstead's views about qualitative method and participant experiences are important to state here:

> The qualitative paradigm perceives social life as the shared creativity of the individuals. It is this sharedness which produces a reality to be objective, extant and knowable to all participants in social interaction . . . In this paradigm individuals are conceptualized as active agents in constructing and making sense of realities they encounter rather than responding in a robot-like fashion according to role expectations established by social structures . . . The qualitative paradigm also includes an assumption about the importance of understanding situations from the perspective of the participants in the situation.†

---

†From Filstead, W. J., "Qualitative Methods: A Needed Perspective in Evaluation Research," in T. Cook and C. Reichardt (Eds.) *Qualitative and Quantitative Methods in Evaluation Research,* Vol. 1, Sage Research Progress Series in Evaluation. Beverly Hills, Calif.: Sage Publications, 1979, pp. 35-36, with permission.

Filstead continues to contrast the two paradigms with the following statements:

> More often than not, the researcher in the quantitative paradigm is concerned with discovering, verifying, or identifying causal relationships among concepts that derive from an a priori theoretical scheme. The assignment of subjects is of concern . . . Data is [sic] collected via established procedures such as structured questionnaires and interviews designed to capture subject responses to predetermined questions with established response options. (Filstead, 1979, p. 37)

Unquestionably, qualitative and quantitative types of method serve different purposes and lead to different paradigms to discover knowledge. If the nurse or health researcher is unaware of such differences there can be confusion and questionable outcomes. The researcher should clearly understand the intended purposes of each prototype. At present, there are only a few studies to determine the outcomes when the two methods are used independently. Studies are also being done in which aspects of the two methods are used in combination with and without awareness of the reasons. Questions remain, such as those that follow:

1. In what ways do the two methods (or aspects) complement each other, or increase validity and reliability?
2. Are the criteria for validity and reliability different for each methodological type because the purposes and goals are different?
3. Under what conditions might the two methods be used in a study?
4. Are there greater advantages in keeping the methods and the paradigms separate or "clean" to grasp a more accurate picture of phenomena under study and the outcomes of each method?

Perhaps some entirely new combined research paradigms need to be developed to use the two methods appropriately according to different purposes and goals. Such weighty questions and others need to be carefully examined by nursing and other health researchers.

Qualitative research findings can be of considerable benefit to quantitative studies in that the findings "put the flesh on" and give meaning to statistical or numerical findings. Qualitative data often provide rich clues for new lines of investigation because qualitative researchers tackle obscure, new, and uncharted areas through direct observation, participation, and other methodological approaches. As a consequence, new theories and hypotheses frequently are generated. How often research consumers say, "So what do all these numbers and statistics mean, as 'significant at the .05 level'? Can you tell me the 'real meaning' of these findings?" More and more, consumers using research findings want more than the magic of numbers or to manipulate figures to fit political situations or the interests of the researcher. Consumers want to understand what the data mean in relevant, descriptive, interpreted, and explanatory ways. Many consumers of research findings still tend to distrust the "numbers game," believing that "the researcher can make the findings say whatever the researcher wants them to say." In other words, there is concern that numbers can always be changed and controlled for someone's gain or benefit. Professional research consumers, too, often find it is difficult to determine and conceptualize

Table 1-2 *Contrasts of Qualitative and Quantitative Methodologies*

Domains	Qualitative Methodology	Quantitative Methodology
Definitional focus	*Quality*: Nature, essence, meaning, and attributes (what it is and characteristics); teleological.	*Quantity*: Measurement focus of a thing, object, or subject (how much).
General research focus	Description, documentation, and analysis of patterns, values, essences, world view, meanings, beliefs, and attitudes. Totality of experiences in natural or particular contexts.	Measurement of controlled or manipulated variables by experimental, quasi-experimental, and other controlled methods. Causal and measurable relationships.
Scope	Generally broad, holistic, and comprehensive; world view. Includes more than excludes phenomena to know totality aspects.	Particularist, narrow, and limited focus. Controlled. Excludes more than includes.
Setting	Naturalistic and generally familiar setting where life patterning frequently occurs.	Often unfamiliar laboratory or artificial settings to control and manipulate variables.
Orientation	Process- and phenomena-oriented. Open discovery, exploratory, comparative, expanding, inclusive, and descriptive. Usually inductive and *emic* discovery approach. Local viewpoints emphasized.	Outcome- or product-oriented. Generally a closed, narrowly defined, and restricted approach. Oriented to reduction and manipulation of control variables. Deductively oriented.
Research goal	Development of understandings and meanings of what one sees, hears, experiences, and discovers through a variety of sensual observation-participation modes. Obtain a full and accurate "truth" from people.	Testing hypotheses to obtain measurable outcomes among variables under study. Precision and objective findings.
Relation to people being studied	Frequently direct involvement and participation with people.	Generally noninvolvement, nonparticipation, and detachment from subjects.
Root source of knowledge	Cultural (ethnography), social, environmental, and philosophical phenomena to obtain patterned human interactions, symbols, values, world views, historical and general ethnographic lifeways.	Logical positivism, with use of human senses. Psychological and biophysical facts and causes of things, objects, or behaviors. Empiricism valued.
Data sought	Seek subjective and objective data. Inclusive.	Seek mainly objective data. Exclusive.

Domains	Qualitative Methodology	Quantitative Methodology
Study focus	Participants, informants, role takers, respondents, and people.	Objects, subjects, cases, data banks, code numbers, and figures.
Domains of analysis	Can reformulate and expand focus of study as one proceeds. No predetermined and no *a priori* judgments. Open discovery. Flexible and dynamic. Moves with people, context, situation, or events.	Predetermined. A fixed design. Prejudgments and *a priori* position taken. Rigid and fixed categories. Nondynamic. Fixed and planned sequence of research design to reduce variances.
"Tools" for investigation	The instrument is mainly the researcher. Uses field study tools as observation guides, open-ended interviews, direct participation, documents, open frames, guides, life histories, audiovisual media, biographies, diaries, kingrams, and many other tools.	Questionnaires, surveys, and special tools to control variables, highly structured interviews, and an array of precise tools to elicit precise responses. Computer is a major tool.
Modes of analysis	Content, symbolic, structural, interactional, philosophical, ethnographic, semantic, historical, inferential, perceptual, and reflexive types of analysis. Diverse and creative modes of analysis to fit context and purposes of research. Diverse qualitative approaches.	Various statistical analysis methods. Predetermined data sets. Must use only what has been collected. Regressive, experimental, and survey analysis. Largely computer analyzed. Inputs and outputs.
Validity indicators	"Truth" as known to the people. Understandings, insight, accuracy, confirmation, completeness of information. The people's viewpoints or world view (*emic*) is mainly sought. A few *etic* inferences for truths.	Statistical significance, alpha-beta levels, measurable, "hard" proof and objective measurements. Internal and external measurable validity factors.
Reliability indicators	Recurrent themes, patterns, lifestyles, and behaviors. Historical and time context, single or small group special features. Difficult to replicate due to unique aspects of context in time and space.	Repeated measures, generalizable to other "cases". Data can be generalized or repeated for large groups. Reproducibility.
Problem areas	Large amounts of qualitative data to analyze.	Defined, controlled, and selected quantifiable data to analyze.

causal relationships between independent and dependent variables without qualitative data.

Granted, quantitative researchers may say they have included qualitative data, but often such data are superficial and stripped of meaning, context, and other accurate interpretations. All too frequently, quantitative researchers tend to devalue, cast aside, or use qualitative data inappropriately. Some quantitative researchers do not wish to use any qualitative data for fear they will contaminate and nullify their objective numerical data. In some instances, qualitative data are used to "fill in" or provide bits of interesting information—what I call "featherbedding findings." Gross signs of what Mishler terms "contextual stripping" may also be found (Mishler, 1979). As noted, even when qualitative findings are used in quantitative research it is to a limited extent, and almost invariably the data are viewed as unimportant compared with "scientifically" measurable findings. Thus, misusing of qualitative data and devaluing the method or findings to a secondary or less important role exists.

Most assuredly, quantitative methods and their findings have an important role in the discovery of knowledge, for numerical and statistical data help to verify and establish facts. Quantitative findings have other strengths as well (see Table 1–2), which must be recognized. The purposes and outcomes of each method need to be understood and used to advantage rather than played against each other. It appears that both methods can help in better understanding the vicissitudes of the human condition and other phenomena. Our challenge, therefore, is to redress the past neglect of qualitative methods and to make this method more fully and completely understood so it can be used appropriately. Only then will we be ready to appreciate the comparative benefits of each type of research. Furthermore, the blind conformist position of accepting only quantitative types of research methods as providing "scientific" or "verified truths" must be challenged. There are other alternatives to knowing establishing truths, and qualitative types of research are an important alternative. Of course, it would be folly to go to the other extreme and rely only on qualitative research methods. Knowing both methods can help the nurse researcher be creative and make wise decisions concerning methods and paradigms in accordance with research goals.

At present, quantitative studies receive federal approval and funding, but most qualitative research is of secondary importance because of the absence of statistical data or measurable tools. Quantitative research studies also tend to be funded by nursing organizations, but qualitative studies seldom gain approval. In addition, there are generally no qualitative researcher specialist or well prepared ones on the review teams. Such realities today make it imperative to have qualitative research known, valued, and rewarded in its own right. It is time to rethink our positions and make redress for the blind overdependence on quantitative methods to the serious neglect of qualitative methods.

With this background, it is enlightening to consider more specifically what has happened in the nursing world in the use of the two research methods.

A LOOK AT NURSING WITH THE TWO TYPES OF METHODOLOGIES

Since the mid-1960s, there has been an increase in the number of nurses with master's and doctoral degrees and a concomitant increase in the number of nurses taught to value and use quantitative types of research and statistical methods. The doctoral (Ph.D.) nurse scientist programs of the 1960s and early 1970s prepared a number of nurses who were competent in the use of quantitative methods, but only a few nurse researchers were prepared in-depth to value and use qualitative research methods. By far the majority of nurses in the nurse scientist programs and within doctoral programs in nursing have focused on quantitative skills and research (Leininger, 1976). Those who conducted qualitative doctoral studies were mainly nurses taught to use different qualitative research methods who were mainly enrolled in anthropology, philosophy, and education programs. Only in the last five to seven years have qualitative methods been slowly gaining recognition in nursing.

It is a matter of curiousity why the majority of nurses with doctoral preparation were groomed to value and use largely quantitative methods. Several reasons explain this situation. First, nurse researchers were eager to be recognized as legitimate and respected researchers with other academic scientists, and so the use of quantitative, scientific methods was viewed as a means of achieving that goal. Many nursing facilities followed the hard-nosed scientific approach based on logical positivism as the desired norm and requirement for completing the research doctoral (Ph.D.) program.

Second, the trend toward scientific methods in the 1960s and 1970s and toward use of quantitative research paradigms became clearly apparent as the model for doctoral programs in nursing, but with little thought to the values, purposes, and goals of qualitative research methods. What effect qualitative research could have in developing nursing knowledge was limitedly explored. Most assuredly, nurses enrolled in Ph.D. programs were not only taught to measure outcomes and arrive at objective empirical findings to fulfill doctoral requirements, but to avoid qualitative research as unacceptable and second-rate research. There were few competent qualitative faculty mentors to guide students. As a consequence, most nurses today believe that any respectable and publishable research must reflect the use of tested instruments, statistical formulas, and numerical computer analysis to be completely acceptable and legitimate. In some colleges it is almost a ritual to follow strict quantitative rules of procedure, using statistical and computer analysis of data, without ever questioning whether alternative methods, such as phenomenological, ethnographic, historical, or other methods might have more value in nursing than the quantification approach. In fact, most doctoral students say they feel guilty and afraid they will not survive the program if they use qualitative research methods. Several have experienced that their supervisory doctoral committee did not approve the use of qualitative methods and so they had to return to the use of quantitative methods. Thus, the current dominant ethos remains in doctoral programs to support quantitative methods and modes of analysis as the reliable and only accepted means for doctoral students to get through the system. Qualitative doctoral studies in nursing are indeed rare.

Third, limited value has been placed on qualitative types of nursing research studies for publication during the past two decades. This can be confirmed by an examination of the major nursing research journals in the United States. Occasionally, and with persistence, a few articles may get accepted, especially if some quantitative data are presented in the research analysis. Only in the last few years have a few qualitative studies been published in nursing research journals, and this has been largely due to persistent pressure by qualitative nurse researchers, especially transcultural researchers. Nurse researchers therefore have had only limited exposure to qualitative types of research in nursing journals, and limited encouragement to use such methods. Most of the active qualitative nurse researchers have had to publish their research in non-nursing journals and books which has seriously delayed other nurses to learn about qualitative methods and use findings from these studies.

Fourth, nurse researchers who were trying to gain national recognition and research funds at the federal level, such as at the National Institutes of Health, Institutes of Medicine, and other biomedical institutes, discovered they had to follow the quantitative and largely medical scientific research model and rules of procedure. Still today nurse leaders hold that the only way to obtain federal funding for research projects is to strictly follow the biomedical research model with quantitative proposals and paradigms. In fact, sometimes special grantmanship sessions have been held for nurses so that they follow the grant rules of procedure and norms. Thus the tendency of many nurses to follow without challenging the national funding trend of medical quantitative research studies to obtain grant approval, funds, and national recognition has been clearly evident. The following statement reflects my concern about such ritualistic behaviors and the outcomes:

> With the marked emphasis upon nurses learning how to develop and use different designs, instruments, statistical methods and computer modes of analysis, one must pause to consider whether such research activities are becoming *ends* in themselves, or getting to the "truths" of nursing. Are these activities ritualistic experiences with limited thought about the essence, central focus or goals of nursing knowledge? Are nurse researchers focusing on relevant, important or epistemological features that characterize or lead to a distinct body of knowledge? (Leininger, 1983b, p. 1)

The above reasons explain, in part, some of the dominant reasons for emphasis on quantitative types of research over the past two decades and the tendency to give less attention to qualitative research methods. This trend has led to the lack of creativity in discovering alternative research methods to the scientific method, and especially failure to discover many of the new and emerging qualitative methods that were being developed and used in the 1960s and 1970s. It has also curtailed the discovery of complex, hidden, and essential components of nursing, such as the nature of care, health, world views, and lifestyles in different environmental contexts. Nonetheless, a few qualitative nurse researchers continued their work; among them are Aamadt, Boyle, Byerly, Dougherty, Evaneshko, Gaut, Glittenberg, Horn, P. and B. Kalisch, Kay, Kroska, Leininger, Munhall, Oiler, Osborne, Raggucci, Ray, and Watson. Most of these researchers are nurse anthropolgists with considerable preparation and field experience in conducting qualitative studies. These nurse researchers have been active in explicating, promoting, and advancing the use of qualitative research methods, such as ethnography, ethnonursing, ethnoscience, and phenomenological, historical, philosophical, and audiovisual research methods. Many more qualitative nurse researchers are needed to discover the richness and potential of qualitative methods to discover different paradigms and to arrive at new or different pathways to nursing truths. For today a definitive and substantive knowledge base in nursing still remains ambiguous; but, some important new leads in human care have been discovered. It is hoped that nursing journals, as well as national research review committees, will give more importance and credence to qualitative research studies in the immediate future.

In the meantime, quantitative research methods remain the dominant method to master in graduate nursing programs and few courses are offered in qualitative research methods. The old descriptive-survey methods are often viewed by faculty and students as the "sum and substance" of qualitative research, and only a few hours are devoted to the qualitative method. One of the most common reasons given to students to not use qualitative methods is because of "uncontrolled threats" to validity and reliability, and so most graduate students are not taught to use such qualitative methods such as phenomenology, grounded theory, ethnography, ethnoscience, oral and written life history, and many others. Thus, there has been a critical deficit in nursing research education to help students learn about and value qualitative types of research. Interestingly, qualitative nurse researchers (as well as many students) know that qualitative types of research methods tend to be far more difficult to master, conduct, and analyze than quantitative methods. As several doctoral students have said, "The rules are well prescribed how to collect and analyze quantitative data, but we get very little on how to collect and analyze qualitative research data."

An important question is, How can nursing faculty who have not been prepared in new and different methods of qualitative research learn to use and value them? Faculty workshops and seminars on qualitative methods are much needed in schools of nursing. National and local funds are needed to prepare a cadre of faculty experts in qualitative methods. Writing qualitative research proposals is no easy task when so few faculty reviewers understand the method. Nurse research clinicians must be prepared in qualitative methods and how to use and interpret qualitative research findings. Steps need to be taken soon to remedy such a serious knowledge gaps; if not, there will be another generation of nurses deprived of a method that has rich and promising potential for discovering nursing's true and meaningful knowledge base.

SOME ISSUES RELATED TO QUALITATIVE RESEARCH

As qualitative types of research methods become recognized in nursing, there are several issues and positions which need to be identified. Presently, two positions are being taken among nurse researchers: (1) the *separatist position* and (2) *combination position*. The separatist (or "clean") position is taken by a few nurse researchers who want to be sure that their quantitative or qualitative method is not unduly contaminated by the other method, to achieve their research goals, and so they maintain that the methods should be kept separated. Most quantitative nurse researchers believe that their scientific method is the best and most valid, and so they prefer to pursue a strictly quantitative approach. Some may ask: Why contaminate the data, design, and analysis with "soft" data or nonmeasurable methods? In contrast, some separatists feel that their qualitative method(s) are the best to obtain truly accurate, truthful and meaningful data, and so they want to use a qualitative method. The qualitative separatists are not persuaded that mastering the scientific rules of procedure and using statistical formulas to measure data will ensure arriving at "truth." Thus, both qualitative and quantitative separatists may prefer their own methods and will limitedly tolerate the other method. The quantitative specialist feels strongly about not having too much "soft" data as it weakens the findings and causal relationships. For the true separatists to use both qualitative and quantitative methods is seen as confusing, imprecise, time-consuming, expensive, and not reliable or valid from their respective stances. In actuality, the separatist is often afraid to use the other method because he or she is not well prepared to use that particular method.

Nurse researchers who greatly value the qualitative method and are trying to establish the worth, legitimacy, and importance of this method, are reluctant to have their research contaminated by quantitative methods. They contend the latter is too superficial, reductionistic, and misses relevant contextual data. These researchers believe that quantitative research never does obtain the truth about phenomena because of the impersonal and nonhumanistic instruments used on subjects. This research methodologist wants the informant's viewpoint and to desire to obtain data directly from the informant in his or her natural and familiar setting. She or he knows that it is much easier to put data into the computer and have the data electronically analyzed by numbers than to spend hours analyzing attributes and context data. So, regardless of the amount of time and higher costs, the qualitative method is upheld to obtain in-depth data of a humanistic, thematic, and descriptive nature.

Of course, there are some nurse researchers who take the combination or "appeasement-like" position, and believe they must use both quantitative and qualitative types of research. They may not be clear *why* they are combining the two methods, other than to say, "It feels right," "It is the thing to do," "It just happened to work out that way," or "I want to please everyone." Combining or merging the two methods tends to fit the cultural norms of nursing in that it is best to get along, meet the expectations of others, and treat both methods equally. Again, the *why*, *what* and *how* of combining the methods may not be clear, but some nurses may say in a general way that both methods strengthen validity and reliability. There are also nurses who combine the methods and give little recognition to one method and much emphasis to the other method. Seldom is equal emphasis and treatment given to both methods in the combination position, nor does the analysis show the results or purposes of using both methods. Usually the quantitative method "wins out" and receives the fullest attention, interpretation, and recognition in the data analysis.

Interestingly, there have been no public written or oral stances made by nurses on the separatist or combination positions; however, individuals do take positions, largely silently, within academic settings. Some healthy open discussion would be helpful to bring the differences of the two methods into relief and to provide insights as to the uses, purposes, and rationale for both types of method.

Cook and Reichardt (1979) discuss some of the vexing issues about dichotomization of the two methods, moving from a separatist position to a position of combining the two methods, but finally state:

> ... a researcher need not adhere blindly to one of the polar-extreme paradigms that have been labeled "qualitative" and "quantitative" but can freely choose a mix of attributes from both paradigms so as to best fit the demands of the research problem at hand. There would seem to be, then, no reason to choose between qualitative and quantitative methods either. Evaluators would be wise to use whatever methods are best suited to their research needs, regardless of the methods' traditional affiliation. If that should call for a combination of qualitative and quantitative methods, then so be it.‡

---

‡From Cook, T., & Reichardt C. (eds.). *Qualitative and quantitative methods in evaluation research*, vol 1. Sage Research Progress Series in Evaluation. Beverly Hills, Calif: Sage Publications, 1979, p. 19.

While these authors have focused on the two methods for evaluation research and conclude that "mix and match" are in order, I hold that the researcher needs to be clear *why* he or she is choosing the method, the purposes of the research, and the pardigmatic views that come from each method. The paradigms do come from different epistemological and ontological sources and have different purposes. Rather than "mix and match" for popular or peaceful coexistence reasons, thought needs to be given the question: What are the purposes and reasons for combining or separating the two methods? The reasons should be evident, whatever stance is taken, whether as a separatist or combination researcher. To quickly embrace one method over the other, or to combine methods *without* knowing the reasons seems highly questionable. It is, of course, possible to have sufficient reasons to use the combination approach. The challenge before us in nursing is to study each method more systematically to determine the fundamental distinctions and outcomes of each type and the paradigms which flow from each. Qualitative methods are invaluable to discover new and unknown knowledge to generate theories and hypotheses and to obtain insight into new and different truths largely unknown in the field. Quantitative methods continue to be valuable to verify known variables and measure them precisely.

The stances of American nurses regarding qualitative and quantitative research reflect our American research norms and differ greatly from those of European social scientists. Rosengren portrays this trend succinctly:

> European social science is often portrayed as philosophical, not to say speculative, while American social science is seen as matter-of-fact or empiricist. Europeans are said to be interested in macro phenomena; Americans in micro phenomena. European research is seen as critical or radical; American as apolitical and, therefore, indirectly conservative. (Rosengren, 1981, p. 10)

A cross-cultural world view is useful for nurses in considering the emphases on each type of method and in realizing how much nursing is influenced by societal and cultural trends. For American nursing research fits the matter-of-fact, empiricist and micro phenomena characterization, and cultural norms, and thus differs from European nurse researcher interests (Leininger, 1970). Moreover, in Japan, China, Oceania, and parts of the Middle East, where only a few nurse researchers exist, their cultural orientations are more congruent with qualitative research and non-Western ideology. However, some American nurses are trying to influence these countries to adopt American quantitative research modes. American nurses need to be aware of tendencies in nursing research and education to impose their own cultural values and allow nurses from different cultures to choose methods and paradigms that fit their cultural beliefs and lifestyles (Leininger, 1978). It is to be hoped that not all nurses in the world will follow American research trends unless they choose to do so, and with good reason. Thus, the critical issue is to value and permit different nursing research methods to evolve so that nursing can benefit from the strengths of different methods, paradigms, and outcomes to advance nursing knowledge.

REASONS FOR USING QUALITATIVE METHODS IN NURSING

In this section, some reasons why qualitative research methods can advance discoveries in nursing and confirm nursing knowledge will be given. Some of the potentials and long-range benefits are important to identify.

The use of qualitative research methods shows great potential to explore new areas of knowledge and to gain fresh perspectives about traditional and new views of the nature of nursing. Discovering nursing phenomena in context, and the opportunity to directly clarify, observe, and confirm data through the use of such methods as ethnographic, ethnonursing, and phenomenological approaches can provide rich sources for data. Ethnofield study methods are invaluable to study people in their familiar and natural settings and to study patterns of behavior in context or in people's home environments. Likewise, phenomenological methods are valuable in discovering the meanings of clinical nursing situations and their relationship to nursing practice. As the reader will discover in this book, a great variety of other kinds of qualitative methods are available that have been tapped and studied only to a limited extent for their actual and potential benefits to discover nursing's unique and distinctive knowledge and practice domains.

But there are other reasons why qualitative research methods are so important to nurses.

First, nursing has philosophical, historical, and epistemological beliefs that are deeply rooted in humanistic services to humankind, and these roots can best be discovered by qualitative methods more than by quantitative "scientific" ones.

Second, the central and unique characteristic of nursing is *care,* and to discover what best defines care requires an array of qualitative methods to tease out and grasp its hidden and culturally based values. This requires such methods as mini and maxi ethnographies, oral and written histories, focused observations, participatory activities, and many other methods. Additional study is needed to document and further explore (and also confirm) a large body of undocumented care and health phenomena from different cultural perspectives. Only by detailed observations, documentation, interpretation, and explanations from informants can nurses truly know the meaning and essence of care within health, care, and illness viewpoints. For the future, it is my belief that care will be the distinguishing and meaningful phenomenon for nursing knowledge and to guide nursing practices. (Leininger, 1970, 1978, 1981, 1983b, 1984).

Third, and differing from the current position of the American Nurses' Association (ANA, 1981), it is my belief that nursing is more than "human responses," and that qualitative research methods will help to reveal the nature and attributes of nursing that go beyond human responses. Human responses are but a small facet to explain nursing. Nursing is more than human responses. It must include the human in context with social structure, aspects of physical environment, historical events, and other factors. Patterned values, world views, subjective beliefs, and unspoken life conditions that vary cross-culturally are also important sources of nursing knowledge that go beyond objective human responses or the measurement of such responses. Qualitative methods are essential to identify, document, know, and confirm intangible, subtle, and unknown aspects of humans. Nurses need first-hand knowledge from people to make intelligent professional decisions or actions.

Fourth, nursing is a humane field of study and practice, and this means that humanistic patterns of care and lifestyles must be identified and studied. Qualitative methods such as phenomenology, ethnocaring, ethnonursing, ethnosemantics, life history profiles, and historical and audiovisual media methods are essential means to discover and understand these rich domains of knowledge. Such qualitative methods enable nurse researchers to get intimate knowledge of the lifestyles and patterns of people. Quantitative methods are generally inappropriate for studying humanistic, subjective, and personalized lifestyles.

Fifth, the qualitative historical research method is important to fully reveal nursing's cultural and social heritage. It would be exceedingly difficult to document and understand nursing's history by quantitative methods alone. Qualitative methods are characteristically descriptive, attributional, and dynamic, and they can facilitate the study of people over time and within an open cultural historical perspective. Furthermore, the discovery and documentation of nursing phenomena requires a deliberate, open posture to permit people's views, situations, and historical events to be revealed.

Sixth, qualitative research methods are essential to gain a holistic perspective to nursing phenomena. The full nature of nursing cannot be conceptualized or grasped by testing isolated aspects. Most assuredly, quantitative methods, with emphasis on mechanistic modes to reduce nursing to parts, have serious limitations; with these methods it is impossible to achieve a holistic view of humans and their care needs and expectations by mechanistic modes. In contrast, qualitative types of research support the study of large gestalts, total expressions, and patterns of behavior. Human beings need to be understood from the totality of their lifeways, bearing in mind the dynamic interplay of these lifeways with social, economic, political, religious, and cultural values within historical and meaningful life events. Discovering holistic patterns and themes of nursing phenomena will become the new way to understand people and their caring lifeways and needs.

In general, qualitative types of research are the essential means to know and understand phenomena of nursing. Nursing knowledge must be closely linked to the cultural lifeways, values, and patterns of human groups. To date, only a few nurses who are knowledgeable and skilled phenomenologists, anthropologists, and philosophers are struggling to learn about the meanings, structure, patterns and purposes of diverse cultural lifeways of families and community groups. These nurse researchers are aware of the wealth of valuable data about people—their subjective and objective meanings and values discovered by the use of qualitative methods. They know that documenting and understanding subjective and intuitive states of human beings, are important areas in which to discover "truths" about human care and health maintenance. Some nurses have valued subjective and intuitive data, but have not been familiar with ways to obtain this data. Qualitative research methods and modes of analysis are well suited to elicit such information on subjective, mystical, religious, and philosophical life experiences. Reflective accounts, semantic data analyses, and attentive listening, observing, and participating in recurrent life situations can be discovered by qualitative research methods.

Today, and more than ever before in our multicultural world, health researchers need to identify document cultural care patterns and lifestyles of people for their optimal health and survival in this world. Qualitative studies on cultural care of individuals, families, institutions, and world cultures are much needed. Qualitative research is the primary method to achieve this purpose and to gain new knowledge with which to understand our complex multicultural world. This is a major and new challenge for qualitative nurse researchers and one that will prove very rewarding.

In this chapter, some epistemological, philosophical, and ontological factors related to qualitative and quantitative types of research for nurse researchers are presented. The goal is to encourage nurses to know, understand, and value the importance of qualitative research methods for discovering many still unknown dimensions of nursing phenomena. Blind conformity and overdependence of many nurses today on quantitative research and the scientific method poses some very serious problems for the full development of nursing as a profession and discipline. Studies of meanings, patterns, attributes, symbols, rituals, and social structural features related to care, health, environment, and human lifestyles of different world cultures must await the discovery of the true nature and essence of nursing. It is time to address the critical need for qualitative research knowledge and expertise so that these methods and paradigms can be used in the future. We need to redress the serious lack of opportunities for the present generation of nursing students to learn qualitative research skills. The turning point has been reached for nurses and especially nurse researchers to chart new directions and methods for alternative way to know and understand human beings. More and more, we shall see that qualitative research will become the method of choice to know fully the health, care, and general lifeways of people. Nurse researchers must awaken to the importance of qualitative methods in order to develop a distinct and relevant body of substantive knowledge in nursing.

REFERENCES

Capra, F. *The turning point*. New York: Bantam Books, 1983.

Cook, T., & Reichardt, C. (Eds.) *Qualitative and quantitative methods in evaluation research*. vol 1. Sage Research Progress Series in Evaluation. Beverly Hills, Calif.: Sage Publications, 1979.

Filstead, W. J. (Ed.). *Qualitative methodology*. Chicago: Markham, 1970.

Filsted, W. J. Qualitative Methods: A needed perspective in evaluation research. In T. Cook & C. Reichardt (Eds.). *Qualitative and Quantitative Methods in Evaluation Research*. (Vol. 1). Sage Research Progress Series in Evaluation. Beverly Hills, Calif.: Sage Publications, 1979.

Frake, C. The ethnographic study of cognitive systems. In T. Gladwin & W. H. Sturtevant (Eds.). *Anthropology and human behavior*. The Anthropological Society of Washington. Washington, D.C., 1962.

Garfinkle, H. *Studies in ethnomethodology*. Englewood Cliffs, N.J.: Prentice-Hall, 1967.

Gaut, D. A Philosophic orientation to caring research. In M. Leininger (Ed.), *Care: The essence of nursing and health*. Thorofare, N.J.: Charles B. Slack, 1984.

Glaser, B., & Strauss, A. *The discovery of grounded Theory*. Chicago: Aldine Publication, 1966.

Kalisch, P., & Kalisch, B. When nurses were national heroines: Images of nursing in American film, 1942–1945. *Nursing Forum*, 1981, *20*(1), 15-61.

Leininger, M. Doctoral programs for nurses: Trends, questions and projected plans. *Nursing research*, May–June, 1976, *25* (no. 3), 201–210.

Leininger, M. Creativity and challenges for nurse researchers in this economic recession. *Center for Health Research News* (College of Nursing, Wayne State University, Michigan), *1*(1), January, 1982.

Leininger, M. Qualitative research methods: A new direction to document and discover nursing knowledge. *Center for Health Research News* (College of Nursing, Wayne State University, Michigan), *3*(2), May, 1983.

Leininger, M. *Convergence and divergence of human behavior: An ethnopsychological comparative study of two Gadsup villages in the Eastern Highlands of New Guinea*. Doctoral Dissertation, University of Washington, 1966.

Leininger, M. *Nursing and anthropology: Two worlds to blend*. New York: John Wiley and Sons, 1970.

Leininger, M. Ethnoscience: A new and promising research approach for the health sciences. *Image* (Sigma Theta Tau Magazine), 1969, *3*(1), 2–8.

Leininger, M. *Transcultural nursing: Concepts, theories and practices.* New York: John Wiley & Sons, 1978.

Leininger, M. Becoming aware of types of health practitioners and cultural imposition. Presented during the 48th Convention, American Nurses' Association, Kansas City, Mo., 1973, pp. 9–15

Leininger, M. Caring: A central focus for nursing and health care services. *Nursing and Health Care,* 1980, *1*(3), 135–143, 176.

Leininger, M. *Caring: An essential human need.* Thorofare, N.J.: Charles B. Slack, 1981.

Leininger, M. (Ed.). *Care: The essence of nursing and health.* Thorofare, N.J.: Charles B. Slack, 1984.

Malinowski, B. Field method, in *Agronauts of the Western Pacific.* New York: Dutton, 1961 (originally published in 1922).

Mishler, E: *Meaning in context: Is there any other kind?* Educational Review, 1979, *19*(1), 1–19.

Morgan, G., & Smircich, L. The Case for qualitative research. *Academy of Management Review,* 1980, *5*(4), 491–500.

Patton, M. Qualitative evaluation methods. Beverly Hills, Calif.: Sage Publishing Company, 1980.

Pelto, P. *Anthropological research: The structure of inquiry.* New York: Harper & Row, 1970.

Polit, D., & Hungler, B. *Nursing research: Principles and methods.* Philadelphia, J. B. Lippincott, 1978.

Raggucci, A. T. The ethnographic approach and nursing research. *Nursing Research,* 1972, *21*:485–490.

Reinharz, S. *On becoming a social scientist.* San Francisco, Calif. Jossey-Bass Inc., 1979.

Rosengren, K. E. Advances in Scandinavian content analysis, in *Advance Content Analysis.* Beverly Hills, Calif.: Sage Publications, 1981, p. 10.

Sjoberg, G., & Nett, R. *A methodology for social research.* New York: Harper & Row, 1966.

Spradley, J. *The ethnographic interview.* New York: Holt, Rinehart & Winston, 1979.

Spradley, J. Participant-observation. New York: Holt, Rinehart & Winston, 1980.

Van Maanen, J. *Qualitative methodology.* Beverly Hills, Calif.: Sage Publications, 1983

Van Maanen, J., Dabbs, J., Jr., & Faulkner, R.R. *Varieties of qualitative research.* Beverly Hills, Calif.: Sage Publications, 1982.

2

The Philosophical Dimensions of Qualitative Nursing Science Research

Michael A. Carter

Nursing science research appears to be firmly fixed upon the horns of a dilemma. Substantial efforts by some of the best nursing researchers are being directed toward the development of a firm scientific base for practice, while at the same time other scientists are questioning the appropriateness of the methodologies used to establish this base. Questions have arisen concerning whether quantitative methods are superior to qualitative methods for answering nursing's many and varied questions.

Part of the false dichotomy that exists between quantitative and qualitative methodologies for nursing science research can be attributed to the continued adherence by some nursing scientists to outdated metaparadigms of the philosophy of science. These paradigms can be shown to be consistent with the logical positivist movement that developed in the early part of this century and which attempted to establish *the* method for scientific research (Suppe, 1977; Watson, 1981; Webster et al., 1981). Difficulties with logical positivism as a metaparadigm for scientific endeavor were evident almost from the inception of the movement, because scientists discovered that important questions could not be addressed through the use of this metaparadigm. The same problems that troubled physicists and other scientists early in their attempts to utilize logical positivism as the ideal method for science are continuing to trouble perceptive and questioning nurses involved in research. The critical element in the débate concerning the superiority of quantitative research over qualitative research seems to be whether mathematics is "the" language of science or whether it is only "a" language of science.

The continued development and evolution of the discipline of nursing requires a cadre of theorists and scholars who understand the restraints imposed by continued adherence to outdated methodologies for establishing truth. It is important to understand several of the key points in the evolution of nursing science in order to better understand the reasons why qualitative nursing science research is so fundamental to further development of the discipline of nursing.

EVOLUTION OF QUALITATIVE APPROACHES

What we commonly call the "scientific movement" began in Europe and specifically in Greece (Whitehead, 1925). Although other civilizations, such as those of China, India, and other non-Western societies, have contributed greatly to philosophy, literature, religion, thought, and art, these contributions differed from those of Western, or European, lines of inquiries. The Ionian philosophers provided some of the first evidence of an intense concern for understanding the logical order and organization of nature (Agassi, 1968). In developing the logical philosophy of nature, the Ionians had a keen interest in mathematics and deductive reasoning. Earlier societies had not developed the use of mathematics to the extent to which the early Greeks had. This early marriage of mathematics and scientific development was to be further strengthened over the next several centuries and continues today.

Thales, Parmenides, Democritus, Aristotle, and Archimedes established a world view that nature consists of irreducible parts or atoms (Agassi, 1968). Atoms were seen as the basic "stuff" or substratum of which the world was made. Pythagoras held the view that the substratum was numbers. The aim of science was to discover just how many different types of atoms could be shown to exist in the world. These early scientists focused very little attention on whether or not interrelationships existed between various and different atoms.

The 17th century saw advances in science unequaled in history to that time. Significant additions to the creative genius of scientists were the major advances made in mathematics (Whitehead, 1925). Galileo, Kepler, Descartes, Spinoza, Newton, and Leibniz depended heavily on mathematics in developing their scientific ideas. Algebra was developed at this time and made possible a new understanding of abstraction in mathematics. The mathematical characteristics of abstraction and generality contributed heavily to scientific advances during this period.

New additions to the theory of atomism were made as well. Nature was now viewed as not merely like a machine, but in fact a very large machine. The basic parts of nature, atoms, were linked to each other through a set of orderly, and potentially understandable, relationships. These parts were independent of each other, were irreducible, and were linked together through a set of mathematically derivable laws (Whitehead, 1925). Humans, for example, could be divided into a mind and body as though these were two separate parts of the same whole, and a set of relationships could be expressed to show the interdependencies. Deductive reasoning and precise measurement were critical elements of the accepted scientific methodology.

The 18th and 19th centuries saw additional dramatic advances in science, including the foundation of modern nursing by Florence Nightingale. Most of these advances were built upon the theory of mechanistic atomism, which was reductionistic and used mathematics as its language. Notable is the fact that Nightingale's work did not reflect the prevalent philosophy of science of her time. Although she utilized mathematics in her work, she did not accept mechanistic atomism as the paradigm on which to establish modern nursing. Nightingale called for nurses to develop an in-depth understanding of man and nature as interacting wholes and also to use quantitative data to support and document situations (Nightingale, 1764). Nursing's paradigm, so well established by Nightingale, began to change to a paradigm that developed in the 1930s and that was more rigid than mechanistic atomism. Qualitative methodologies did not fit this new scientific dogma and were, therefore, dismissed as not useful for scientific progression.

THE "RECEIVED VIEW"

In the 20th century, for over 30 years a consensus existed among scientists concerning just what constituted acceptable scientific methodology. This methodology, or *the* scientific method, was useful in advancing fields such as physics and biology. The consensus as to what constituted appropriate methodology in science grew out of the work of the Vienna Circle of the 1930s and is associated with Carnap and others (Suppe, 1977). Their work was sarcastically labeled the "received view," (Putnam, 1962), since only work that conformed to the dogma of this position was acceptable for publication in the respectable journals of science, and only persons who espoused the position could hope to gain employment in respectable universities.

Several positions of the received view continue to be held today as prescriptions for the only acceptable methodology for research. The tenets of the received view were rejected as being unsound, however, by the very individuals who initially proposed them. This rejection was not heard by scientists in disciplines that were not in the mainstream of philosophy of science (Watson, 1981).

Webster and others (1981) have summarized the hallmarks of the original received view. Of these hallmarks, the ones that seem to dictate the superiority of quantitative methodologies over qualitative methodologies are the following:

1. The more mature and developed theories must be capable of being expressed in the language of mathematics and symbolic logic. This means that research whose purpose is to test theories must have the same characteristics of mathematical language and symbolic logic.
2. Theories to be tested by research must also be axiomatized after the model of Euclidean geometry.
3. The physical sciences, especially physics, are basic to the other sciences.
4. Observational terms used in the research process should be distinguished from the theoretical terms or language.
5. The context of discovery is unimportant for the evaluation of the scientific findings.
6. The purpose of science is to predict the occurrence of events by developing and combining descriptive laws with statements of antecedent conditions.
7. Science has nothing to say about value.
8. Science progresses by reducing earlier theories to later theories, and by reducing less basic to more basic sciences.
9. There is a single scientific method.*

---

*Adapted from Webster, G., et al.: Nursing theory and the ghost of the received view. In M. C. McCloskey & H. Grace (Eds.), *current issues in nursing*. Boston: Blackwell Scientific Publications, 1981, pp. 29–30.

The advocates of the received view assumed that matter was primary and that a real, objective world exists independent of the individual perceiver. There was thought to exist one set of objective, universal truths that could be discovered by scientists who searched with sufficient diligence and persistence.

The received view continues to pose a problem for nursing today, but only because some nursing scientists have failed to realize that this dogma no longer holds. There is evidence that the message is being received by some scholars in the field, but remnants of this powerful school of thought still exert control over the acceptance, funding, and publication of the results of nursing research. Work is still evaluated with respect to how well the scientist is able to show congruence between his theoretical and operational terms, how well he follows the scientific method in the design of the study, and how well he understands the use of statistical manipulations of the resulting data for the purpose of producing predictions of future events (Treece & Treece, 1977).

The received view also troubles us with some strange dichotomies. How does one distinguish between objective and subjective? What is the real difference between quantitative and qualitative methods? These troublesome dichotomies can take nursing away from its unique focus upon wholes in our sphere of concern—the person, family, society, health, environment, nature, illness, and so forth. These wholes are understood in a very different way when they are examined through reductionism. This is not to say that reductionism does not yield very useful information; rather, a focus on the whole results in substantially different information than a focus on a part of the whole. There is hope, however, that new methodologies are gaining respectability and acceptance in research. Philosophers such as Thomas Kuhn (1970), Larry Laudan (1977), and W. H. Newton-Smith (1981) propose alternatives to the restrictive positions of the received view, and these alternatives support qualitative research.

Perhaps the most misleading assumption used to support quantitative methods over qualitative methods in nursing science is the notion of prediction. Growing out of the received view and rooted in mechanistic atomism is the idea that quantitative methodologies will ultimately allow the scientist to predict the subsequent occurrence of phenomena. Extensions of this idea include allowances for prescribed actions to produce or control the desired outcomes. While this view has some utility in other sciences, it is far too restrictive as a single focus for nursing science and is particularly flawed when given close scrutiny. In the words of Whitehead, "Nothing ever really recurs in exact detail" (1925, p. 5). True prediction is, therefore, not possible. What is possible is forecasting. Forecasting differs from predicting in that forecasting is the probabilistic estimation of the likelihood that an event will occur, whereas predicting is based upon the mechanistic view that events can be foretold with certainty. Much as a weather forecaster would state the likelihood of rain for tomorrow, the nursing scientist forecasts the occurrence of particular phenomena after close study and sufficient repetition of measurement. Such forecasts carry with them the probability that the event will actually occur. Generally, the farther into the future, as well as the more detailed the forecast, the lower the confidence of the scientist in the forecast.

Forecasts in nursing science cannot be made from results obtained by quantitative research methodologies. The building of a science of nursing, which is predicated on a focus on wholes in the life experience, fundamentally requires qualitative research methods. Research methods based upon reductionism can never capture the elusive qualities of phenomena that nurses know exist. These qualities are more than and different from the sum of the parts and cannot be understood by any attempt to study only the parts.

DIRECTIONS FOR THE FUTURE

The major thrust of nursing research in the last two to three decades was to focus on what nurses do, as they care for their patients. In a developing profession, this focus is not unusual. The methodologies used in these early studies were borrowed, for the most part, from the fields of education and sociology, both of which lie outside the mainstream of science. Researchers in these fields failed to realize that the tenets of the received view were no longer the only acceptable ones for the development of science.

In the next stage in the development of nursing research questions focused on relationships among and between sets of phenomena. The methodologies used at this stage were heavily influenced by the behavioral sciences. Logical analysis and axiom format for theories that directed the research were viewed as mandatory.

The recent rapid proliferation of nursing doctoral programs and centers for nursing science research meant that new directions in research could be explored. There now appears to be a concerted focus among some nursing scientists to understand the rich and subtle characteristics of the basic phenomena with which nursing is concerned. Research focused on increased discernment of nursing phenomena is now viewed as a fundamental activity and one for which only nurse scholars are suitably prepared to undertake. The human experience as it relates to health and illness is the proper field of study for these scholars.

Many scientists in nursing, however, who have been taught the scientific method know that mathematics is merely *a* language, not *the* language of science. They know that there are no real differences between subjective and objective data. Yet these scientists mistakenly believe that unless they cling to the outdated tenets of the received view, they are not true scientists, or at the least they will be viewed with suspicion by other scientists. Encouragement is necessary to assist these researchers in the development of new directions in research using qualitative methods to understand nursing's phenomena. Editoral boards of nursing research journals need members who are supportive of a broader view than exists at present if these scientists are to find a forum for disseminating the results of their efforts. Areas in which a logical positivist methodology is appropriate should be defined and continued, but the weaknesses of this methodology should also be recognized and used with caveats.

The evolution of the discipline of nursing is predicated on adopting more expansive methodologies for discovering truth. Nursing scientists who are willing to take the bold steps of new and different approaches to research will advance nursing's evolution most rapidly and will emerge as the true leaders of the profession. These new, evolutionary approaches will maintain nursing's time-honored focus on wholes in the human experience, while providing greater understanding of the phenomena of specific interest to nurses. Examples of these new approaches include the developing work being done in ethnographic studies and the beginning science base for nursing being developed by theorists such as Leininger (1979), Newman (1979),

Rogers (1970, 1980), Watson (1979), and others. There are, of course, other promising examples, with new ones emerging each year.

Reorienting the masses of nurses to think in new and expansive ways is a task that appears to be matched by no other discipline. These new ways of thinking are not always congruent with the paradigms of other health professionals concerned with care delivery. Nurses have shown themselves capable of meeting the challenging task of evolutionary thinking and of mastering quality research work.

We have not even conceived of the ways in which the human experience of health and illness will change in the years ahead. Reliance upon restricted and outdated methods for answering our questions will not help nursing move rapidly into the future. Qualitative research methods will provide an important component to our evolving science base by helping scholars and clinicians to discover, describe, document, and know those subtle attributes that make people the unique beings that they are, and that reveal the true nature of humankind.

REFERENCES

Agassi, J: *The continuing revolution.* New York: McGraw-Hill Book Company, 1968.

Kuhn, T. S. *The structure of scientific revolutions.* Chicago: University of Chicago Press, 1970.

Laudan, L. *Progress and its problems.* Berkeley: University of California Press, 1977.

Leininger, M. *Transcultural nursing.* New York: Masson Publications, 1979.

Newman, M. *Theory development in nursing.* Philadelphia: F. A. Davis, Co. 1979.

Newton-Smith, W. H. *The rationality of science.* Boston: Routledge and Kegan Paul, 1981.

Nightingale, F. *Notes on nursing: What it is and what it is not.* Philadelphia: J. B. Leppencott, 1964.

Putnam, H. What theories are not. In E. Nagel, P. Suppes, & A. Tarski (Eds.), *Logic, methodology and Philosophy of Science. Proceedings of the 1960 International Congress.* Stanford, Calif: Stanford University Press, 1962, pp. 240–251.

Rogers, M. *An introduction to the theoretical basis of nursing.* Philadelphia: F. A. Davis, 1970.

Rogers, M. Nursing: A science of unitary man. In J. Reihl, & C. Roy (Eds.), *Conceptual models for nursing practice, 2nd ed.* New York: Appleton-Century-Crofts, 1980, pp. 329–337.

Suppe, F. (Ed.): *The structure of scientific theories, 2nd ed.* Urbana: University of Illinois Press, 1977.

Treece, E., & J. Treece, Jr. *Elements of research in nursing.* St. Louis: C. V. Mosby, 1977.

Watson, J. *Nursing: The philosophy and science of caring.* Boston: Little, Brown, & Company, 1979.

Watson, J. Nursing's scientific quest. *Nursing Outlook, 1981, 29*(7), 413–416.

Webster, G. et al. Nursing theory and the ghost of the received view. In M. C. McCloskey, & H. Grace (Eds.), *Current issues in nursing.* Boston: Blackwell Scientific Publications, 1981, pp. 26–35.

Whitehead, A. N. *Science and the modern world.* New York: Free Press, 1925.

3

Ethnography and Ethnonursing: Models and Modes of Qualitative Data Analysis

Madeleine Leininger

Discovering and using new or different research methods to study nursing phenomena is an important challenge today. Several nurse researchers have been active borrowers of research methods and instruments from sociology, psychology, and the physical sciences during the past three decades. Interestingly, until recently they have paid less attention to anthropological, philosophical, and historical research methods. Most importantly, only a handful of nurses have given thought to the creative development and examination of nursing research methods tailored to study nursing phenomena. As nurses recognize that different research methods might provide new insights and facts about nursing situations or events, they may be less dependent upon borrowed research methods. Recurrent, ambiguous, sparse, and questionable research findings are often indications that new or different methods need to be explored.

It is my belief that nurse researchers in this decade will begin to explore such diverse research methods (comparable to different nursing theories) in order to grasp nursing phenomena more precisely or fully. In this chapter, two major research methods will be explored that are known and used only to a limited extent in the field of nursing today, namely, ethnography and ethnonursing. These methods offer some of the greatest hopes for developing substantive, empirical, and abstract nursing data in the field. The methods are designed to obtain basic "raw" data from the client or person(s) under study and to also make abstract deductions from the findings.

The methods are conceptualized from a *macro-range* perspective discovery of knowledge to *middlerange* and *micro-range* research studies. The nature and scope of the research varies with the purposes and goals of the researcher. Such methods help the researcher to conceptualize different types and varying perspectives of research methods to study key nursing questions, domains of inquiry, or problems of special interest to the nurse researcher.

Ethnonursing research is essentially a new method to most nurse researchers; however, the method was developed and has been used by the author and other nurse researchers for several years. Likewise, the ethnographic method is essentially new in nursing, but has been known and used in anthropology for nearly a century. These two types of primarily qualitative research methods are discussed further in other chapters in this book as well as in other sources cited in this book.

A few general statements are in order here to help the reader understand the importance of ethnography and ethnonursing methods for nursing and the health field. Probably the most important reason is to learn that these methods are powerful means of obtain facts, feelings, world views, and other kinds of data that reveal the real world, truths, and lifeways of people. They are methods that enable the researcher to obtain extremely rich and comprehensive data about people, places, symbols, rituals, and patterns. Both ethnonursing and ethnographic methods help the researcher enter the world of the informants to obtain their recurrent and familiar world views, meanings, attitudes, and lifeways. Getting to the "truths" of the *what, why,* and *how* of people's lifeways and the thoughts, feelings, and actions that accompany such living can be discovered by using these methods. Each method relies on focused observations, in-depth interviews, and degrees of participation with the people in their known or natural living environments, or wherever the individuals find themselves. These two methods get to the heart of how people live and experience events over short or longer periods of time. In fact, the researcher using ethnographic and ethnonursing methods can become quite close to the client or people, in their world of wellness, sickness or whatever their state of well-being. Such methods seem most congruent with nursing's desire to discover holistic, total or personalized care modes of people in different environmental settings. In general, the ethnographic and ethnonursing methods appear most promising to discover the real world of people and their health and care lifeways in order to assist people with their health needs, human conditions, and lifeways.

This chapter has two major parts, dealing with discovering ethnographic and ethnonursing research methods (Part I) and describing modes of qualitative data analysis (Part II). The purpose is to provide an overview of ethnographic and ethnonursing methods and the different ways to analyze qualitative types of research data. This chapter also gives a general introduction and provides background for other types of research presented in the book, especially regarding differential modes of data analysis. Because the ethnoscience method has special methodological features, it will be presented in a separate chapter to provide a full description of the nature and methods of ethnoscience.

PART I: DISCOVERING ETHNOGRAPHY AND ETHNONURSING RESEARCH METHODS

"Mini" and "Maxi" Ethnographies

During the past two decades, a new awareness and appreciation for the ethnographic field study has arisen in nursing as some nurse researchers are beginning to learn about the ethnographic method, its purposes and uses through anthropology and transcultural nursing courses. The ethnographic method has been of particular interest to some nurses because of its comprehensive focus and nursing's goal to obtain personalized and total nursing care data. Moreover, the idea of doing "mini" or "maxi" ethnographic studies have appealed to nurse researchers because of their growing interest to undertake clinical institutional and community field studies as types of holistic care. Use of the ethnographic method in nursing has been promoted and used largely by nurse anthropologists the past two decades, but the method is now being recognized by other nurses as a means to understand people of different cultural backgrounds and from time and place perspectives. The trend toward the use of clinical and community field studies, mainly by transcultural nurses, is attracting nurses who want to try new methods to gain fresh insights about old nursing problems.

Ethnography, in the broadest and simplest sense, can be defined as the systematic process of observing, detailing, describing, documenting, and analyzing the lifeways or particular patterns of a culture (or subculture) in order to grasp the lifeways or patterns of the people in their familiar environment.

The author has identified two types of ethnography that are useful for nursing and the health fields, namely, (1) a *mini ethnography* and (2) a *maxi ethnography* (Leininger, 1968–1983 field work). A *mini ethnography* is defined as a *small-scale ethnography focused on a specific or a narrow area of inquiry.* For example, a mini ethnography could focus on health and caring practices of ten Philippine informants* in their home. Alternatively, a mini ethnography would study postpartum care rituals of mothers and their newborn infants in a particular culture. A limited or narrow selective focus is used for a mini ethnography, at the same time giving attention to the general lifeways of the people living in their specific environment.

In contrast, a *maxi ethnography* is defined as a *large and comprehensive study of general and particular features of a designated culture.* For example, the researcher would study caring and health rituals in relation to social structure factors as the political, economic, kinship, religious, and ecological factors of two cultures. The communication modes and material and nonmaterial symbols of health care rituals would represent another maxi study. A maxi ethnography of social structure features of care rituals requires that the researcher have some background knowledge of the people being studied and the meaning of the social structure features. Some basic preparation in ethnography methods in transcultural nursing or anthropology will be of great assistance to complete a maxi research investigation successfully. A mini ethnography does require less cultural knowledge, but this type of study can lead the novice nurse researcher to new kinds of insight. Unquestionably, the most successful and well-executed mini or maxi ethnography studies are performed by researchers prepared through formal courses and under the guidance of an experienced nurse ethnographer. Moreover, the researcher should know how to enter, remain in, and appropriately depart from a community in which an ethnographic study is done (see Chapter 9).

The distinctions between mini and maxi ethnographers help clarify for the researcher the scope and nature of the research and other expectations with each

---

*In qualitative research the persons taking part in the study are referred to as "informants" rather than "subjects" to acknowledge the importance of their contributions and roles in research studies.

type of study. At present, most anthropological literature regarding ethnographies does not differentiate between maxi and mini types of ethnographies. However, this classification is proving most useful to nurses and other health personnel who have less time or more time for conducting ethnonursing or ethnographic studies. The mini ethnography, moreover, is well suited to the goals of several kinds of health care studies; it is also a method of choice for nursing students who have less time for major long term field studies, yet want to experience the richness of entering and studying the real world of people.

The Ethnographic Research Method

Ethnography is an old research method to anthropologists, who have developed and used the method since the early part of this century with the pioneering work of Franz Boas (1920), B. Malinowski (1922), and Margaret Mead (1929). It has been the principal anthropological method to discover unknown facts and lifeways of most people in the world. Without the ethnographic field method, there would be limited knowledge about hundreds of different cultures. Indeed, anthropologists have been the researchers who have developed and extensively used the ethnographic or field study method for more than a century to discover anew (or restudy) the lifeways and material culture of people in the world.

Using the general (or maxi) ethnographic field method, the ethnographer focuses on obtaining the broadest and most detailed view of the lifeways of people of a particular cultural or subcultural group, such as the Afro-Americans, Amish, or Cree Indians. An ethnographer documents, describes, and analyzes physical, cultural, social, and environmental features as these factors influence people's patterns of living.

Ethnographers study how people live in the daytime and at night, and how they communicate and interact with one another. Material and nonmaterial goods are of interest to the ethnographer, as are the folk tales, symbols, rituals, and expressive arts. Social structure features, such as political, religious, kinship, legal, educational, and technological factors are studied to determine how they influence general patterns of living. A general ethnographic study is the principal research means for obtaining a holistic view or total perspective of people in their physical and sociocultural environments. It means studying obscure, unexplained, or known happenings and activities. Identifying, explaining, and being able to predict human lifeways are outcomes of a well-executed, comprehensive maxi or mini ethnography.

Ethnography is an excellent means to capture and understand human lifeways within specific environmental and cultural contexts. Using primarily an inductive method and then speculating about obscure or unexplained facts, the ethnographer is able, in time, to grasp the world view and lifeways of people. It is a challenge to put large and small pieces of lifeways together.

Ethnographies are used to generate both real life (grounded) and abstract theories about people and general phenomena. Ethnographic findings usually generate many new research questions and diverse theories to stimulate researchers for a lifetime. Glaser and Strauss, as sociologists, have recognized the value of ethnographic data as a vital means to develop theories that are "grounded" in empirical data (Glaser and Strauss, 1967). The author believes that "once an ethnographer, no other research methods can satisfy a true researcher interested in people." This statement appears true, as nurse ethnographers and others continue to discover the most ambiguous and mundane human life phenomena. Such researchers value the privilege and excitement to discover new or old human relationships and lifestyles of people. Getting close to people, knowing their intimate secrets, and experiencing how they live their lives brings many satisfactions to both the novice and seasoned ethnographer.

Ethnographic data and findings have multiple uses. The data can be used to get fresh new insights, interpret behavior, or to guide changes in a variety of projects. It is fascinating to see ethnographic data used over-time for comparative historical studies or for current day studies. Conscientious and carefully documented ethnographic field studies can be valuable for many years and the data should be preserved to compare past and present lifeways or human conditions.

Although the ethnographic method and findings remain known only to a limited extent in nursing and among members of health disciplines, the potentials still exist for using ethnographic data to understand care, health, and human ways. For example, Spradley's studies of alcoholic skid row bums (1970), cocktail waitresses' life patterns (1975), and the way the rich and poor live (1972) offer new insights about health needs of people. Indeed, Spradley's writings and those of several transcultural nurses are being used as models of how to undertake sound ethnographic studies and use the research findings in health care changes or policy development. Readers are encouraged to study Spradley's substantive and informative ethnographic works (Spradley, 1970, 1979, 1980). These books and others (Beattie, 1970; Chance, 1966; Hostetler, 1980; Estroff, 1981) provide information on how to do ethnographies and offer rich insights about common and unique life experiences seldom identified, known or documented. The Holt, Rinehart, and Winston publication series of different cultures in the world demonstrate the general ethnographic method, and at the same time provide findings with which to gain different perspectives of human health and cultural life patterns of people. The ethnographic method has been used to study practically all cultures of the world, and many of these classical ethnographies are valuable models for nurse researchers and other health personnel.

To date, the ethnographic method in nursing has been used primarily by nurse anthropologists who have been prepared in anthropology and transcultural graduate nursing programs to use the ethnographic method in their field studies. Some examples of these substantial (maxi) ethnographies to serve as nursing research models can be found in the works by Aamodt (1976), Boyle (1983), Byerley (1968), Dougherty (1978), Glittenberg (1979), Horn (1978), Kendall (1968), Leininger (1966, 1968, 1978, 1984d), Ragucci (1974), Sohier (1981), Tripp-Reimer (1983), and others. These studies and others are identified in the recent reference publication by Leininger (1984).

With the introduction of "mini" ethnographics, nurses have begun to use this method more frequently than the "maxi" general ethnographies because of time factors involved and because their limited knowledge and experience preclude a "maxi" ethnography. Some examples of "mini" ethnographies by nurses are the following: (1) study of Amish child care practices; (2) study of street drug problems of the adolescent in a particular community; (3) study of caring and health practices of a hospital unit; (4) study of specific Soviet immigrant health care problems; and (5) documentation of health care practices of five Vietnamese families in a rural community. Each of these mini ethnographies has limited scope and includes a partial study and analysis of social structure, world view values, and environmental factors;

whereas a maxi study is a full scale study of these dimensions. Mini ethnographies are predicted to gain in value and use in nursing research in the near future.

Comparison of Ethnonursing Methods

Turning to the relatively new method of ethnonursing, there are slight differences from a general ethnography in purposes and uses. The author, as the founder and major leader of the transcultural nursing field, developed the ethnonursing method in the mid-1960s. Since then, the method has been used to study explicit nursing phenomena from a cross-cultural perspective. I have defined *ethnonursing as the study and analysis of the local or indigenous people's viewpoints, beliefs, and practices about nursing care phenomena and processes of designated cultures* (Leininger, 1978, p. 15). While this method is derived from the general ethnographic method, the formulation and focus is different in that the goal is to discover new nursing knowledge as perceived or experienced by nurses and consumers of nursing and health services. (Consumers are viewed as actual or potential users of nursing services.)

Ethnonursing methods show some similarities to ethnoscience method; however, there are differences in that *emic* and *etic* data are studied together in ethnonursing, with primary focus on the implications for nursing. Moreover, *ethnoscience* is a specific and rigorous classification method which is only partially used in ethnonursing method. Not all nursing data can be systematically classified with the ethnonursing method, but all such data would be classified in an ethnoscience study.

In general, ethnonursing and ethnoscience are different and should not be construed as the same method. A separate chapter is devoted to ethnoscience in this book, but a definition can be cited here to show differences with ethnonursing. *Ethnoscience refers to a rigorous and systematic way of studying and classifying emic (local or inside) data of a cultural group's own perceptions, knowledge, and language in terms of how people perceive and interpret their universe* (Leininger, 1970, pp. 168–169). Ethnoscience has become a highly systematic mode of eliciting, documenting, and classifying the informant's data in order to grasp the person's "inside views" about a specific phenomenon under study. (Further descriptions of the ethnoscience method are found in Chapter 15). In contrast, *ethnonursing* has been *conceptualized*, developed and used as a *specific research method focused primarily on documenting, describing, and explaining nursing phenomena*. Ethnonursing is the search for the obscure, elusive, or obvious phenomena of nursing related particularly to care, health, prevention of illness, and recovery from illness or injury. Thus, ethnonursing is viewed as a special nursing method to explicate and document specific nursing care data from the clients, nurses, or nursing or health situations. The focus and purposes are specific to document personalized, interactional, and environmental care meanings and attributes, which may not require formal linguistic classification of all data as noted in ethnoscience studies.

In considering further the ethnonursing method, both *emic* and *etic* data are used to obtain *inside* and *outside* knowledge about nursing phenomena. *The emic dimension of knowledge refers to the local or indigenous cognitions and perceptions about a particular phenomenon, such as caring and nursing care;* whereas the *etic dimension of knowledge refers to the more universal or outside knowledge related to care phenomenon under study* (Leininger, 1978, p. 15). For example, Southern rural Afro-Americans' *emic* view of care was expressed as *concern for my "brothers and sisters,"* whereas the *etic* view refers to "all strangers who care for strangers." With the ethnonursing method, *emic* care knowledge is sought from informants by what they say verbally, how they explain events or interpret their meaning, and the action modalities. Other observational, in-depth interview and participatory experiences are incorporated into ethnonursing studies. Selected features of social structure, world view themes, and environmental factors are also included in ethnonursing studies. As already noted, whereas the steps of discovery are similar to those in a general ethnography, the goals, purposes, scope of investigation, and research strategies differ.

General Indications for Ethnography and Ethnonursing Methods

There are several reasons for use of ethnography and ethnonursing research methods.

First, both methods are used when there is *virtually no knowledge or very limited knowledge about a phenomenon.* When one attempts to discover *what* is happening, *how* it is happening, and the *meaning* or *interpretation* of what is happening, ethnography and ethnonursing methodologies are most valuable. They are initial detection methods to discover obscure or unknown knowledge about people in areas previously not studied. There are many unexplored and unknown areas about nursing, care, and health that require the use of the ethnonursing methods and techniques. Some examples of questions to be answered include, *What* is nursing? *How* is nursing given? *What* is the meaning of nursing to nurses and to different cultural groups in the world? The discovery of unknown nursing phenomena is the goal of ethnonursing. It is often the first step to study nursing phenomenon, but it is also a method to reexploring a new specific phenomenon.

Second, both ethnonursing and ethnographic methods are used when the researcher wants to grasp the *totality of a human lifestyle* or of a *broad* worldview *about individuals, families, and cultures* from *their* viewpoints and *their* modes of knowing and understanding life. What the researcher observes and experiences is also included in these methods. Obtaining a world view of people and of nursing is important, and ethnonursing and ethnographic methods help to reach this goal.

Third, these two methods are used when the researcher wants *data relating to some quite new or different types of questions that have not been asked by scientists or humanists.* For example; Do human groups need care? Does a nursing culture exist? What does care mean to a Lebanese family? These are ethnonursing types of research questions. Ethnography and ethnonursing research methods are thus used to clarify unknown, ambiguous, incomplete, and conflicting data previously obtained by quantitative research methods, such as the experimental or survey method, or to explain findings when data are obviously missing. In general, both methods are used to ask questions or study situations, people, or conditions that are largely unknown or only partially known.

Fourth, ethnography and ethnonursing methods are used to obtain *meanings-in-context* data, and *meanings-in-familiar or recurrent environmental* contexts. The "maxi" ethnographic method focuses on broad holistic meanings in context whereas ethnonursing method focuses on narrower aspects of human care contexts. Thus, the methods help to restore data that have been stripped of their meanings by other methods, such as experimental or survey methods. Context discovery as interpretation is an integral part of the ethnography and ethnonursing methods.

Fifth, ethnography and ethnonursing methods are frequently used to *generate concepts, theories, and hypotheses* or *to identify salient variables that have not been identified or that merit study.* For example, the author's ethnonursing study of the couvade phenomenon with professional nurse midwives in the early 1970s led to several hypotheses and stimulated other nurses to study couvade and its relationship to nursing care practices. The author's ethnonursing studies of care phenomena found to be culturally expressed and defined has led to new hypotheses and theories about differential nursing care. (Leininger, 1984c). The theory of cultural care diversity and universality has been under investigation since the mid-1960s and has generated many studies, theories, and hypotheses about cultural care and health (Leininger 1984a).

Sixth, both methods are highly appropriate for *cross-cultural comparative study of human and nursing care phenomena.* The methods are useful to obtain comparative viewpoints of human conditions, cultural family patterns, caring, health and illness, and qualitative life features. Discovering a particular phenomenon leads to contrasts of *similarities* and *differences* by the use of ethnography and ethnonursing methods, and it also leads to new insights with increased explanatory and predictive power. Nurse researchers will discover that the two methods can yield comparative findings about infant-mother feeding patterns, cultural care values, ways to preserve health, and contrasts of health care practices among cultures. Ethnonursing studies by transcultural nurses the past two decades are leading to a growing body of comparative health and care findings. As more nurse researchers are prepared to use ethnomethods, comparative data from most cultures and nursing situations have potential to greatly expand basic and applied nursing knowledge. Hence, the comparative features from the methods are important to nursing.

Seventh, ethnography and ethnonursing methods are used to *identify recurrent and patterned lifeways of people.* This is one of the most promising outcomes in using these two methods. Identifying *patterning* in care, in lifeways, and in dealing with crises provides a broader framework to know and predicting nursing care. Bringing "bits and pieces" of unrelated findings into larger gestalts of information in order to obtain a sequenced picture of human actions is an important new direction in nursing. It replaces the heavy emphasis on traits and symptoms and encourages the identification of cognitive patterns of human expressions. For example, Chinese clients prefer care patterns that include the family rather than self-care patterns. The Truk people believed one should not be touched by non-Trukese people when ill or well. This has led to development of other-care practices through which nurses may work with kinsmen to provide care. The discovery that *care is culturally defined, patterned and expressed* (Leininger 1978, 1981, 1984a, c) stimulated the discovery of some entirely different patterns of nursing care. Moreover, patterns of care are generally more satisfying to clients when they are expected and predicted to fit their lifeways.

Eighth, both ethnography and ethnonursing methods are used to provide *detailed accounts of events, situations, and circumstances* that are usually difficult to discover by other research methods. In-depth observations, interviews, and participatory experiences are unique to these two methods. In nursing, such detailed and documented data are essential for building a sound, reliable, and valid base of nursing knowledge. Unquestionably, there are other uses of ethnography and ethnonursing methods (depending upon the specific research goals of the investigator), but the eight reasons just identified help the reader to recognize their importance to nursing and the health fields.

As ethnography and ethnonursing methods become more known, valued, and used in nursing, nurses will gain comprehensive and in-depth knowledge about nursing and health care. There will be more substantive or fundamental knowledge of nursing and newer perspectives about the essence, nature, and basic structure of nursing knowledge. Replication and comparative ethnonursing studies, should increase the amount and quality of data generated about nursing. Nursing research should move from the use of basic to applied knowledge in a more significant way than previously noted in nursing's historical development.

Conceptualizing Ethnography and Ethnonursing Research Phases and Levels

Before initiating an ethnography or ethnonursing research study, the researcher needs to conceptualize not only the major features of the method but also the phases and levels of the research study. Developing a new or choosing a conceptual framework helps the researcher to see the components and their relationship to each other. The scope, phases, and levels of research are other essential considerations to conduct an ethnographic or ethnonursing study.

In any research investigation, the conceptual framework, or configuration of ideas serve as a blueprint for the study, and should be related to the purpose(s) of the investigation. Discovering accurate information about certain phenomena should always be foremost in the researcher's mind. The general domain of inquiry is of central interest to the researcher and is the basis for generating ethno-philosophical questions to be explored. It is common for the ethnographic and ethnonursing researcher to identify only one *domain of inquiry* and formulate a few major questions before launching an ethnographic and ethnonursing study. (This is in marked contrast to experimental studies, which always have a stated theory, problem, and hypotheses at the outset.) In conceptualizing ethnographic and ethnonursing studies, the researcher expects to generate theories and hypotheses at the *end* of the study. Although the ethnonurse researcher always has some broad theoretical notions about the phenomena under study, the theory should not be generally tight and explicit with a number of stated hypotheses at the outset.

With ethnographic or ethnonursing studies, the researcher is often aware of some general and vague features of the culture under study. He/she has general ideas and knows how to enter, remain with, and leave a culture; this is the broad and open research conceptualization and process used by the researcher. The researcher, however, does not know everything about the people nor have fixed and predetermined views about the findings. Instead, an open learning and discovery attitude prevails, in which the researcher becomes more of a learner and on-spot discoverer than a teacher or proclaimed a priori scientist. This is a different conceptual view from most research role expectations. Researchers who have some general knowledge about a culture become better discoverers as they take their cues from people and listen and observe rather than having no general knowledge of the culture. This, however, may not be possible if a culture has not been studied. Being alert to some gross cultural features may cue the researcher to grasp features such as the economic and political aspects of care. General ethnographic data already available from anthropological studies help the researcher anticipate some general features, but the nursing and health dimensions are usually not explicated. In addition, an open and humble learning attitude with the people is the key to performing successful ethnographic type of research. If nurse researchers are not prepared to assume such a learning attitude, much valuable data may be missed.

During the past few decades, the author has identified two major phases to guide ethnonursing research, namely, phase 1, discovering *substantive basic knowledge*, and phase 2, to *applying basic knowledge* to nursing and health contexts. Figure 3–1 depicts these two phases of ethnonursing research and should help the researcher understand that it takes time, patience, and goal-directed steps to move from basic to applied knowledge in nursing. Moreover, this model affirms that nursing is not an applied field; but it is also a basic field of study, with substantive knowledge applied to nursing situations, contexts, or interventions. Without basic scientific and humanistic knowledge a discipline of nursing cannot be established; only a quasi-professional one exists. Hence, much of the author's research work the past two decades has been directed largely toward basic and epistemological knowledge of nursing, so that nurses will be able to apply nursing knowledge—unique to our discipline. Conceptualizing these differences in research methods makes a difference in the research process and outcomes. The two phases for generating research knowledge summarized in Figure 3–1 are valuable to guide the nurse to realize his or her role in developing both basic (or fundamental) and applied knowledge. Moreover, it is hoped that the knowledge gained may be shared with other disciplines, such as *generic care knowledge* in contrast with *professional* nursing care knowledge (Leininger, 1981, 1984a, c.).

To conceptualize the research process further, nurse researchers need to consider different levels of research and theory to generate knowledge. Figure 3–2 shows different levels of research and theory generation from "macro" to "micro" levels. The researcher is free to choose which level of theory and research suits his or her own interests, preparation, and skills.

Being aware of different levels of research and theoretical abstractions helps to clarify the researcher's goals and the probable duration of investigations. For example, an ethnonursing study of 12 clients' views of care in a hospital unit might be viewed as a *micro-scope* study with low-level empirical data. In contrast, an ethnonursing research study of health and illness patterns of a large Polish-American community would be viewed as a *macro-scope* research study, with the researcher using macro theory and hypodeductive formulations. The level of theory and the research scope may not always be the same. For example, the researcher may conduct a macro-level study of the Amish community, but use middle-range theory rather than macro-theory. Hence, variations in research theory, type and scope of method do exist. The researcher should be aware of his or her own levels of conceptualization to share such scope and theoretical interests with others. Moreover, the level of theory and the research scope influence the research design tools and ways of proceeding with the study.

Since nursing is in the process of discovering its unique and distinctive discipline domains, there are benefits to using both ethnographic and ethnonursing research studies, as the former helps to establish the epistemological bases for basic knowledge, and the latter contributes to both basic and applied knowledge. In addition, nursing research studies at all levels of theory abstraction and methodologi-

Figure 3-1. Leininger's Phases of Generating Research Knowledge From Basic (Substantive) to Applied Knowledge

Phase 1	Phase 2
Discovering Substantive Knowledge (Basic Science Focus)	*Applying the Knowledge to Practice Situations* (Professional Focus)
Focus is upon discovering basic or substantive knowledge to know phenomenon fully	Focus is upon critical testing of knowledge for practical or applied uses
Research goals include 1. Discovering mainly unknown knowledge in-depth 2. Generating theories or hypotheses relevant to the phenomenon 3. Examining the phenomenon critically to know all aspects of it 4. Rechecking and validating basic knowledge with the people or in the context of the study 5. Heavy use of qualitative research methods to discover essence or nature of the phenomenon	Research goals include 1. Critical examination of questions or problems to professional situations 2. Testing theories and hypotheses related to the *use* of basic knowledge to applied situations 3. Reexamining findings and theories with different applied interests 4. Use of both qualitative and quantitative methods (depending on goals) to practice situations. 5. Explicit analysis of applied interventions to outcomes

Figure 3-2. Macro, Middle, and Micro Research Scope and Theory Levels

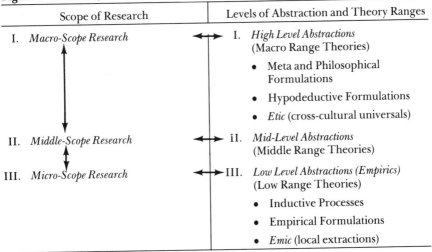

Scope of Research	Levels of Abstraction and Theory Ranges
I. *Macro-Scope Research*	I. *High Level Abstractions* (Macro Range Theories) • Meta and Philosophical Formulations • Hypodeductive Formulations • *Etic* (cross-cultural universals)
II. *Middle-Scope Research*	II. *Mid-Level Abstractions* (Middle Range Theories)
III. *Micro-Scope Research*	III. *Low Level Abstractions (Empirics)* (Low Range Theories) • Inductive Processes • Empirical Formulations • *Emic* (local extractions)

cal scope should be encouraged to establish nursing knowledge. It is also important to realize that some nurse researchers are skilled at macro theories and macro-levels of conceptualizing research, whereas others are skilled at handling empirical studies or middle-range theories. Using nurses different abilities should be encouraged rather than attempting to make all nurses middle-range or macro-theorists. Diversity in theories and methods is essential to discover the true nature and essence of nursing knowledge and practice.

Still another model to consider in theory and research generation is the "Sunrise Model" of Transcultural Care Diversity and Universality (Fig. 3–3). This model illustrates a differential conceptual, theoretical, and research method to study diversity and universality of care phenomena. It also incorporates ideas presented in Figure 3–2 relating to macro, middle, and micro range approaches to research and of high to low levels of abstraction. The researcher can choose where to enter and leave this conceptual model. Macro-scope and micro-scope researchers and theorists will undoubtedly pursue all levels of research as programs of care research are established in nursing, with plans to study research findings from each level of analysis. This model has been developed during the past two decades and is being used by several nurse researchers and graduate students. It is the only known model in nursing to combine both theory and method and to distinguish differential levels of abstraction and methodological approaches. The focus of the model is to generate knowledge concerning basic and applied health and illness. Theoretical premises, assumptions, and postulates, along with research data from 40 cultures, are under publication in another book (Leininger, 1985). The model is presented here to help researchers conceptualize ethnonursing type of research and to point out the value of conceptualizing macro, middle, and micro types of research theory and methodological approaches. It is also a model to study holistic nursing phenomena.

Conducting Ethnonursing Research: Steps and Process

Since the ethnography method of anthropology has been quite fully described (and by steps) by Spradley (1979, 1980), Pelto (1970), and some other authors, the primary focus in this section will be on the ethnonursing and ethnographic research methods and process was used in nursing.

Since the ethnonursing method primarily focuses on obtaining *emic* or people-centered data, after which some *etic* data revealed from observations and other sources are used, the researcher's goal is to obtain the world view, attitudes, meanings, and experiences of the people so that truths and realities can be known. *Emic* or local information serves as a baseline of knowledge, in contrast with *etic* or more universal views and explanations of nursing, care, health, and illness phenomena. Comparative *emic* and *etic* differences are sought. Throughout the ethnonursing study, the researcher is cognizant of detailing, documenting, describing, and analyzing nursing data from basic and applied perspectives.

It is helpful to consider ethnonursing research process according to:

Step 1. Identify a Domain of Inquiry, Area, or Phenomenon to Be Studied

The researcher asks, What do I need to know about the nature and essence of nursing? What domain has not been explored or has been studied only superficially that could yield nursing knowledge? The domain of inquiry can be large or small

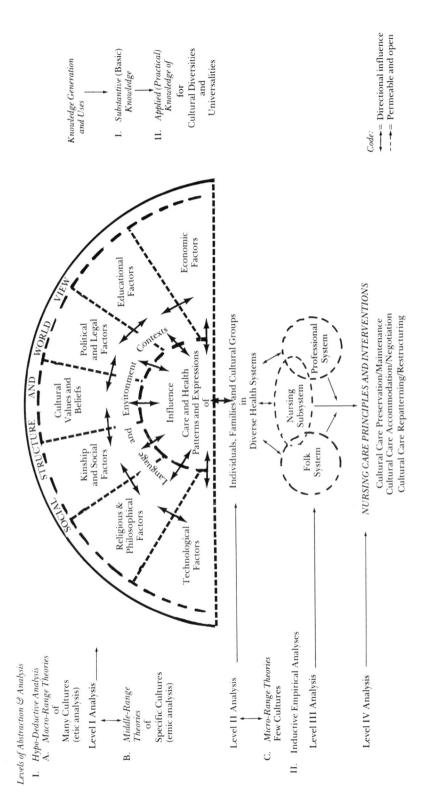

Figure 3-3. Leininger's "Sunrise" Theoretical/Conceptual Model of Transcultural Care Diversity and Universality. This model has been developed and used by Leininger since 1965 to the present.

45

for systematic investigation. For example, care is a large domain of inquiry when pursued in depth and from a comparative or cross-cultural stance. This encourages the researcher to investigate the phenomenon as fully as possible and with a vigorous in-depth approach so that multi-faceted aspects of it are explicitly known. Sometimes specific research questions are used with the domain of inquiry. The researcher usually has some general theoretical ideas to predict directionality, and often the theory is broad to accommodate subtheories or to develop a substantial theory after the ethnonursing study is completed. Ethnonursing follows the qualitative perspective and contrasts with theories used in quantitative types of experimental studies which are more explicit and tight than ethnonursing and ethnography research. Broad heuristic questions are valuable in ethnographic research to guide the researcher's thinking and identify the purposes and subareas of inquiry. Some types of broad questions used in ethnonursing research might include the following: What is the meaning of care in this particular culture? What are the characteristics of care phenomenon? What are the differences in the way care is perceived and known to men and women? What are some differences between a caring and a noncaring nurse? How do cultural values and practices define generic care? Such broad questions are deliberately used to let discoveries be made without having fixed or preestablished expectations of responses or studying only predetermined variables. The greatest discovery is often what the researcher least expected to find. The informants provide and control the data, not the researcher. Having a domain of inquiry permits an openness to discovery and an openness to document and analyze emic data in context. Ethnocare has been a rich and stimulating domain of inquiry, and many of the questions asked above have guided my research for nearly two decades (Leininger, 1966, 1978, 1983, 1984c, 1985).

Step 2. Explore Available Literature on the Domain or Area of Inquiry

Before initiating the study, a literature search about the domain or area of inquiry is important. This search helps to reveal what has or has not been studied in the domain. Current electronic computer retrieval methods are of much help to identify information and research of specific cultures or phenomena under study. Such preliminary literature search is essential to build upon, reaffirm, replicate, or pursue an entirely new line of inquiry—often with time and context differences.

Step 3. Prepare Research Instruments, Plans, and Approvals

Preparing for an ethnonursing or ethnographic research study of a cultural group, hospital unit, health department, or whatever chosen group, event or place requires thoughtful consideration before initiating the study. Depending upon the nature and focus of the study, equipment, instruments, material goods, cost, time and many other aspects need to be considered. For example, in one ethnocare study of the southern rural people, an open-ended interview guide, drawing materials, photographic equipment, and selected *etic*, culturological, and psychological tests were assembled prior to entering the field. In addition, field note books, tape recorders, films, games, paper, and personal supplies were also collected for the field study. While the researcher may decide not to use every tool and piece of equipment brought into the field (for various reasons and because of unexpected circumstances), it is better to have the materials readily available to meet time contingencies and ways of explicating data related to the domain of study, especially if you are a great distance from home. Generally structured (etic) interview tools are usually pretested, whereas *emic* interview tools are open or semi-structured and are seldom pretested unless a replication study is planned. General questions and broad areas of inquiry are identified to guide the researcher. Previsits with the people are made with ethnonursing and ethnographic studies to get general information and a feel for the community, and to plan general strategies for the study. If the researcher plans to live in or near a community to study the people, a place to live with the people (with the advantages and disadvantages of the living location) must be made; in addition, other factors must be considered carefully by nurses to assure safe and successful field studies.

As with other research studies involving humans, ethnonursing research requires committee review and approval. Generally, ethnography and ethnonursing studies are viewed as "low-risk" or exempt because there are no physical intrusive procedures or medical types of body or mind treatments. It is, however, important to obtain appropriate institutional or community approval for this type of research. Obtaining approval and informing others about the study should be done in an open and honest manner. Some cultures stand behind a "yes" verbal approval and decline a written approval.

These preliminary plans and considerations are important steps to take before collecting data; they also insure that the study can be followed through without major interruptions. If the researcher is a rigid and compulsive person and likes to have every detail planned in advance, and if he or she is reluctant to adapt to changing circumstances as a result of quantitative scientific orientations, one can reasonably predict this person will have difficulty in using the ethnonursing (or ethnography) methods. The ethnonurse researcher must be flexible and both ready and willing to adapt to changes and unexpected circumstances almost daily in the field to get data. Most importantly, the ethnonurse researcher must be able to adjust to changing lifeways (sometimes catastrophic) as one studies the lifeways of a culture group, a hospital, or community or whatever is being studied.

Step 4. Identifying and Choosing the People to Be Studied

In ethnonursing research studies, attention is given to obtaining a representative sample, but this is nowhere near as meticulous and detailed as a sample for a quantitative study. This is because of the different purposes and conceptual paradigms for qualitative type of research and nature of the study (see Chapter 1). Ethnomethodologists are concerned with choosing informants who represent the community by virtue of their roles, status, age, sex, and experience. Even the philosophical orientation and view of others who know "good informants" are given consideration by the researcher.

As noted earlier, the term "informants" is used to recognize personalized attributes and the important role of these persons, rather than the impersonal term of "subjects" which is used in quantitative research. Both *key informants* and *general informants* are chosen because of their knowledge and experience about the domain or phenomena under study. A *key informant* is most knowledgeable about the domain. This informant is considered among possibly ten key informants or possibly among 200 possible informants because of their areas of knowledge, status, role, sex, and years of experience with or about the domain of inquiry. Thus, selection of informants rests more on the careful identification of persons, often in advance, who are *representative* of the culture and who show potential to reveal substantive data (with similar or different viewpoints) on the domain of study. It is possible that some key informants may be missed by a random number assignment of quantitative methods but may be identified later as the researcher begins to study the people. A randomized sample may also exclude key and general informants because role, knowledge, and experiences are generally not considered. Sometimes additional informants may be added as the study progresses in order to open up an undiscovered and important area related to the subject. Pelto and Pelto offer the general rule "when addition of informants has little effect on the general structure of a complex pattern of data, then the present sample is satisfactory" (Pelto & Pelto, 1979, p. 139). Indeed, in qualitative studies, it is far wiser to involve key informants who are knowledgeable about a topic or domain than hundreds of general informants who are not. It is fascinating how a community or village knows who are key and general informants and will help to identify these persons when they want accurate information. The author has often noted that researchers who present questionnaires to community groups are often annoyed with the tool, and the researcher often gets inaccurate and limited information because key informants have not been included in the sample. Informants dislike being just another statistical number of a large group. Perhaps quantitative researchers will begin to reexamine their samples in light of the experiences of ethnographers in conducting community and institutionally based studies. Examining thousands of subjects may be of limited help in truly knowing, understanding and verifying phenomenon or problems under study.

In ethnonursing research, the focus is on gaining *in-depth* qualitative knowledge about a domain, hence the concept of *key informant* is important. In general, ethnonursing key and general informants are few in number to meet the purposes and goals of qualitative research. During the previsit in the community or setting, the researcher attentively listens to key informants as they are interviewed about subject areas; whereas general informants may have a less intense interview and provide general information. By being alert and observant, and by listening to ideas presented by the people, key informants can be identified by the researcher, but not all are chosen for the study. Frequently, key informants appear equally qualified. When this occurs, their names may be drawn from a hat by sex, role, status, and age. But if key informants are few in number and their input much needed, then all key informants may be used. It is also well to keep in mind Pelto's statement that "key informant interviewing is used to best advantage when it is closely integrated with participant observation" (Pelto, 1970, p. 97).

In-depth interviews, observations, participant experiences, and other methods and techniques are used in combination with data supplied by key informants to study particular phenomena. Depending upon the scope and purposes of the ethnonursing study and on the domain of inquiry, about 10 to 15 key informants and 30 to 60 *general* informants constitute a desired number of informants. In-depth participant interviews, along with other confluent methods, i.e., several methods that contribute to the goals of the research, can provide adequate reliability and validity for qualitative research studies.

Step 5. The Research Process of Observing, Participating, Interviewing, and Validating Data

Entering to learn and document data from people. Nurses and other health personnel unfamiliar with ethnographic field research method often ask, How does one enter and remain in a community or institution over a period of time? This is an important question in conducting ethnonursing research. Figure 3–4 and Table 3–1 illustrate stranger-friend models which have been developed by the author and used for nearly two decades. These models help the researcher to anticipate some common response expectations when entering the field as a stranger, and later in becoming a research friend.

Both the general model (Fig. 3–4) and the detailed model (Table 3–1) were conceptualized from some of Berreman's insightful ideas in *Behind Many Masks* (1962). However, I modified and further developed the stranger-friend models to fit the ethnonursing research method. Having lived alone for more than a year in the Eastern Highlands of New Guinea, these models gave me additional ideas about entering, participating in, and leaving field research with human groups. The models have been used and examined with several transcultural nursing and anthropology students in the field and in institutions to show what a researcher can expect. Transcultural nursing and other field students have found that the model has repeatedly validated their experiences and helps them to work through or respond favorably to the research process. As one student stated, "This model [Table 3–1] helped me to know the facades, hidden and true realities to make research more interesting, challenging and successful." The goal is to move successfully from the "Front stage" to the "Back Stage," where truth in the real world prevails.

As the researcher moves into a community or institution, there is a front stage and a back stage. The front stage has many protective facades; it is characterized by

Figure 3-4. Researcher as Stranger to Friend: Knowing the Facades and Realities

Front Stage	Back Stage
(Many Protective Facades)	(The Real World)
Goal: ──────────────────────────→ Get to Back Stage	
Researcher Enters as a *Stranger*──→ Moves to──→ A *Trusted* Research *Friend*	
Behavior Expectations:	Behavior Expectations:
1. Many facades and withholding of rich data to researcher	1. The local world of reality opens to the researcher as a trusted friend
2. Testing the researcher	2. Mutual trust and acceptance evident between researcher and informant
3. Protective-management strategies by informants	3. Reveals intimate secrets and treasured data to researcher
4. Distrust of stranger's motives and use of data	4. Shares in an open manner with researcher
5. Disguising reality to researcher	5. Informant wants researcher to have accurate facts
6. Misinformation to researcher and non-caring attitude	6. Caring attitude about data, people, and researcher by informant
7. Uncertain in sharing local truths	7. Shows pride in sharing truths to researcher

Table 3-1 Leininger's Stranger-Friend Ethnographic/Enthnonursing Field Process Model*

Front Stage: Entering as a Stranger	Back Stage: Established as a Friend
Stranger: A person who is unknown, unpredictable, and not familiar to a particular group or community.	*Friend*: A person who is generally known, accepted, and trusted by others.
As a stranger, one can expect:	As a friend, one can expect:
1. To be watched attentively and fairly continuously.	1. Less observation and being trusted to move about.
2. Local leaders are protective of their territory and cautious, suspicious, and guarded of a stranger.	2. Leaders and followers are not guarding and protecting their territory as much as when they are with friends.
3. Signs of distrust prevail, i.e., questioning and watching.	3. Signs of trust are evident, i.e., being accepted, participating in activities, and mutual sharing.
4. Limited invitations to participate in common and recurrent community or home activities.	4. Invitations to participate in daily life activities, ceremonies, and the people's activities.
5. Facade behavior that is not genuine but more "impression management" (Berreman phenomenon).†	5. Open sharing behavior and reality presented as it is experienced daily.
6. Signs of noncaring behavior, i.e., exposure to harmful or nonbeneficial events.	6. Signs of caring behavior, i.e., efforts to be protective, sensitive to needs, and supportive of friend.
7. Behavior tested in various ways.	7. No testing; rather acceptance and helping.
8. Guarded in sharing information. Messages often vague and not accurate or complete.	8. Accurate information shared and available without a lot of queries. Efforts made to give accurate information.
9. Deliberate protection of cultural secrets, sacred rites, and ceremonies.	9. Spontaneous sharing of cultural secrets, ceremonies, and rituals with pride and respect.
10. Different ambiguous explanations about phenomena.	10. Efforts to give clear, detailed, and consensus interpretations, validating and checking data.
11. Subtle, hostile jokes, and humorous statements with local idioms and covert meanings.	11. Participation in jokes, humor, and cultural activities with a sense of special privilege.
12. Sense of being uncomfortable, frustrated, and exhausted.	12. Relaxed and enjoying the people as respected and valued friends.

*Developed and used in field studies of several cultures (1960 to present time). High qualitative validity and reliability.
†Berreman, G. *Behind many masks.* Ithaca, NY: Society for Applied Anthropology Monograph #4, 1962, pp. 4–24.

such behavior as testing the researcher's motives and goals; protective management strategies; distrust of the researcher; disguising and hiding reality; providing misinformation; and general ambivalence whether or not to reveal their truths to a stranger. Nurses and other researchers are "professional strangers" until proved otherwise (Agar, 1981).

A researcher who is aware of these front stage and back stage expectations will not become unduly frustrated but will allow time to become trusted and known as a research friend. Patience, time, sensitive participation, and self-appraisals are important for the ethnographic and ethnonurse researcher. With time and thoughtful consideration of and respect for the people, the researcher can become a trusted research friend. Some researchers are tested a lot before being accepted by the people. Once accepted, the informants are generally willing to share their intimate secrets and treasured knowledge. Entering the real world of the informants is no small and simple task; the rewards, however, are great as the doors open when people feel comfortable with you to share their *emic* knowledge and world views. Once the back stage is reached, the researcher checks and rechecks to see that the data are accurate as this increases validity of the study. The researcher will know when he or she has passed into the back stage because the quantity and quality of data are rich in amount and meaningful in the back stage; whereas the data are sparse and ambiguous in the front stage.

Often researchers unaware of front stage and back stage differences will get data from the front stage that is highly questionable. Impersonal mail surveys or questionnaires often reveal front stage data that are not as truthful as back stage. Such data, when compared with rich ethnographic research data, point to such obvious differences in quality and quantity of data obtained. In fact, local people have often told the author that they give "survey people" false information to get them "out of their hair or the community." Considerably more thought concerning the validity of their findings is needed by researchers who use questionnaires or survey data collection techniques when the people deliberately give false data. The front stage data are generally impressionist, false, superficial, controlled or protective responses; back stage data are of a different kind. These two models help the ethnonursing researchers and others strive for accurate, back stage data and to seriously question the validity and reliability of front stage data. Hence, ethnonursing research has some built-in data checks on validity with these models.

In general, the models in Figure 3–4 and Table 3–1 need to be studied and used to envision what can be anticipated as the researcher moves into an unknown community, institution, or group to do research. Knowing front stage and back stage behavior can be a means of checking the quality and quantity of responses and the accuracy of the responses by other data sources, instruments, and methods used. It may also provide clues for physical safety of the researchers.

Most assuredly, cultural groups have a way of responding to, protecting, and testing strangers. Strangers can become friends and greatly facilitate research when signs of *trust, acceptance,* and *respect* replace fear and distrust. The quality and quantity of research tends to vary inversely with degree of trust and acceptance in stranger-friend relationships. Likewise, validity and reliability factors are increased where signs of trust and friend relations are evident in the research process. Truth or validity of data becomes more apparent when the researcher is obtaining information especially regarding religious, kinship, and economic, political, and health experiences, which are often intimate or secretive knowledge domains related to care, health, and illness.

Observation-participation: essential to ethnonursing research process. Since the days of Malinowski (1922), a famous field researcher, the participant-observation method has been a central method of anthropologists to study people virtually everywhere in the world. The participant-observation method described by Kluckhohn more than three decades ago continues to be used, developed, and refined as an integral part of many ethnographic research studies (Kluckhohn, 1949; Kluckhohn & Strodbeck, 1961). Malinowski and Kluckholn laid the cornerstone to participant-observation methods to discover and validate human thoughts with actions. Qualitative research depends heavily upon this method in studying people and in their natural environments. Qualitative researchers can greatly sharpen their observations and participation skills through direct field experiences under skilled mentors. It is amazing to see variations in how researchers observe the same phenomena and see differences in detailing and responding to humans and environmental clues. Such differences are largely related to lack of education in the participant-observation method. Accordingly, biases and selective observations can be noted by observers who are unskilled in observation and participation; skilled researchers are aware of these tendencies and can correct them.

In the field of nursing, participant-observation has been an expected part of the nursing process and activity. However, ways to perfect and make explicit the participation and observation techniques as a research skill have only recently been explored as nurse-anthropologists and ethnographers bring their expertise to bear upon nursing research methods. Explicating the central issues and devising ways to increase reliability and validity of participant-observation are taking place to a greater extent in schools of nursing today. The work of nurse researchers on the participant-observation method is documented in writings such as those of Boyle (1981); Byerly (1968); Dougherty, 1978; Germain (1979); LaFargue (1981); Leininger (1966, 1968, 1984); Ragucci (1974); Ray (1981); and Tripp-Reimer (1983).

During the past two decades, the author has questioned the traditional focus of the participant-observation method and has reversed the terms from observation (first) to participation (later), which reflects a more logical and practical approach in ethnographic research. In addition, the process phases have been extended to help the researcher grasp a more accurate and realistic picture of what transpires with the method. Figure 3–5 illustrates the four phases of this process. With *observation* as Phase I is observation followed by primarily observation and some participation

Figure 3-5. Leininger's Sequenced Phases of Observation-Participation Field Method

Research Phases of Observation-Participation Method			
1	2	3	4
Primarily Observation	Primarily Observation with some participation	Primarily Participation with some observation	Reflective Observations of impact

(phase II); and then primarily *participation* and less observation, and finally the *reflective observation* phase.

In thinking about this model, especially as an essential part of ethnonursing research method, each phase is emphasized to help the researcher become aware of the role and to study collected data in a systematic manner. This helps to establish the method in an explicit manner for future replication studies and guides the researcher in the investigation. Let us consider each phase.

Initially, (phase 1) the researcher focuses on making observations close at hand and farther away. Observing and listening are major parts of this phase. The researcher obtains a broad view of the situation and gradually makes detailed observations. Allowing some time to make detailed and documented observations is essential before interacting or participating more directly with the people because it permits the researcher to establish what is occurring *before* influencing the situation as a participant. It also permits the people some time to observe the researcher at a distance and to "size up" his or her behavior as a stranger in the people's living context. Testing of the researcher begins by the people at this time.

In phase 2, observation continues as the major focus, but some participation occurs. The researcher begins to interact more with the people and observes their responses.

In phase 3, the researcher becomes a more active participant, and observation tends to decrease because it is often difficult to observe fully all aspects that are occurring while participating in the informants' activities. What it means to participate in specific activities, such as a ritual of healing, may best be understood by actively taking part to grasp the feeling for the activity and to experience the ritual directly. While participating in an activity or event, it remains important to maintain a role as observer. Recall that generally the researcher does not participate in the research in quantitative experimental researchers because of the desire to control for biases. However, with qualitative research, the researcher participates in varying degrees to learn from the people and to feel, experience, and learn by direct involvement in activities. Accordingly, the qualitative researcher describes, explains, and accurately documents what transpires during participant-observation experience, instead of avoiding these naturalistic happenings. The researcher explains what happens.

In the last phase of the observation-participation process, the researcher does reflective observations to determine the actual or potential impact upon the people in the situation and event. Reflective observation means to "look back" thoughtfully on what happened and to recapture the situation and total process of what happened and how the people responded to the researcher. Understanding what transpired between researcher and the people being studied is essential to get an accurate and full account of the situation or event. Reflective observations help the researcher to appraise his or her own influence and the influence of others; such observations also help to synthesize the total encounter in sequential and particularized ways to obtain an accurate picture and to report data honestly.

In the observation-participation process, the researcher takes an *active learning role* as informants instruct the researcher about the situation or topic under discussion. Letting go to learn from others—rather than controlling others and their responses—is a crucial feature in qualitative research. Learning about, listening to, and observing are the dominant role expectations of the ethnonursing researcher.

Hence, the observation-participation method differs considerably from quantitative experimental methods and yields quite different research outcomes. The ethnonursing researcher should know such methodological differences and be ready to defend the approach to ensure valid and reliable qualitative data.

Interview methods and techniques.   Since the ethnonursing method focuses on documenting and understanding the meaning of what is heard, seen, and observed from people and environments, interview methods are important. Spradley has written three helpful chapters about interviewing in his book, *The Ethnographic Interview* (1979, pp. 78–92; 120–131; 155–172). The reader is encouraged to study carefully this material and to review additional materials available and presented by the author below on conducting quality interviews.

Essentially, there are three major types of interview, which will be described briefly. The *first* type is called the *open-ended interview,* which is an unstructured type of question (an interview item) or topic area for discussion. The interview stem encourages the interviewee to complete the statement and to provide information about the subject from his or her viewpoint and experiences. This type of interview is an important and dominant approach used in ethnonursing and ethnographic research because it lets the informant's ideas, world views, and information be revealed rather than those of the interviewer. Essentially, the open-ended interview type is ideal to elicit *emic* data and get "inside the head" or obtain the world view thoughts and experiences of the informant. It is truly an art and skill for the interviewer to listen actively and patiently after posing an open-ended stem to the interviewee. Some examples of open-ended stems are the following:

1.   You believe health means _____.
2.   You view care as _____.
3.   You get care from _____.

With an open-ended interview, the interviewer does not ask questions that lead to fixed or predetermined responses. Instead, the stems encourage talking about, clarifying, and giving examples. Folk and life history stories may be generated. Since many Americans are becoming resistant to fixed questions and "fixed" responses, the open-ended interview is reassuring to the interviewee that his or her own ideas and creative responses are valued. This traditional anthropological and ethnonursing interview type has yielded much rich material from people and reaffirms the intent to learn from the informant. It helps interviewees direct the communication and to tell their stories, facts, or truths in their cultural styles and frames of reference rather than meeting the researcher's style and data expectations. Being ready to document the informants' local cultural expressions, verbatim statements, and folk stories is expected with the open-ended interview method.

The *second* type of interview is referred to as the *structured and closed interview.* In this approach the questions are phrased in order to elicit specific responses to specific questions. This type of interview is more often used in quantitative than in qualitative research in order to control responses to fit specific variables, and to ask the same questions to all interviewees. For example, one might ask: (1) How many people live in your home? (2) Who takes care of you? and (3) How many days were you ill? While structured types of interview questions may be used in ethnonursing research, they are more rare than usual. Such structured and closed interview items elicit specific responses but limit or control what the interviewee may wish to share with the interviewer. Thus an opposite approach is used in qualitative research to let the informant "talk out" or relate his ideas in his own style of talking.

The *third* type of interview is called the *semi-structured interview*. This type of interview is a combination of both the open and closed types of interview. It is designed to elicit both definitive and unexpected kinds of information from the interviewee. In ethnonursing research this type of interview is used almost as frequently as the open-ended type. Some examples of semi-structured interview items are (1) Could you tell me about your ideas of care and give some examples of good caretakers in your family? (2) Care often has different meanings to people; what does care mean to you? (3) As you tell me about your typical day, specifically when do get up and go to bed?

In the process of obtaining ethnonursing data, it is helpful to have some general knowledge beforehand about the informant's life or home context. Such knowledge helps to clarify what is being perceived. Or if the researcher is in a comparable situation (with no information), the researcher can approximate ideas about the informant's behavior or response. Framing interview questions or topic domains helps the interviewee to know from where the interviewer comes or the contextual situation and its implicit or explicit meanings. Then, to obtain informant contextual data requires that the interviewer give thought to ways of structuring questions so that the interviewee will share specific and general information. This requires a degree of empathy to enter the informant's world, culture or situation. For example, a researcher might say, "I understand you have no car and are also living where there is no public transportation or train service, so I am wondering what you do when members of your family become seriously ill?" With this statement, the context of the situation was established so the informant could readily identify with and respond. Because people are exposed to many different actual or changing contexts, it is well to be clear which context is being referred to in order to document responses accurately.

Problems of "contextual stripping," or posing questions and taking ideas and responses out of the informant's world view, has been discussed by Mishler (1979). He tells us that contextual stripping is a serious problem in research and in working with people (1979). He also says, it is a "key feature of our standard methods of experimental designs, measurement, and statistical analysis" (Mishler, 1979, p. 2). Implicit and explicit statements, cultural referents, and environmental factors may be absent or misunderstood unless the contextual referents are carefully noted and supported. *Meanings in context* and the use of symbols and rituals are excellent means to know people. Contextually framed questions and areas of familiar inquiry help the informant to recall situations and to clarify, explain, or elaborate ideas in ways that are meaningful to him or her. They also help the researcher enter the informant's world. Historical and cultural data help to provide or ensure a contextual frame of reference between the interviewer and interviewee (or informant).

Allowing the informant to interpret, *demonstrate, clarify, verify* or *confirm* data is most essential to the ethnonursing interview method. It is amazing how much well or sick people like to explain or interpret experiences in their own way without being interrupted with a host of questions or interpretations that may not be close to the informant's line of thinking, knowledge or life experiences. Listening to and then repeating a statement or question with context referents permits the researcher to share accurate and meaningful data. Often validity responses are confident revelations or secrets and disclosed in informant's words or communication modes. They usually provide continuity in thought about the subject or topic under discussion. For example, if the informant says, "care is presence," the interviewer picks up this statement to grasp all the implied or known meanings from the informant. Without cultural and social context, data have limited meaning and there is increased potential for error. Hence worldwide population samples or mass household samples of 2000 to 3000 subjects taken out of sociocultural context seem highly questionable to obtain validity data, and such samples are used quite extensively in quantitative types of research. Reducing or eliminating contextual stripping and preserving meaning in context are important in ethnonursing and qualitative research.

A valuable interview technique used by the author in ethnonursing research is called the "Tell me" or "I would like to learn (or hear) about" interview approach. It is encouraging to see how helpful these lead-in stem phrases are in working with strangers, especially under stress. "Tell me" and "I would like to hear (or learn) about" statements tend to open the "idea gate" for people who need to be heard. These stems permit the informant to tell the story in his or her own way and style. For example, "Tell me about your recent experiences in the hospital." "I would like to learn about the kind of nursing care you received during your recent stay in the hospital." "I am interested to hear about the ways you coped with your handicap while growing up." These are what I call "big lead-in" questions, in contrast to "little lead-in" questions such as "Tell me how you got here." "I want to hear about your aches." Big lead-in questions let the informant tell the story in his or her own way. The little lead-in's are used when time is a constraining and real factor. With either technique the informant supplies the information more easily and makes it unnecessary for the researcher to ask literally hundreds of questions, and often get less information. Moreover, this type of inquiry is generally less annoying and more satisfying to the informant. This approach has been validated by the author repeatedly as informants state their preference for the "open lead-in" questions in ethnonursing research and in doing culturological care and health assessments (Leininger, 1978, p. 85–106).

Whatever the type of interview, the interviewer needs to try to relax the informant and listen attentively to the major ideas, themes, patterns, and statements in response to each area of inquiry. Jotting down these ideas in an unobtrusive or undisrupting way is important. Tape recording of interviews may be done to ensure accurate and full accounts if the informant grants permission and is comfortable with the idea. More and more people are resisting tape recording for a variety of reasons. The approach and genuinely interested attitude of the interviewer has much to do with the researcher's success in moving from front stage to back stage data and in obtaining accurate and reliable data. The researcher's methods of documenting, recording, confirming, and rechecking data are important. Time needs to be allocated to reconfirm or recheck data during and later in the ethnonursing research process. Additional validating interviews techniques are often used such as the use of Q-sort statements, replaying taped data, or restating informant ideas to confirm data. Spot checks on specific responses to ideas that were not clear is done during the two to three visits with the key informants (often of 2 to 3 hours' duration) and with general informants (often only one visit, 1 hour long). The researcher will soon discover that many ideas begin to converge, "make sense" or reaffirm each other. When this occurs, the researcher knows that validity and reliability in qualitative ways are occurring. Unusual responses are always carefully recorded and saved for divergent analysis representing acculturation variabilities.

PART II: MODES OF QUALITATIVE DATA ANALYSIS

Ethnographic and ethnonursing data can be analyzed in a variety of ways with the use of several confluent or compatible methods. Some of these methods can be also used to analyze other types of data. In this section several qualitative methods will be presented among them, thematic, hermeneutical, componential, symbolic, textual, value, semantic, kinetic, and semiotic methods.

During the past decades, different types of qualitative research methods have been developed and are being used to reaffirm the importance of meanings, attributes, and other features of qualitative research. Efforts are also being made to avoid reducing data to numbers unnecessarily and to prevent contextual stripping. This trend has been clearly evident in America and Europe in recent years with the thinking of Cook and Reichardt (1979); Leininger (1970, 1978, 1981, 1984a, b); Mishler (1979); Maanen 1983 *et al*, Rosengren (1981), Spradley (1970, 1979), and many other qualitatively oriented researchers. In addition, some myths have been challenged, such as the view that qualitative data are not good for explanatory and predictive features.

The author predicts that by the end of this decade many new types of qualitative data analyses will be developed, and these methods will become more explicit and valued by researchers. As the types of analyses increase in numbers, quality researchers will be challenged to find new ways of presenting their findings, with perhaps less emphasis on numbers and statistics and more emphasis on attributional, humanistic, and meaning inferences. The imbalance in emphasis between qualitative and quantitive analyses will be redressed with more divergent methods and more thought given to utilizing alternative methods for specific research purposes.

In this decade and the next, qualitative methodologists are expected to:

1. Explicate the modes of qualitative data analysis so the methods can be used by other researchers for some types of replication studies.
2. Make known the theoretical underpinnings, and research frameworks of qualitative studies.
3. Explicate research findings in as clear and succinct ways as possible, especially to reduce misinterpretation of data.
4. Identify and explicate the explanatory and predictive powers of qualitative research methods to change the traditional beliefs and views that qualitative research has only descriptive value or purposes.
5. Arrange for qualitative data to be processed by electronic computers with new types of soft and hardware equipment to retain the essential attributes and purposes of qualitative research.

At present, the types of qualitative data analysis identified in the section are known and used by some qualitative researchers, but the methods are continually being developed and refined. Only brief accounts of each type of analysis can be given here, but the reader is directed to study illustrative examples offered in this book by other authors and to consult the extensive references cited.

Ethnographic Data Analysis

This method of analysis is primarily focused on the use of ethnographic *(emic)* cultural data obtained directly from the people, through mainly the observation participation method. The method includes also *etic* and other general observational data obtained while studying people over a short or long period of time. In addition to a general ethnographic data analysis of observational and participatory data, textual, structural, sematic, value, and other kinds of analysis will be used to explicate the findings. (These methods will be discussed later.) The ethnographic data analysis is best demonstrated by ethnography studies done by cultural and social anthropologists. Perhaps the most detailed, explicit, and oldest example is Malinowski's ethnography, *Argonauts of the Western Pacific* (1922). A more recent analysis of ethnographic data is Hostetler's *Amish Society* (1980). Chance's book, *The Eskimo of North Alaska* (1966), and Benet's study, *Abkhasians: The Long-Living People of the Caucasus* (1974), offer some classic illustrations of how ethnographic research is analyzed. There are hundreds of other anthropological ethnographies to examine for patterns of ethnographic data analysis, and several are cited in a new reference source book (Leininger, 1984b). Some specific examples of ethnographic analyses by nurse-anthropologists with a focus on the lifeways of people are Dreher's *Working Men of Ganja* (1982); Dougherty's *Becoming A Woman in Rural Black Culture* (1978); Leininger's *The Gadsup of New Guinea* (1978 pp. 375–399) and *Southern Culture* (1984c, pp. 133–161); Kendall's *Maternal-Child Nursing in an Iranian Village* (1968); and Horn's *Study of the Muckelshoot Indians'* child-rearing practices (In Leininger, 1978, pp. 223–238).

Ethnonursing Data Analysis

The ethnonursing analysis focuses on examining selected nursing and ethnographic data that are related to care, health, prevention of illness states, illness, and other nursing care phenomena. Some examples of ethnonursing data analysis are found in this book in Chapters 13 (Wenger) and 18 (Leininger). This type of analysis includes the identification of themes and patterns of care (or health), classification of semantic health care expressions, and an *emic* and *etic* interpretive analysis of the data. Daily or recurrent life experiences (ethnographic components) are analyzed to provide a broad framework to understand nursing phenomena related to health, care, environment, context, and related nursing and human expressions. Ethnonursing analysis includes *etic* and *emic* data related to the purposes of the study and general theoretical interests of the researcher. What is said, and observed and the action patterns of people are analyzed and brought together to get a total view of the phenomenon. Data from several key informants are compared, using in-depth interviews and general observations made by the researcher. Differences and similarities of the phenomenon are made, often using both quantitative and qualitative analysis of data. In addition, the author include social structure aspects (political, kinship, social, economic, religious, and cultural values, beliefs, and practices) that appear to be influencing health and care practices in the ethnonursing analysis. Understanding how social structure, world view, environment, and folk and professional health systems influence nursing is essential to obtain a holistic picture of the people and their actual or potential nursing care needs. The use of different qualitative methods and tools is frequently combined to obtain a thorough and comprehensive view of ethnonursing data. Data from these methods converge to help the researcher know and understand fully all the findings.

Phenomenological Data Analysis

Phenomenological analysis refers essentially to analyzing specific components of data for their meaning of life experiences, subjective feelings, attributes, and intentionality. In this book, Chapters 5 (Lynch-Sauer) and 6 (Ray) provide examples of this method. The phenomenological method is valuable to obtain subjective feelings, experiential meanings, and intentional data. There is a growing interest both in the phenomenological method and in combining ethnographic data with phenomenological data. Nurses prepared in the phenomenological method are active in explicating this method for clinical and community health care research. Accordingly, variations in methods of analyses are becoming evident to fit the purposes or goals of the nursing researcher. Some nurse researchers are using selected research techniques and methods from ethnography and ethnonursing in their phenomenological analysis because of some similar goals and research purposes. This method of analysis is of much interest to many nurses because of the need to understand client life experiences, subjective feelings, intuitions, and meanings.

Philosophical Data Analysis

It is encouraging that more nurses in doctoral programs are taking philosophy courses. With this trend, nurses are discovering the importance of philosophy through humanistic and scientific analysis of research data as well as the application of such knowledge to nursing situations. Philosophical analysis includes logical, existential, epistemological, ontological, and related aspects of philosophical data analyses. Philosophical analysis is concerned with the use of logical reasoning, modes of knowledge acquisition, and the "why" of human thoughts and actions. In this book, Chapter 4 (Gaut) provides an excellent example of philosophical analysis; Zderad's book (1967) is another type. Much of the data are analyzed by systematic and logical reasoning of oral or written statements of subject matter. For example, Gaut analyzes the meaning and reasoning of nurses about care, using logical inferences and kinds of implicit and explicit meanings. This method requires preparation in philosophical methods, but it may also be learned by reading the many works of research philosophers and several works now available by nurse-philosophers. It is an important method for grasping the nature of human thought and reason, especially of nursing phenomena, nurses, and the meaning of nursing decisions and actions.

Structural-Functional Data Analysis

The structural-functional method of data analysis is derived primarily from social anthropologists, especially the British social anthropologists beginning in the 1940's. The goal of the structural-functional method is to analyze social phenomena for the structural form for organizational attributes of social institutions and to relate these finding to the purposes, uses or functions that such structures serve in society. Social structural units are important and include the political, economic, legal, kinship, and cultural systems of Western and non-Western societies (Evans-Pritchard, 1973;

Nadel, 1957; Radcliffe-Brown, 1952), with a thought to nursing data. A critical assessment of the function of these systems is made in relation to needs and structure of each system.

The structural-functional method of analysis is an extremely valuable way to grasp totality nursing in a society or culture; but the nurse researcher needs substantive knowledge in social anthropology to do a competent and accurate structural-functional analysis. At present, very few nurses have been prepared to use the structural-functional analysis method. Instead, many nurse researchers have only partial knowledge and misinformation, such as the method being a static mode of analysis rather than the dynamic and comprehensive feature of the method. Structural-functional analysis actually provides one of the highest level of abstractions to analyze complex and large amounts of data such as the political and economic systems and their relation to nursing and care phenomena. Nurses who are low-level abstractionists or who can only deal comfortably with empirical, simple, and concrete data will find the structural-functional method difficult to comprehend and use. Some of the best conceptualizers, theorists, and abstractionists in nursing should consider this method to understand nursing's diverse and holistic attributes. It is a method of choice for many transcultural nurse researchers who have been well prepared in social anthropology. It is a method the author has used, in part, in her conceptual model and transcultural nursing theory. Unquestionably, this method will be used more in the future when nurse researchers fully understand the theory and its concomitant method.

The author's "Sunrise" Model (Figure 3-3) in this chapter reflects the importance of social structural features and of looking for the interrelatedness of each system as it influences care, health, and nursing goals. As one studies this model, the multiple factors that influence care can be seen, and it becomes obvious how important it is to give thorough attention to these factors. As an ethnonursing methodologist, the author have used different levels of analysis (macro, middle, and micro range) and have indicated different levels at which the researcher might study care. This model was developed over a period of two decades as a nursing model to fit the author's theory of care diversity and universality and of how to develop cultural specific and universal nursing care. Graduate students are finding this model extremely valuable to obtain a holistic view of care and to analyze diverse cultural and social systems, influencing folk-professional care systems.

Thematic and Pattern Analyses

The roots of thematic and pattern analyses stem mainly from the creative work of the anthropologist Ruth Benedict (1948) and the psychologist H.A. Murray (1938) in their analyses of cultures and human behavior. This mode focuses on the analysis of different cognitive and identifiable themes and patterns of living or of behavior. Raw data are analyzed by identifying and bringing together components or fragments of ideas or experiences, which often are meaningless when viewed alone. Much creative thought and analytical ability is needed to literally "put the pieces together" so that a theme or synthesis of behavior is formulated that is congruent to the people being studied. Themes should be verified by the people, but the total gestalt or coherence of ideas rests with the analyst who has rigorously studied how different ideas or components fit together in a meaningful way when linked together.

The author has developed and used the following sequential conceptual steps for thematic and pattern analysis of nursing and ethnonursing data.

Step 1.   Identify and list descriptors (pieces of raw data) of nursing observations and experiences or domain under study.

Step 2.   Combine raw data and descriptors into meaningful sequential units or into larger units, known as patterns.

Step 3.   Identify mini or micropatterns and determine how they relate to patterns and themes.

Step 4.   Synthesize several patterns to obtain a broad, comprehensive, and holistic view of the data as themes and subthemes.

Step 5.   Formulate theme (or pattern) statements to test or reaffirm further nursing phenomena.†

Step 6.   Use the confirmed themes for hypothesis, decisions and nursing interventions.

In studying the meaning of care for six Filipino families, I discovered, that the dominant theme was "caring is harmony with others and with our families," as expressed in recurrent oral statements as well as repeated explanations by the people. This care theme was confirmed by my and other researchers' observations and was a pattern that could be validated in day-to-day living modes of the people.

While thematic and pattern analyses are closely related, they are not precisely the same. Patterns are generally small units of sequential behavior that contribute to themes. Themes are large units of analysis derived from patterns which can explain multiple aspects of human behavior. Thematic and pattern analyses have only recently been used in nursing as an explicit data analysis method. This method has promise for nurse researchers (especially clinical researchers) who are disposed to analyzing client, staff and administrators' behaviors in large units or themes of behavior. Nurses also combine separate small observations and experiences into larger units to get a total picture of the client.

Value Data Analysis

Closely related to thematic and pattern analysis is value analysis. However, *value analysis is focused upon the abstraction of preferences, choices, any thing or idea that is viewed as desirable, and implicit or explicit forces that tend to guide human thoughts and actions.* Kluckhohn defines value broadly as "a conception, explicit or implicit, distinctive of an individual or characteristic of a group, of the desirables which influence the selection from available modes, means, and ends of action" (1961), p. 395 .

The author has used value analysis directed toward identifying repeated cognitive actions and thoughts that give direction to a person or group. Values are also identified that reflect recurrent experiences chosen or linked with a person's philosophy or explaining his or her behavior. Generally, emotional expressions are connected with values that have meaning and importance to the person or group. Values of care-giving, values of the cost of care, and values such as preferred ways of coping with illness or maintaining health are a few examples of qualitative values to be analyzed. The method of value analysis is often done by content, linguistic and context analysis. Data from semi-structured questionnaires, and other data collecting

---

†The use of "tests" or "testing" in qualitative research is generally different from quantitative research. Testing with qualitative research refers to confluent modes of confirming and validating data under repeated similar or varient conditions of systematic examination.

forms are used in value analysis. Often qualitative and quantitative combined methods are used to explicate values.

Nurses need to develop different ways to analyze health and care values, with thought to cultural values in different life situations or environments. My studies of cross-cultural care values points to many qualitative differences in care among different cultures (Leininger, 1966, 1978, 1984a, 1985). Kluckhohn and Strodbeck's method for studying cultural values with a health and care focus remains a viable paradigm in analyzing values (Kluckhohn and Strodbeck, 1961). Different instruments and modes of analyzing nursing care values are just beginning to be studied. Value analysis is a powerful means to explain, interpret, and predict human care and nursing behaviors.

Content or Textual Analysis

Content analysis is a very old and familiar method of analyzing almost anything communicated between people. Berelson (1952) is best known for his early work in describing and analyzing content objectively and systematically. Holsti (1968) has also been an authority in content analysis, and he refers to content analysis as a quantitative and objective examination of primarily written and spoken communications. Quantification and objectivity have been the usual and traditional expectation of content analysis with qualitative analysis receiving less consideration. Content analysis includes analysis of messages, books, reports, films, drawings, letters, and related kinds of data. The ideas are often reduced to numbers or an enumeration of specific variables (Polit and Hungler, 1978, p. 380). The modes of analyzing the content tend to vary, with all data analyzed into explicit units or parts.

In recent years, content analysis has been advanced by the work of European leaders such as Lindkvist (1981), Rosengren (1981), linguists, and others who have done a thorough study of ways of performing content analysis. Social philosophers and linguists have focused on preserving the meaning of qualitative data through linguistic, semantic, and related data analyses. Most of all, these content specialists have given careful attention to the original text and to the development of precise textual categories, their interpretations and meanings.

Structural text analysis, by classifying the structure of text data into groups of different functional elements, has been promoted in content analysis so that events, persons, and processes are grouped according to similarity. Cultural data such as values are delineated and analyzed by their position in the system and by their semantic meanings. Lindkvist (1981) identifies four types of content analysis, namely: (1) general content analysis; (2) analytical semantics; (3) structuralism; and (4) hermeneutics. Content is primarily analyzed by the qualities of structural features and meanings rather than focusing on quantification or descriptive data per se, which characterizes the American approach. For example, analytical semantists (largely of the Scandinavian tradition of analytical philosophy) analyze textual data to determine the meaning of each script. "Reasonable interpretations" of a text are sought, with focus contextual claims of an empirical, linguistical, logical, and semantic nature. Sentences are noted to have different functions and can be interpreted independently of the formal nature of a sentence. The principle of reconstruction replaces the principle of testability (Lindkvist, 1981, p. 29), and the relationships among textual categories in the original text are made distinct and clear through precizations.

Other ways in which content is analyzed may be found in the work of Rosengren (1981), Berelson (1952), Holsti (1968), and several semantic linguists.

Hermeneutical Data Analysis

Hermeneutical analysis refers to the theory of interpretation. The names of Gadamer (1960), Hirsch (1967), and Ricoeur (1974) are commonly associated with hermeneutical analysis. For example, Gadamer holds that the text itself points to the method by which the material is to be interpreted (Lindkvist, 1981, p. 32). He believes that some methods tend to block our understanding of the truth. Gadamer speaks of people having a "horizon" or certain knowledge and preunderstandings so that every new text extends the interpreter's horizon. Lindkvist states, "The interpreter must have a genuine respect for the text. He does not create the meaning of the text, but is a receiver of it and the tradition it mediates" (1981, p. 32). The text is "truth" revealed through positive horizon extending features, whereas "method" may destroy the text. Hirsch and Ricoeur have challenged Gadamer's theory. Ricoeur tries to obtain the meaning of the text by freeing it from the "tutelage of mental intention" or from the intention of the author to the "world of the work." Hermeneutics has a phenomenological orientation, with focus on thoughts and ways to articulate preunderstandings. In general, hermeneutic analysis is largely unknown in nursing analysis as a formal and special mode of analyzing data. This method has had stronger developments in Europe than in the United States, and qualitative analysis is emphasized in the theory of interpretation.

Ethnoscience Analysis

Ethnoscience analysis is a formal, explicit, and systematic method of analyzing data to determine semantic and structural relationships of domains of knowledge. Because this method is important and a complex mode of analysis, it is discussed in Chapter 15 of this book.

Grounded Theory Analysis

This method of analysis was developed and named by Glaser and Strauss (1967). Discovering theory from data by means of comparative analysis is the goal. There are similarities and differences between this method and the anthropological ethnographic method. Grounded theory was developed in the mid 1960's, well after the ethnographic method was established, and these methods also have common features. Grounded theory analysis is discussed in Chapter 10 in this book.

Componential Analysis

Componential analysis is a complex, rigorous, and systematic mode of analysis to determine the semantic and structural relationships of particular emic-derived components or concepts and to formulate abstract statement(s) derived from the components. While the method may be used separately to analyze data, it is generally used in association with the ethnoscience method. It is discussed in Chapter 15 (Leininger) in this book.

Historical Analysis

This mode of analysis refers to the systematic investigation of past longitudinal historical data for various purposes or goals of the researcher. External and internal analyses of primary and secondary data over time periods are undertaken to identify events, patterns, and processes, that are time-spaced based. The historical analyst has the responsibility of reconceptualizing and restructuring fragmented events in order to identify certain relationships among facts and events. Accuracy with verification of primary sources of data increases the dimensions of truth. Quantitative analysis of certain numerical data may also be part of this method, but in-depth analysis of qualitative data is important to provide meaningful conclusions. Historical research is generally difficult to replicate, although comparative analysis of fairly similar event contexts may be studied for hypothesis and theory generation. The historical method is of growing importance to nurses seeking to document and understand past events and developments in nursing and their relationship to present-day practices. Chapter 7 (Kruman) in this book covers the historical method, and its purposes and modes of data analysis.

Life History Profile Analysis

A relatively new and valuable research method in nursing and other health disciplines is to used and analyze life history profiles of individuals, families, or groups to assess lifestyles and health and care patterns. Chapter 8 of this book provides an explication of this method. The method focuses on analyzing normal or abnormal life history events, patterns, and their relationship to health maintenance. This method was borrowed from the anthropological life history method, but it has been modified and reformulated to fit nursing and health care studies. The early work of Langness, *The Life History in Anthropological Sciences, Series of Studies in Anthropological Method* (1965) and Langness and Frank's book (1981) *Lives: An Anthropological Approach to Biography,* provide substantive information on this mode of analysis. An analysis of life history events is extremely relevant to nursing as it helps to identify longitudinal patterns of living related to wellness, caring, health maintenance, critical life events, and other struggles related to human health care.

Individual Health Study Analysis

Individual health study analysis focuses on a particular individual's mode of maintaining health, patterned illness, or other styles of survival through long (or short) spans of time in different (or the same) environmental contexts. Individual studies require both breadth and depth of focus to discover factors influencing the person's health status, lifestyle, and coping ways. This mode of analysis is important to (1) obtain intimate and detailed knowledge about the individual; (2) identify health, care, and illness patterns; (3) identify actual and potential factors leading to illness; and (4) gain a comprehensive view of the individual's environment and lifestyle over short or long periods of time. In doing qualitative research studies, the human being is viewed with respect as an individual of worth, and special interest.

The author uses the term "individual study" instead of "case study" analysis, because in qualitative research the individual is viewed as a unique or special person, not as an object, case, or statistic. Most assuredly, professional nurse researchers are familiar with the term "case studies," but now they need to rethink the use of this depersonalized term and consider analyzing individuals, and their health, illness, and care patterns in a personalized way. Analyzing individuals by life historus or by thematic, pattern, and contextual (or situational) methods is valuable to obtain a full and accurate picture of the individual within contrasting individual lifestyles. Documenting individual's qualitative lifeways can help nurses learn healthy and less healthy patterns of living. Because nurses have always valued and cared for (with) individuals, this method of analysis is a natural one and should be used frequently in qualitative research, but without reference to depersonalized "case studies." Different modes of individual studies of clients await discovery on nursing.

Configurational Analysis

Ruth Benedict (1956), a cultural anthropologist, was an early proponent of this method. Configurational analysis resembles componential, pattern, and theme types of analysis; however, it uses larger molar units for analysis and brings complex cultural themes and patterns into a configuration or molecular design to grasp the culture, system, or collective behavior.

Configurational analysis focuses on bringing together major structural units, themes and patterns of people such as the relationships of compliant, normative behavior (theme) with kinship and political systems. For example, child rearing patterns may be linked with authority or ecological systems to reflect a configuration or major mosaic design showing relationship among the structural units under study. A configurational analyist looks for obscure patterns that transcend particular individual features. Again, a high level of abstraction is required with this method. The findings make sense with cultural realities or in institutional practices. Benedict's work, *The Chrysanthemum and the Sword* (1956) provides an example of configurational analysis. To date, this method is essentially unknown to most nurse researchers and health care professionals, but its potentials for obtaining comprehensive views of human health lifestyles are clearly great.

Symbolic Analysis

Symbolic analysis refers to the analysis of different signs, messages, icons, material objects, and other forms of human expression. However, symbol analysis is again meagerly used in nursing and health research. In the health field many forms of symbols can be studied and analyzed to guide health practices; examples include the white uniform, nurse's cap, stethoscope, and other special signs used daily by nurses. Clients, too, use symbols to communicate their beliefs, values, and lifestyles to others. For example, an Arab child may wear a blue stone to protect himself from harm while in the hospital. An Afro-American may have a string with thirteen knots around the abdomen to protect herself from illness while in the hospital. Analysis of symbols requires knowledge of their cultural meaning of objects, icons and other media used by the person of a particular culture. Nurse researchers need to study the values, uses, and richness of symbol analyses in nursing care, rituals, and other activities within and outside the hospital environment.

Drawings, Games, Picture Tests, Play Modes, Story Telling, and Photographic Data Analysis

These expressive human methods are important ways of analyzing qualitative data. They are used to document and access individuals and group feelings, attitudes, and patterned expressions. Drawings, tests, stories, play, and other modes mentioned help the researcher identify patterns and specific expressions of values, motives, needs, and human responses. Child play and story-telling analysis offer free-form expressions of roles, attitudes, needs, and emotions of children and adolescents. There are various cognitive, psychoanalytical, culturological and other theories regarding the role of drawings, games, and photographs to interpret cultural and other data accurately. Projective testing continues to be challenged because of the culture-bound nature of the tests. Aggression, submission, and other human responses tend to vary with cultural values and must be examined within a culture; generalizations to all human cultures must be made cautiously. Hence, projective tests and responses to stimuli still have questionable value with respect to universal meanings.

In the future, electronic computer games will be used to analyze child and adult behavior. How people solve problems, cope with losses or wins, and express fears and goals are some of the kinds of data that can be obtained from the computer technology.

It is to be hoped that games will be developed to study people's choices and reasons for health care services. Computer machines are already available and should be valuable in identifying people's feelings and needs. Structured and unstructured games analyzed within particular cultural contexts can reveal much about an individual, family, and cultural representatives. Detailed observations and analysis of such data should lead to special insights about care, illness, and health care experiences.

It is rare for transcultural nurses or pediatric nurse researchers not to use play and photographic equipment today with their field studies. Bateson and Mead's work (1942) may serve as a model for nurse researchers in demonstrating the importance of pictures and play to document and know artistic expressions of human groups.

Drawings, photographs and other expressive forms reveal people's views and are qualitative types of research data to be analyzed. Chapter 20 (Leininger) of this book provides more information on the use of drawings and photographs as well as ways to analyze such data.

Computer Data Analysis

With modern technology has come the rapid development, expansion, and use of electronic computers. This is the "age of computers" and the "age of numbers." Most researchers are expected to analyze their data by computers "to be accepted and acceptable researchers," especially as modern quantitative and qualitative data analyzers.

The role of electronic computers in analyzing quantitative types of data is quite clear; however, their value in analyzing qualitative data is less clear at this time. Preserving meanings, attitudes, characteristics, symbols, rituals, and many other aspects of qualitative data remains a major area for development by computer scientists and qualitative analysts. Reducing statements to numbers, specific variables, or other kinds of reductionistic modes tends to destroy the meaning and purposes of the qualitative data. The author recalls the attempt of a computer scientist to reduce a birthing care ritual to three lines of numbers. It took hours to decode and interpret, and the meaning of the ritual was completely lost. The author believes, however, that in time there will be computer breakthroughs for qualitative data analysis that preserve the content. This is occurring now with the author's ethno-graph software and it is great to eliminate the current tedious recording and manual analysis of volumes of rich qualitative field and clinical data. The challenge to nursing phenomenological, philosophical, and other qualitative researchers to develop and perfect qualitative software and sound computer programs without reducing all qualitative data to numbers unless meanings are explicit remains a stimulating one.

Other Modes of Analysis

These computer methods should help the researcher envision the many creative possibilities in analyzing clinical, field, institutional, cultural, and other types of qualitative data. Such modes of analyses are also valuable in generating theories and new lines of research. There are, however, still other types of data analysis methods that need to be considered such as the following:

Role, Family, and Institutional Analyses
Cognitive-Mapping and World View
Symbolic Interactional Analysis
Comparative or Cross-Cultural Analysis
Ethical and Moral Analyses
Participatory Analysis
Attributional Analysis
Ecological Care Analysis
Genealogical Analysis (with kingrams)
Material and Nonmaterial Data Analyses
Semantic and Semiotic Analyses
Combined Qualitative and Quantitative Analyses
Health Calendar and Health Diary Analyses

Interpreting, Summarizing, and Reporting the Findings

The final phase of any research endeavor is to interpret, summarize, and report the findings to others. This requires considerable creativity, intellectual abilities, and attentiveness to the original purposes of the study. Much thought must be given to the best way to communicate and publish the results. This goal is generally more difficult to achieve for qualitative than for quantitative research. One reason for this is because of the importance of preserving volumes of rich data needed by research consumers concerning meanings, attributes, values, world view, and structural and other components that characterize human styles. In addition, there is no effective mechanical or electronic means to handle large volumes or small amounts of qualitative data. As indicated earlier, qualitative data is far more difficult to analyze and present than quantitative types of research data. Furthermore, more time, creative thought, and analytical abilities seem to be required to interpret, summarize, and report qualitative findings.

In the process of interpreting the findings, the researcher must keep close to the goals, purposes, or intent of the study. Generally, qualitative findings are emphasized to help the reader grasp the qualitative features and results of the study. Demographic and any quantitative findings are appropriately woven into the report; examples are found in the reports of Wang (1982), Tripp-Reimer (1983), and others. Most importantly, the findings and report should be written clearly; they should have both scientific and humanistic information that can be understood by the public and research users. Qualitative studies remain of great interest to the public because they "make sense" as they are generally written in phrases people use. The art of combining humanistic and scientific data in a qualitative report requires much skill and creative writing. It is also important to realize that qualitative articles require more publication space, and publishers should not expect the same space requirements as for quantitative reports. At present, this is a serious problem with publishers who are unaware of and lack appreciation for the differences in reporting findings from two different types of research. Hence, reducing a qualitative report to the space norms of a quantitative study often leads to the omission of material that is needed to understand qualitative findings. It is to be hoped that there will be more editors and publishers knowledgeable about qualitative research in the future to remedy this problem as well as authors discovering ways to be concise and still communicate the essential ideas.

Validity and Reliability Criteria for Qualitative Research

Before bringing this chapter to a close, the critical issue of what constitutes validity and reliability for qualitative research needs to be addressed. This is a matter that merits more attention, study, and debate. The critical question is, Can or should the same criteria be used to determine validity and reliability for qualitative research as are used for quantitative research? I do not believe so, as the purposes, goals, and intent of these two types of research differ. Different criteria therefore are required to appraise validity and reliability. At present, qualitative researchers are expected to meet the validity and reliability definitions and implied criteria for quantitative types of research; the logic and rationale tend to be overlooked.

As mentioned in Chapter 1, there are *differences* in the *purposes* of the two types of research. Cook and Reichardt (1979), Patten (1980), and Van Maanen, Dobbs, and Faulkner (1983) point to these substantive differences. Consider the popular definitions of validity and reliability. In quantitative research, validity refers to the degree to which an instrument measures what it is supposed to be measuring (Polit and Hungler, 1978, p. 434); measurement is the focus. In contrast, I contend that *validity* in qualitative research *refers to gaining knowledge and understanding of the true nature, essence, meanings, attributes, and characteristics of a particular phenomenon under study. Measurement is not the goal; rather, knowing and understanding the phenomenon is the goal.* Qualitative validity is concerned with confirming the truth or understandings associated with phenomena. The *criterion-related* approach to qualitative validity assessment does not focus on the validity of the instrument or on "how well the tool is *measuring* a particular thing"; instead, the emphasis is on establishing the *existence* and *nature of the phenomenon with its meanings, attributes, and contextual features.* Hence, qualitative *construct validity* focuses on *identifying and knowing the nature, essence, and underlying attributes of the phenomenon* under study rather than validating the instrument to measure the object or thing. Still other points of difference must be stated.

In quantitative research, *concurrent validity* refers to the *ability of the instrument to measure and distinguish individuals who differ with respect to some objective measures.* This definitional criterion seriously limits the purposes of qualitative research. In qualitative research, *concurrent validity* should refer instead to the *ability to show congruency, meanings, and syntactical relationships of findings with respect to subjective, inferential, intuitive, symbolic, objective (empirical), and other quality factors under consideration.* Thus *qualitative validity* should rest upon *knowing and understanding the phenomena as fully as possible* rather than on the adequacy of the instrument and measuring the results. Again, the qualitative *predictive validity* criterion should rest upon the *ability (including knowledge and skills) of the researcher to differentiate abstracted experiential and empirical phenomenon under study in order to predict human lifeways or behavior;* should not rely on the adequacy of instruments per se to measure behavior or subjects.

With respect to the criterion of *reliability*, in *quantitative research* again is the focus primarily upon the measuring tool or on its ability to guage *"the degree of consistency or accuracy with which an instrument measures an attribute"* (Polit and Hungler, 1978, p. 445). In *qualitative research*, however, *reliability* focuses on *identifying and documenting recurrent, accurate, and consistent (homogeneous) or inconsistent (heterogeneous) features, as patterns, themes, values, world views, experiences, and other phenomena confirmed in similar or different contexts.* Reliability as internal and external consistency and recurrency is important, to the extent that the phenomena under study consistently reveal meaningful and accurate truths about particular phenomena.

As can be judged from the foregoing formulations of the two major types of research, it is time to recognize and give serious attention to the validity and reliability criteria for qualitative and quantitative research. Otherwise, all qualitative research gets reduced to quantitative data, and the heart or flesh of the data is lost. The author contends the criteria have a different focus as the outcomes of the types of research are different. At present, students of research are taught to use quantitative validity and reliability for qualitative studies. As a result, confusion, conflict, and other problems are evident today. In addition, many qualitative nurse researchers face problems in obtaining grants and in getting their research results published when validity and reliability factors that fit quantitative research are being used. To use qualitative validity and reliability will require bold and active leadership to change current traditional research normative practices in nursing and in other fields. The pendulum is fortunately swinging to qualitative research methodologies so nursing and other health disciplines will undoubtedly be moving soon to meet this world-wide trend.

REFERENCES

Aamodt, A. Observations of a health and healing system in a Papago community. In M. Leininger (Ed.), *Transcultural health issues and conditions for health care dimensions.* Philadelphia: F. A. Davis, 1976.

Agar, M. H. *The professional stranger: An informal ethnography.* New York: Academic Press, 1981.

Bateson, G., and Mead, M. *Balinese character: A photographic analysis.* New York: New York Academy of Science Special Publication, 1942.

Beattie, J. *Bunyoro: An african kingdom.* New York: Holt, Rinehart & Winston, 1960.

Benedict, R. *The chrysanthemum and the sword.* Boston: Boston Press, 1956.

Benet, S. *Abkhasians: The long-living people of the Caucasus*. New York: Holt, Rinehart & Winston, 1974.

Berreman, G. *Behind many masks*. Ithaca, N.Y: Society for Applied Anthropology, 1962.

Boas, F. The methods of ethnology. *American Anthropologist*, 1924, *22*, 311–321.

Boyle, J. Illness experiences and the role of women in Guatemala. In J. Uhl (Ed.), *Proceedings of the Eighth Annual Transcultural Nursing Conference*, 1983, pp. 52–71.

Boyle, J. An application of the structural-functional method to the phenomenon of caring. In M. Leininger, *Caring: An essential human need*. Thorofare, NJ: Charles B. Slack, 1981, pp. 37–49.

Byerly, E. L. The nurse-researcher as participant-observer in a nursing setting. *Nursing Research*, 1968, *18*(3), 230–236.

Chance, N. *The Eskimo of North Alaska*. New York: Holt, Rinehart & Winston, 1966.

Cook, T. & Reichardt, C. (eds.). *Qualitative and quantitative methods in evaluation research*, (Vol. 1). Sage Research Progress Series in Evaluation. Beverly Hills, Calif.: Sage Publications, 1979.

Dougherty, M. C. *Becoming a woman in rural Black culture*. New York: Holt, Rinehart & Winston, 1978.

Dreher, M. C. *Working men of Ganja*. Philadelphia: Institute for the Study of Human Issues, 1982.

Estroff, S. *Making it Crazy: An Ethnography of Psychiatric clients in an American Community*. Berkely, California University of California Press, 1981.

Evans-Pritchard, E. E. Social anthropology: Past and present. In P. Bohannan & M. Glazer (Eds.), *Highpoints in anthropology*. New York: Alfred A. Knopf, 1973.

Gadamer, H. G. *Wahrheit und Methode*. Tubingen: J. C. B. Mohr (Paul Siebeck), 1960.

Germain, C. *The cancer unit: An ethnography*. Wakefield, Mass.: Nursing Resources, Inc., 1979.

Glaser, B. G., & Strauss, A. L. *The discovery of grounded theories: Strategies for qualitative research*. Chicago: Aldine Publishing Co., 1967.

Glittenberg, J. E. An ethnographic approach to the problem of health assessment and program planning: Project Genesis. In P. Morley (Ed.), *Developing, teaching and prac-ticing transcultural nursing*. Salt Lake City: University of Utah, 1981.

Glittenberg, J. K. Fertility patterns and child rearing of the Ladinos and Indians in Guatemala. In M. Leininger (Ed.), *Transcultural nursing: Proceedings from four transcultural nursing conferences*. New York: Masson Publishing Company, 1979, pp. 140–155.

Hirsch, E. D. *Validity and Interpretation*. New Haven, Conn.: Yale University Press, 1967.

Holsti, O. R. Content analysis. In G. Lindzey, & E. Aronson (Eds.), *The Handbook of Social Psychology* (2nd ed.). Reading, Mass.: Addison-Wesley, 1968.

Horn, B. Transcultural nursing and child-rearing of the Muckleshoot people. In M. Leininger, *Transcultural nursing: Concepts, theories and practices*. New York: John Wiley & Sons, 1978.

Hostetler, J. *Amish Society* (3rd ed.). Baltimore: The Johns Hopkins University Press, 1980.

Kendall, K. W. Personality development in an Iranian village: An analysis of socialization practices and the development of the woman's role (unpublished dissertation). Seattle: University of Washington, 1968.

Kluckhohn, C. *Mirror for man*. New York: McGraw-Hill Book Company, 1949.

Kluckhohn, F. R., & Strodbeck, F. L. *Variations in value orientations*. Evanston, Ill.: Row, Peterson Co., 1961.

LaFargue, J. Those you can count on: A social network study of family organization in an urban Black population (unpublished doctoral dissertation). Seattle: University of Washington, 1981.

Langness, L. *The life history in anthropological science, series of studies in anthropological method*. New York: Holt, Rinehart and Winston, 1965.

Langness, L. & Frank, G. *Lives: An anthropological approach to biography*. Novato, Calif.: Chandler & Sharp Publishers, Inc., 1981.

Leininger, M. *Convergence and divergence of human behavior: An ethnopsychological comparative study of two Gadsup villages in the Eastern Highlands of New Guinea*. Unpublished doctoral dissertation University of Washington, Seattle, Washington, 1966.

Leininger, M. *Nursing and anthropology: Two worlds to blend*. New York: John Wiley & Sons, 1970.

Leininger, M. Study of the health-illness system of Spanish-Americans in an urban community. Denver, Col: Unpublished, 1968.

Leininger, M. Transcultural nursing: Concepts, theories and practices. New York: John Wiley & Sons, 1978.

Leininger, M. (Ed.). Transcultural nursing: Proceedings from four transcultural nursing conferences. New York: Masson Publishing Co., 1979.

Leininger, M. Caring: An essential human need. Thorofare, N.J.: Charles B. Slack, 1981.

Leininger, M. Transcultural care diversity and universality: A theory of nursing. Thorofare, N.J. Charles B. Slack, 1985.

Leininger, M. Reference sources for transcultural health & nursing. Thorofare, N.J.: Charles B. Slack, 1984b

Leininger, M. Care: The essence of nursing and health. Thorofare, N.J.: Charles B. Slack, 1984c

Leininger, M. Ethnohealth, ethnocaring and ethnonursing of six cultures. Detroit, Mich.: Wayne State University, 1984d (In press).

Levi-Strauss, C. Social structure. In P. Bohannan & M. Glazer (Eds.), Highpoints in Anthropology. New York: Alfred A. Knopf Co., 1973.

Lindkvist, K. Approaches to textual analysis. In K. Rosengren (Ed.), Advances in content analysis. Beverly Hills, Calif: Sage Publications, 1981, pp. 23–42.

Malinowski, B. Argonauts of the Western Pacific. New York: E. P. Dutton, 1961 (reprinted), London: Routledge, 1922.

Mead, M. Coming of age in Samoa. New York: New American Library, 1929.

Mishler, E. Meaning in context: Is there any other kind? Educational Review, 1979, 19(1), 1–19.

Murray, H. A. Explorations in personality. New York: Oxford, 1938.

Nadel, S. F. The theory of social structure. Glencoe, Ill.: Free Press, 1957.

Patton, M. Q. Qualitative evaluation methods. Beverly Hills, Calif.: Sage Publishing Company, 1980.

Polit, D., & Hungler, B. Nursing research: Principles and methods. Philadelphia: J. B. Lippincott, 1978.

Pelto, P., & Pelto, G. Anthropological research. New York: Harper & Row, 1979.

Pelto, P. Anthropological research: The structure of inquiry. New York: Harper & Row, 1970.

Radcliffe-Brown, A. R. Structure and function in primitive society. Glencoe, Ill.: Free Press, 1952.

Ragucci, A. T. Health and illness beliefs and practices in a southern Italian community: An ethnographic study. Philadelphia, PA: American Philosophical Society, 1974.

Ray, M. A. A study of caring within an institutional culture (doctoral dissertation). Ann Arbor: University of Michigan, 1981.

Ricoeur, P. Metaphor and the main problem of hermeneutics. New Literary History, VI, I, 1974.

Rosengren, K. R. (Ed.) Advances in content analysis. Beverly Hills, Calif.: Sage Publications, 1981.

Sohier, R. The influence of Mormon socialization in gender development in childhood (unpublished thesis). Chicago: University of Chicago, 1981.

Spradley, J. The cocktail waitress: Woman's work in a man's land. New York: John Wiley & Sons, 1975.

Spradley, J. Participant-observation. New York: Holt, Rinehart & Winston, 1980.

Spradley, J. You owe yourself a drunk. Boston: Little, Brown & Company, 1970.

Spradley, J. Down and out on skid row. In S. Feldman & G. Theilbar (Eds.), Lifestyles: Diversity in American society. Boston: Little, Brown & Company, 1972.

Spradley, J. The ethnographic interview. New York: Holt, Rinehart & Winston, 1979.

Tripp-Reimer, T. Retention of folk healing practices (Matiasma) among four generations of urban Greek immigrants. Nursing Research, March–April 1983. Vol. 32, 97–101.

Van Maanen, J., Dabbs, J., Jr., & Faulkner, R. Varieties of qualitative research. Beverly Hills, Calif.: Sage Publishing Company, 1983.

Wang, J. Caretaker-child interaction observed in two Appalachian clinics. In M. Leininger, Care: Essence of nursing & health. Thorofare, N.J.: Charles B. Slack, 1984.

Watson, J. Nursing: The philosophy and science of caring. Boston: Little, Brown & Company, 1979.

Zderad, L. T. Humanistic nursing. New York: John Wiley & Sons, 1967.

4

Philosophical Analysis as Research Method

Delores A. Gaut

A task widely assumed to be distinctive of philosophy has been to assess and systematically relate from some integrating perspective the diversity of human knowledge and experience. This conception of philosophy recognizes that a class of questions exists that are generally regarded as characteristically philosophical because the questions deal with foundational problems of knowledge, being, or value. The more traditional philosophical approaches attempt to provide a comprehensive and systematic view of reality and of the meaning of life itself (Soltis, 1978, p. 80).

A fairly new approach to philosophizing about ideas and phenomena is that of the analytic philosopher, wherein the techniques of analysis are utilized for improving an understanding of important human endeavors by the clarification of language. Analysts are concerned with clarifying the arguments and methods employed by human beings in their speech and thought. Techniques of analysis can force abstract and vague ideas into concrete and more meaningful contexts (Scheffler, 1958, p. 1).

Whereas the empirical researcher may ask questions that require explanation of events or causes, the philosopher asks questions that pertain to logical relationships and statements of justification. Nagel explains further the tasks of analysis:

> Analysis not only seeks to clarify concepts for the sake of clarification, but also to criticize cognitive claims in order to suggest alternative ways for organizing portions of knowledge. While philosophy is not an empirical enterprise, it can make research more successful by clarifying the concepts used in empirical research. (Nagel, 1960, p. 75)

QUALITATIVE RESEARCH METHODS IN NURSING
ISBN 0-8089-1676-9

To call for the application of philosophical methods to nursing research is to call for a clarification of the concepts chosen for study as well of the ways in which we formulate beliefs, arguments, assumptions, and judgments in nursing research. Serious interest in nursing concepts and research may be fused with serious concern for philosophical clarity and rigor. The basic significance of philosophical activity lies in the rational reflection, critical analysis of arguments and assumptions, and systematic clarification of the fundamental ideas that its methods address. In applying philosophical methods of analysis, we are concerned directly with solving intellectual rather than practical difficulties and with removing the perplexities that arise in our attempts to say systematically and clearly what we are doing in nursing research and why.

The purpose of this chapter is twofold: (1) to acquaint the reader to philosophical analysis as a research method, and (2) to demonstrate three techniques utilized in concept analysis: generic type, differentiation type, and conditions type.

CONCEPT ANALYSIS

In concept analysis, the purpose is to identify categories based on the use of the concept in normal language. The goal is not to develop concepts, but rather, through analysis and explication of broad and comprehensive concepts, to become aware of the various types of referents for the term. In addition, analysis provides a clear set of conditions or criteria to be met if a concept is strictly applicable in any particular context.

Clarifying concepts is not the same as ascertaining facts or making value judgments. The point of analytic strategies is to clarify conceptual rather than value or empirical issues, in a search for a conceptual perspective that will help in theorizing or problem solving. Soltis identified three types of analysis, the generic type, the differentiation type, and the conditions type, each with differing questions and aims. The following analytic strategies are drawn primarily from Soltis's work (Soltis, 1978, pp. 98–105).

Strategies for clarifying conceptual issues include asking a certain kind of prior question depending on the kind of information being sought. For instance, a generic-type analysis aims at finding the necessary conceptual features or properties of a thing and tries to answer, "What is an X?" or, "What features make something an X?" If the analyst is interested in identifying and separating basic senses of meaning, a differentiation-type strategy is used, and the prior question would be, "What are the different uses of the term X?" or, "What are the various types of X?" Lastly, a conditions-type analysis would attempt to answer the question, "What are the contextual conditions under which it would be correct to say that someone is X-ing?" or, "What conditions govern the proper use of the term X?"

The following section is presented in the hope that the steps and examples will not only assist the reader in a further understanding of the strategies, but also encourage and enable the reader to attempt concept analysis.

Generic-Type Analysis

The concept requiring clarification is the geometric term 'square'.* The prior question would be, "What features must a two-dimensional figure have to be called a square?"

---

*The single quotation marks are used when referring to a word as a word or concept.

Step 1. Drawing from your general knowledge of squares, identify a necessary feature of all squares.

Step 2: Test for necessity and sufficiency of the feature through the use of examples and counterexamples.

Step 3: Keep, modify, or reject the feature on the basis of the necessity and sufficiency tests.

Step 4: Repeat steps 1, 2, and 3 for each identified feature. These features or conditions then serve as the criteria for the proper use of the term 'square.'

Example of Generic-Type Analysis

Step 1. The necessary features of all squares include the following:
A square must have four sides.
A square must have four right angles.
A square must have four equal sides.

Step 2. Test each feature for necessity and sufficiency.

There are two ways to test the features identified. The first is by asking if the criteria are necessary features of square. For example, can you draw a square that does not have four sides? If not, then having four sides is a necessary characteristic of squares. The second test has to do with sufficiency. Having four sides may be necessary, but is it possible to draw a four-sided figure that isn't a square? The answer is yes, because a rectangle has four sides. Therefore, although the four sides is a necessary feature, by itself it is not sufficient to determine a square from other four-sided figures. Additional features must be sought.

In addition to a square having four sides, a square must also have four right angles. This feature of four right angles is necessary, for if one right angle was eliminated, the figure would no longer be a square. Nevertheless, having four sides and four right angles, although necessary for a square, are not sufficient, because a rectangle also has four sides and four right angles. Another feature must be found that will discriminate a square from other four-sided figures that have four right angles.

The last feature added to the description is that a square must have four equal sides. This is a necessary feature of square, for if three sides were long and one side short, the figure would not be a square. But are features 1, 2, and 3 when taken together sufficient to distinguish a figure as a square? No counterexamples can be found that include all three features— four sides, four right angles, and four equal sides—that are not squares.

These three features when taken together, serve as the criteria for the proper use of the term 'square.' The point of this type of analysis was to identify those features which logically must obtain to identify 'square' from all other two-dimensional figures.

This example of analysis of 'square' was fairly straightforward, for the features of squares are invariant. Regardless of the context or situation, the proper use of the term square is always guided by the above-stated features. In this sense, 'square' is a monomorphic term, whose features are easily identified and tested. However, polymorphic terms or concepts, such as 'teaching' or 'caring', also exist and can be analyzed in a similar way, but because they are context-bound or dependent they require more than a generic-type analysis. For example, whether a certain action will count as caring depends not only on what the action is, but also on the context in which it is done.

The questions that must be addressed with a concept such as caring include not only what must be true to distinguish caring from noncaring, but also how caring activity is distinguished from all other activity. Such analysis requires both differentiation among the senses of caring, and the examination of the contextual conditions. These requirements call for both a differentiation-type analysis which asks, "What are the basic different meanings of caring?" and a conditions-type analysis, which asks, "Under what conditions would it be true to say that S is caring for X?"

Differentiation-Type Analysis

Given that the concept 'caring' seems to have more than one standard meaning, and the bases for differentiating them are not clear, the first step in this analysis will be to search for dominant standard uses of the concept. In analyzing caring as an activity, the aim is not to invent some new concept or idea of caring or even to specify what people ought to mean by caring. The goal is rather to study, clarify, and more thoroughly understand the idea of caring as it already exists in our language (Green, 1971, p. 3).

The analysis begins with the following questions:

1. How is the word caring employed in normal usage? How does it differ from non-caring?

2. What examples can be given to demonstrate the use of 'caring' and 'non-caring'?

Example of Differentiation Strategies

The search for the meanings of caring begins with consideration of the term as a word in common usage over time. Using the Oxford English Dictionary, for example, the word 'caring' can be traced from the Old English and Gothic words *carian* and *kara* or *karon* (c. A.D. 1000), meaning charging the mind with concern, heed, or attention as in "attend to this matter with due care." With the later addition of the preposition "for," the sense of attending to also becomes one of "regard for."

Further examination of the word indicated no clear-cut rules for the use of the term, but rather a general family of meanings all related to the notion of caring in three senses: (1) attention to or concern for; (2) responsibility for or providing for; and (3) regard, fondness, or attachment. The negative sense of the word, "not to care" or "uncaring," adds additional credence to those three senses, for 'noncaring' is used to convey the notion of disregard, inattention, or indifference.

Utilizing the three identified senses of 'caring', a next step might be to examine the literature that speaks of caring, to identify any special or extended use of the concept not found in normal usage. For example, a review of selected writings from the nursing literature revealed that the discussion of caring in nursing related directly to the values and attitudes existing at any given historical period. The term caring, in the early nursing literature, speaks of the physical care of the sick (Nightingale, 1964; Taylor, 1934). This notion later evolved into the discussion of nursing as a caring process within the nurse-patient relationship (Orlando, 1961; Peplau, 1963), and the recent literature speaks of caring as the essence of nursing (Leininger, 1977).

A review of various sources of nursing literature revealed that although the heritage and traditions of nursing are firmly rooted in the value and practice of caring, little if any attempt had been made to understand the nature and essence of the concept of caring as a basis for nursing theory, research, and practice. At a time when the nursing profession is attempting to develop its own body of knowledge as an academic discipline, it becomes imperative that the language used to define theoretical concepts be precise, unambiguous, and readily communicated; thus the concern for philosophical analysis and the clarification of concepts.

Having reviewed the general literature, it became evident that the statements about caring were contemporaneous with the common word 'senses.' The next step in the analysis could be to search for standard uses of the concept by means of examples, and then to classify or categorize the uses identified into types. Caring can be differentiated by the three identified senses: caring as giving attention to or having concern for; caring as being responsible for or providing for; and caring as having regard or fondness for, or attachment to. From the examples of situations of caring, it becomes obvious that 'caring for,' in the sense of providing for or being responsible for, can be talked about apart from any sense of 'caring about.' However, 'caring about' brings a quality to the relationship between the carer and the cared-for. 'Caring about' eliminates the apathy, indifference, obligation, withdrawal, isolation, manipulation, and possession so possible in situations of providing for or being responsible for.

It became obvious that as a concept caring does not have one determinate definition or singular meaning in all contexts. Although the analysis did provide some general rules regarding the correct use of caring, the question remains, "Under what conditions would it be true to say that caring is present, or that S is caring for X?" The strategy useful in addressing such questions is a conditions-type analysis.

Conditions-Type Analysis

In order to arrive at a clearer idea of the contextual dimension of caring or any other concept, one would follow these steps:

Step 1. Identify a feature of the concept, such as caring, that seems to be a necessary condition to say that S is caring for X.

Step 2. By altering the context or situation, try to find an example in which the condition holds, but caring does not.

Step 3. Revise or modify the condition to meet the context problem, or tease out from the altered context another condition and test it as in step 2.

Step 4. Test the necessity and sufficiency of the conditions arrived at as in generic-type analysis.

Example of Conditions-Type Analysis

The following analysis of caring is offered as an example of the conditions-type strategy. In this analysis, caring is considered an action a person engages in or is occupied in doing, and as such, the action is directed toward a goal. Caring as action is to be understood in this example as S providing something for X. For the sake of precision and objectivity, the analysis considers S caring for an object rather than a person.

Question: What must be true to say that S is caring for X?

Situation: S represents a teacher. X represents the teacher's office walls that are in a state of disrepair.

First condition: S must be aware, either directly or indirectly, of the wall's state of disrepair.

Discussion: It seems necessary that for S to be said to be caring for the wall, S must first be aware of the state of disrepair. If S is on leave in another country, or if the disrepair is not visible, it would be unlikely we would speak of S as caring or not caring for the walls. However, if the walls are cracked and peeling, and obviously in disrepair, then for S to be considered caring for X, S must be aware of the need for care. Awareness, then, is necessary to speak of 'caring,' but is it sufficient? It would appear not, for S could walk into the office and say, "I see the office walls are in disrepair, but I don't know what to do about it." Something more than awareness is needed. Let us consider a second condition.

Second condition: S must know that certain things could be done to improve the situation.

Discussion: It does not seem likely that S would be considered as caring for the wall unless S knew something about walls, and knew what kinds of things might be done to improve the situation, or at the very least knew who to call for advice and expertise.

Given that S is aware of the need for care, and S knows what needs to be done, is that sufficient to say that S is caring for X? Probably not, for S could walk into the office, see the condition of the walls, know they need to be painted and still say, "I see the walls are in disrepair, but I don't intend to do anything about it." Something more than awareness and knowledge are required. Let us consider a third condition.

Third condition: S must intend to do something for X.

Discussion: To intend to do something for X requires, at the very least, a disposition to choose some action, or purpose, or plan to meet the need for care in X. S must not only be aware of the need for care and know that something could be done, but also must intend to do something relative to the need for care. It would be contradictory for S to say "I am caring for X, but I do not intend to do anything for X."

Even though the conditions of awareness, knowledge, and intention are necessary conditions, they still are not sufficient to say that S is caring for X.

Consider another example: S walks into the office and exclaims, "These walls are in bad shape, and if I have time, I'll paint them with the old cement-floor paint I have in the basement to save money. S is aware of the condition of the walls, knows the walls need painting, presumably knows how to paint walls, and states an intended activity. Even though the first three conditions are met, S's actions would make the caring questionable on two counts: (1) The "if I have time" statement allows of the possibility that the intended action will never be carried out, and (2) the choice of paint designed for cement floors for use on wooden walls to save money would not seem to account for what would be good for X. What seems to be required is a condition that will take into account both the implementation of the intended activity and the purpose or goal of such activity.

Fourth Condition: S must choose an action intended to help bring about a positive change in X, and then implement that action.

Discussion: The positive change for X is to be understood in the sense of making a difference in X's state or welfare of the object or person being cared for, and that difference must in general be considered to be good for X. S must not only intend some action, but also intend that action to serve as a means for bringing about a positive change in X. In addition, S must implement, either directly or through an agent, the action chosen. But if S does implement the action chosen, can we say that S is caring for X? It is possible that the action chosen, although it may appear to make a difference in the state of the wall (a new coat of paint), was perhaps not a positive change, for there is the possibility exists that the reason for choosing the action was based on what S knows is good for walls in general, but not this particular wall. Or S may have chosen the action because it was the easiest for S to accomplish, and the welfare of the wall was not the primary consideration. What seems to be required is a condition, that will take into consideration a nonarbitrary measure of what may be considered a positive change in X.

Fifth condition: The positive change in X must be judged on the basis of what is good for X rather than S or some other agent or object (Y or Z).

Discussion: To say that S is caring for X would require that S be aware of the needs of X as a particular kind of thing, requiring certain kinds of doings that are perhaps different from the requirements of other types of things. Prior to implementing the action, then, S must not only intend the doings as a means for bringing about a positive change in X, but that positive change must be directly related to what is generally considered good for all walls versus cement floors or other paintable objects, as well as what is good for this particular wall with its particular needs.

This discussion of caring distinguished between S's caring or not caring for an object in the sense of providing for. Five logical conditions were identified—awareness, knowledge, intention, positive change, and welfare of X—that allow one to say S is caring for X if, and only if, those five conditions prevail. To the end of refining the analysis even more, and extending the consideration of caring for persons, the following questions could be addressed:

1. In what sense must S be aware of X in order to care for X?
2. What must S know in order to care for X?
3. What is the relationship between the intended action and the need for care?
4. What would count as a positive-change direction for X?

This chapter has attempted to demonstrate that in addition to empirical questions, which most often receive the attention of researchers, there are other kinds of questions and problems that require consideration if we are to understand and improve the enterprise of nursing research through philosophical analysis.

REFERENCES

Green, T. F. *The activities of teaching.* New York: McGraw-Hill, 1971.

Leininger, M. Caring: The essence and central focus of nursing. The phenomenon of caring. American Nurses Foundation Nursing Research Report, Part V, 1977.

Nagel, E. Philosophy in educational research. In F. W. Banghart (Ed.), *First annual symposium on educational research.* Indianapolis: Phi Delta Kappa, 1960.

Nightingale, F. *Notes on nursing: What it is and what it is not.* Philadelphia: J. B. Lippincott, 1964.

Orlando, J. *The dynamic nurse-patient relationship.* New York: G. P. Putnam, 1961.

Peplau, H. Interpersonal relations and the process of adaptation. *Nursing Science,* 1963, *11,* 272–279.

Scheffler, E. *Philosophy and education.* Boston: Allyn and Bacon, 1958.

Soltis, J. *An introduction to content analysis.* Boston: Addison-Wesley, 1978.

Taylor, E. Of what is the nature of nursing? *American Journal of Nursing,* May, 1934.

5

A Philosophical Method to Study Nursing Phenomena

Marilyn A. Ray

A new movement is occurring within the scientific community of nursing. Many researchers and theorists are becoming disillusioned with the scientific method of positivistic—empiricism as the dominant mode of scientific inquiry. The typically used experimental method, which infers the existence and direction of causal relations as well as assumes linearity (Tinkle and Beaton, 1983), is being questioned. This heightened awareness has led researchers to recognize and acknowledge that a contradiction exists between nursing philosophy and nursing research. Munhall states that "nursing philosophy almost universally includes a belief about holistic man.* The holistic view of man insists that man possesses an integration that does not allow analysis by breaking him down into reducible parts and piecing him back together" (Munhall, 1982, p. 176). Furthermore, Munhall claims that each person experiences his own "reality," and is autonomous. This apparent disparity between the nursing beliefs of individualism and holism, and the limitations of a methodological inquiry, that gives little information about how to fit the parts back into the dynamic whole of lived experience in historical and cultural settings, has guided researchers to examine the value of the qualitative method.

Qualitative research includes the study of individuals and groups as well as cultural-historical factors through such anthropological methods as ethnography, ethnoscience, and grounded theoretical methods from sociology, all of which have

---

*Although Munhall uses the term man, this author also implies the use of the term woman.

been identified as appropriate research approaches to develop and structure nursing knowledge. More recently, however, the phenomenological method—expressed as a philosophy, approach, and method—has been introduced into nursing research by the concepts or works of Davis (1978), Oiler (1982), Omery (1983), Paterson and Zderad (1976), Ray (1979) Reeder (personal communication, 1983), Stevens (1971), and others. Since phenomenology attempts to provide a method from which to study human experience as it is lived, including a description of the meanings that these experiences have for individuals who participate in them (Omery, 1983), it is both relevant and necessary as a qualitative research method for the nursing profession.

The nursing discipline has both scientific and humanistic care dimensions. In the past few decades, researchers have made progress in developing and structuring the scientific knowledge base of nursing. The humanistic identity of the nursing discipline, however, has received less attention. Inherent in humanism are beliefs and values, which as Munhall remarks "are found in such expressions as becoming, freedom, self-determination, autonomy, and human potential" (1982, p. 176). In nursing, many theorists have referred to these humanistic expressions. For example, Leininger (1978) encourages and reinforces the evolution of humanistic knowledge along with scientific knowledge in the study of transcultural nursing (the study of caring values and behaviors of different cultural and subcultural groups). Moreover, Leininger and others hold to the position that caring is the central construct of nursing (Leininger, 1978, 1981). Accordingly, since caring, in its most significant sense, is defined as helping another to grow and actualize herself or himself (Mayeroff, 1971) or to achieve human potential, the way to understanding humanistic expressions is by the description and explication of the meaning of nursing care in lived experience.

What is needed in nursing is a way in which the concepts of humanism (or helping another to grow through caring) can become known while at the same time maintaining a scientific attitude or approach in the investigation of nursing knowledge. Nursing is not the only discipline that is engaged in a process of reexamination. Science in general has come to a new point in history. The old idea of a static universe is now incompatible with the newer conception of the world as a dynamic process. A crisis of consciousness has been articulated through the crisis in science, and Anshen notes that "underlying the new ideas, including those of modern physics, is a unifying order, but it is not causality; it is purpose, and not purpose of the universe and of man [woman] but purpose 'in' the universe and 'in' man" [woman] (1971, p. xiv). Influenced by the idea of a dynamic conception of man and woman "in" the universe, as advanced in the study of transcultural nursing and anthropology; and influenced by readings in phenomenology, the author believes that the phenomenological approach as the explication of meaning in experience is one of the most promising of the qualitative methods by which to capture the interrelationship and interdependence of humanism and science in nursing.

ORIGINS OF PHENOMENOLOGY:

In a discussion of the phenomenological philosophical approach to the structuring of nursing knowledge, the following historical aspects need to be considered.†

In 1900, Edmund Husserl, a European philosopher, introduced the idea of

---

†The author wishes to express gratitude to Dr. P. Haanstad, Associate Professor of Philosophy, University of Utah, Department of Philosophy, Salt Lake City, Utah, for his critique of much of the content of the following phenomenological approach.

phenomenology because of his belief that the study of philosophy should have not only "rigor" but also a new humanism. Husserl was disenchanted with the scientific position that the final truth lay in facts alone (Kockelmans, 1967). At the turn of the century, the positivist-empiricist approach in the natural sciences, with its emphasis upon context-free generalizations, influenced scientific thought significantly enough that research in the human sciences was also divorced from influences of the "reality" of the individual in his or her sociocultural context. Omery claims that "the phenomenological method in philosophy began to crystallize in reaction to the denigration of philosophical knowledge, and objectification that was taking place in relation to the human sciences" (1983, p. 51).

Husserl specified how the philosopher can recover by phenomenological reduction (structured reflection), the ability to describe with scientific exactness the life of consciousness in its original encounter with the world. In his philosophy of humans in their life-worlds, Husserl showed how phenomenology attempted to explain *meaning*‡ in a rigorously scientific manner. Hence, phenomenological reduction is concerned with the demonstration and explanation of the activities of consciousness—a true science of the mind (Schutz, 1967). Madison remarks that "for Husserl, his phenomenology was the actual working out of universal science, the science of the Totality, of all encompassing unity of all that is" (1977, p. 250).

EVOLUTION OF PHENOMENOLOGY

A number of scientists have criticized the use of philosophy as a research method. Omery (1983), however, points to the fact that, contrary to opinions that phenomenology is ambiguous and ill-defined, philosophical phenomenology can be differentiated as a viable and valuable qualitative research method. Many interpretations and modifications of this method have been developed. "The aim of the phenomenological approach is to *describe* experience as it is lived" (Oiler, 1982, p. 178). Historically, cultural and social anthropologists and nurse-anthropologists have been advocates of the description, understanding, and explication of the meaning of behavior within social and cultural contexts. However, it is only recently that *serious* questions have been raised in relation to the definition of meaning in anthropology, the role of reflexivity in ethnographic understanding, the importance of the idea of intentionality, and the extent to which Western thought and methods shape the interpretation of other cultures (Parkin, 1982). The questioning can be attributed in part to the increasingly important role that philosophical phenomenology is contributing to the context of traditional qualitative research methods. Omery (1983) reports, according to Spiegelberg, the historian of the phenomenological movement, there are six common steps in the modifications of the philosophical method that are used. They include the following:

---

‡A theory of meaning according to Husserl includes the following features: Meanings are characterized by a sort of identity and contextual independence; they can be shared and communicated intersubjectively, so that it is legitimate to say they are objective; they are related to thoughts, feelings, and intentions; they serve as a medium of reference to things, events, persons, places, and processes in the world; they are in physical expressions and in language; they are signs; and they are united with the meanings they signify (Mohanty, 1977).

1. Descriptive phenomenology (includes presuppositions, direct investigation, analysis, and description).
2. Essential or eidetic phenomenology (probing of the phenomena for typical structures).
3. Phenomenology of appearances (watching for clarity of phenomena).
4. Constitutive phenomenology (exploring the way in which phenomena are constituted in consciousness).
5. Reductive phenomenology (suspending the belief in the reality or validity of the phenomena).§
6. Hermeneutic phenomenology (interpreting the concealed meanings in the phenomena).

Although some social science researchers who support and use the phenomenological method choose less restrictive steps, that is, they approach the phenomenon with no preconceived expectations, other researchers, such as Van Kaam, Giorgi, and Colaizzi, have developed more definitive methodologies (Omery, 1983). Nurse-researchers choosing the phenomenological method also have developed definitive methods. Paterson and Zderad (1976) explicated their humanistic nursing theory through the phenomenological method by defining theory as an approach that aims at the reality of a person and how he or she experiences his or her world. Their method is directed primarily toward the description of the clinical experiences of the nurse and the client.

Oiler (1982) uses Spiegelberg's outline of the essential operations of the phenomenological method. This includes bracketing, intuition, analysis, and description. Oiler states, however, that "the phenomenological approach for nursing research does not offer a well-defined set of methods or procedures that establish it clearly as a paradigm to its critics" (p. 18). Omery, however, asserts that "as long as an experience has meaning, the potential is there for the phenomenological method to be utilized" (1983, p. 59).

THE "MEANING" OF PHENOMENOLOGY FOR NURSES

Philosophy deals not only with scientific presuppositions but also with a valid knowledge of things derived by rigorous, critical, systematic, and intellectual investigation. Phenomenology is a fundamental method through which the philosopher, at the beginning, secures an absolute foundation for himself or herself (Kockelmans, 1967). For the philosopher, this absolute foundation is the cumulative consciousness of his or her life-world made explicit by means of the rigorous process of structured reflection, and which now informs and structures the way he or she views and experiences the ever-changing world of present experience. Philosophy, essentially phenomenology, offers a means by which the nurse can constantly rediscover his or her awareness of the world. Phenomenology, then, can offer a means by which the lived experiences of the "life-world" of nurses can be studied and understood.

Leininger (1978) emphasizes that universal and nonuniversal caring knowledge

---

§Reality for phenomenologists is subjective and perspectival—a matter of appearances (Oiler, 1982).

must be identified. To permit the discovery of universality, and to explicate the meaning of holistic values and comprehensive approaches to caring, not only empirical observations are necessary; the discovery and explication of caring phenomena through phenomenological reflexive inquiry is essential. A new "humanism" about the nature of nursing that already is a large part of transcultural nursing knowledge must also form the structure of the reality of nursing in general. Leininger (1976) reiterates the importance of the humanistic notion of nursing by posing a challenge to nurses to systematically study humanistic attributes, human values, and lifeways of people. Moreover, Leininger stresses that a broad humanistic philosophy is needed, which accommodates both general and diverse cultural beliefs to improve the health status of persons from different cultural backgrounds. In this process, the constituents of cultural caring for the nurse can be defined more clearly. Although nursing has made some inroads into the study of caring (Leininger, 1981, 1984), the objective and cognitive components of caring tend to be examined rather than the equally important internal (intersubjective) structures of caring, which are essential attributes for the clinical nurses to know. Hence, a systematic phenomenological study that employs structured reflection to lived experience, and one that elicts subjective meaning, has the potential to reveal humanistic and nonhumanistic values in relation to nursing phenomena. In other words, by the use of the phenomenological method, what may be considered humanistic caring by the nurse in one social context may not necessarily be humanistic caring in another. Nursing must pursue the humanistic elements of nursing care by discovering the meaning of caring for individuals, families, and groups. If certain humanistic attributes—for example, empathy, sympathy, compassion, comfort, trust, support, love, and protection—have been identified as caring phenomena, what meaning do they have in the reality of clients? More rigorous efforts toward this identification are needed in nursing. The meaning of a client's reality through the phenomenological approach will reveal to the nurse the qualities of each individual's existence, which subsequently will provide a more comprehensive understanding of the nature of nursing itself.

THE PHENOMENOLOGICAL METHOD AND ITS CONDITIONS

Phenomenology is a dialectic between two extreme positions of scientific development (represented by Fig. 5–1), and it utilizes both analytical and concrete inquiry.

Spurling (1977) discusses that analytic inquiry as a process is concerned with the grounds (underlying principles, laws, and assumptions) that make things intelligible, and that it is the reflexive mode of inquiry. By contrast, Spurling writes that concrete inquiry is the process of looking at phenomena themselves, where inquiry is conceived of as a description (reporting or reproduction) of what appears. Simple description or empirical inquiry exemplify this type of inquiry. In other words, Spurling reports that the distinction between the two inquiries is that of the transcendental** and the descriptive (immanent/real). This is the constant dialectic to be maintained in phenomenology.

Kockelmans (1967) reports that individuals who have been educated in the domi-

---

**Transcendental refers to a description of matter and objective things as products of the subjective mind (*Concise Oxford Dictionary*, 1956, p. 1356).

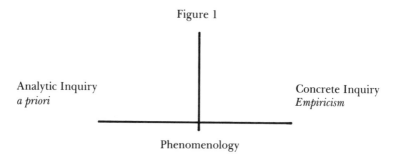

Figure 1

Analytic Inquiry   Concrete Inquiry
a priori   *Empiricism*

Phenomenology

Figure 5-1. A constant dialectic is maintained in phenomenology between the two extremes of analytic *(a priori)* and concrete empirical inquiry.

nant mode of positivistic science have certain prejudices regarding the supposed original object of experience. Positivism's claim is that an object is an object as it manifests itself through exact description and determination of the sciences. Tinkle and Beaton remark that "the critical assumption of this position is the belief in the existence of an independent, autonomous ordering of facts that are ahistorical and acontextual" (1983, p. 28). However, phenomenologists believe that to reach reality, individuals must try to locate meaning as it is immediately given in original experience (Kockelmans, 1967). In other words, as Kockelmans suggests, a return to the world as it manifests itself in original experience—the natural world, or the world of immediate experience—is the achievement. It is the task of phenomenological reduction (structured reflection) to lead us back to the original world of life from the idealized world of the natural positivistic sciences.

The fundamental idea of phenomenological reduction and its relationship to nursing can be represented by a conceptual model manifesting the analytic and concrete modes of inquiry (Fig. 5–2). A description of the terms will follow.

The Concept of World View

In an explication of the phenomenological approach to nursing, the concept of "world view" developed by Redfield (1953) provides a helpful analytical basis from which to argue for the congruency between science and philosophy in nursing. "World view refers to the way individuals or cultures grow, perceive, and know their world about them" (Leininger, 1981, p. 5). More specifically, Redfield characterizes the world view as the way people look outward upon the universe, a definition that includes forms of thought and the most comprehensive attitudes toward life. He asserts that a world view involves a matter of systematic and highly specialized reflective study and development. Redfield's notions of world view support the belief that a systematic study through the phenomenological method of the nursing of individuals and groups must consider the way in which nurses look outward upon the

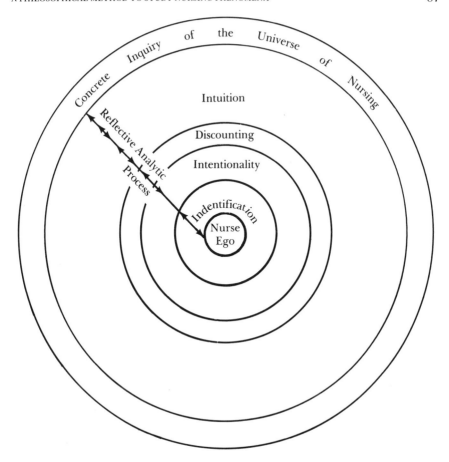

Figure 5-2. A "world view" model of the phenomenological approach to the study of nursing. Although visual models are not considered to be relevant to genuine intellectual inquiry in phenomenology, they are useful for clarification and application to nursing pedagogy.

"universe" of nursing (caring), and also employ highly specialized, structured reflection in order to intuit and describe the nature of the meaning of health and illness, as well as the meaning of the reality of caring for both clients and nurses. Thus, Redfield's concept of world view is a helpful conceptual tool to identify the steps used in both the analytic (reflexive) and concrete (empirical) positions of inquiry in the phenomenological method.

The conceptual model (Fig. 5–2) illustrates the constituents of inquiry—ego, identification, intentionality, discounting (bracketing), and intuition, with the final position as the empirical reality of the lived experience of nursing (caring, health or illness behavior, or other phenomena under study by nurses). This model utilizes the constituents of phenomenological reduction, and the direction is both outward (empirical or concrete) and inward (reflective or analytic). The model demonstrates that the process is both transcendental (describing objects as part of the subjective mind) and interactional (acting on one another through the sequencing of the different constituents of phenomenological inquiry).

From this conceptual framework, nurse researchers can develop an awareness of how the phenomenological approach encompasses a universe of nursing and caring of which he or she is a part. Concrete inquiry has been utilized in the descriptive and ethnoscientific research methods of transcultural nursing, but even more study is needed to understand the significance of lived experience within all areas of nursing. A more complete approach to nursing should utilize the phenomenological method so that the two processes of reflective inquiry and empirical inquiry can be interrelated to present a comprehensive world view of the full meaning of nursing phenomena. The main issues and questions include the following: How is meaning constituted for the client who is under the care of the nurse, and how is meaning constituted for the nurse in the process of care? Will nurse researchers move forward with the use of the phenomenological approach or are they too entrenched in positivism as the scientific method of inquiry?

Phenomenological Reduction Process in Nursing

Description of Terms

Phenomenology, as posited by Husserl, is a philosophy of "rigorous science" that is born from different mental attitudes. Phenomenology is in an entirely different dimension from positivism, with an entirely new starting point and method. For Husserl's phenomenology is a philosophy which has as its starting point a field of originality in which induction and deduction do not take place; intuition based on exact analysis and description is the sole feature. The fundamental principle with this method is that every original intuition is a legitimate source of knowledge (Kockelmans, 1967). (It should be noted that "intuition" is a technical term, and the end point of the process of analytic phenomenological reduction.)

Phenomenological reduction is referred to as "transcendental" (describing matter and objects as part of the subjective mind) because it uncovers the ego.†† Wartofsky (1977) clarifies this notion by stating that the subject-object relation is a relation of and by a subject:

> In this way the other is always a clue to the character of the subject: the object can always be "read back" so to speak, as revealing the primordial or necessary conditions or structures of subjectivity itself. (pp. 305–306)

---

††For clarification, ego in Husserlian phenomenology evolved from the philosopher Emmanuel Kant, who proposed a transcendental unity of apperception "whereby the ego as a thinking entity is necessarily present to itself, and the idea of the identity of the ego has a necessary correlate in the necessary uniformity in the world of objects" (Elliston & McCormick, 1977, p. 240).

In addition, as Kockelmans (1967) states, phenomenological reduction is called "reduction" because it leads individuals back to the source of meaning of the experienced world insofar as the world is experienced by uncovering intentionality. Thus, phenomenology is reflective enterprise or mental activity.

For the nurse researcher, in the process of analytic inquiry, the preliminary investigation consists of the examination of human experiences in which there is "sense constitution," that is, "sense" (meaning and significance) is made out of a nursing situation to achieve objectivity. What does a human experience in a health-related context or a cultural context mean to the client and the nurse? Below is a description of the terms used in systematic, analytical inquiry in interaction with the concrete inquiry of nursing.

Constituents of Phenomenological Reduction

The phenomenological reduction approach includes the method, guidelines, and rules that allow for the determination or the ability to make assertions about the grounds of meaning in nursing phenomena. The method equips the nurse with a way of knowing about nursing through the use of the reflexive mode. Scientific validity cannot be imposed. Validity is formulated in light of a client's conception of himself or herself in the world; for example, the descriptions of meaning, to be valid, should be recognized as true by those who live the experience.

The constituents (units in the experience) of phenomenological reduction are as follows:

Ego.   Nurse is the phenomenologist-researcher, or nurse clinician.

Identification.   This is a process by which the nurse as a clinician or a researcher uncovers the constituents of an experience. By being aware of the client as a total being, and of the nurse herself as a total being, perceptions in relation to an experience can be revealed. For example, through identification with a client dependent on alcohol, a researcher can help to uncover the experience of alcoholism for the client himself or herself, and at the same time, identification can help to reveal the feelings of empathy or disgust on the part of the nurse in relation to the experience of alcoholism as expressed verbally or behaviorally by the client.

Intentionality.   This is essentially a character or a property of acts that is always directed toward an object. Consciousness is intentional, that is, consciousness is always consciousness of something. The intentional activity of the adult both constitutes and is constituted by meaning, which is the way in which something relates to the whole world view. For the clinical nurse or researcher, the intentional activity is directed toward caring for a client or toward uncovering the meaning of the specific caring interaction (the lived experience of nurse and the client).

Discounting (bracketing).   This is holding in abeyance those elements that are irrelevant to nursing; for example, defining the limits of an experience. For the clinical nurse or researcher, discounting is important particularly when the nurse is uncovering a phenomenon of which he or she knows a great deal. For example, pain is an area well known to clinical nurses. However, in understanding the meaning of pain for a client, the nurse must not impose "pain knowledge" on the client, but allow the reality of the client's experience to be fully expressed.

Intuition.   This is a technical term relating to the mode of awareness in which the object intended by it (nursing care in relation to the identification of a client's specific health need) is not only "meant" but originally given. To possess the character of intuition, one arrives at knowledge (of caring) which grasps the ideal (essence). An act of intuition is an act of reason. By intuiting, the nurse is able to know the necessities imposed by reason of their own nature (components of nursing care to be rendered), without being obliged to go back to premises, and without having to justify these components of nursing care by deduction. Husserl believed this direct vision of intuition to be the first phenomenon of intellection and the end point of analytic, phenomenological inquiry (Kockelman, 1967). Intuiting the components of nursing care can provide both the nurse and the client with a mutually satisfying and knowledgeable experience. For the clinician or researcher, the structure of nursing care has meaning. It is constituted in the reality of both the client's and the nurse's world views.

Thus, phenomenology as a whole becomes a self-explanation of one's own ego taken as the subject of all possible knowledge (Kockelmans, 1967). Moreover, Kockelmans remarks that "the goal of analytic phenomenology, therefore, is to explore the intimate structure of objects, and clarify the essential categories that constitute them" (1967, p. 98).

Another point in the phenomenological approach is description. Descriptive techniques have been clarified by Giorgi (Omery, 1983) and Paterson and Zderad (Oiler, 1982).

Giorgi suggests a procedure for communicating the language of experience into scientific concepts, that is, the classification of experiential data. Giorgi's steps include reading the entire description of the experience to get a sense of the whole; rereading the description; identification of the transition units of the experience, called constituents; clarification or elaboration of meaning by relating them to each other and to the whole; reflection on the constituents in the concrete language of the subject; transformation of that concrete language into the language or concepts of science; and integration and synthesis of the insights into a descriptive structure of the meaning of the experience (Omery, 1983, p. 61). Communication to clinicians for the planning of care or to researchers for criticism is the final point in the phenomenological approach.

Paterson and Zderad's technique to aid description (Oiler, 1982) includes comparing and studying instances of the phenomenon wherever descriptions of it may be found (putting descriptions in a log book); imaginatively varying the phenomenon (the idea is to imagine the phenomenon, after the common elements of it have been identified); for example, pain, identifying the phenomenon's central characteristics (those elements that make the phenomenon what it is); explaining through negation (a way of getting the central characteristics of the phenomenon across: for example, explaining that loneliness may be different from being alone); explaining through analogy and metaphor (for example, "a patient is all tied up in a knot"); and classification of the phenomenon (establishing a category or hypothesizing about the phenomenon: for example, suggesting a new category for stress).

It should be noted that while phenomenology is a relatively new approach in nursing, there are some similarities, especially in the descriptions of human behavior, to the method of participant-observation (ethnography, ethnoscience, and ethno-nursing) used principally in social-scientific and transcultural nursing investigations. In his comparison of the phenomenologist and the participant-observer, Bruyn (1970) remarks that:

if this inner perspective [structured reflection] were combined with the exter-nal perspective of the scientific tradition in the context of social research, the result could have a significant effect upon sociological theory [nursing theory] in comprehending man [woman] in his [her] wholeness during the latter third of the twentieth century. (p. 287)

In addition, Tinkle and Beaton (1983) have called for a convergent definition of science that provides opportunities for the higher organization of the opposites in the experimental and the sociohistorical paradigms of research methods. Phe-nomenology is an answer to that call.

SUMMARY AND CONCLUSIONS

In this chapter, an attempt has been made to explain and provide methodologi-cal guidelines related to the phenomenological method. The analytic process (phe-nomenological reduction, with its components of ego, identification, intentionality, discounting [bracketing], and intuition) and the concrete process (the concept of empirical reality) of inquiry were explained and represented by a conceptual frame-work modeled after the notion of "world view" postulated by Redfield. Paterson, Zderad, Leininger, and others have reiterated the humanistic positions of nursing; they have also presented ideas of what humanistic nursing care is and have described the challenges facing nurses to explicate the philosophical and scientific positions underlying the claims to be a humanistic science of nursing. By using the components of structured reflection of the phenomenological method, the nurse can describe the life consciousness of caring. Phenomenology is a way to recover and maintain the humanistic and scientific claims nursing posits.

Strasser states that "the phenomenological philosopher who locates essential insights into human existence, may be able to make a contribution to the theoretical justification of the new form assumed by their scientific knowledge" (Kockelmans, 1967, p. 532). And, as Strasser (1967) indicates, the role of the phenomenological philosopher will be "to act as 'midwife' at the birth of *a new ideal of science*" (p. 532). Thus, for nursing this new ideal of science needs to be developed. A meaningful way to unite subjectivity and objectivity in the science of nursing is through pheno-menology. As an approach to nursing research and practice, phenomenology can offer continued growth and revelation, attentiveness, and awareness; it will expli-cate the meaning of nursing as that meaning continually comes into existence. In this way, phenomenology is an answer to the enduring process of the ever-experienc-ing, ever-changing reality of those involved in the world of nursing.

REFERENCES

Anshen, R. N. (Ed.) Introduction, World perspectives: What this series means (Vol. 43). In M. Mayeroff, *On caring.* New York: Harper & Row, 1971.

Bruyn, S. The new empiricists: The participant observer and phenomenologist. In W. Filstead (Ed.), *Qualitative methodology.* Chicago: Rand McNally, 1970.

Davis, A. J. The phenomenological approach in nursing research. In N. Chaska (Ed.), *The nursing profession: Views through the mist.* New York: McGraw-Hill Book Company, 1978.

Elliston, F., & McCormick, P. (Eds.). Husserl: *Expositions and appraisals.* Notre Dame, Ind.: University of Notre Dame Press, 1977.

Kockelmans, J.J. (Ed.). *Phenomenology: The philosophy of Edmund Husserl and its interpretation.* New York: Doubleday & Co., 1967.

Leininger, M. (Ed.). Humanism, health and cultural values. In M. Leininger (Ed.), *Transcultural nursing: Theories, concepts and practices.* New York: John Wiley & Sons, 1976.

Leininger, M. (Ed.). *Caring: An essential human need.* Thorofare, N. J.: Charles B. Slack, 1981.

Leininger, M. *Care: The essence of nursing and health.* Thorofare, N.J.: Charles B. Slack, 1984.

McCormick, P. Phenomenology and metaphilosophy. In F. Elliston & P. McCormick (Eds.), *Husserl: Expositions and appraisals.* Notre Dame, Ind.: University of Notre Dame Press, 1977.

Madison, G. Phenomenology and existentialism: Husserl and the end of idealism. In F. Elliston & P. McCormick (Eds.), *Husserl: Expositions and appraisals.* Notre Dame, Ind.: University of Notre Dame Press, 1977.

Mayeroff, M. *On caring.* New York: Harper & Row, 1971.

Mohanty, J. Husserl's theory of meaning. In F. Elliston & P. McCormick (Eds.), *Husserl: Expositions and appraisals.* Notre Dame, Ind.: University of Notre Dame Press, 1977.

Munhall, P. Nursing philosophy and nursing research: In apposition or apposition? *Nursing Research,* 1982, *31,* (3), 176–177, 181.

Oiler, C. The phenomenological approach in nursing research. *Nursing Research,* 1982, *31* (3), 178–181.

Omery, A. Phenomenology: A method for nursing research. *Advances in Nursing Science,* 1983, *5* (2), 49–63.

Parkin, D. (Ed.). *Semantic anthropology.* New York: Academic Press, 1982.

Paterson, J., & Zderad, L. *Humanistic nursing.* New York: John Wiley & Sons, 1976.

Ray, M. Phenomenology: A method for the study of nursing care. Unpublished paper, University of Utah, Salt Lake City, 1979.

Redfield, R. *The primitive world and its transformations.* Ithaca, N.Y.: Cornell University Press, 1953.

Reeder, F. Personal Communication, 1983.

Schutz, A. Phenomenology and the social sciences. In J. Kockelmans (Ed.), *Phenomenology: The philosophy of Edmund Husserl and its interpretation.* New York: Doubleday & Co., 1967.

Spurling, L. *Phenomenology and the social world.* London: Routledge & Kegan Paul, 1977.

Stevens, B. A phenomenological approach to understanding suicidal behavior. *Journal of Psychiatric Nursing,* 1971, *9* (5), 33–35.

Strasser, S. Phenomenology and the human sciences. In J. Kockelmans (Ed.), *Phenomenology: The philosophy of Edmund Husserl and its interpretation.* New York: Doubleday & Co., 1967.

Tinkle, M., & Beaton, L. Toward a new view of science: Implications for nursing research. *Advances in Nursing Science,* 1983, *5* (2), 27–36.

Wartofsky, M. Consciousness, praxis, and reality: Marxism vs. phenomenology. In F. Elliston & P. McCormick (Eds.), *Husserl: Expositions and appraisals.* Notre Dame, Ind.: University of Notre Dame Press, 1977.

6

Using a Phenomenological Research Method to Study Nursing Phenomena

Judith Lynch-Sauer

. . . it is a question not simply of defining a specific method, but rather, of recognizing an entirely different notion of knowledge and truth. (Gadamer, 1979, p. 13)

Nursing researchers need to be aware of the differences between the two perspectives of research, namely, quantitative and qualitative (or interpretive) research. It is likewise important to understand the distinction between the realist or idealist positions and how these positions influence the way the research is conceived and conducted. Broadly speaking, quantitative research may be viewed as a realist position based on an objective reality that is external to the self, whereas qualitative research may be viewed, in part, as an idealist position in which reality lies partially within the self.

Unfortunately, the quantitative method has assumed ascendancy in the Western world, and as a result, the value of most research is measured by the criteria of this approach. An important area for nursing researchers to address is whether a "unity of science" exists that dictates the use of quantitative research standards for all research, or whether standards for qualitative research exist, or need to be further developed. Nurses should not be deterred from using the qualitative types of research in nursing. The inability of quantitative research in the social areas to achieve "an intellectual and material mastery of its subject matter similar to that of the physical sciences" points to the need for competitive and alternative research methodologies (Smith, 1983, p. 13).

Nursing is a young profession, and it does not need to automatically follow the footsteps of the more traditionally focused disciplines and the scientific method. Instead, nursing can thoughtfully choose the research approaches and methods that can lead to human understandings which are most beneficial to persons under nursing care, especially understandings which have a direct application to practice. This means searching for alternative research methods and approaches specifically directed toward increasing our knowledge of the significance and meaning of human experiences.

Human science, the antithesis of natural science, is a paradigm well suited to nursing. Phenomenology, a particular philosophically based approach to research, offers a methodology that can lead to systematic explication of human experiences and human science paradigms. How does phenomenology differ from other qualitative methods, such as ethnography and ethnomethodology? Is there a specific method associated with phenomenology? How can a researcher prepare to conduct phenomenological research? Can phenomenology be described as a process? How does one use phenomenological methods? What are the strengths of this type of research, particularly for nursing? These questions are addressed in this chapter.

After a brief discussion of how phenomenology differs from some other well known qualitative research methods, the phenomenological method of the Utrecht School, one of the major schools in the United States will be described. Following this, examples from my own preparation and research will be given to help the reader understand phenomenology and its uses in nursing research.

COMPARISON OF PHENOMENOLOGY WITH ETHNOGRAPHY AND ETHNOMETHODOLOGY

The heightened interest in qualitative research may result in some confusion regarding differences among research methods and their purposes. For example, in comparing phenomenology with ethnography and ethnomethodology, it can be seen that the processes of doing research have some similarity with other qualitative methods in that, as Van Manen identifies, "all use participant observation and life-experience material, as well as employing an 'interpretive methodology,' and various applications of ethnomethodological inquiry . . . are closely aligned to the interpretive method of phenomenological research."* For example, children's assumed competencies in interpretive skills are used by teachers in classroom teaching, yet these skills are "seen but unnoticed" (1978–79, p. 53).

Van Manen also says that phenomenology, as practiced by the Utrecht School, does have some commonalities with ethnography and ethnomethodology. However, it is more closely related to existential phenomenology and philosophical anthropology (p. 53). The purpose of phenomenology is to understand a human experience.

---

*Martinus Langveld founded the Institute for Didactic and Pedagogic Studies at the University of Utrecht. His work is central to the philosophical content of social and intellectual thought in which the phenomenology of the Utrecht School has been established.

PHENOMENOLOGICAL METHOD

The phenomenological method which the author is most familiar is the Utrecht School as taught and practiced by Martinus Langveld[1] in the Netherlands. The aim of this method is to uncover the ground structures of certain phenomena by analysis of situations (e.g., being in the hospital, having a baby, having a terminal illness). Van Manen (1978–79) describes a situation as "any worldly complex of meanings in which a person finds himself and to which he simultaneously assigns meaning" (p. 59). Through the analysis of descriptions of experiences, "the ground structures . . . of situations are 'uncovered.' The phenomenologist continuously appeals to the *sense* we have in *common:* he invites us to insert our own experiences in a reflective dialogue" (p. 59). You as the reader "are invited to collaborate in the construction of analytic descriptions" (Van Manen, 1978–79, p. 59).

The concept of ground structure is not "some kind of product or achievement," but rather "an interpretive instance in an ongoing dialogue of interpretive method" (p. 54).

PREPARING TO CONDUCT PHENOMENOLOGICAL RESEARCH

Van Manen states: "one might argue that experimental research can be done by any social science student who has taken some statistic courses—but the method of phenomenology may require some less 'trainable' competencies" (Van Manen, 1978–79, p. 59).

There are different ways to learn how to do phenomenological research, and what follows is a description of one method. This particular method was developed by Beekman and his colleagues of the Utrecht School; for two summers I had the experience of being Beekman's student in the Netherlands.

First step. Each student writes a protocol, an account of a single experience. The goal is to use descriptive language as much as possible and to avoid evaluative and interpretive statements. Examples of experiences are: fear of the dark; waking up; waiting for someone. The following is my own protocol "Fear of the Dark."

FEAR OF THE DARK

I am about fourteen years old and have just been to a basketball game—my first in high school. I walk out into the night with a group of my friends. I laugh and talk with them—I feel secure and happy—almost heady with my newly acquired independence. I am no longer a child.

I wave goodbye to my friends at the end of the first block and start my long walk home alone. I walk for about a block thinking of what I've just experienced—I walk on the sidewalk. Gradually I become aware of the stillness of the street—there are no people in sight, no cars, and I notice how dark it is. My hearing gradually becomes more acute, and I hear what I think are faint footsteps. I turn and look but no one is there. Then I begin to notice shadows of trees and shrubs—suddenly they look like the shadows of a man hunched up, waiting to jump out at me. My heart begins to beat more rapidly and my breathing quickens. I dart out into the middle of the road so I no

longer see the shadows on the sidewalk. Now no one can surprise me by jumping out of the foliage. I walk faster now, almost running—I feel afraid.

As I turn to walk up the long hill to my house, I begin to relax. My heart
slows down as well as my breathing, and I walk on the sidewalk again. I know
the shadows of the trees here and I feel safe. Now I think about Jim and Dave
and how happy I am that they made the team. I open the door and walk into
my house.

Second Step.   Have one student's protocol used to study meaning of the analysis
(the foregoing description will be used as the example). The analysis is carried out by the
class, and the analysis itself consists of listing the descriptions of thoughts, actions, etc.,
using the same language or as near as possible to that which the account writer used. To
derive themes it is important that the writer be present and can clarify for the class
whether or not the analysis expresses the meaning of account. If not, the writer may
elaborate further to be sure the class understands her/his intention. When all the themes
are listed, they are compared with the accounts of all the other class members. (Those
themes common to all accounts are noted, as were those that vary.) The themes which
vary from those held in common are very much in flux during this process, as they often
move from the unique to the shared and back again as their meanings become clear
to the group. Unique or different themes often "throw into relief the meanings which
are present in the common forms" (Barritt, Beekman, Blecker, & Mulderij, 1983, p. 11).
For example, the themes from the author's "Fear of the Dark" are the following:

> (1) My long walk home alone; (2) I become aware of the stillness of the street;
> (3) I notice how dark it is; (4) My hearing becomes more acute and I hear faint
> footsteps; (5) I turn and look but no one is there; (6) I notice shadows of trees
> and shrubs like the shadows of a man hunched up, waiting to jump at me; (7)
> My heart begins to beat more rapidly, and my breath quickens; (8) I dart out
> into the middle of the road so no one can surprise me by jumping out of the
> foliage; (9) I walk faster now, almost running—I feel afraid; (10) As I turn to
> walk up the long hill to my house, I begin to relax; (11) My heart slows down
> as well as my breathing . . . I open the door and walk into my house.

When these common themes and their variations are generated, further comparisons may be made using sources from literature, drama, cinema, and music.

Third step.   Write a description of the ground structure of the experience of
fear of the dark. For example, fear of the dark is an experience with the following
structural elements:

> (1) The threat is coming from all sides; (2) cannot (always) identify it; (3) the
> heightened sensory awareness; (4) the threat to the rear; (5) seeing human-
> like faces and shapes everywhere; (6) bodily sensations (holding one's breathe);
> (7) seeing things negatively. (Beekman & Mulderij, 1977, p. 43–44. As trans-
> lated by Loren Barrett.)

Understanding of a given phenomenon comes about "through exhaustive description (rather than through causal explanation)" (Van Manen, 1978–79, p. 58).

Another aspect of learning to do phenomenological research is the intensive study of phenomenological philosophy and its application to human sciences; this aspect will not be discussed here.

PHENOMENOLOGY AS PROCESS

As phenomenological researchers, the goal is to systematically examine human experience and from this examination derive consensually validated knowledge. Reinharz (1983) notes that there are many ways of changing experience into knowledge (e.g., "artistic, experimental, human scientific"), but we are concerned with one special way, that being the phenomenological method.

Every research method has as its goal obtaining consensually validated knowledge. Not all methods are concerned with how one carries out the change process. Reinharz (1983) sees phenomenologists as being particularly attentive to the process of transformation because it is seen as affecting the "validity of their claims to knowledge." According to Reinharz, there are five steps in the phenomenological transformation:

1. A person's experience is transformed into actions and language that becomes available to him/her by virtue of a special interaction s/he has with another person(s). In this case the other is a phenomenological researcher who creates a situation or context in which the person's inchoate lived experience becomes available to him/her in language. That's the first transformation.

2. The researcher transforms what s/he sees or hears into an understanding of the original experience. Because we can never experience another person's experience, we rely on data the subject produces about that experience, and we produce from that our own understanding. That is the second transformation.

3. The researcher transforms this understanding into clarifying conceptual categories which he or she believes are the essence of the original experience. Without doing that, one is simply recording, and recording is not enough to produce understanding.

4. The researcher transforms those conceptual categories that exist in his/her mind into some sort of written document (or other product such as a picture, poem) which captures what s/he has thought about the experience that the other person has talked about or expressed in some way. That's another transformation. In all these transformations, something can be lost and something gained.

5. The audience of the researcher transforms this written document into an understanding which can function to clarify all the preceding steps and which can also clarify new experiences that the audience has. This is where the inductive principle leads. (Reinharz, 1983, pp. 78–79).

AUTHOR'S PHENOMENOLOGICAL METHOD†

The situation analyzed here is to demonstrate the author's phenomenological method. It is focused on couples having a planned first child later in life than is usual in their culture. The women in this study are 29 years old or older and see

---

†This example of how to conduct phenomenological research study was part of my doctoral thesis, and the information was provided by the women subjects as examples of data analyses.

themselves as invested in a career (Lynch-Sauer, 1981). This situation was studied in order to more clearly understand a poorly delineated topic in the life cycle of a modern woman, that is, the timing of childbearing.

Description of the Method Used

In order to obtain a rich descriptive data base, I had extensive encounters with three couples as they lived through the last three months of a delayed pregnancy, childbirth, and the first three months of parenthood.‡ Two other women in a similar situation were interviewed during the last month of pregnancy.§ I also used descriptive diary entries from Phyllis Chesler's book, *With Child: A Diary of Motherhood,* to expand my data base. As I became pregnant toward the end of this study, I (consciously delayed) used some of my own and my husband's experiences to highlight the final descriptions.

All interviews were taped. The interviews with the three couples were transcribed and the diary entries made in written form. This was my descriptive material. The couples were asked to reflect upon and relate their experiences as they unfolded. The two women interviewed in the pilot phase (whose data are included later in the study) were asked specific questions regarding their experiences; then they were allowed to continue talking about their experiences until they had related all they wanted to say. The diary entries were chosen to illustrate some common themes which emerged from the study as well as some variations. My own and my husband's experiences were self-selected, again to illustrate common themes and their variations.

During the research process, I kept a log of my experiences, which were used to help me understand what was meaningful and to make phenomenological transformations.

Phenomenological Transformations with Log Entries
from the Encounters

The first transformation was to create a context in which each informant would be able to make his or her experiences available to me. The encounters took place in the informant's homes. The following entry from my log is a reflection on an encounter:

What is different about me when I'm a researcher rather than a friend? The first thing is that the meeting between the two of us is set up for a specific purpose and at first it seemed it was my only purpose. However, soon after we began talking I realized she was getting something out of our encounter. She was having a chance to reflect on her meaningful experiences with someone who wanted to hear them. Once that became apparent to me, I relaxed and began to enjoy hearing what she had to tell. I realized she didn't have to say

---

‡I chose not to include interviewing here as a special skill that is necessary for phenomenological research, as it could be a chapter in itself, but preparation in interviewing is essential to conduct phenomenological research.

§These two women were originally in the pilot phase of the study. Their related material was later included in the study itself.

anything she didn't want me or others to hear so had a lot of control over our exchanges. This eased my anxiety over dealing with a very intimate and personal experience.

In determining how best to conduct the interactions, I used the amount of information as well as the ease with which we talked as a gauge of a successful encounter. What eventually evolved was a flexible, close to natural conversation with each informant. The initial interactions did not go as smoothly as the ones that followed, as reflected in the following personal log entry. My reflections on the first interview with Alan:

The encounter goes smoothly but I find I'm asking a lot of questions. There's a bit of awkwardness at first as evidenced by his silences. He seems unsure of what he should be saying. I pick this up and ask questions.

First meeting with Barbara:

I feel more relaxed—after all this is the second time I have met with an informant. The interaction is similar to Alan's. There are many pauses and she looks to me for direction. I ask her questions and she responds. Now I'm beginning to feel that they both are trying to give me what they think I want. I have to be clearer about how I'd like the encounter to proceed. I'd like this to be more like a natural conversation rather than a questions and answer period. The encounter still is not meaningful to them. It is being carried out only to meet my goals for research. Can I expect otherwise?

First interview with Dana:

Dana structures her reflections chronologically. She is able to articulate and organize what she wants to say. I feel as though I don't have to say anything— she continues to talk until she's through. Only then do I ask her a few questions, mainly to clarify what she has already said. This is my first really successful encounter. The idea of letting people say what they want to say is a good one. I think of all I would have lost by structuring this interaction. The level of self-revelation and reflection is so much deeper when the individual is able to structure her own thoughts and how she expresses them.

The style of encounter, however, seemed to do very little to change the amount of information obtained. Rather, this seemed to be more dependent on the nature of the experience they had just lived through. More information from the women was given while they were pregnant and immediately after delivery, and less when the baby reached three months of age. For the men, the longest conversations were right after the birth of the baby.

By giving the informants copies of the written transcriptions of our encounters, I hoped to engage them in the research process. I wanted them to be sure the information eventually used in the study was clear, was understandable, and expressed what they meant to say. I also wanted them to have the opportunity to remove material from the transcripts which they did not want used in the study.

Two examples of informant feedback follow: One subject said that what she had stated in one transcribed interaction was "garbled," and she was able to make a correction. Another subject who read the transcription was upset because he thought that what he had said sounded very disorganized. He had not finished reading the transcription and told me that although he really would like to drop out of the study, he would not, as he had already made a commitment. We talked about how the spoken word is very different when it is written and how this might have made the transcription appear to lack smooth transitions from thought to thought. The rest of the informants had little to say about the transcriptions other than that they were accurate. No one deleted any material. After the study, however, one of the women who was contemplating having another child reread her transcriptions and said they helped her to realize what a difficult period she went through with her first child. The transcriptions provided a backdrop for this woman in making a decision about having another child. The transcriptions were given very different meaning by each informant who chose to use them. In retrospect, what I really needed to give them was feedback about the analysis of these transcriptions as well, so that they could validate my interpretation of their experiences.

Understanding of the Original Experience

Analysis of the dialogues at first seemed an overwhelming task, as reflected in my comments:

> Spent the day in the library beginning to get the data together. I'm overwhelmed! Started to pull out themes each person brings up—so many.
> I spend weeks reading and rereading the transcripts with the goal of becoming very familiar with what these people had told me. I need to tie these reflections together in some meaningful way—a way which is grounded in their lived experiences.

At the time I was involved in the phenomenological transformation process, I was introduced to Kurt Wolff during his visit to the University of Michigan. I read his paper on "Surrender and Community Study" and attended his lecture. I was struck by how similar his "surrender" is to what I am doing in explicating the phenomenon of transition to parenthood. He talked about the difference between "surrender" and "surrender to," and the fact that "surrender to" may ultimately become a "surrender." He made these statements:**

> In surrender, an individual becomes involved, undifferentiatedly and indistinguishably, with himself, with his act or state, and with his object or partner. (p. 238)
> In surrender, a person's received notions are suspended including those that he feels in any way bear on this exploration—for instance, his belief in the plausibility of theories, the appropriateness of concepts, the validity of assumptions and generalizations. (p. 238)

**From Wolff, K. Surrender and community study: The study of Loma. In A. Vidich, J. Bensman, & M. Stein (Eds.), *Reflections on community studies*. New York: Harper Row & Co., 1964, pp. 238–243. With permission.

Surrender is unforeseeable, unpredictable, happens, befalls, whereas surrender-to is concentration, dedication, devotion, attention. With surrender it shares involvement, the "pertinence of everything," identification, and the risk of being hurt, but only to the extent that these can be willed or consciously risked. If surrender-to unexpectedly grows into the "infinity" of its experience, it becomes surrender. (pp. 238–243)

"Surrender-to," then, is very similar to the dropping of presuppositions as spoken of by phenomenologists. Wolff gives a very good description of this mode of analysis.

The "catch" or the "invention" is what one arrives at after an experience of "surrendering" or "surrendering-to." This might be looked upon as similar to Strasser's "vision," "a synthesizing conception which endows a number of experiences with a meaning that transcends these experiences" (Strasser, 1963, p. 50).

Wolff talks about "the irony of surrender":

This is the opposition of the idea of surrender-to our official contemporary Western, and potentially world-wide, consciousness, in which the relation to the world is not surrender but mastery, control, efficiency, manipulation. Such a relation, furthermore, is "virile" rather than womanly. Non-virile, and in this sense womanly, relation is another polemical connotation of "surrender," for we tend to think of women, not of man, as surrendering, as giving; and of man, if he does surrender, as forfeiting his virility.

"Invention" is synonomous [sic] with "catch." But as "surrender" has a feminine ring, "invention" has a masculine one. Yet to "invent," that is, "to come into" most poignantly in the tabooed word "come has a bisexual flavor: it is the same that "surrender" intends, even though it does not have the meaning in linguistic custom.††

As I reflected on Wolff's statements, I agreed with him and thought about the affinity of this type of thinking with feminine rather than masculine intellectual skills. This idea was also expressed by Shule, another participant in my research, as noted in my log:

Shule brings up a point that I've often thought of, i.e., the feminine way of thinking being more apropos to this method of doing research.

I experience "ups and downs" as I slowly work through my explication of the experiential material. The "ups" occurred when I seemed to clearly understand how to explicate thematic material, the "downs" occurred when the sheer amount of material overwhelmed me.

Classification of Conceptual Categories

I began by using Beekman's analysis format in which the form (theme) of components of the experience are noted and related for each informant. The exact words of the informant were used as much as possible. Table 6–1 gives an example of the analysis of the transcribed encounters of one informant.

---

††Ibid., p. 262.

The forms in Table 6–1 were used to relate each informant experience. The forms were then compared with other informants' transcripts. Using the first transcript analyzed for comparative purposes, similar forms across transcripts were noted as well as variations of the same form. Table 6–2 provides an example of comparisons of one particular form across transcripts.

The reader will note in Table 6–2 that the informant whose transcript was chosen for comparative analysis with those of other informants is somewhat different in that she had not planned to have a baby before, while the other informants had this goal in mind.

An example of the similarities among informants may be noted in Table 6–3.

Table 6-1   *Thematic Material From One Informant*

- in a sense it (the pregnancy) was planned and in a sense unplanned in that I just stopped taking Ovulum*

- mixed feelings of becoming pregnant

- when I found out I was definitely pregnant, I had more positive feelings about it

- when I examined why I would do such a drastic thing like stop taking Ovulum, I realized it had to do largely with my age and the realization that if I didn't make this decision in some way, I probably wouldn't have children, and the immediacy of making this decision really had to do with being 35

- fear of missing experience of having baby (could be had no other way)

- reasons for delay (desire for perfection: fear of replication of problems between own mother with child; not having a perfect marriage; difficult to give up career for child)

- perceptions of what mothers should do (be available to child at all times without compromise)

- shift in thinking regarding perfection; maybe wouldn't repeat what own mother had done; could have a child even if marriage wasn't perfect; saw examples of working mothers

- could fit child into life of career woman

- changing body (enjoys this)

- future hard to envision (delivery, care of child, changes in life)—can only think of pleasant things because can't envision difficult ones

- care of baby frightening (very little prior experience)

- projections of self as mother (feels competent about emotional aspect of mothering)

- financially no problems (can hire others to do housework and part of child care)

- career can be managed

- open to idea of not working when child older (thinks age of child has something to do with amount of time mother's presence will be needed)

- might enjoy being mother full-time—hard to give up idea of working full-time

- baby being helpless is scary idea

- changing body—feels like somebody else is inside of me

- baby—I know its sex, he has a name—this makes him more of a person—he has an identity separate from me already (questions whether this is a different experience because I have this information from the amniocentesis—age)
- reaction of others to pregnancy—lots of attention because of age—particularly if didn't want child before
- relationship with husband doesn't change feelings about pregnancy and having baby—separate vein of life
- sense of loss that mother ill
- baby viewed as part of extended family, yet separate
- thinks having baby a narcissistic gratification
- sees child moving away—fantasy of having ideal parent-child relationship of closeness and distance
- feared other women at work my age would get pregnant and leave
- feels I'm role model at work—other women have told me I aroused thought in them of whether to get pregnant or not—non-married women became depressed as their situation didn't allow for children—age and being alone makes this problematic for many people
- staff wants me to bring baby to work—this probably will happen
- how viewed at work—being a women and boss—nobody could imagine me pregnant (desexualized)—pregnancy
- pregnancy sexualized me—hard for others to absorb
- receive rather than give nurturing
- later the staff will complain when I'm not there
- now I have become perfect for some staff, for others my being pregnant is a fault
- no one expected me to stop working (my close staff)
- people on periphery of those I work with ask me when I'm leaving
- lower middle class people ask me how long I'm going to work before I quit for good—they assume I'm not going to continue working—I wonder why I let them know my plans
- aware of wanting the amniocentesis to make sure baby not mongoloid—age
- anticipated being more tired
- perceive myself as very healthy person
- fears birth regardless of age—anticipates pain
- thinks of being an older mother—what will child think of this—I had younger mother
- thinks of body as very young
- chose obstetrician for very definite reasons—motherly, uses Leboyer birth method—trust my body and child with him
- specific plans for birth—no strangers there; Lamaze
- anticipation of having to have cesarean delivery; even though no physical reason for this to happen

*Exact words as much as possible by informant. From Lynch-Sauer, 1981.

Table 6-2 *Comparison of Themes from One Informant with Other Informants*

Theme	Variations
1.* reasons for not having a baby before now: • desire for perfection • fear of replication of problems between my own mother with the child; not having perfect marriage; difficult to give up career to care for child . . . so although at the back of my mind was always a thought it would be nice to have a child—but it was kind of a romantic ideal rather than a real one. I mean I don't really know that it was a really well-thought-out idea about what it could be like.	2. I don't know if I could really feel like a woman unless I could have a child. . . . I was always trying to keep these feelings away because they would be too threatening, I felt, because it just wasn't suitable to have children when you are in graduate school. . . . This was a planned pregnancy . . . we had decided this was the time we wanted to have a baby. 3. I always saw myself as having children the same as I always saw myself having a career and I guess I put it off in many ways because there always seemed like there was lots of time, and the other reason was I hadn't found anybody for a long time that I wanted to have a child with . . . so, after about a year of marriage I decided that I really wanted to have a child. I said it was about time. 4. Wanting to have a child—that was about ten years ago. But a lot of things, I mean, there were a lot of reasons why we couldn't and decided not to. . . . I am glad we waited . . . his (my husband) finishing school had a lot to do with finally making the decision.

*Numbers denote informants.

Table 6-3 *Examples of Similarities of Themes*

1.* I selected him (obstetrician) because he does the Leboyer thing . . . it's almost going to seem like a home birth. Even though it's in a hospital, there aren't going to be any strangers there. . . . It won't feel like there are any professional, distant people, but all people who are really very personally involved.

2. I go over my final list with Frederic. My conditions: that your father room in; that I'm not put into stirrups or strapped down in any way; that I hold you and breast-feed you before they clean you up or inject silver nitrate into your eyes; . . .†

3. I've been going to Lamaze classes and . . . I feel so much more in control than I did. . . . I feel I can go in there and have that baby and that I'm having that baby—that it's not going to be someone else's task to deliver the baby. And that's very important to me too. . . . Being in control over my environment. . . .

*Numbers denote informants.
†From Chesler, P. *With child: A diary of motherhood.* New York: Thomas Y. Crowell, 1979, p. 94.

The examples I have chosen of the forms (themes) show how the researcher begins to organize and make sense out of related lived experience. It is at this point in the transformation process, that is, after the themes are compared and organized under the headings of "Themes" and "Variations," that the ground structure or clarifying conceptual categories begin to be realized. In bringing this thematic material together, I began to understand that planning seemed to stand out against the background of these informants' lived experiences. Hence, I described the following as one of the ground structures of the experience of delayed parenthood for women over the age of 29 years who are involved in a career.

ingfulness of transition to parenthood becomes more understandable for these individuals. For with planning goes a sense of control, something with which these older individuals have had a lot of experience, in both their personal and professional lives. They were not the type of individuals who just "let things happen." These individuals "planned" to have a baby as they planned other aspects of their lives. Expectations about how they would feel as they lived through the experience were very much a part of the plans. Hence, their reflections often revealed shock, surprise, and disbelief as the actual experience was compared to the one anticipated. They discovered that the experience of one's body during pregnancy, in childbirth, and after birth was not easy to anticipate. Even though plans were made and carried out to ensure control over their bodies during childbirth, the women found this a somewhat uncontrollable situation. The anticipation of pain did not accord with the reality any more than did the anticipation of parenthood. The relationship with the new baby was an unknown which could not be calculated beforehand.

HOW PHENOMENOLOGICAL RESEARCH FITS NURSING

In the works of the great phenomenologists, thoughtfulness is described as a minding, a heeding, a caring attunement . . . of what it means to live a life. For us this phenomenological interest of doing research materializes itself in our everyday practical concerns as parents, teachers, educators, psychologists. (Van Manen, 1983, p. ii)

Research as practiced by proponents of the Utrecht School of phenomenology is considered by Van Manen (1978–79) to be a practical science. The goal is to understand human beings not only to know how they "are," but to understand them "in order to know how to act." Science, in Langeveld's use of the word, is best translated as "the science of the human mind and human experience." As in the Western world's usage of this term, "science", according to Langeveld,

makes claims to objectively, but this objectivity is grounded not positivistically, but hermeneutically—in interpretation theory. Consequently, . . . 'science' in the usage of the Utrecht School has unfamiliar connotations; it focuses on the subjectivity of . . . situations, on the interpretation of the inner experience and on the ground structures of the lived world. (Van Manen, 1978–79, p. 51)

Nursing, as a science, has a goal to understand those individuals being cared for in order to know how to care for them. For example, my phenomenological nursing study showed that those caring for a woman who has delayed having a child should understand the importance of planning in her life. Knowing this would help to provide care when all goes as expected as well as when unexpected crises arise. Yet, it is not always so simple to link nursing practice to phenomenological knowledge. Van Manen raises the question of what kind of knowledge "contributes to the grammar, the deep structure, which makes pedagogic competence possible" (Van Manen, 1978–79, p. 63). He says that children learn the deep structure of grammar not by studying grammar, but by hearing speech, i.e., the "deep structure of grammar incarnates itself in active speech competence" (Van Manen, 1978–79, p. 63). Carefully analyzed descriptions of the life world may in a similar manner serve as " 'examples' of what figures as concrete embodiments of the grammar of pedagogic competence in curriculum practice" (p. 63). So, too, may descriptions of the lived world of the patient provide examples of the "concrete embodiments" of the "grammar" of nursing competence in nursing practice.

LIMITATIONS AND STRENGTHS OF PHENOMENOLOGICAL METHOD

Phenomenology is not without its critics; Barritt, Beekman, Blecker, and Mulderij (1982, p. 4–11) summarize their criticisms with these comments:

1. It is difficult to replicate a descriptive study of experience;
2. A phenomenological study is too subjective;
3. In a phenomenological study, researcher bias interferes with clean results;
4. The language of phenomenological research is too vague and ephemeral;
5. There are no procedural guidelines for conducting phenomenological research;
6. The phenomenological method is ahistorical; and
7. Phenomenological research is frequently based on the memory of informants.

Most assuredly, one can argue that these limitations are the great strengths of phenomenology and the attributes that uniquely distinguish the phenomenological and other qualitative research methods from the traditional and prevailing quantitative methods, which select only certain variables and measure their outcomes. Qualitative research methods serve different purposes and should not be measured by criteria of quantitative research methods.

In this chapter, some basic ideas about phenomenological nursing research as it is known and evolving today were presented. In addition, the author's research method and clinical raw data were used as examples of how to use the phenomenological research method in nursing. This method has some similarities to ethnographic, ethnonursing, and grounded theory methods, but it still has some differential features that make it worthy of consideration in its own right, as it brings special insights to understanding nursing phenomena and building nursing knowledge.

REFERENCES

Barritt, L., Beekman, A. J., Blecker, H., & Mulderij, K. *Handbook for phenomenological research in education.* Ann Arborn, MI: School of Education, University of Michigan, 1983.

Beekman, A. J., & Mulderij, K. Beleving en

Ervaring: Werkboek Phenomenology voor de Sociale Wetenschappen. Meppel: Boom, 1977.

Chesler, P. *With child: A diary of motherhood*. New York: Thomas Y. Crowell, 1979.

Gadamer, H. The problem of historical consciousness. In P. Rabinow, & J. Sullivan (Eds.), *Interpretive social science—A reader*. Berkeley: University of California Press, 1979.

Glaser, B., & Strauss, A. *The discovery of grounded theory: Strategies for qualitative research*. Chicago: Aldine Publishing Co., 1967, p. 67.

Lynch-Sauer, Judith. Delayed first-time parenthood: A small sample phenomenological study. Michigan, Ann Arbor, University of Michigan (Unpublished Dissertation, 1981).

Reinharz, S. Phenomenology as a dynamic process. *Phenomenology and Pedagogy*, 1983, *1*, 77–79.

Smith, J. Quantitative versus qualitative research: An attempt to clarify the issue. *Educational Researcher*, March, 1983, *12* (3), 3–13.

Strasser, S. *Phenomenology and the human sciences: A contribution to a new scientific ideal*. Dequesne Studies, Psychological Series I. Pittsburgh: Duquesne University Press, 1963, p. 50.

Van Kaam, A. L. *Existential foundations of psychology*. Pittsburgh: Duquesne University Press, 1969.

Van Manen, M. An experiment in educational theorizing: The Utrecht School. *Inter change*, 1978–79, *10*, 48–66.

Van Manen, M. Invitation to phenomenology and pedagogy. *Phenomenology & Pedagogy*, 1983, *1*, i–ii.

Wolff, K. Surrender and community study: The study of Loma. In A. Vidich, J. Bensman, & M. Stein (Eds.), *Reflections on community studies*. New York: Harper and Row, 1964, p. 233–263.

7

Historical Method: Implications for Nursing Research

Marc W. Kruman

WHY SHOULD NURSES STUDY HISTORY?

Why should nurses study history and use historical methods in their research? The answer to this question is manifold; virtually all modern research techniques have been derived from historical study. The very roots of the word "history" lie in the Greek word "historiai," which translates as "researches" (Barzun & Graf, 1970, p. 47). If any of the methods suggested in this book are adopted in your future research, you will be employing techniques derived from historical methods. Therefore, it would be well for you to know about their origins.

This is not the only reason why nurses should understand history and historical methods, however. First, in their everyday activities nurses are writing history. They do it, for example, when they write a report on a patient. Of course, they believe themselves to be writing about the present; but at the moment that they put pen to paper, they describe the past, no matter how recent. Thus, all report writing is essentially historical writing. Second, the study of history enables the student of nursing to understand how the past impinges upon the present. Without a past, there is no meaning to the present, nor can we develop a sense of ourselves as individuals and as members of groups. As Barzun and Graf put it, "Without this developed sense of the self, and without words in which to record experiences, man would be doomed to live entirely from moment to moment, like a cow in a field" (Barzun & Graf, 1970,

The author would like to thank Professors Samuel F. Scott and Sandra F. VanBurkleo for their criticisms of an earlier draft of this chapter.

p. 46). Stated differently, the study of nursing history or of pioneer leaders is a way for nurses to study themselves and their profession, because both are necessarily products of their past (Nugent, 1967, p. 27; Christy, 1969, 1970). The study of history also enables nurses to place contemporary American nursing practices in a broader comparative context: how has nursing been conducted in other places at other times? Finally, the use of historical methods allows nurse researchers to strike an appropriate balance between humanistic and scientific practices. Historical methods will enable them to break the impasse between the two because they combine the humanistic with the scientific. As Nugent points out, "History deals with people, both humanistically because of its attention to the individual and the unique event and scientifically because it deals with people in groups and as the focus of long-term trends" (Nugent, 1967, p. 24). For all of these reasons, an understanding of the past and of the way in which we study the past is important for research in nursing.

THE EVOLUTION OF MODERN HISTORICAL STUDIES

History, as Barzun and Graf have written, grew out of people's "awareness of continuity." That awareness fueled a desire to understand their past. The earliest conceptions of Western historiography (i.e., the writing of history) date back to the works of the great ancient historians, Herodotus and Thucydides. Herodotus sought to understand and teach the moral lessons of the past, whereas Thucydides shunned morality and thought of history as an examination of past politics. Such rival conceptions are still with us, although they have been enormously modified over the centuries. With the spread of Christianity, Thucydides's concerns receded into the background, the moral purposes of history became paramount, and most history was devoted to chronicling the progress of God's worldly kingdom. Only with the secularization of life in Europe during and after the Renaissance did a critical historiographical tradition emerge. These events and processes set the stage for the development of modern historiography, which emerged in the 19th century, after the French Revolution and with the dissemination of the theory of evolution. The French Revolution sparked the overthrow of kings throughout Europe and led new rulers, the people, to seek a fresh understanding of their past (Barzun & Graf, 1970, p. 57). The triumph of evolution as a scientific theory in Victorian Europe and America led people to seek out their "genetic" or historical origins. It prompted them to look to the past to comprehend who they were. Now everything had to be traced back to its origins as historians tried to write "scientific" history. In so doing, they tried to write definitively about one subject, in a style now called monographic. Although few historians today would argue that such definitive histories are possible, most of us still write monographs within a "scientific" tradition (Bergan & Graf, 1970, p. 57; Higham, 1965, pp. 89–144). More will be said later about this matter.

WHAT IS HISTORY?

The foregoing sketch of the evolution of historiography leads us to ask the question: What is history? Laymen often view it as something immutable; like a photograph, it is fixed and not subject to change. Thus, all the historian of a particular problem need do is gather all of the facts and they will arrange themselves automatically, along a perfectly linear stream of time. Social scientists who view history in this manner will often take a particular American history textbook, which marshals facts in chronological order, as their sole source for analyzing the American past. If, indeed, history is something fixed and unchanging, then one honest author's general textbook on the American past would be enough. Such a conception of history might lead nursing researchers to believe that the excellent text by Kalisch and Kalisch (1978) is all the nursing history that one will ever need.

But history is much more than an assemblage of facts that speak for themselves. It would be more appropriate to describe history as facts (ideas, events, social and cultural processes) filtered through human intelligence. Most historians believe in the "objective relativism" of history. In other words, they imagine the existence of an objective reality, but also acknowledge that the different experiences of different historians will produce different historical interpretations (Nugent, 1967, pp. 109–110; but see Kousser, 1980). Thus, another historian might view some or much of what Kalisch and Kalisch (1978) have to say in a very different light. This "relativism" is taken to be a good thing: it allows insights and breakthroughs alongside occasional errors. Just as scientific theories change, then, so does the past in the hands of different historians.

METHODOLOGICAL STEPS TO DO A HISTORY

At the outset, the historian must define a topic (Shafer, 1980, p. 43–44). This may be framed as an hypothesis or, perhaps more usefully, as a question or series of questions (Fischer, 1970, pp. 3–39). For example, what role did Florence Nightingale play in the establishment of the modern nursing profession? As your research evolves and your perspective is altered, the topic itself may shift somewhat, and so will your questions. Without some clearly delineated questions, however, your research will be aimless and ultimately fruitless. A researcher cannot simply gather nuts and berries forever without a plan.

Once you have outlined a preliminary hypothesis or set of questions, you should locate a few books or articles on your subject. A good place to start would be in the extensive bibliographies supplied by Kalisch and Kalisch (1978) or Winchell (1967). Before delving into these books, you should obtain some notion of how they have been received by other scholars by examining reviews in major nursing journals. Do not try to read all of the books on your subject. At this point, all you want to obtain is an understanding of the broad outlines of your project and what historians have said about it (Shafer, 1980, pp. 45–48). Upon what points do the authors agree? On what do they disagree? What kinds of evidence do they use? Is the evidence of one more trustworthy than another?

Take, again, the question of Florence Nightingale's role in the establishment of the modern nursing profession. First, one might ask what are the characteristics of modern nursing? Second, what did Nightingale do that has led historians to conclude that she was the first modern nurse? If, indeed, she was the first modern nurse, then how did she find a number of competent nurses to serve under her during the Crimean War? Third, how important is education in the shaping of the modern nursing profession? If you deem it crucial, and it would seem to be of some significance, then perhaps the historian of 19th-century nursing would place more emphasis on the nursing school established in Kaiserwerth, Germany, in 1836, and less upon one of its students (Kalisch and Kalisch, 1978, pp. 32–45). By asking substantive questions during your preliminary reading, then, you begin to give shape to your research.

Your next step is to build a bibliography by using the bibliography and footnotes of the works you have already consulted. Now use the library's card catalogue. Check the author's dates, the subtitle, the date of publication, and sometimes the number of pages. A careful examination of the card will save you some time. A 100-page history of nursing may not be worth examining in your study of the role of Florence Nightingale; on the other hand, it might be indispensable. Once you decide that a book requires further study, first check its preface and introduction to see what kinds of questions the author is asking; they survey the table of contents and the index. Although a good index will convey to the reader the subjects discussed in the book, the researcher should be wary because indexes are usually prepared in haste just before a book is bound, often by publishers rather than authors. For books that are indexed superficially, examine the first and last few paragraphs of the chapters. This will give you a better idea of the substance and emphases of the book. Whether or not you find a book or article useful, enter the full bibliographical information on 3 x 5 inch index cards or slips of paper. Be sure to make a brief notation on the card of the potential usefulness of the sources. When you have long forgotten that you had reviewed a book and found it to be worthless for your purposes, a quick check of your bibliography file will save you considerable time.

As you are constructing your bibliography, you are also starting the process of fact-gathering. What are facts? Historians accept no single definition; however, fact might be said to include objects, actions, ideas, and values (Shafer, 1980, pp. 73–76). Historians might agree about some "conventional" facts like the dates on which Florence Nightingale arrived at and left the Crimea (Barzun & Graf, 1970; Shafer, 1980), but one might ask what those conventional facts might mean when joined together. Such linkages depend upon the judgments and values of individual historians.

Be sure to avoid an error common to beginning researchers: do not try to gather every fact so that you will be "certain" about your conclusions. Two problems are connected with such an approach. First, researchers who try to gather everything possible on a subject are often never satisfied that they ever have enough information, so they never write their reports. Second, and more important, we cannot gain absolute certitude. It simply is not accessible; all we can hope for is to obtain probability (Barzun and Graf, 1970, p. 155).

As you uncover relevant facts, a dialectical relationship will develop between you and your sources. You will find facts that do not fit your tentative hypothesis. Then, other facts, seemingly irrelevant before, will take on new meaning, and a new hypothesis and new questions will emerge. As you locate useful information, you must make careful notes, and follow the same mechanical procedures as before. The description given here is one way of taking notes, borrowed from Shafer (1980). However, you may develop a different method that suits your personality. Whatever procedures you follow, be consistent throughout your project. If you start with 4 x 6 inch index cards, continue using them. When you record your notes, put the same kinds of information in the same place on the card. Try to record only one thought or quotation on each card. You also might reserve the upper left-hand corner for the author, title, and page number and the upper right for a brief description of the note. A description will make it easier to file the note and to check its contents readily. In addition, some historians employ cards of different colors for different purposes (notes, bibliography, and so forth).

Next, organize your notes. You may find it easiest at first to simply file the notes alphabetically by the sources used. As you become more familiar with your topic, or after you have largely completed your research, you will need to rearrange your notes by subject. For my own recent book (Kruman, 1983), I found it helpful not to reorganize the notes until the end. That gave me a chance to read carefully through all of my notes in their original order, thus refreshing my memory and making it easier to file the notes in the appropriate places. Notes that refer to more than one subject should be cross-indexed. It may appear that I have made much ado about the seemingly trivial mechanics of note-taking, but if you do not attend to these details, you will have to waste time running back to the library to find the page of the book from which a note was taken or look frantically for that note that you know is there *somewhere.* Sometimes a source you consulted is in far-away archives. You may not be able to check it again at all, and the note will be useless.

Addressing the Evidence: Primary and Secondary Sources

Once you have mastered the mechanics, it is time to address the evidence. Historians deal with two kinds of sources: primary and secondary (Schafer, 1980, pp. 77–78). Primary sources are those that participants or observers provide and may (unlike evidence heard in a court of law) include hearsay evidence. These are the original sources of information. Secondary sources are all other accounts, once removed from actual participation, even those by contemporaries. Some documents can be both primary and secondary sources. In a study of *Florence Nightingale,* for example, a history written in 1858 by a non-participant is a secondary source. But in a study of *histories* of Florence Nightingale, that same account becomes primary.

The sources themselves, of course, may be of many kinds, ranging from hospital architecture and old nursing uniforms to oral interviews and documents. Although the lifeblood of most historians is documents, students of the nursing profession's recent past may find oral interviews and artifacts helpful. Remember that oral history has to be conducted systematically, and that other kinds of sources should be consulted at the same time. A few tips may be in order here (see also Hoover, 1980). Ask similar questions of all interviewees. When you try to elicit information from participants, begin with uncontroversial matters that make the interviewee think anew about the subject and to display your own grasp of the subject. Only then should you move on to problematic subjects. Throughout the interview, try to keep the discussion on the subject and not let the interviewee ramble. Otherwise, you will end up with a useless document (Shafer, 1980, p. 91).

As you examine each piece of evidence, you will evaluate it in two ways: for veracity and for meaning. The problem of veracity may be beyond the abilities of the beginning researcher to tackle, but its importance became apparent recently in the exposure of a hoax involving purported diaries of Adolph Hitler. Most researchers, though, even the most experienced, spend less time deciding on the authenticity of a document than on its meaning. The historian's most pressing task is the evaluation of the meaning of a source—a feature of qualitative type of research.

The first obligation of the historian is to understand the literal meaning of the document. You must be careful to understand the words as the author intended them to be understood. Definitions of words change over time. In order to understand the changing meaning of the word "nurse" (or almost any other English word), for example, consult the unabridged *Oxford English Dictionary*. Once you understand the document, be careful not to take parts of it out of context. A soldier writing about Florence Nightingale's activities during the Crimean War said that "she was all full of . . . fun." Such a statement might suggest that she regarded her work with some frivolity, and one might conclude that, for her, nursing in the Crimea was a lark. But the researcher would not come to such a conclusion if the comment is examined in its context: "She was all full of life and fun when she talked to us, especially if a man was a bit downhearted" (Kalisch & Kalisch, 1978, p. 39).

Now you are ready to evaluate the evidence. In their examination of an event, historians rely upon participants and witnesses. First, you should determine how *reliable* your observer is. Were there any physical problems, like impaired vision, that prevented the witness or participant from observing accurately? More frequently, an observer might have social, cultural, and mental problems that make it difficult for him or her to interpret the meaning of what is happening. Such problems would include prejudices or an untrained eye and ear (Shafer, 1980, p. 154). What would you do, for instance, with an uncomplimentary account of Nightingale's skill as a nurse, written by a contemporary physician who thought that women should not be nurses?

Next you have to evaluate the observer's ability to report his or her observations (Shafer, 1980, pp. 155–156). That ability is often influenced by the "conventions" of the time in which the observer lived. Take, for example, how medical researchers considered a corpse "defective" if it provided evidence that contradicted the views of the ancient Roman physician Galen (Kalisch & Kalisch, 1978, p. 8). In addition, when you evaluate evidence, be aware of the observer's biases as well as your own. When was the observation written down relative to the event? Why did the witness or observer record the observation? Was it recorded consciously for posterity or unconsciously (Shafer, 1980, pp. 156–157)? One motivation is no better for the historian than another, but it will influence the way the evidence is evaluated. The kind of presentation made and the kind of distortions in the evidence will be influenced by the audience for which the author is writing. Florence Nightingale's account of her experience during the Crimean War would surely be different if she were writing for other nurses, for public support for nursing schools, or to her mother.

Once you have evaluated a simple piece of evidence, you have but begun. You must now compare it with other evidence to see if your original piece of evidence can be corroborated. The amount of corroboration needed will depend upon the size and nature of a subject and upon the availability of evidence. An account of Florence Nightingale's activities in the Crimea will perhaps require less confirmation than a study of her impact on the profession of nursing. A large topic will require more corroboration than a small one; and an evaluation of a person's attitudes will require more than a single physical act or instance. If a lot of evidence is available, you generally will be able to corroborate a conclusion more easily than if you had only a few extant sources. But it is sometimes true that a hundred unreliable sources are no better than one or two excellent ones.

Before you have completed the process of corroboration, you will have already begun to synthesize your evidence. In fact, you began the synthesis when your research began. In this part of the research, your own prejudices and life experiences can be crucial. Subjectivity and biases are to be understood, not eliminated. As part of our very humanity, we have attitudes, feelings, and flaws. They will influence the way we perceive the world. As Barzun and Graf (1970) write: " 'Subjective' and 'objective' properly apply not to persons and opinions but to sensations and judgments. Every person, that is every living subject, is necessarily subjective in *all* his sensations. But some of his subjective sensations are *of* objects . . ." (p. 165). Because only inherently subjective persons can know objects, the researcher's task is to ask, as Barzun and Graf do, "Is this an object in the outer world?" In order to answer that question, the researcher seeks corroboration. In the end, the researcher reaches a judgment approaching objectivity. As Barzun and Graf conclude, "An objective judgment is one made by testing in all ways possible one's subjective impressions so as to arrive at a knowledge of objects" (Barzun & Graf, 1970, p. 165).

Hence, subjectivity is not a synonym for "bias." It includes a good many other things as well. But, as with "subjectivity," the researcher should not look askance at "bias." As defined simply by Barzun and Graf, "Bias is an uncontrolled form of interest." We cannot eliminate our biases, but we can understand and acknowledge them. As Gaetomo Salvemini has put it: "Impartiality is a dream and honesty a duty. We cannot be impartial, but we can be intellectually honest" (Barzun & Graf, 1970, p. 181). An Anglophobe might be unwilling to give Florence Nightingale the credit that she deserves, but as long as the report written is based upon rigorous research methods, readers can filter out the author's bias. As you engage in your research, try to be aware of the ways in which your biases influence the way in which you treat a subject.

The problem of bias has profoundly influenced the writing of history and prevents there ever being any "true" history. One historian (A) of Florence Nightingale's role in the evolution of nursing practices will criticize the work of an earlier historian (B), only to be criticized by a later student (C) of her activities. Viewed narrowly, each criticism of a predecessor expressed conflicting biases. But viewed broadly, the third historian (C) likely found some value in the work of B, restored it, and added yet a new layer of understanding. Over time, we learn more about Nightingale's role, but because of our biases, we never will know the truth about her role. Thus, Barzun and Graf can assert confidently that "the past cannot help being reconceived by every generation, but the earlier reports upon it are in the main as good and true as they ever were. . . . The revisionism of historians, rightly considered, does not substitute; it subtracts a little and adds more" (Barzun & Graf, 1970, p. 185).

Having recognized that you are a subjective creature with biases, you proceed with your research and bring it to a conclusion. Ultimately, you will review all of your research notes and set about the task of writing. The subject of history-writing is beyond the scope of this chapter, but useful suggestions may be found in Barzun and Graf (1970) and in Strunk and White (1979). Remember that the most excellent research effort is wasted if you cannot convey your findings clearly to your readers.

AN EXAMPLE OF HISTORICAL RESEARCH
AND WRITING

Because the foregoing description abstracted the process of historical research and writing, it may be worthwhile to present one concrete example of the process. What follows is an account of the death of Silas Deane, a middle-echelon American diplomat during the revolutionary era. It relies heavily on the work of Boyd (1959) and Davidson and Lytle (1982).

Silas Deane's life followed the mythical American dream of going from rags to riches. Success in business led him into politics and eventually to France, where the Continental Congress sent him to buy supplies for the Revolutionary War effort. While in France, he helped to negotiate the Franco-American treaty of 1778. That success was later marred by charges that he had lined his own pockets while procuring supplies. Although he was recalled by the Congress, his guilt remained unproved.

In 1781, Deane, with exquisitely poor timing, wrote a letter to a friend urging that Americans seek a reconciliation with England short of independence. Intercepted and made public, the letter appeared to be nothing less than treason to revolutionaries, who were on the verge of winning their independence. Unwelcome at home, Deane drifted around Europe and eventually made his way to England. Within a few years, he was but a poor drunkard with a few remaining American friends, among them Edward Bancroft, his private secretary during the Paris negotiations. Deane eventually tired of his grim existence in London and, in 1789, determined to return to the United States. His ship set off in mid-September, encountered a storm on September 19, and turned back. A few days later, on September 22, as the captain waited for the weather to clear, Deane became ill and within four hours lay dead.

At this point, one might conclude that the story is over; but Deane's life and death created controversy. Thus, for the historian the work has just begun. Some writers at that time, for example, speculated that Deane committed suicide. The most important of the writings is a letter from John Cutting, a New England merchant, who reported the rumor to Thomas Jefferson. According to Cutting, Edward Bancroft suspected that Deane had taken "a sufficient quantity of Laudanum [a form of opium] to ensure his dissolution." (Davidson & Lytle, 1982, p. xvii). In the same letter, Cutting explained the plans that had been made by and for Deane:

> A subscription had been made here chiefly by Americans to defray the expense of getting [Deane] out of this country. . . . Dr. Bancroft with great humanity and equal discretion undertook the management of the *man* and his *business.* Accordingly his passage was engaged, comfortable cloaths and stores for his voyage were laid in, and apparently with much reluctance he embarked. . . . I happened to see him a few days since at the lodging of Mr. Trumbull and thought I had never seen him look better. (Davidson & Lytle, 1982, p. xix).

One careful historian, Julian Boyd, was puzzled by the apparent contradiction between Deane's happy state before leaving and the notion that he was a miserable creature bent on suicide.

The historian, curiosity piqued by the apparent contradiction, will want to know more about Deane's state of mind on the eve of his departure. This desire will lead the researcher to the library's card catalogue to look up works by and about Deane under author, title, and subject. The search reveals that most of Deane's personal papers have been published (Deane, 1887–1891, 1930). His letters reveal an optimistic man excited about the possibility of reviving his fortune in the new nation. Why then would he commit suicide? And why, if he was determined to kill himself, did he wait until he was on board the ship for a week?

The historian will now want to learn more about Deane and his acquaintances. One can trace the lives of many of Deane's friends; but eventually the historian will need to pay close attention to Edward Bancroft, who was a scientist of some repute and who became a member of the exclusive Royal Society of Medicine. In 1776, Deane had contacted Bancroft on the advice of Benjamin Franklin, who had earlier befriended the young scientist. Franklin and Deane thought that Bancroft would help Deane in supplying the war effort, and, when he was back in England, he could spy on the British. Bancroft agreed.

In addition to those activities, Bancroft joined Deane to speculate at the expense of the Americans. Davidson and Lytle provide one example: "Deane . . . sometimes sent ships from France without declaring whether they were loaded with private or public goods. Then if the ships arrived safely, he would declare the cargo was private, his own. But if the English navy captured the goods on the high seas, he labelled it government merchandise and the public absorbed the loss" (Davidson & Lytle, 1982, p. xxii–xxiii). Not all of their speculations were as successful as those, and they probably did little better than break even.

One other aspect of Bancroft's life during the revolutionary years, (not learned until a century later) should be mentioned. He was a double agent. Throughout the war, he either sent letters directly to England or passed along notes written in invisible ink to the English ambassador to France. In these ways, Bancroft kept the British aware to the negotiations going on between the revolutionaries and the French. Although American diplomats realized that there were some leaks from their ranks, few suspected Bancroft of double-dealing. Deane apparently was not a double agent, but he may have protected his partner and secretary.

Bancroft, despite having been implicated earlier in a plot to burn down the British navy, returned to England at the end of the war with his reputation intact on both sides of the Atlantic. Parliament even raised the lifetime annual pension he was promised for spying from £200 to £1000.

We are now ready to ask anew about the circumstances of Silas Deane's death. Who started the rumors about Deane's suicide? According to Cutter, it was none other than Bancroft. Would Bancroft have had any interest in hastening Deane's demise? Would he have anything to fear if Deane returned to the United States? Indeed, he would have. Deane might expose Bancroft's spy activity or his association with the aforementioned incendiary plot. If his treasonable activity were exposed, it is unlikely that Parliament would have continued Bancroft's pension or granted him the monopoly he was then seeking for a new dye process. Thus, Bancroft had a motive for killing Deane; but did he have the ability to do it at long distance? Remember that Bancroft was taking care of Deane in England and had arranged the plans for his return to the United States. Bancroft himself wrote to Thomas Jefferson that he was helping Deane with "advice, medicines and money for his subsistence." Maybe the physician slipped something into Deane's drugs that would have killed him but which might not be ingested for days. But did Bancroft know enough about poisons to do it? Again, the answer is yes. Bancroft had gained his reputation as a scientist by publishing *An Essay on the Natural History of Guiana and South America*, based upon his observations while living in Surinam. In the book, he revealed his considerable knowledge about the poison curare. Did he bring any of it back with him to England? We don't know.

Nor will we ever know conclusively about Silas Deane's death unless new evidence is uncovered. The way in which the foregoing facts have been arranged and presented leads the reader to conclude that Bancroft may well have murdered Deane. But what has been presented is not the truth. Rather, in this instance and in virtually all other kinds of qualitative research, we deal in probabilities. In sum, how the tale of Deane's death is told depends upon the kind of disciplined research done by the historian—from the framing of a question, the construction of a bibliography, and systematic note-taking to the evaluation of the veracity and meaning of the evidence. But it also depends upon the exercise of historical imagination transcending the use of good common sense, and the way the historian interprets, synthesizes, and arranges the facts. In other words, the research and writing of history is not an impersonal process by which the unvarnished facts present themselves. Instead, it is the product of the historian's labor and intelligence acting directly and systematically upon the evidence.

REFERENCES

Barzun, J., & Graf, H. F., *The modern researcher* (rev. ed.). New York: Harcourt, Brace & World, 1970.

Boyd, J. Silas Deane: Death by a Kindly Teacher of Treason? *William and Mary Quarterly*, 3rd Ser., 1959, *16*, 165–187, 319–342, 515–550.

Cantor, N. F., & Schneider, R. I. *How to study history*. New York: Thomas Y. Crowell, 1967.

Carr, E. H., *What is history?* New York: Alfred A. Knopf, 1962.

Christy, T. E. Portrait of a leader: Lavinia Lloyd Dock. *Nursing Outlook*, 1969, *17*, 72.

Christy, T. E. Portrait of a leader: Lillian D. Wald. *Nursing Outlook*, 1970, *18*, 50.

Davidson, J. W., & Lytle, M. H., *After the fact: The art of historical detection*. New York: Alfred A Knopf, 1982.

Deane, S. *The Deane papers*, New York Historical Society *Collections*, XIX-XXIII. New York: New York Historical Society, 1887–1891.

Deane, S. *The Deane papers*, Connecticut Historical Society *Collections*, XXIII. Hartford: Connecticut Historical Society, 1930.

Fischer, D. H. *Historians' fallacies: Toward a logic of historical thought*. New York: Harper & Row, 1970.

Hexter, J. H. *Doing history*. Bloomington: Indiana University Press, 1971.

Higham, J. *History: The development of histori-* cal studies in the United States. Englewood Cliffs, N. J.: Prentice-Hall, 1965.

Hoover, H. T. Oral history in the United States. In M. Kammen (Ed.), *The past before us: Contemporary historical writing in the United States*. Ithaca, N.Y.: Cornell University Press, 1980, pp. 391–407.

Kalisch, P. A., and Kalisch, B. J. *The advance of American nursing*. Boston: Little, Brown, and Company, 1978.

Kousser, J. M. Quantitative social-scientific history. In M. Kammen, *The past before us: Contemporary historical writing in the United States*. Ithaca, N.Y.: Cornell University Press, 1980, pp. 433–456.

Kruman, M. W. *Parties and politics in North Carolina, 1836–1865*. Baton Rouge: Louisiana State University Press, 1983.

Nugent, W. T. K. *Creative history: An introduction to historical study*. Philadelphia: J. B. Lippincott Company, 1967.

Shafer, R. J. (Ed.) *A guide to historical method* (3rd ed.). Homewood, Ill.: The Dorsey Press, 1980.

Strunk, W., Jr., and White, E. B. *The elements of style* (3rd ed.). New York: The MacMillan Company, 1979.

Winchell, C. M. *Guide to reference books* (8th ed.). Chicago: University of Chicago Press, 1967.

Woodward, C. V. The age of reinterpretation. *American Historical Review*, 1960, *46*, 1–19.

8

Life Health-Care History: Purposes, Methods, and Techniques

Madeleine M. Leininger

The purpose of taking an oral or written life health care history is to obtain a personalized and longitudinal account of an individual's health, care, and illness patterns from a lifetime perspective. The life history method is a special way of obtaining a chronological sequence of an individual's ideas and experiences from their particular viewpoint. It is a self-disclosure method based upon personal recall or reminiscences of the person's own subjective and objective life experiences. Life histories may serve many and different purposes, depending upon the researcher's goals, skills, and interest areas.

A life history can be taken at any age (usually beyond the age of ten years), but it is especially rich and productive in content with individuals in middle and advanced years of life. Before initiating an oral or written history, the researcher usually spends some time with the individual to establish a trusting and favorable rapport so that the history taker is viewed as trustworthy and genuinely interested in the person's life story. Most importantly, the history taker is knowledgeable and skilled in the purposes, uses, and methodological considerations of the oral and written history method.

Life histories may be conducted as an autobiography or a biography of an individual. An *autobiography* refers to a self-disclosure by presenting a person's own life history as known and experienced by the individual, and in his or her own particular style of sharing the written information or research data. A *biography* refers to a written account of an individual's chronological life experiences as revealed to the researcher (or history taker), who records, produces, and analyzes the individual's life history. Hence an autobiography is a self-disclosed and self-produced account of an individual that is produced by the history taker in his own style of communication. In contrast a biography is done by another person (e.g., history-taker) brings together the individual's story with primary and secondary data to reconstruct an accurate account of the individual's life. Both methods are valuable because they generally reveal the person's own viewpoints, life experiences, and events told in their world view (*emic*) perspective. Due to language factors, a biographer may need an interpreter, and the researcher must check for accurate translations and interpretations. The essential difference is that an autobiography is written or produced by the story tellee and the biography is produced by another person, a researcher.

Since the goal of a biography is to produce a comprehensive, recollected and sequenced view of an individual's life history, the researcher must try to obtain an accurate account by remaining an active and empathetic listener and must have the ability to write another person's life history. Developing an accurate and reliable life history of another person is an art and a skill. *Validity* is obtained by continual assessment of oral and written content, getting truths, and using documents from the informant. *Reliability* is obtained through re-checking of information, rephrasing of questions, probing, and the use of supplementary data or documents. Anthropologists have used oral and written life histories for decades (Langness, 1965) and have established the validity and reliability criteria for doing and using biographical and autobiographical data.

An individual is chosen as representative of the culture for a life history and because of special interests of the researcher. Both a biography and autobiography are life histories of qualitative types of research and can provide extremely rich, particularized and indepth information about an individual's life history.

At the outset, it is important that the researcher state the purposes of the oral or written history. Besides a recording and ordering the person's life history chronologically, the researcher may select a particular focus throughout the life cycle, such as a focus on health, care, and illness patterns (recommended by the author for nurses doing and using life histories for research and teaching purposes). Nurses with graduate preparation in social science usually can conduct a full life history because they have learned how to identify and abstract broad social structure and complex life events affecting health and care practices in society. For example, the author has used the life history method for comparative life profiles of cultural representatives of five different cultures to determine differences and similarities related to ethnocare and ethnohealth patterns (Leininger, 1960–1961, 1968, 1978, 1984). Comparative and in-depth single life histories are extremely valuable to understand patterns and meanings of health and care patterns of all age groups, but especially the elderly.

Life histories are often referred to as reminiscences, self-disclosure, self-constitutional, and personalized documentaries of individuals to disclose chronological life experiences, events, conditions, or patterns of living. Life histories are used to obtain some of the most intimate, humanistic, and scientific sequenced data by an individual in order to ascertain chronological knowledge about human beings over time and their particular life experiences. Because a life history is potentially a rich source of data for health scientists and humanists, it should be used more as a research method and as an option to traditional quantitative methods to identify and document health and patterns of clients, families and cultural groups who use professional health systems. Transcultural nurse researchers who have used the life history method for several decades can give helpful information to other nurse researchers.

This qualitative type of nursing research method has much promise for generating care, health and other kinds of nursing knowledge.

The purpose of this chapter, therefore, is to encourage, promote, and help nurse researchers to understand and use life histories as another qualitative type of research method to study nursing phenomena. Most of the ideas presented in this chapter come from the author's knowledge and experience in using the life history method as known and used by anthropologists and modified to fit nurse researchers' interests and goals.

HISTORICAL BACKGROUND: USES OF LIFE HISTORY METHOD BY SOCIAL SCIENTISTS

Since 1900, life histories have been used by anthropologists and other social scientists for different reasons and purposes, such as the following: (1) to provide a full account or life portrait of an individual; (2) to identify cultural trends and historical development through individual lifestyles; (3) to identify culture changes or stability factors in predicting historical trends; (4) to disclose personality features of leaders and followers in different cultures; and (5) to understand human and environmental conditions impacting upon individuals (Becker, 1970; Dollard, 1935; Gottschalk, Kluckhohn, & Angell, 1945; Langness, 1965; Langness & Frank, 1981).

The relevance of life histories has been well documented by many renowned social scientists, and there has been considerable interest in the use of biographies to achieve certain research goals. At present there is a growing, resurgent interest in the method (Langness & Frank, 1981; Paul, 1983). Researchers are expanding their methodological options, and the life history method is being discovered anew to know more fully particular individuals in order to gain insights about their behavior, cultural lifeways, human conditions, and so forth. Autobiographies and biographies are being viewed as choice methods to obtain accurate and reliable portraits of individuals as members of cultural groups and particular societies. Diverse life span roles of individuals functioning in key leadership, political, economic, and top executive positions, as well as in common daily life roles, are of special interest to researchers. The longitudinal perspective brings refreshing and different views to survey and questionnaire types of studies, which emphasize the present time. Hence, the life history is becoming an important and relevant research method among scientists and humanists (Paul, 1983, p. 19) and needs to be established as a legitimate method by health researchers.

Some of the classic life histories of the past can serve as valuable guides for the development of the method, especially as it relates to nursing research. Life history examples from researchers in social sciences and transcultural nursing are especially relevant in studying health and caring patterns such as those listed below.

Dyk's *Son of Old Man Hat* (1938), Underhill's study of a Papago woman (1936), Simmons's *Sun Chief* (1942), and Williams' recorded *Reminiscences of Ahuia Ova* (1939) are outstanding biographical classics to depict the life history method. Radin's *Crashing Thunder* (1926) and LaFarge's work, *Laughing Boy* (1929), are outstanding accounts to show cultural history changes, personal life styles, and qualitative attributes and characteristics of individuals.

Life histories of women were begun early with Parsons's study in 1919, *American*

Indian Life. Bowen's book, *Return to Laughter* (1954), and Mead's book, *Blackberry Winter* (1975), revealed emotional, cultural, and social patterns of women adapting to different life situations. Myerhoff and Simic's recent work on aging (1978) is also of interest to grasp different views of aging women.

In the past four decades, several life histories have been done by anthropologists in collaboration with psychologists to study interrelationships of culture and personality. The work of Dubois, *The People of Alor* (1944) and Kardiner's book, *The Psychological Frontiers of Society* (1945) are examples of the use of life histories. Later some innovative and descriptive life histories were written by Lewis (1959, 1961), namely, *Five Families* (1959), and *The Children of Sanchez* (1961). Most of these life histories are viewed as literary masterpieces and valued research documents to disclose individual and family life history events, daily life experiences, and human conditions of cultural groups. These histories can serve as early and excellent prototypes of the life history method for nurse researchers, and to learn about health promotion, illness prevention, life care values, beliefs, care, deviant behavior, personality, culture, and other areas of interest to nurses. Other life history accounts by social scientists have been identified in a recent comprehensive work by Langness and Frank (1981), and the reader is encouraged to study these works to gain an understanding of the importance and methodological features of life histories.

STATUS OF LIFE HISTORIES IN THE HEALTH FIELD

In the health field, written or oral histories for research purposes are used by nurses and other health personnel only to a limited extent, even though brief health and illness (or disease) inquiries are done by nurses and physicians. These types of histories are generally not the same as longitudinal in-depth life histories of a person, but instead tend to focus on recent symptoms of physical and emotional illnesses by a series of questions that fit the nurse's or physician's knowledge of types of illnesses and diseases. The client's longitudinal life history is seldom obtained systematically in medical or nursing histories.

Nurses have written a few historical vignettes of past nursing leaders, but very few have used the life history method as discussed in this chapter. Christy's work comes the closest to reflecting some features of the life history method; however, her writing reflects a historiographical account of selected early nurse leaders (Christy, 1975). Other examples of partial historical vignettes can be found in *One Strong Voice: A Thousand Nurses Tell Their Story* (Flanagan, 1976). This book gives brief and incomplete accounts of several nurses, but it does not include their life histories, nor is it reflective of the life history method *per se*. Other kinds of quasi-"histories" have been done by nurses to elicit mental illness and symptom characteristics. Again these "histories" are not the same as obtaining a full and comprehensive life history because the focus is too narrow and superficial. They do not capture the life account of an individual from his or her past life experiences, and questionable documents for research purposes.

As nurse researchers begin to take life histories of adults and young adults for research purposes to obtain chronological care and health patterns, they will discover some entirely new or different sources of knowledge in nursing, which are helpful to guide nursing practices. For example, the author obtained life histories to study the Gadsup of the Eastern Highlands of New Guinea, Mexican-Americans in Denver and Detroit, the Southern Afro- and Anglo-Americans in the United States, and the Mormons of Utah (Leininger, 1960–1961, 1968, 1978, 1984). These life histories included longitudinal health, care and illness patterns of cultural representatives as well as social structure, acculturation, and ecological factors. As a consequence, the author has developed a Life History Protocol to guide nurses and other health professionals in the use of the life history research method within a health care and nursing frame of reference. This protocol can be used not only for research but also for teaching and guilding clinical practice interventions. It can be used to provide comparative data when the protocol and general method are used by several health researchers in studying cultural representatives of the same culture or different ones when purposes or goals of the research are similar. In time, the life history method can be refined, tested cross-culturally, and checked for validity and reliability features. But before the Life History Profile is presented for research purposes, one needs to consider the actual and potential purposes of the life history method in nursing and the health fields.

PURPOSES AND POTENTIAL USES OF LIFE HISTORIES IN NURSING AND HEALTH RESEARCH

Life histories can serve different research and clinical purposes for nurses and other health professionals, and some of the most evident uses are the following:

1. Life histories provide a *chronological picture* of an individual's life and lifeways, including normal life encounters, daily and yearly living patterns, unanticipated crises, and stresses and as a reconstructed account.
2. Life histories are an important means to *pinpoint certain ways* people maintain health and prevent illness patterns.
3. *Folk and professional care patterns can be identified that* have helped an individual regain and preserve health.
4. Often life histories uncover some *unexpected and unusual health or illness experiences that are unknown* through other nursing and medical research approaches. (These unknown dimensions often stimulate new lines of inquiry and theoretical propositions (i.e., "mushroom madness," "folk health," "planned death").
5. Research data from life histories are highly *individually centered* and can, therefore, provide in-depth data about a person in ways that "make sense" because the history is usually told within the individual's familiar and natural life context. It is, indeed, the individual's *own history* and told in his or her *own way*.
6. A life history can provide an *accurate* and *meaningful processual account of health,* illness, and care behaviors throughout the life span and within a particular holistic ecological, social structure and cultural context. To date, few quantitative research methodologists attempt processual and historical change studies.
7. Life history data often provide *new sets of explanations* to older theoretical views about birth, living, growing old, and dying.
8. Life history data can be used to generate *specific care plans* in relation to the individual's longitudinal life values, experiences, and patterned needs.
9. In the process of obtaining life histories, the author and others have noted the *therapeutic value to individuals* of recalling and reminiscing on certain life events.

At the same time, there may be aspects of the life history that are painful and anxiety-producing, which need to be noted and recorded. Hence, the joys and achievements as well as the sad and less favorable life events may be found in a life history (Bramwell, 1981; Ebersole, 1978; Leininger, 1968, 1978, 1981, 1984; Liton & Olstein, 1969).

10. Life history data provide information on *life career changes* and changes in social structure features that can influence the health status of individuals and groups.

11. From life histories come *recurrent life patterns* and *non-recurrent* (or deviant) events that can often be understood as health-promoting or illness-inducing.

12. A number of life histories of individuals of a culture or population are valuable historical documents for *comparative studies* on health, cultural patterns, and social structure that can be used over time to study current trends and predict future changes (diachronic and synchronic historical changes).

13. Life histories can be used as *collaborative or supplemental* data to explain quantitative findings as they often brings obscure and numerical facts into focus with time and contextual meanings.

14. Life histories can provide *primary and secondary* research data to document ambiguous and mythical statements about health and nursing care situations.

15. Life histories can have many *therapeutic features,* such as heightened morale and self-esteem, expansion of conscious awareness or positive health patterns, and rediscovery of old ways of dealing with current life and health concerns (Bramwell, 1981; Leininger, 1975).

GUIDELINES FOR OBTAINING A LIFE HEALTH-CARE HISTORY (LEININGER PROTOCOL)

The guidelines developed in this section by the author may be useful to nurse researchers in developing their knowledge and skills to prepare either a biographical or an autobiographical life history.

The general purpose of the life health care history is to document and identify longitudinal pattern(s) of an individual's perceived, known, and experienced health, care, and illness lifeways within particular cultural and environmental contexts.

In using the life history method, nurse researchers with preparation or experience in ethnographic and social science research would be good persons to tap for the life history method as these researchers are generally most familiar with the method. They know the ways to proceed and what traps to avoid for sound research practices. The field study method of anthropology is a natural one for incorporating the life history method because the researcher is working with the people and knows many aspects of the people's lives. Hence, life histories are often done with the ethnographic and ethnonursing field methods described in this book, and the findings are often reported in full ethnographic research studies.

After identifying the purposes or goals of the study, the researcher asks about potential key informants (see chapter 3 on key informants), who would be knowledgeable, accurate, and reliable story-tellers in studying the phenomena of care, health, illness, values, and other aspects of special interest to nursing. Often the nurse researcher asks people in the community about "good story-tellers" regarding health practices and lifeways. Sometimes the researcher has already done research in the community or knows about the people. Several names may be proposed; the researcher then may use convenience or random informants by criteria such as age, sex, and social, economic, and cultural factors. Usually eight to ten detailed life histories are taken from a cultural group; the number may vary, however, depending on the goals or purposes of the study. These informants represent a specific culture or population when identified with the community over time.

In choosing the informants, try to choose those who are willing and volunteer to be raconteurs (story-tellers) and who seem most interested to share their life histories with health personnel to improve people's care. Generally, these individuals realize they have rich data to offer and will show pride in sharing their ideas with others. If informants are uncomfortable in story telling, or if they have never assumed such a role, they will need time to reflect upon different facets of their life from birth to the present time. It is fascinating how cultural groups know who are the key informants, who would be able to represent them well about certain phenomena. There fore, do not underestimate the ability of community members to select their own best raconteurs. If their suggestions not considered, problems may occur and the accuracy and extent of histories may be limited for typical and nontypical life histories.

From the beginning, it is important to keep in mind that the *reliability* of the life history can be increased by the careful selection of informants and how representative they are of the culture or population. *Validity*, too, will be strenthened as one seeks raconteurs who tend to be honest, well-informed, and willing to produce an accurate history. The informants should know their culture and environmental features, but there will be some variability in life histories.

When people discover that researchers are genuinely interested in their life histories and respect the history-sharing, the author has found that pride, willingness, and real satisfactions can be noted with those who are chosen. Documenting the life views and special experiences of "chosen informants" is often a most rewarding experience, with many beneficial outcomes.

Although the researcher's goals may vary, it is extremely important not to treat a life history like a "one-shot" quick questionnaire or survey study in response to a predetermined set of questions. Much time, patience, active listening, and genuine interest are essential to assure an accurate and reliable life history. Confidence that informants will tell their story is important, as is allowing time for the informant to come to know and trust the researcher. The informant needs to feel important and have his or her ideas (story) valued.

Keen observation and interview skills are most essential for the researcher. He or she must also have the ability to be an active listener and to enjoy hearing life accounts; if this is not evident to the informant and if the researcher is restless, nonproductive accounts can be anticipated. The researcher must be constantly alert to what the individual is saying and doing and understand the cultural referents. The "Tell me" and "I would like to learn from you" are key phrases to facilitate life history taking.

In the actual conduct of a health and care-centered history, the guidelines given in Table 8-1 are important to consider.

Throughout the sessions, the researcher trails or follows the client's story and does not impose his or her views. Remaining as neutral as possible about subject matter such as politics, events and conditions is important. Saying, "I am not sure I

Table 8-1 *Leininger's Life History Health Care Protocol*

1. Introduce yourself and explain that you would like to obtain the person's life and health history. Indicate how such a history could be helpful to health personnel and of interest to him or her. Answer questions or clarify concerns of the individual. Obtain written permission from the individual for the autobiographical or biographical health history study (clarify the differences in these methods).

2. If the individual wishes to write his or her own life history (an autobiography), encourage him to write in his own style, but ask him to include his views and experiences about health, care, and illness patterns in order to help him and others benefit from such knowledge. Clarify how you plan to use the research findings.

3. If you are writing the individual's health and care history biographical account, proceed as follows:

   A. Plan to record the information *before* initiating the interview. Use unobtrusive materials so that you do not distract the informant in telling his history. If you are using a tape recorder, choose one hour tapes to prevent disruption in the flow of the life history with the informant. Written permission must be obtained from the informant prior to any recording (follow the requirements of the committee for human subjects research). If you use ethnographic field notes, you may wish to use the guidelines already described by the author in this book, or use Spradley's suggestions for record keeping (Spradley, 1979, 1981). It is important to note that some informants are not comfortable with having their life history taped and their request must be respected. If an informant consents to taping, offer him or her a copy of the tape without cost. (Usually the informant does want a copy.) If taping is not agreed to, use a stenographer's pad and record words and an outline of what you are observing and talking about. *Immediately* after the history taking, write in detail what you observed, heard, and talked about. Do not wait hours or days, as recall is difficult and accuracy decreases.

   B. Use primarily the ethnographic open-ended type of interview method described in this book or in Spradley's book (1979) to encourage and promote an open flow of information. The researcher's introductory comment might be, "I would like to learn about you and how you have known and experienced health, caring, illnesses, or disabilities." "As a nurse, I am interested in your past and present lifeways so I can learn what has made you healthy or less healthy, and who you believe have been caring persons in your life." "Feel free to offer special stories or events as you recall ideas important to you." (Clarify as needed how this information may be helpful to nurses to improve nursing care.)

   C. Suggest some life history domains or topic areas on which to focus, using with lead-in statements with a sequence, such as the following:

      (1) "Let us talk about where you were born and what you remember about your early days of growing up, keeping well, or experiencing illnesses."

      (2) "Can you recall special events, experiences, and health practices during childhood and adolescent years that were especially important to you in keeping well, or that limited your wellness or healthiness?"

      (3) "Let us talk about your special health care experiences that were particularly clear and pleasant (or unpleasant) to you regarding these periods in your life" (encourage use of folk stories, humorous tales, and descriptions of special events):

a. Early childhood days
b. Adolescent years
c. Mid-life years
d. Older years

(4) "Give some examples of healthy caring activities or ways of living by your family, cultural group, or significant people who helped you."

(5) "As you think about your life experiences to date, what do you recall about these experiences and what did you value most or least about":

a. Going to school (primary, secondary, and college days) and your health status.
b. Employment experiences and how you viewed or experienced them as healthy or less healthy.
c. Marriage or remaining single throughout life (stresses or nonstresses).
d. Sudden (or gradual) death of loved persons and how such experiences influenced your thinking and health status.
e. Accident or illness events to you, your family, or friends and the care expressions.

(6) "I would like to hear about your general philosophy of keeping well and how you believe your religion, political, and cultural values have helped (or hindered) your life goals and health. Can you tell me what beliefs or values have especially guided you to remaining well or become ill? (Give examples.)"

(7) "Can you recall special folk or professional health and caring experiences that were most important to you during your life regarding the following topics?"

a. Staying well (or becoming ill).
b. Becoming disabled (and maintaining/getting well).
c. Experiencing or dealing with healthy patterns of living.
d. Recovering from a traumatic experience as perceived by you.

(8) "Can you recall who you believe were 'good caretakers' in the past (and today) and what made them such good caretakers? What noncaring persons influenced your lifestyle or made life difficult or unhealthy for you? What caregivers were important in your life and what made them so? Can you tell me about nurses as caretakers?"

(9) "Throughout your life, what factors seemed to keep you going, living, or establishing healthy patterns of living for yourself and others?"

(10) "What have been some of the greatest rewards or joys in your life? The least rewarding and why? How are these joys related to health or illness?"

(11) "Feel free to tell me other aspects of your life so I can understand it as fully as possible. You can tell me stories, jokes, healing practices, and any special events you believe I should know about to understand you."

D. *Writing and Checking the History.* Covering the above life history points (and others the researcher wishes to include) will take several sessions—usually three to four. Upon completion of the history, you should carefully review and check the history, and then clarify vague points immediately while fresh in the mind of the informant. Use the informant's own words and accounts as much as possible. Thank the informant and make plans to confirm and share the written (biographical) account. If the account is autobiographical, return and go over

(continued)

Table 8-1   *(continued)*

the written account to be sure it is understandable and readable, suitable for reproduction as a written document. Express appreciation for the informant's time and information. Present a copy of the tape(s) to the informant. Be sure to provide sufficient time after you have written the account to clarify, confirm, reexamine, or explicate ideas from the informant.

E. *Analysis of Data.* Analyzing the data is a creative art and skill in that the researcher must consciously preserve the informant's statements, but still identify salient themes and synthesize life events in context. It is also an art and skill to both write a health and care life history and keep it accurate and interesting. The verbatim and sequenced account is preserved. Generally thematic, semantic, contextual, and general textual analyses of the data are done with life histories as part of the researcher's separate but special analysis. (See other chapters in this book on these methodological approaches.) Try to identify and analyze patterns of health, care, and illness (if present) so that a synthesis of ideas can be readily identified and used by research consumers. The researcher may wish to present the raw biographical data to the informant and retain theoretical and complex data for the researcher, still sharing dominant findings with the informant at the end of the study.

understand what you are saying" is always an important strategy for the researcher to use in clarifying and checking what is being said. Checking and cross-checking are important, but do not stop the informant's flow of ideas. Disrupting the flow or the story is always annoying to a raconteur. The informant may shift to what he or she thinks the researcher wants to hear when questions are inserted or interruptions occur. It is well to follow the open-ended, active listening method and to use the different inquiry modes as revealed in this book elsewhere and (Spradley, 1979, 1981) in doing sound ethnographic studies.

In the protocol given in Table 8-1, you will note that the ethnonursing approach is chosen to elicit the informant's *emic* views, such as, "Tell me," "Let's recall," "Can you recall or remember?" Broad and open-ended lines of inquiry are used rather than asking many focused questions. This helps to maintain an open interview method and to encourage the flow of information from the raconteur, so that he or she will present ideas and experiences in his or her own way. The informant's views, perceptions, and experiences must be understood in his or her world view, and not in the researcher's. Taking a life history requires research skills not only in choice of words, but also in thoughtful tone of voice, body language, and gestural manner of the researcher. The art of holding the informant's interest through several sessions is an important consideration.

You will also note that the life health and care history differs from an individual (or case) study in that (1) the life history focuses explicitly on longitudinal or sequenced life events, not on a few specific events; (2) the informant and interviewer "trail" or "track down" events, activities, and experiences throughout the life cycle, do not focus on just a few specific symptoms, (3) the life history is broad and detailed, not limited to medical symptoms, disease encounters, or researcher's views; and (4) the life history reconstructs and synthesizes life events through time.

ETHICAL AND METHODOLOGICAL ASPECTS

In obtaining a quality life history focused on health and care, ethical and other methodological problems will be found. Langness and Frank (highly experienced life historians) identify some central issues about life histories and note that "maintaining an informant's privacy, or reputation, is perhaps the most obvious ethical problem in life history research" (1981, p. 119). Unquestionably, the researcher must not probe for disclosure of information that is truly secret and private unless the informant wishes to share it with the researcher. Using undue pressure or coercive techniques to probe without informant's consent is unethical and a violation of human rights. Revealing secrets or private information about an individual, family, or even cultural group may cause harm, as persons may be subjected to ridicule or be threatened by loss of employment. At the same time, some autobiographical or biographical accounts have brought fame and other gains or benefits to the informants. The purposes and the way in which the writer has presented the life histories are important.

Sometimes life history data are influential in establishing health care and public policies. For example, Oscar Lewis' well-known book, *The Children of Sanchez* (1961), which focused on the culture of poverty, was used in formulating public policy. Whether this was helpful to Mexico and to the family portrayed is debatable. The consequences of making certain aspects known need to be anticipated, because poverty, for example, as political negligence, is an unfavorable societal image and repugnant to societal values. Life history data must be considered carefully to protect the individual and family; hence fictitious names and places must be used.

Since life histories include detailed and private accounts, appropriate use of the data must be considered at the outset. It is also wise for the researcher to check the accuracy of the written account to prevent future problems and to be sure it is acceptable to share with public or private groups. Identities must be protected, and it will require skill to share the salient ideas with others. It may be difficult for the researcher to identify the sensitive parts of a person's life history, but he or she should try to be alert and respond sensitively to them. The informant should always be free to comment on and check the document before publication to be sure it protects him.

Other ethical and general methodological research questions include the following: (1) How much detailed or private information should be included? (2) What is excluded and why? (3) How much editing can be done and still portray an accurate life history? (3) If private and detailed aspects are deleted, can the life history be truly accurate? (5) What ethical problems are related to constructing a life history with a focus on health, care, and nursing?

Unless the researcher has some knowledge of the native language, the use of interpreters may also pose special problems. Sometimes the interpreter may omit what he thinks is irrelevant and miss important and subtle points, leading to inaccurate data. To prevent distortions and inaccurate interpretations by the translator, the researcher should know the informant's language.

Sometimes ethical problems arise concerning the role of the researcher in publishing life histories or in follow-up expectations of the health researcher. Occasionally misunderstandings arise about the researcher's ability to do something about the informant's chronic illness, inadequate nursing care, medical treatments, or other factors. The researcher should clarify his or her role before initiating the study, making it clear that interventions may not be possible and giving reasons why. When a story of poor health care to the researcher, the informant may expect quick action or explicit help. Expecting nurses to act on their findings is often an ethical problem with consumers, especially with life histories. Hence, it is important to clarify your primary research role at the beginning. If, upon completion of the life history, you can guide the informant to get help, this should be considered, since in qualitative nursing research, the researcher is not expected to remain totally detached and nonresponsive to the people being studied. Helping people can often be done upon completion of the research, as action research intervention studies.

Political, social, legal, and cultural problems may also arise if the informant asks the nurse researcher to "take sides" or support the informant. The researcher should try to remain as neutral as possible to get an accurate account. But the researcher must accurately portray the informant's position on political, legal, and cultural issues.

Any quality life history account should reflect the humanistic dimensions of living and the health and care implications. With the qualitative research method and using participant-observation and life history accounts, the researcher becomes close to peoples' intimate past and present lives. Disturbing intrusions, harmful exposure and exploitations are important moral and ethical problems to guard against in research. Protecting the individual, family, and cultural group should be foremost in the researcher's mind although at the same time he or she should report as truthful and full an account as possible to show patterned behaviors. Getting close to the informant's private data or perceived "strange behavior" may frighten the researcher, which in turn may curtail the informant's sharing of life experiences. In order words, an informant may not be as frightened as the researcher in disclosing the use of certain folk healing aids. For example, take a client who has always used herbal medicine to treat stomach conditions or massage to heal an injury. Remaining nonjudgmental and listening with genuine interest may be most difficult for some health researchers who have strongly ethnocentric ideas of healing or curing illnesses within the professional norms and who view folk cultural (or popular) remedies with suspicion.

BENEFICIAL OR THERAPEUTIC OUTCOMES

The author has repeatedly noted marked therapeutic effects on informants in the process of doing life histories. A researcher who is genuinely interested in an individual's health and lifeways may make the raconteur feel valued and of worth, and help to increase his or her self-esteem. Valuing folk and cultural lifeways for minorities that have been recognized and understood only to a limited extent by health professionals may also be beneficial. Giving full attention to an informant with four to five open types of interviews may indeed be a gift. Langness and Frank identify this gift as:

> The anthropological life history offers a positive moral opportunity to pass on stories that might otherwise never be told. For those who are bearers of a tradition, the opportunity to tell their story can be a gift: reassurance that they are indeed still alive, that their voices will be heard and that their cultures can survive. It is a gift of equal importance for those generations to come who will take up that tradition and shape it to their own needs as the future unfolds. (Langness & Frank, 1981, p. 136)

Because nurses and health professionals have not fully recognized the therapeutic benefits of doing a life history, more education is needed in this area.

Beneficial consequences may occur simply through the disclosing of life history data. Recovering from a grave illness and starting life anew may occur in an unknown and almost miraculous way. The researcher too may be startled or led to disbelief by doubting or being uninformed about different therapeutic healing ways of different cultures (Leininger, 1978). Disclosure about the meaning of health and care to different families and cultural groups through an in-depth and longitudinal life history account may provide entirely new insights to the informant and to nurse researchers. Understanding the therapeutic role of music, art, and cultural rituals in healing and maintaining health or recovering from illness may be another new discovery from life histories. Comparative investigations about health, care, and illness of different individuals may provide fresh data or new approaches to nursing care. The discovery how people can help themselves in culturally prescribed and effective ways to care for themselves may be new to nurse researchers. Effective care-giving methods by nonprofessionals can offer new insights about the phenomena of care, self-care, and care by others that are not provided by professional nurses. What, then, is the role of the professional nurse as a caregiver with families?

Life histories of both rich and poor people can be most beneficial for understanding the meaning of health and care from different viewpoints and within social structural, language, and ecological contexts. The individual variability and humanistic patterns of health and care revealed through life histories may lead to new theories and hypotheses about human beings and how they live and cope throughout life.

In general, there is great potential for the life history method in qualitative nursing research. Life histories, both biographical and autobiographical, can yield much rich information that is not obtainable by experimental, survey, and other types of quantitative research methods. Life portraits are excellent ways to get to the heart of knowing people and to accurately document their health and care needs. Nurse researchers need to give much serious thought to the use of life histories, their purposes, and the contributions to be made to understand and know people from a longitudinal and in-depth viewpoint. Nurses will, however, need to develop their skills in obtaining life histories, in writing, and in analyzing the data. It takes time to develop the skills to construct good life histories; in addition, much patience and good interviewing skills are required. Ethical and moral issues related to private or secret information are important and need further study. The author contends that the life history method is one of the richest untapped sources for knowing people and their health and caring patterns, a method that still limitedly is known and used in nursing and the health fields today.

REFERENCES

Becker, H. S. The relevance of life histories. In N. K. Denzin, *Sociological methods: A sourcebook*. Chicago: Aldine Publishing Company, 1970.

Bogdan, R. *Being different: The autobiography of Jane Fry.* New York: John Wiley & Sons, 1974.

Bowen, E. S. *Return to laughter.* New York: Harper & Row, 1954.

Bramwell, L. Exploration of the effects of producing a tape-recorded life history on elderly individuals: A transcultural approach, field study proposal, N820 (unpublished). Ann Arbor, Michigan: Wayne

State University, College of Nursing, 1981.

Christy, T. Portrait of a leader: Sophia E. Palmer. *Nursing Outlook,* 1975, *23,* (12),746–751.

Dollard, J. *Criteria for the life history* (with analysis of six notable documents). New Haven, Conn.: Yale University Press, 1935.

Dubois, C. A. *The people of Alor.* Minneapolis: University of Minnesota Press, 1944.

Dyk, W. *Son of old man hat: A Navaho autobiography recorded by Walter Dyk.* With an introduction by Edward Sapir. New York: Harcourt Brace Jovanovich, 1938.

Ebersole, P. A theoretical approach to the use of reminiscence. In I. M. Burnside (Ed.), *Working with the elderly: Group process and technique.* North Scituate, Mass.: Dunberry Press, 1978.

Flanagan, L. (Ed.) *One strong voice: A Thousand Nurses tell their story.* American Nurses Association. Kansas City, Mo.: The Lowell Press, 1976.

Gottschalk, L., Kluckhohn, C., & Angell, R. (Eds.). *The use of personal documents in history, anthropology, and sociology.* New York: Social Science Research Council, Bulletin 53, 1945.

Kardiner, A. (with collaboration of R. Linton, C. Dubois, and J. West). *The psychological frontiers of society.* New York: Columbia University Press, 1945.

LaFarge, O. *Laughing boy.* Boston: Houghton Mifflin Co., 1929.

Langness, L. L. *The life history in anthropological science.* New York: Holt, Rinehart & Winston, 1965.

Langness, L. L., & Frank, G. *Lives: An anthropological approach to biography.* Novato, Calif.: Chandler & Sharp Publishers, 1981.

Leininger, M. Field research with the Gadsup of the Eastern Highlands of New Guinea (unpublished biographies, Papua–New Guinea), 1960–1961.

Leininger, M. Field research with Mexican and Spanish-Americans health care in an urban community (unpublished biographies, Denver, Colorado), 1968.

Leininger, M. Therapeutic dimensions of reminiscence through the life history method (unpublished paper, Salt Lake City, Utah), 1975.

Leininger, M. (Ed.). *Transcultural nursing: Concepts, theories and practices.* New York: John Wiley & Sons, 1978.

Leininger, M. *Caring: An essential human need.* Thorofare, N. J.: Charles B. Slack, 1981.

Leininger, M. *Care: The essence of nursing and health.* Thorofare, N. J.: Charles B. Slack, 1984.

Lewis, O. *Five families: Mexican case studies in the culture of poverty.* New York: Basic Books, 1959.

Lewis, O. *The children of Sanchez: Autobiography of a Mexican family.* New York: Random House, 1961.

Liton, J., & Olstein, S. Therapeutic aspects of reminiscence. *Social Casework,* 1969, *5*(5), 263–268.

Mead, M. *Blackberry winter: My earlier years.* New York: William Morrow and Company Inc., 1975.

Myerhoff, B., & Lufte, V. Life history as integration. *Gerontologist,* 1975, *15*(12), 541–543.

Myerhoff, B., & Simic, A. (Eds.). *Life's career—aging: Cultural variations on growing old.* Beverly Hills, Calif.: Sage Publications, 1978.

Opler, M. E. *An Apache lifeway.* Chicago: University of Chicago Press, 1941.

Parsons, E. C. Waiyautitea of Zuni, New Mexico. *Scientific Monthly,* 1919, *9,* 433–457.

Paul, A. "Biography" is one sign of what may be new life in the art of recounting lives. *Chronicle of Higher Education,* 1983, *19,* pp. 20–21.

Radin, P. (Ed.). *Crashing Thunder: The autobiography of an American Indian.* New York: Appleton-Century-Crofts, 1926.

Simmons, L. W. *Sun Chief: The autobiography of a Hopi Indian.* New Haven, Conn.: Yale University Press, 1942.

Spradley, J. P. *The ethnographic interview.* New York: Holt, Rinehart & Winston, 1979.

Spradley, J. P. *Participation-observation.* New York: Holt, Rinehart & Winston, 1981.

Underhill, R. *The autobiography of a Papago woman's memoirs.* Millwood City, New York: Kraus-Thompson Organization, Ltd., 1936.

Williams, F. E. The reminiscences of Ahuia Ova. *Journal of the Royal Anthropological Institute,* 1939, *69,* 11–44.

9

Entrée Strategies for Nursing Field Research Studies

Veronica Evaneshko

The sun was setting as I drove over deeply rutted dirt roads to meet my first American Indian informant, and the view was spectacular enough to almost allay my fears over whether my diabetic research project would be understood and accepted by people who were traditionalists and who spoke no English. I had spent months seeking the necessary approvals for my transcultural nursing field research project from an incredible number of subcommittees, the tribal council, the Bureau of Indian Affairs, and the local health authorities. The dirt road I was driving on was taking me into the challenging world of field research and I would need to make a favorable entrée if my project was to succeed.

This chapter focuses on the ethnographic fieldwork method of data collection, and on different considerations with which nurse researchers should be cognizant when using a qualitative research method such as ethnographic fieldwork. A brief discussion of ethnographic fieldwork as a method for nursing studies, a description of the use of field research in nursing, and an overview of general fieldwork considerations are included in this chapter. Some preparatory activities for field research covered in this chapter include selection of the community, literature review, and appropriate timing of the fieldwork. Field research strategies are also discussed; these include initial contact, community expectations and attitudes, living and working arrangements, establishing an identity or role, identifying respondents, developing trust and rapport, and providing reciprocity.

ETHNOGRAPHIC FIELD RESEARCH METHOD

Ethnographic field research differs in several ways from such common research approaches as the historical, survey, and experimental methods. These differences include purpose(s) of research, time orientations, qualitative aspects of human behavior, control over data, and selection of data collection techniques, (Babbie, 1979; Fox, 1976; Junker, 1968; Smyth, 1981).

Ethnographic field research may involve the generation of past, present, or future oriented research data. Unlike the other methods, which require prior judgments and clear-cut, carefully defined data collection techniques, field research permits creative and innovative use of a number of different methods and techniques as the situation warrants (Smyth, 1981). Examples of such methods and techniques include participant-observation, case studies, in-depth interviews, and surveys.

Fieldwork generally is not directed at the testing of theories and hypotheses. Rather, attempts usually are made to identify new and unexplored data in order to understand ongoing processes that cannot be predicted in advance (Leininger, 1977; McElroy, 1982). The end result of ethnographic field research is the generation of hypotheses and theories that may require the use of other types of research approaches (Babbie, 1979; Smyth, 1981). Stated another way, in situations in which knowledge and information are sparse, fieldwork permits the fieldworker to discover what are the appropriate, meaningful questions to ask. Once this is done, other research tools, such as surveys and questionnaires, can be used to standardize results for the purpose of testing hypotheses (Junker, 1968).

FIELD RESEARCH IN TRANSCULTURAL NURSING STUDIES

The use of field research in transcultural nursing studies and other areas of nursing is particularly appropriate because of its comprehensive perspective. When health and illness attitudes and behaviors need to be understood within their natural (i.e., cultural) setting, ethnographic field research is the method of choice. Transcultural nursing mainly focuses on the cross-cultural caring behavior, nursing care, and health/illness values, beliefs, and patterns of behavior for people to determine culture-specific nursing care needs (Leininger, 1981). The goal of transcultural nursing has been identified by Leininger (1978) as the identification, testing, understanding, and utilization of a body of transcultural nursing knowledge and practices that are culturally derived. In other words, the basis of transcultural nursing, as of all professional nursing, is research; in this case, however, research features culturally distinct or similar groups.

Field research is the preferred research method by a number of scholars who have studied culturally distinct groups (Maykovich, 1977; Tsukashima, 1977; Warren, 1977; Weiss, 1977) because it "sensitizes the investigator to the parameters and nature of the community and its members including language, . . . customs, and habits that make for a better understanding of a community" (Montero, 1977, p. 7).

A salient feature of field research that is especially important for transcultural nursing studies is the setting. People are observed in situ or in their normal, everyday environment or naturalistic setting (Smyth, 1981). Depending on the nature of the research, the fieldwork setting can be an ethnically distinct group's neighborhood, *barrio,* or incorporated town, or it can be any clinical setting, including hospital, nursing home, county health clinic, neighborhood health center, school, or home.

The value of conducting nursing field research in a naturalistic setting provides the researchers with understanding about cultural and social phenomena during their natural enactment. Constantly fluctuating situations cannot be duplicated exactly, and preset research designs could not allow for the many variables that continually influence situations during daily activities (Babbie, 1979; Smyth, 1981).

FIELDWORK CONSIDERATIONS

Fieldwork generally can be conceptualized as the four stages of preparation, initial contact or entrée, accomplishment, and completion. Most fieldwork discussion tends to focus on the third stage (accomplishment), whereas only a few discussions over preparation, and fewer yet address the problem of initial contact or completion. As Wax (1975) notes, this is unfortunate since it is during initial contact that the ultimate character, scope, emphasis, and success of the research is likely to be determined. Before discussing essential features of entrée strategies in nursing field research, a few caveats are appropriate.

First, fieldwork implies intrusion, which requires minimizing the effects of invasion (Cohen, 1970; Junker, 1968; Middleton, 1970). In the general use of fieldwork methods and techniques, the researcher attempts to prevent any changes in people's behavior and cognitions that might occur as a result of the fieldworker's presence. The degree and type of change resulting from a fieldworker's presence will vary depending on such factors as size of community, degree of acculturation, community perceptions and attitudes, role identification, and the personality and actions of the researcher.

A nurse researcher entering a small Eskimo community to study clinic utilization patterns is likely to be seen by most residents many times each day. Another nurse researcher doing fieldwork among Indians on a remote part of a Navajo reservation may find widely dispersed extended family units, which require extensive traveling and infrequent contacts. In a third nursing study the nurse researcher may be studying interpersonal relationships in a Jewish nursing home. Each of these nurse researchers will have the task of understanding the effect of his or her presence on the community and the responsibility of minimizing the intrusion (Junker, 1968).

There are no set, hard-and-fast rules for entrée into the field, but rather general guidelines that have been used by anthropologists and transcultural nurses for some decades. The usual activities of daily living, in which field observations of human behavior are made, encompass so much variation, both within and among groups, that no manual or set of detailed rules could serve (Junker, 1968; Middleton, 1970; Wax, 1975). Add to this variation the different interests, educational preparation, and temperaments of each fieldworker (Middleton, 1970) and another set of constraints has to be considered. Given such variability factors in field research, Wax (1975) suggests that the neophyte would do well to read reports of various fieldwork situations to "get a handle" on the ways in which other fieldworkers have proceeded; in other words, develop a sort of repertoire of options from which to draw.

The very nature of fieldwork decrees that the fieldworker's basic research tool is himself. Fieldwork observation as a science "has not yet separated the instrument of observation from the instrument of analysis" (Newman, 1965, pp. 3–4). Consequently the aims, expectations, hopes, and attitudes that the researcher brings to the field will influence what is seen and how it is observed (Powdermaker, 1967; Turnbull, 1972). Subjective perspectives must be taken into consideration by the researcher and incorporated into the research report.

The issue of a fieldworker's potential for subjective bias has been discussed, analyzed and compared with the positivist-quantitative approach's presumed tight control of the observer's influence. There is a growing realization that all researchers are a part of the research process and as such influence their data (Gould, 1981; Leininger, 1978; McElroy, 1982; Spradley, 1979). Unlike the Heisenberg effect, in which the observer's influence is assumed to be unmeasurable, or the Hawthorne effect, in which the observer's influence is acknowledged as a limitation, fieldworker deliberately utilize the influence of their participation to guide them in the collection and analysis of their data (Aamodt, 1982; Cassell, 1980; Leininger, 1978).

A common error made by neophyte fieldworkers is to develop identity confusion. Entering a community with no set rules as to how to proceed, having skyrocketing anxiety levels over being accepted and being able to complete a study, and not knowing the group's behavioral norms and expectations often produces an intense desire for acceptance. Under these conditions a fieldworker may try to win acceptance by "going native" or becoming a member of the cultural group being studied (Polsky, 1967; Whyte, 1955). This is neither necessary nor desirable since such behavior runs the risk of being interpreted as rude, presumptuous, insulting, or threatening (Wax, 1975).

Complete acceptance by a community is not a requirement for successful fieldwork. While studying Eskimo culture, Rainey (1947) noted that the people perceived him as an exotic, albeit accepted, addition to the community. Weiss (1977), on the other hand, made the mistake of assuming that, because he had been extended the hand of friendship by the Chinese people he lived among, he was "accepted" in the full sense of the word. When he was severely chastised by his Chinese friends for presuming to speak out on questions of racism, prejudice, and identify, he realized that he had forgotten who he was: "a white anthropologist who mistakenly assumed he was no different from his Chinese friends, who thought he could comment on issues as if he was speaking to others of his kind" (p. 126). "Let no fieldworker ever fool himself that he has become a complete member of his community," warned Middleton (1970, p. 228).

The need to remain somewhat an outsider has other advantages besides objectivity, however. Respondents often will talk more readily with an outsider (Beattie, 1964), and the fieldworker can effectively adopt the role of naive learner or interested and informed student (VanStone, 1970).

PREPARATION

There is no clearcut differentiation between what could be labeled preparatory fieldwork activity versus actual entrée activity. However, at least three issues are likely to need consideration before actual entrée occurs: selection of an appropriate community or site, review of the relevant literature, and timing of when the fieldworker enters the community or site.

Community Selection

One of the first decisions in preparing for fieldwork is selecting a community that is suitable for the research and in which it is feasible to do the study (Smyth, 1981). Suitability issues include availability of a representative sample with all the necessary characteristics, such as income, ethnicity, age, and health knowledge or condition. Feasibility issues include time, money, availability and accessibility of the community, transportation, training, and professional skills. Obtaining permission from the committee on human subjects research is also important.

At the time of this writing; the author was involved in a diabetic research project on an American Indian reservation. One of several foci to the research was the development of a diabetic profile. In order to conduct this study, access was needed to a representative sample of adult male and female Indians, living primarily on a reservation, and having a longitudinal health history record. My "community" was found in the inpatient and outpatient records of a hospital located on the reservation, and its suitability was confirmed.

Since the reservation was approximately a six-hour drive through mountainous terrain on secondary roads, and I had a fulltime teaching position, I needed to determine whether I had the necessary time, money, and transportation means to undertake this project. An additional concern was whether I had the professional skill, in particular, the advanced methodological expertise, needed to successfully complete all phases of the project. After weighing each feasibility concern, I did undertake the fieldwork, recognizing that it would need to be conducted over an extended period of time and that statistical consultation was available.

Literature Review

Another preparatory step in fieldwork is a search of relevant literature. This is standard operating procedure for all research but is sometimes questioned in fieldwork because of the potential for selective perception (Babbie, 1979; Langness, 1970). Prior readings may lead to biased observations—however unconscious—of only those things that confirm preconceived notions. On the other hand, most fieldworkers have found that one of the most successful ways of gaining entrée into a field situation is to become as well informed as possible about the community, area, or site (Babbie, 1979; Newman, 1965; Van Stone, 1970; Leininger, 1977).

Acquaintance with the literature permits the researcher to anticipate what might be found in the field situation in a general way; how to begin solving the research problem; expected behaviors and attitudes; and practical needs for self-maintenance. Background preparation about the culture often eases entrée into the community. Accurate knowledge of the culture may impress community members, influencing individuals to take the researcher and the work seriously. VanStone (1970) reported that the elderly Eskimo in his study were intrigued by his knowledge of the past, while other family members appreciated his informed dialogue on topics they were interested in and knowledgeable about.

Timing

An area for consideration in fieldwork that is frequently ignored is the timing of a project. Most research can be conducted at any time of the year, but the implementation of some projects depends on a student's or professional academic's summer break. Some culturally distinct groups' or subgroups' activities are seasonally influenced. For example, a nursing study on migrant health behaviors will need to consider the migratory movement and pathways of these seasonal planters and harvesters.

While a nursing study on Black folk health traditions among the urban clientele of a county health department clinic may not reflect any serious seasonal fluctuation, a similar study among Native Americans on an Indian reservation may be jeopardized by the large number of ceremonies which draw participants from considerable distances at different times of the year, for periods of one to twelve days. The nurse researcher has a responsibility to conduct fieldwork observations or interviews without interfering unduly with essential subsistence activities (VanStone, 1970).

ENTRÉE STRATEGIES

Since there is no rigid or prescribed way to guide the researcher's entrée into the field, the researcher is advised to minimize any potentially intrusive aspects of fieldwork. Admonished about the perils of "going native"; and cautioned about the potential for subjectivity, the fledging nurse field researcher is now ready to make that initial contact.

Initial Contact

The first contact with the community is likely to be a formal letter of entrée addressed to the appropriate leaders or authorities. Smyth (1981, pp. 168–169) has identified six essential components of the letter of entrée:

1. The purpose of the proposed study.
2. How it will be conducted.
3. When it will be completed.
4. The part the community will play in the study.
5. A request for an interview.
6. The name of the sponsoring institute or agency.

I would add the following items to this list: information on who will be responsible for conducting the study or doing the actual field work; the researcher's pertinent credentials; and what is to be done with the results of the study. Many culturally distinct groups are asking researchers to identify the nature of potential benefits for the community.

Direct contact with authorities or community leaders is highly recommended by fieldresearchers (Adair & Deuschle, 1970; Brownlee, 1978; Crane & Angrosino, 1974; Paul, 1953; Trimble, 1977; VanStone, 1970). A few researchers have advised against any formal identification with regional or local authorities in field situations, on the grounds that to be associated with them could jeopardize the fieldworker's standing in the community. Despite the fact that members of culturally distinct groups may not have respect for some regional or local authorities, such persons may be instrumental to ensure successful completion of the fieldwork (VanStone, 1970). Certain kinds of fieldwork may not require a formal request for permission to conduct research (i.e., traditional folk healers) but will depend on the successful development of rapport with key leaders in the community (Johnson, 1978).

Community Attitudes

The nurse researcher should be aware of some of the common attitudes that different cultural groups may have. The nature and history of a community's contacts with outsiders may have lead to suspicion, hostility, extreme shyness, or apathy (Crane & Angrosino, 1974; VanStone, 1970). Some communities that have had less contact with the dominant Euro-American culture may be relatively unsophisticated, which may make it difficult for the nurse researcher to adequately explain his or her presence.

Researchers and quasi-official personnel who preceded the fieldworker may have left a residue of distrust and misunderstanding. Some communities may feel they have been "overstudied," do not perceive that they have benefited from previous research, or cannot see the benefits of research projects whose results have no direct application to the people.

On the other hand, if the nurse researcher can explain his or her purpose in ways that make sense to the community members; if community members can perceive potential benefits of the study; if community members are encouraged to participate in the planning and implementation of the study when appropriate; if previous researchers have left a good impression; or if the community has managed to develop or maintain a sense of pride in its cultural heritage, then the community's attitudes may be quite supportive, and members may be actively interested in the proposed fieldwork.

Living and Working Arrangements

An early practical matter for fieldworkers who will be living in the community to study people directly is making living and working arrangements. The decision whether to live with the people or outside the community is based on such factors as the nature and duration of the fieldwork, availability of housing, local politics, customs, and traditions, or serendipitous factors (Crane & Angrosino, 1974; Mead, 1972; VanStone, 1970; Wax, 1975).

Ideally, the fieldworker's living and working arrangements should reflect the type of research being conducted. If the research is concerned with adolescent nutrition and exercise, for example, then arrangements which permit daily observations of normal adolescent activities would be desirable. A study on an American Indian tribe's diabetic clinic utilization patterns could be done while living off the reservation or in the government housing compound away from intimate daily contact with community members. Studies of short duration may permit temporary living arrangements in the heart of the community, as when fieldworkers pitch tents during summer months or park a camper alongside a Navajo hogan. Studies of longer duration may require a more permanent residence arrangement.

The decision to live with a family in the community or to rent a house often depends on short or long-term field studies as planned as well as on other factors. Among some cultural groups, the houses are small, families may be large, and some usual amenities, such as hot and cold running water, are nonexistent. Living with a family often entails taking part in family responsibilities, some of which can be quite pleasant and rewarding, in addition to being an excellent opportunity for specific data collection. On the other hand, meeting family responsibilities may take away from the researcher's data-collecting activities; may make demands on his or her ability to adjust personally; may make it difficult to find the privacy needed to write up notes; and may restrict contact with other community members. Some nurse researchers may live at home and travel to and from the group or individuals under study.

Field workers may prefer to rent a house or build a hut in order to have the personal privacy needed at some time during an extended stay among people who do not have the same attitudes, beliefs, values, and customs. The residence is preferably centrally located within the community to permit observation of daily comings and goings and to allow formal and casual visitors to have private talks or interviews. One field researcher (Wax, 1975), after several misadventures in house hunting, moved into an abandoned schoolhouse; another (Mead, 1972) found an ideal central location on the back veranda of the community's medical dispensary.

In some field situations, local authorities may have a major influence on where the fieldworker resides. A field researcher in Africa was viewed as having a social position above that of the people he was studying and was not permitted to live in the village, whereas another tribal group with whom he worked insisted he live among them as an equal (Crane & Angrosino, 1974; Wax, 1975). Custom and tradition decreed that a White fieldworker (Powdermaker, 1967) could not live in a Black informant's home or Black section of town, while another White fieldworker (Wax, 1975) was unable to live among her Japanese-American informants in their evacuee quarters.

Attitudes and traditional rules of conduct may work against lone fieldworkers, especially women, who attempt to find housing. Unattached individuals who live alone are a rare occurrence in most ethnic communities where transcultural nursing studies are likely to be conducted. A female fieldworker living alone may be perceived as "loose" or aberrant (Crane & Angrosino, 1974), thereby placing herself or her work, or both, in jeopardy.

Establishing an Identity or Role

Pragmatically, the fieldworker is constrained by the role or social position which the local people assign (Crane and Angrosino, 1974; VanStone, 1970; Wax, 1975). Many communities are familiar with certain categories of outsiders: missionaries, schoolteachers, traders, health care personnel, government workers, and law enforcement agents. There may be a tendency for the community to place fieldworkers in one of these categories and to interact with them on the basis of this categorization. More sophisticated communities will have an expanded view of potential categories and may be clear in their identification of the fieldworker's role as researcher.

Other types of roles of a more informal nature also are likely to be imposed on nurse fieldworkers during their initial contacts. Wax (1975) comments on some roles which Native Americans have used, including White thrill-seeker or Indian-lover who pays large sums of money for the opportunity to participate in "genuine full-blooded life"; eccentric, but reasonably decent employer; rich tourist willing to buy local crafts; cultural broker (i.e., go-between or interpreter of the dominant society's rules and regulations); and respectful learner of traditions.

Researchers' roles, over which the nurse fieldworker has more of a choice, include the various options available in the participant-observation set of social roles. The four roles which encompass participant-observation are complete participant, participant-as-observer, observer-as-participant, and complete observer (Gold, 1969; Junker, 1968). See Chapters 3 and 18 (Leininger and Wenger) in this book for a slightly different approach.

As a complete participant in a group's activities, the nurse fieldworker subordinates objectivity for an in-depth understanding of why the group believes and behaves as it does. A nurse researcher interested in the influence of religion on health care practices among Native Americans could fully participate in a Native American Church peyote meeting, beginning with a donation of food or money; assisting with the premeeting preparation of food, chopping of wood, and raising the teepee; attending the entire all-night ceremony; joining the church members for an early morning breakfast; and assisting with the clean-up activities. As a complete participant, the nurse researcher will need to be aware of how her involvement may affect the sociocultural phenomenon in which she participates.

As a complete observer of a group's activities, the nurse fieldworker reconsiders the insights of subjective understanding to scientifically objective knowledge of how the group behaves or what they say they believe. A community health study involving observations of an elderly male Japanese population's activities in a neighborhood park could produce useful information on social interaction patterns, which might be helpful to the nurse interested in social support networks. This role would produce objective data but not the subjective interpretations and understandings which participants would have.

The roles of participant-as-observer and observer-as-participant combine aspects of the two role extremes, emphasizing one or the other as the situation requires. Nurse field researchers using either combined role could conduct a study on the application of transcultural nursing principles in hospital settings. Thus, a nurse clinician, in the role of participant-as-observer, could participate in his or her usual role as staff or head nurse while collecting data on how colleagues apply transcultural nursing principles in the development and implementation of nursing care plans. Subjects in the study would be aware that such data were being collected during the researcher's normal job duties.

A nurse researcher in the role of observer-as-participant could collect similar data primarily as an observer and restrict participation in the hospital setting to such things as helping visitors, transporting patients, running errands, or, as Byerly (1969) did, performing a few nursing jobs on an ad hoc basis. In the role of participant-as-observer, data collection is subordinated to nursing activities as participant, whereas in the observer-as-participant role, a researcher's activities are subordinated to data collection efforts. Variations in the anthropological participant-observation method are being developed, modified, or transformed by Leininger to fit ethnonursing research method. Also see Chapter 3 (Leininger, 1977) of this book.

Identifying Respondents

There are no set rules for identifying appropriate respondents in nursing field research studies, since so many factors influence this process, including the focus of the research; its design; sampling procedures; initial contacts; where or with whom one lives; and just plain serendipity or luck. As usual, a few caveats are in order.

Some respondents who are "marginal" to their own culture may be particularly eager to volunteer their knowledge, especially during the researcher's early entrée, before familiarity with the community is acquired. These marginal people may be attractive to the fieldworker because they are likely to have spent some time away from their own cultural group and may know the researcher's language and some of his or cultural ways, thereby bridging the gap of "alienness." Because of these experiences outside their own culture, marginal people sometimes are not fully accepted within their community and may be eager to initiate interaction with the newcomer. Their marginality does not automatically preclude their usefulness as informants, for they may understand their culture as well as, or better than, fully accepted members. If they are critical of their community, the nurse researcher may acquire a category of data not otherwise obtainable.

While collecting data on a housing improvement project, I acquired valuable insights from an Indian reservation's group of marginal people (Evaneshko, 1974; 1976). These Native American men and women, who were not on that reservation's tribal rolls, had married tribal members but were treated as outsiders and not permitted to buy or inherit houses on the reservation. The families' opinions with regard to accepting the housing improvement plan were of critical importance to my understanding of the issues associated with the project's ultimate defeat.

Many culturally distinct groups have administrators or others in authority who are quite knowledgeable about the people for whom they are responsible. It would be a grave error to ignore these leaders, even if community residents voice disapproval of them. On one Indian reservation, I was advised by residents during early entrée activities that I would not need to present my research project to the tribal leaders, for "they were just old men whom many of the people didn't listen to anyway" (Evaneshko, 1974, pp. 30–31). While it is true that I probably could have conducted my study without their approval, I considered this unethical; in addition, the leaders turned out to be knowledgeable informants as well as helpful expediters of my fieldwork requests.

Most culturally distinct groups today, among whom nursing field research is possible, are likely to have a mix of acculturated and nonacculturated or traditionally oriented members. The inexperienced fieldworker might seek out the more acculturated members as being "more cooperative" or easier informants with whom to work, thereby missing out on the opportunity to learn the wealth of traditional lore which the nonacculturated still retain. An obverse error would be to ignore the acculturated informants as not having meaningful data to contribute to the study.

Similar issues concerning who has the kind of cultural knowledge that would make for a good informant include the demographic characteristics of age and sex. Whereas younger people may be more amenable to the researcher's request for information, they are not as likely to have certain kinds of knowledge. Older people are likely to have more responsibilities; may not speak the researcher's language; and may not understand or support the need for research. With regard to sexual differences, men are not as likely to know as much as women on such subjects as childbearing, whereas women will be less likely to have detailed knowledge of male-dominated sacred ceremonies.

The nurse researcher may feel very fortunate if the field situation seems to include informants who are eager to help. Caution is needed in this situation to determine to what extent the informants are telling what they think the researcher wants to hear. Similarly, there are always some informants who may have a biased perspective because of emotional, political and other reasons. Other informants may deceive, sometimes deliberately, sometimes inadvertently, because they are too embarassed to admit ignorance.

Finally, a major informant problem for the field researcher in many communities is the issue of factionalism. The fieldworker's initial contact with certain informants may serve to alienate the researcher from subsequent contacts with groups of people or individuals who are "at odds" with the informants contacted earlier. Once the researcher is identified with a faction, it may be difficult for others to perceive him or her as either neutral or interested in the views of the opposing factions. In one field research study, I was quickly categorized by most community members as sympathetic to and interested only in the more acculturated nontraditional community members by virtue of my living arrangements (Evaneshko, 1974). Since the only housing available was with a Baptist Christian family who did not participate in traditional ceremonies, the less acculturated community members thought I was not interested in their views, knowledge, and opinions. Although it took time, I was able to convince both factions that I was neutral in my opinions—or perhaps more accurately, nonjudgmental—and my data collection was enhanced by free access to both groups.

Fortunately, the very nature of fieldwork allows the field researcher to overcome the potential pitfalls in identifying appropriate informants. Living in or becoming involved in the community encourages a depth of knowledge of members which permits the fieldworker to become aware of potential biases and to validate data by cross-checking with other informants.

Trust, Rapport, Reciprocity

Underlying the concern over identifying appropriate informants are the issues of validity and reliability. As Becker succinctly puts it, "To what degree is the informant's statement the same one he might give, either spontaneously or in answer to a question, in the absence of the [researcher]?" (1958, p. 652). Trust and rapport are assumed to be essential ingredients for fieldwork validity and reliability. Rapport concerns the development of a harmonious affinity or accord between informant and fieldworker, whereas trust involves the development of confidence by the fieldworker in the informant's integrity and veracity; that is, the truthfulness and accuracy of responses.

Factors influencing the development of trust and rapport are too numerous to mention, but various fieldworkers have provided some examples. Adherence to, or at the very least, respect for, local rules of conduct and etiquette is likely to be viewed as a gesture of friendliness, caring, consideration, esteem, or worthiness (Crane & Angrosino, 1974). Showing interest in the children and working side by side with the adults in economic pursuits were among several devices Uchendu (1970) used to develop rapport with his Navajo informants. Tsukashima (1977) discovered in his fieldwork among urban Blacks that it was essential to identify and use the informants' self-definition of their race if rapport was not to be damaged.

Experienced fieldworkers who possess more knowledge and information than many of the community members need to be very careful not to offend the local people by contradicting their statements or playing the "expert" and demonstrating superior wisdom on a topic (VanStone, 1970). Being willing to live in the community, even though it was with a family who was considered marginal to many of the group's commitments and interests, helped me establish rapport on one American Indian reservation (Evaneshko, 1974).

Some nurse field researchers may need to overcome the mistrust that develops from poor past experiences with others of the researcher's cultural group (Brownlee, 1978), or from the evolvement of a superior-subordinate relationship between the group and the dominant society (VanStone, 1970). On the other hand, the fieldworker may be able to benefit from the rapport that a previous researcher in the community developed (VanStone, 1970). Including community members in the planning, implementation, and analysis of a research project is becoming more essential in transcultural settings (Bengtson, Grigsby, Corry & Hruby, 1977; Evaneshko, 1976, Montero, 1977; Trimble, 1977). The nature of the questions and how they are asked may interfere with the development of trust or rapport (Brownlee, 1978; Crane & Angrosino, 1974). Direct questioning; eye-to-eye contact; timing; who is permitted to ask what; sensitive topics; and clarity of questions all need to be considered.

The technique of reciprocal exchange can be quite valuable in developing rapport and trust (Wax, 1952), as well as being an essential ingredient in the moral and ethical obligations which many culturally distinct groups now believe should be incorporated into any fieldwork which is done among them (Bengtson, Grigsby, Corry & Hruby, 1977; Gladwin, 1972; Kahana & Fenton, 1977). The reciprocity element in fieldwork occurs at both a macrolevel and a microlevel.

At the macrolevel some field researchers believe that, in exchange for conducting research, they have a responsibility to concentrate on issues and problems reflecting the community's interests and needs, or to conduct studies which have a potential for practical rather than theoretical application in resolving a community's problems.

At the microlevel, reciprocal exchanges are more individualized and concern the fieldworker's relationship with individual community members. Some fieldworkers become informants to the people they are studying (Evaneshko, 1974; Nader, 1970; Uchendu, 1970) by providing information on the researcher's culture or on another group in whom the local people are interested. Wax (1975) has utilized a wide range of reciprocal techniques in her many fieldwork studies, including being a friend (p. 87), a willing learner (p. 77), providing temporary accommodations, food (p. 255), and transportation (p. 228), being an arts and crafts buyer (p. 230), and paying for services rendered (p. 232); in short, performing the usual acts that identify a good neighbor in most cultures by being reasonably friendly, unpretentious, and courteous (p. 272).

In my own fieldwork experiences, I have helped prepare for community affairs; provided transportation to social events and for medical attention; acted as an "expert" on the White man's culture; and assisted individuals in handling the red tape (my Indian friends call it white tape) involved in the dominant society's institutions. I like to believe that the most important exchange I have offered is to provide a role model of the White person who respects the rights of other cultural groups. A fifth grader's essay concerning me, written during my first fieldwork experience on an Indian reservation in the Northeast, indicates I may have had some success:

My opion [sic] about whites isn't uncommon. I say some whites are good like a white lady I know. I don't classafie [sic] her as white but as a full blooded seneca Indian on our reservation. She helps her brothers and sisters on the reservation. (Evaneshko, 1974, p. 41)

In summary, both informants and researchers influence fieldwork interaction (Cassell, 1980). The researchers have a responsibility for minimizing—or at least being knowledgeable about—the potential effects of their entrée and continued presence. Since fieldworkers are their own measuring instrument, their preparation, interests, expectations, and attitudes will influence how they approach their entrée into the field situation. Entrée behavior, then, will vary among fieldworkers as well as for the individual researcher who implements nursing field research projects in different settings.

The many preparatory activities for entrée into nursing field research include community selection, a review of literature, and timing of entrée. Actual entree activities start with the initial contact, usually in the form of a letter to the appropriate personnel, detailing the field researcher's proposed project. At this stage the field researcher should be sensitive to potential community attitudes regarding the value of the research project and the fieldworker's presence. Arrangements for living and working quarters during the early entrée stage may affect the study's ultimate success. Whether to live in the community, with whom, and where could prove to be critical, as is the selection of informants and the use of community leaders during the entrée stage.

The development of different roles which the fieldworker may wish to cultivate and the assignment of roles by the community are likely to begin during the entrée stage. While trust and rapport take time to develop, the fieldworker's initial entrée activities are likely to have a great effect on their subsequent development. Sensitivity to customs and traditions, respect for differing values and attitudes, and adherence to local rules of conduct and etiquette will also be critical.

Since fieldwork research features human interaction between observers and observed in all its richness, variety, and contradiction (Cassell, 1980) researchers must take into consideration this existential situation in their fieldwork entrée strategies. A statement by Langness (1970) on fieldwork can be quoted to summarize many of the issues on entrée into nursing field research that have been covered in this chapter:

Boldness in [entering] field work is sometimes necessary, but not at the expense of rapport; good manners are essential, but not at the risk of being wishy-washy; prior training and knowledge are admittedly advantageous, but not if they result in bias. (p. 224)

REFERENCES

Aamodt, A. M. Examining ethnography for nurse researchers. *Western Journal of Nursing Research*, 1982, *4* (2), 209–221.

Adair, J., & Deuschle, K. *The people's health: Medicine and anthropology in a Navajo community.* New York: Appleton-Century-Crofts, 1970.

Babbie, E. R. *The practice of social research* (2nd ed.). Belmont, Calif.; A: Wadsworth Publishing Company, Inc., 1979.

Beattie, J. *Other cultures: Aims, methods and achievements in social anthropology.* New York: Free Press of Glencoe, 1964.

Becker, H. S. Problems of inference and proof in participant observation. *American Sociological Review*, 1958, *23*, 652–660.

Bengtson, V. L., Grigsby, E., Corry, E. M., & Hruby, M. Relating academic research to community concerns: A case study in collaborative research. *Journal of Social Issues,* 1977, *33* (4), 75–92.

Brownlee, A. T. *Community, culture, and care: A cross-cultural guide for health workers.* St. Louis: C. V. Mosby Company, 1978.

Byerly, E. L. The nurse researcher as participant-observer in a nursing setting. *Nursing Research,* 1969, *18* (3), 230–236.

Cassell, J. Ethical principles for conducting field work. *American Anthropologist,* 1980, *82* (1), 28–41.

Cohen, R. Introduction. In R. Naroll & R. Cohen (Eds.), *A handbook of method in cultural anthropology.* New York: Columbia University Press, 1970, p. 220.

Crane, J. G., & Angrosino, M. V. *Field projects in anthropology: A student handbook.* Morristown, N. J.: General Learning Press, 1974.

Evaneshko, V. Tonawanda Seneca ethnic identity: functional and processual analyses. Tucson: Department of Anthropology, University of Arizona, 1974. Ph.D. dissertation.

Evaneshko, V. Tonawanda Seneca cultural persistence and economic adjustments. Paper presented at American Anthropological Association meeting, Washington, D.C., 1976.

Fox, D. J. *Fundamentals of research in nursing* (3rd ed.). New York: Appleton-Century-Crofts, 1976.

Gladwin, T. Comments. *Human Organization,* 1972, *31* (4), 452–454.

Gold, R. L. Roles in sociological field observation. In G. J. McCall & J. L. Simmons (Eds.), *Issues in participant observation.* Reading, A: Mass.: Addison-Wesley, 1969, pp. 30–39.

Gould, S. P. *The mismeasurement of man.* New York: W. W. Norton & Company, 1981.

Johnson, J. M. *Doing field research.* New York: The Free Press, 1978.

Junker, B. H. *Field work: An introduction to the social sciences.* Chicago: University of Chicago Press, 1968.

Kahana, E., & Fenton, B. J. Social context and personal need: A study of Polish and Jewish aged. *Journal of Social Issues,* 1977, *33* (4), 56–74.

Langness, L. L. Entree into the field: Highlands New Guinea. In R. Naroll & R. Cohen (Eds.), *A handbook of method in cultural anthropology.* New York: Columbia University Press, 1970, 220–225.

Leininger, M. Ethnonursing Research: New Method and Process for Nurses. Lecturer material for graduate seminars, University of Utah, Salt Lake City, 1977.

Leininger, M. *Transcultural nursing: Concepts, theories, and practices.* New York: John Wiley & Sons, 1978.

Leininger, M. The phenomenon of caring: Importance, research questions and theoretical considerations. In M. Leininger (Ed.), *Caring: An essential human need.* Thorofare, N.J.: Charles B. Slack, 1981, pp. 3–15.

Maykovich, M. K. The difficulties of a minority researcher in minority communities. *Journal of Social Issues,* 1977, *33* (4), 108–119.

McElroy, A. (Ed.) Culture and ethos. *Anthropology and Humanism Quarterly,* Washington, DC: June–Sept., 1982, 4–5.

Mead, M. *Blackberry winter: My earlier years.* New York: Simon and Schuster, 1972.

Middleton, J. Entree into the field: Africa. In R. Naroll & R. Cohen (Eds.), *A handbook of method in cultural anthropology.* New York: Columbia University Press, 1970, pp. 225–230.

Montero, D. Research among racial and cultural minorities: An overview. *Journal of Social Issues,* 1977, *33* (4), 1–10.

Nader, L. From anguish to exultation. In P. Golde (Ed.), *Women in the field: Anthropological experiences.* Chicago: Aldine Publishing Company, 1970, pp. 97–116.

Newman, P. L. *Knowing the Gururumba.* New York: Holt, Rinehart & Winston, 1965.

Paul, B. D. Interview techniques and field relationships. In A. L. Kroeber (Ed.), *Anthropology today.* Chicago: University of Chicago Press, 1953.

Polsky, N. *Hustlers, beats, and others.* Chicago: Aldine Publishing Company, 1967.

Powdermaker, H. *Stranger and friend: The way of an anthropologist.* New York: W. W. Norton and Co., 1967.

Rainey, F. G. The whale hunters of Tigara. *Anthropological Papers of the American Museum of Natural History,* 1947, 41 (pt. 2).

Smyth, K. Field research: Entry into the community and inherent problems. In S. D. Krampitz & N. Pavlovich (Eds.), *Readings for nursing research*. St. Louis: C. V. Mosby Company, 1981, pp. 167–173.

Spradley, J. P. *The ethnographic interview*. New York: Holt, Rinehart & Winston, 1979.

Trimble, J. E. The sojourner in the American Indian community: Methodological issues and concerns. *Journal of Social Issues*, 1977, *33* (4), 159–174.

Tsukashima, R. T. Merging fieldwork and survey research in the study of a minority community. *Journal of Social Issues*, 1977, *33* (4), 133–143.

Turnbull, C. M. *The mountain people*. New York: Simon and Schuster, 1972.

Uchendu, V. C. Entree into the field: A Navajo community. In R. Naroll & R. Cohen (Eds.), *A handbook of method in cultural anthropology*. New York: Columbia University Press, 1970, pp. 230–237.

VanStone, J. W. Entree into the field: Arctic and subartic North America. In R. Naroll & R. Cohen (eds.), *A handbook of method in cultural anthropology*. New York: Columbia University Press, 1970, pp. 237–245.

Warren, C. A. B. Fieldwork in the gay world: Issues in phenomenological research. *Journal of Social Issues*, 1977, *33* (4), 93–107.

Wax, R. H. Reciprocity as a field technique. *Human Organization*, 1952, *11* (3), 34–37.

Wax, R. H. *Doing fieldwork: Warnings and advice*. Chicago: University of Chicago Press, 1975.

Weiss, M. S. The research experience in a Chinese-American community, *Journal of Social Issues*, 1977, *33* (4), 120–132.

Whyte, W. F. *Street corner society*. Chicago: University of Chicago Press, 1955.

10

Using Grounded Theory Method in Nursing Research

Phyllis Noerager Stern

Nurse scientists who use grounded theory find it ideal for tracking nursing problems, for finding solution to those problems, and for applying the findings to nursing settings. Because the scientist generates constructs (or theory) from the data rather than applying a theory constructed by someone else from another data source, the generated theory remains connected to or *grounded* in the data. Hence the name, "grounded theory," coined by Glaser and Strauss.

By the time Glaser and Strauss published "The Discovery of Grounded Theory" in 1967, they had already worked with nurse–doctoral students in the second D.N.Sc. degree program in the United States at the University of California, San Francisco. Their research method has generated a number of recurrent problems for the researcher. Glaser and Strauss, both sociologists, wrote their book using the jargon of their profession—a language all but incomprehensible to the unitiated. On the one hand, this language problem has given rise to a number of interpretations of the method which bear only faint resemblance to the original work. On the other hand, some nurse scientists more accustomed to a linear, step-by-step approach, declare that this foreign method, (grounded theory), written in a foreign tongue (*sociologize*), is consequently unscientific and unsound.

Beginning in 1980, the author attempted to translate grounded theory into standard English, in order to make the method more understandable to the serious nurse scholar who wishes to identify, track, and provide applicable solutions to nursing problems (Stern, 1980; Stern, Allen, & Moxley, 1982; Stern & Pyles, 1985). In this chapter the author will briefly discuss methodological issues of grounded theory regarding validity, reliability, and predictability, and describe the research process and variations in the method.

DEFINITION OF GROUNDED THEORY

Grounded theory is a research method used to search out factors (factor searching) or to relate factors (factor relating) that pertain to the research problem at hand. The term "grounded theory" refers to data grounded in fact and generating theory from that data. The grounded theorist looks for the processes involved rather than static conditions. Data are generally gathered using field techniques consisting of interview and observational methods. Additional data come from documents and publications. These data are examined and analyzed through a system of constant comparison until the investigation generates a number of hypotheses. As the investigator develops hypotheses, he or she consults the literature for already developed theories that relate to the emerging hypotheses of the study in progress. However, at no time does the investigator attempt to impose a theory from another study onto the study data. In grounded theory method, theory comes from data. The basic assumption of grounded theory is that not everything has been discovered yet: Hypotheses are linked together so that the investigator is able to present an integrated theory to explain the problem under study. The developed theory, consisting of related factors (or variables), should be suitable for testing.

VALIDITY, RELIABILITY, AND PREDICTABILITY: RECURRING ISSUES AND QUESTIONS

Nurse researchers increasingly acknowledge grounded theory as a credible method of scientific investigation. Still, the nurse who presents her or his findings from such a study must be prepared to answer a few questions which inevitably arise about the validity, reliability, and predictability of the findings.

Validity

Other chapters in this book have explained the inherent validity of a naturalistic approach to research. Like the ethnographer, the grounded theorist makes no attempt to remove herself or himself from the scene. As the theory is derived from the data, it must be valid and it must look at the problem at hand. As Hutchinson (1983, p. 3) states, "Such a theory is inherently relevant to the world from which it emerges, whereas the relevance of verificational research varies widely."

Reliability

Can a grounded theory study be replicated? The answer is no. This method is meant to discover factors. The discovery process resembles the searching for clues (or factors) of a detective, and in this way, each situation studied by an individual researcher is unique. The discovered factors, however, may be tested.

Is such a method reliable? Can the method be used to predict? The answer is yes to both questions. Reliability is established by asking the respondents who participated in the study to evaluate the findings. The researcher asks, "Is this how it is?" "Does this describe the problem?" The actors, or participants, in the study serve as the most reliable judges of their reality of the situation under study. They are the real experts. If you grasp the *truth* in your analysis of the data, your participants reward you with a physical response to your findings: they react with a start or a gasp. You will find your study participants equally easy to read when you have gone astray. They not only tell you you are off the track, but often shake their heads, and frown. The serious researcher, and that includes all of us, continues with the grounded theory investigation until he or she produces that gasp, that start in the audience that signifies the reliable truth.

Thus it can be said that a grounded theory is reliable. The test-retest procedure occurs as study participants are asked about emerging hypotheses. The investigator tests and retests the hypotheses by asking study participants if what was true for other participants is true for them. Testing need not consist of paper and pencil instruments coded for statistical analysis. Rather, in reporting the findings, the investigator describes variations in the hypotheses using standard English prose instead of reporting numerical findings of levels of significance, standard deviations, and the like.

Predictability

How can grounded theory be thought of as a method to predict? Scientists use grounded theory to discover processes that involve individuals. Processes can be thought of as timeless. A few examples can make this point clear. Suicide, for example is a process. Whether the year is 1902 or 2002, the process remains the same. The number of suicides, ethnic types, and choice of instrument may change, but the process of dying involved in suicide is a stable entity. To this end, Durkheim's work *Le Suicide,* first published in 1897, holds relevance for us today. Durkheim used a method other than grounded theory to reach his conclusions, but he described conditions which surround the process of suicide. An accurate description of a process lasts, thus it can predict processes in similar situations.

Of more recent vintage, the author's own work with stepfather families (Stern, 1978, 1982a, 1982b, 1984) endures because I looked at the process involved in integrating a new member, the stepfather, into an ongoing family system of mother and child. The integrative processes discovered in the stepfather study predicted the processes of integration in other stepfather families. Another example is the process through which a nurse gains high-level expertise (which its discoverers named "the nursing gestalt" [Pyles & Stern, 1983]); this remains constant even though the actors and the contexts change. Once one has discovered such a process in a substantive area, the identified process can be transferred to other contexts to predict what will happen there. In this way, a grounded theory can be thought of as one that is predictive.

Definition and Clarification of Terms

The word "factor" as it is used here means "element." That is to say, what are the elements involved in this research problem? The factors (elements) and discrete parts the researcher searches for in this kind of factor-searching study are *processes.*

The individual processes (factors, elements, parts) are compared with one another in order to understand how they are related. Related processes joined together are called *concepts* or hypotheses. The investigator hypothesizes that certain processes are related to one another in a given conceptual way.

In this chapter, the related concepts (made up of processes, i.e., factors, elements, parts) are fully integrated with one another, and are called a grounded theory or *conceptual framework*. The terms theory and conceptual framework are used interchangeably in grounded theory. This is done to help the researcher become familiar with hypothesis-testing techniques and to understand what a grounded theorist discovers; as well as what the theory can be used for. In other words, the factors (processes, elements, parts) of a grounded theory related in a conceptual way are hypothesized by the researcher to form a conceptual framework (or theory), which explains the problem under study and can be tested.

THE PROCESS OF GROUNDED THEORY

Process can be simply described as "The man walked from point A to point B." However, a visitor from a foreign planet who wanted to learn how to walk would gain little help from that description. Walking itself takes pages to explain carefully, and even then, something is lost because walking is a total endeavor which involves the whole person at once. Grounded theory is the same: the processes in the method all occur at the same time. The reader should bear in mind that what follows has been teased out into a series of numbered steps, but in real life, the steps may occur out of sequence and they may be repetitive, may overlap, and may evolve as a series of gestalts, or hypotheses, that are linked together in such a way to explain phenomena.

The Prodrome

The investigator for any study will have thought about the general area for some time before the actual study begins. Usually, scientists talk to their colleagues about a study area until some sort of focus is gained: an idea of what to look at and what is manageable. The wise investigator visits the study site, or talks with a few potential subjects, in order to find out "if there's anything there" (Chater, 1974).

The researcher must first write a plan of how she or he proposes to study the problem. If no funding is involved, one must at least give the committee to protect human subjects some idea of what is being sought and how the investigator expects to find it. If the investigator is a student, her or his research committee will require a proposal complete with literature search, research question, and number of subjects. Those who know the method well and who have experience in using it know that a conceptual framework is discovered from the data and that the appropriate literature to search, the research question, and the number of subjects are determined by the data.

The purist will argue that the proposal has little to do with the completed study, and later in this chapter the author will explain why. For now, it should be remembered that the finished thesis, the funded research, and the approval of the committee on human subjects research all begin with a proposal. How does the researcher write a grounded theory proposal? First, as accurate a guess as possible is made. The proposal becomes the stated null hypothesis for the study. Paradoxically, although the aim is to be as precise as possible, the proposal really describes how the study will probably *not* be done. This paradox can be understood more clearly by examining the literature search, the research questions, and the number of subjects.

Literature search. A prestudy literature search is disadvantageous for three reasons: (1) the search may lead to prejudgment and effect premature closure of ideas and research inquiry; (2) the direction may be wrong; and (3) the available data or materials used may be inaccurate.

The researcher hardly goes into the field to discover something with a tabula rasa posture. Either natural curiosity or the researcher's committee forces the investigator to read something about the subject beforehand. Too much knowledge of behavioral theory, however, may lead the researcher to prejudge the study participants. If for example, the nurse has read that alcoholism is a serious problem among the Inuit Indians of North America and goes to the site and finds drinking in the Northern Territories, he or she may say, "Yes, that's it" and then go home and write about it. This would be called premature closure. In other words, the researcher has not discovered anything else about the people or the problem. What are the conditions, contexts, and consequences of drinking? Who avoids it? What makes those persons different? What do the people of the North see as a bigger problem? What do they do to solve it? These kinds of questions need to be answered.

Second, there is the problem of inaccurate aim. The study may begin with one focus then shift to another. In the stepfather study, for example, the author began looking at factors causing disequilibrium in these families. After three interviews, the author realized that discipline of children was the factor discovered and a literature search began in this area.

The third problem with a primary search is that the literature sources may be partially or wholly inaccurate. For example, the literature on Filipinos describes them as shy and deferring, and the author believed that description for some time, despite the fact she many Filipino immigrants who did not match this description. One of the chief informants finally explained to the author that immigrants become more assertive "as soon as we learn your ways" (Stern, 1981, p. 89). In this instance, while literature on either residents of the Philippines or recent immigrants was important, the author found that temporal conditions—length of residency in the United States—modified the variable of acting shy. A literature search may be made prior to the study, but a second and third search will surely follow as the study proceeds.

Developing the research question. In a grounded theory study, the scientist develops the research question from the data. This means that the purpose of the study is to identify problems, and discover what the actors themselves see as solutions. Problem identification cannot take place prior to the study; therefore, a problem statement is impossible to make, and a truly accurate research question is impossible to ask prior to the study. Scientists will, however, need some focus. The researcher should not state (as I once did), that he or she wants to study "stepfather families," because then one is asked, "What about them do you want to study?" "Everything" is a little too much for any researcher to take on. The prestudy question, then, fences off a field for study. Grounded theory is a method for searching out factors. The study question becomes, "What are the factors involved in X?" The final refined research question comes at the end of the study, when you have discovered the factors with which the problem is involved, and perhaps have related those factors to solutions. The author wrote the research question in the stepfather study after discovering the factors which made discipline a difficult problem in these families and had related those to solutions some families had found. Thus, the post-study research question became, "Given the problem of the discipline of children, how do stepfather families manage to become integrated?"

Number of subjects. The scientist keeps asking questions until she or he is satisfied that a conceptual framework is developed that is integrated, testable, and explains the problem; in other words, the truth. The number of questions and the number of subjects are unknown quantities prior to the study. Therefore, the researcher proposes a number of subjects that seems to be respectable (enough), feasible (not too much), and appropriate for the study (whether a master's, doctoral, or funded study). For example, for a master's thesis, the proposal might involve three individuals followed over a four-month period. In contrast, a doctoral study might involve the interviewing of 20 stepfather families. A funded study might include 100 or 200 people in the sample.

Collection of Empirical Data

Data may be collected from interviews, observations or documents, or from a combination of these sources (Schatzman, 1973). The method works well because it follows the same pattern that people use to figure out what they do not understand, that is, it is the way people think. Gathering data follows this same pattern. If you fail to understand how something is done, you ask, "How do you do that?" Later, if you think you missed part of the explanation, you telephone the subject and say, "I need a little more information." Still later, you may find an article or news clipping that sheds some light on the subject. As Strauss says, "Everything is data" (Strauss, personal communication, 1975).

The beginning researcher may feel more comfortable using some sort of interview guide for the first encounter. Soon, however, you realize that the interviewee is the teacher, and you are the learner. "Teach me" is asked of your subject, and if you attend well, the respondent will act like a professor.

The tape recorder and note taking controversy needs to be clarified here. If the researcher tape records interviews, a word-for-word reproduction is obtained (provided that the words are not muffled and the recorder is working properly). A taped interview must be transcribed and requires resources, In other words, a typist and funds. If the researcher can afford a typist, there may be pages and pages of data. Much of this recording will be filler: meaningless and unimportant parts of the conversation that must be read through to find the real data. The author found it desirable to be a short-note researcher. Instead of taping, it is best to write down key words, a few phrases, and type the interview or observations as soon as possible.

As the researcher types, he or she thinks about the data, codes it, and intersperses the interview data with some hypothetical notions derived from the codes. The researcher should label whether the notes are interview, code, or hypothesis. Observed behavior is also labeled. Schatzman and Strauss (1973) use such labels as "ON" for observational note, and "TN" for theoretical note. The researcher can establish his or her own labels and codes.

A fact sheet on which to collect demographic data seems helpful for most researchers; this may be a running tally in the form of a chart to record such things as age, sex, race, or whatever demographic variable, which saves time later in describing the sample.

Finally, data are like pure gold, which you keep secret. The wise scientist keeps two copies of the data: one in the office, and one at home. In case of fire or flood, your data will not be lost. The credible scientist also maintains the anonymity of the subjects. Informants are protected with code names, numbers, or letters. One may even want to change the name of a small town if the researcher's subjects live there and their privacy might be invaded.

Some researchers interview and observe alone, however. For this reason, the next steps described may be done by the lone researcher. An easier and better study analysis usually develops when a group of colleagues, or a seminar of grounded theorists work together, at least part of the time. Discussing a nursing problem with other nurses gives the data more scope, meaning, and accuracy.

Concept Formation

In the next stage the investigator begins to label, hypothesize, and cluster data. These are the first steps in forming a tentative conceptual framework. Coding, hypothesizing, and categorizing are discussed in the next sections. Subsequent steps (concept development, modification, and integration) follow.

Coding. Coding data means labeling it to note what is going on. These codes are called substantive codes because they label the substance of the data. In coding the researcher uses gerunds, those words ending in "-ing" that indicate action. Side-stepping, tuning in, tuning out, labeling, selling, or teaching might be substantive code words. If a researcher has trouble thinking of a code word, she (he) can read the work of another researcher until appropriate code words come to mind.

Hypothesizing and Categorizing. Another name for the grounded theory method is constant comparative analysis because every datum is compared with every other datum rather than comparing totals of indices. As coded data are compared, patterns or categories begin to take shape. People tend to categorize data in everyday life, for example, and place things in alphabetical or other order. As another example, a person can decide that certain activities are normally nighttime or daytime appropriate, or that a patient's problem is either a true emergency or one that can be placed on hold for a time. Placing data in categories helps the individual to organize them. It is a hypothetical process, as a guess is made about what coded data belong in which categories. If a categorizing scheme is incorrect, the researcher generally recognizes this fact while collecting more data. The researcher may hypothesize that data belong in a certain category and may prove or disprove the hypothesis of categorization by collecting more data. If the investigator's stated hypothesis is wrong, it is rejected. A scientist detective keeps looking until the truth is discovered.

Concept Development

By now the researcher knows the parts (factors, elements, and processes) of the framework being generated from the data and the categories, but nothing seems connected. At this point, the researcher develops a working title that says what the study is about. The working title may relate to the core variable, or central theme, which may be discovered later in the analysis, or it may not. At this stage a title provides the focus needed to continue. Three processes help the researcher retain or reject the hypothetical title: reduction of categories, selective sampling of the literature, and selective sampling of the data. Through these processes the core variable is discovered.

Reducing Categories.   Reducing categories provides a way of connecting concepts. When categories and incoming data are studied, a higher-order category can be found that describes several original categories. For example, when studying a nursing gestalt, the authors found that nurses developed the ability to generate a nursing gestalt from an experienced nurse and one who served as teacher, role model, motivator, and friend (Pyles & Stern, 1983). This process was termed the "gray gorilla syndrome," in which a "gray gorilla" refers to a wise and experienced nurse who teaches neophytes the nursing gestalt. Later the authors found more categories fit the "gray gorilla" concept.

Selective sampling of the literature.   In developing the elements of the conceptual framework, the researcher searches the literature to see what has been written about the concepts under study. Once Pyles generated the concept of "gray gorilla" syndrome (1981), for example, she needed to know more about mentoring relationships and used literature to fit the emerging concept, rejecting that which was extraneous.

Selective sampling of the data.   As the investigator brings the higher-order category together with relevant literature, the conceptual framework begins to take shape. Now the coded and categorized study data seem to make some sort of a conceptualized whole. However, it soon becomes apparent that some of the component parts of the framework are incomplete or absent. The investigator may have solved one part of a puzzling problem, only to find that other parts of the puzzle are missing. More data must be collected, selected on the basis of what one already knows about the study problem; hence the term selective sampling. For example, Graham (1983) found that in northern Nova Scotia elderly people living with a partner have better dietary habits than those living alone. Graham also found that some older persons living alone also practice good nutritional habits. Graham's selective sampling consisted of asking people in this group how they developed their values about nutrition. In Graham's study, the researcher asked the question: What factors influence dietary habits in the elderly? Once the researcher had found that some single elderly persons eat well, she needed to collect more data to determine how these single elderly people developed their values about nutrition.

Emergence of the core variable.   Core refers to center or heart. Variable can be defined as "any factor, characteristic, quality, or attribute under study" (Notter, 1974, p. 147). In other words, the question is, What is the heart of the matter being studied? What guiding principle or process explains what is occurring in the scene?

As explained earlier, the factors or variables being sought in a grounded theory study are processes. The core variable, then, is the central process that seems to dominate the scene. This central process (core variable) will be a composite process that encompasses several supporting processes. It can be seen that the process must be complex in order to describe central themes of social interaction and one that transcends a variety of contexts. As an example, when Harris studied the ways in which parents come to a decision about whether or not to circumcise their child (Harris, 1985), she found that their values were determined by the culture into which they were born, the one in which they lived, and the one in which they aspired their son to live. The process Harris found to be the heart of her study (the core variable) was cultural decision making. She was able to construct a decision-making model (tree) that predicts what decision parents will make about circumcision for their baby—a complex model that encompasses several processes. This model guides the nurse when parents ask, "What do you think we should do?"

Concept Modification and Integration

After identifying a core variable and knowing X, (a given fact) the researcher describes the conceptual framework in a way that is theoretical, integrated, and tight. Every part of the framework must fit together. A completed grounded theory must be testable, and therefore the researcher moves the conceptual framework from a descriptive to a theoretical one by using theoretical codes. Memoranda are made to keep track of the analysis. As the nurse arrives at a theoretical statement, thereby increasing the theory's abstraction, he or she writes memoranda about the statement.

Theoretical coding. Theoretical codes were so named by Glaser and Strauss (1967) because they were intended to help the research move from a descriptive frame of reference to a conceptual one. Hence, the codes help the researcher develop theory out of description.

(Parenthetically, it should be noted that one of the problems researchers have with grounded theory is its terminology.) Glaser and Strauss come from a sociological perspective and use sociological terminology to describe their method. Researchers struggling with the method may have difficulty with labels such as theoretical codes, core variables, and theory integration. Moreover, both Glaser and Strauss and Schatzman and Strauss (1973) tend to use "conceptual" and "theoretical" interchangeably, as well as to mean "abstract," "speculative" or "hypothetical." A similar problem with use of selected terms occurred in Selye's (1974) work, in that after his "stress theory" had caught on, he realized that a more accurate term would have been "strain theory." However, once the theory became popular, it was too late to change the terminology. The same may be said about grounded theory's terminology—although imperfect, and sometimes confusing, one may at times be stuck with it.

Theoretical codes, then, help to define concepts more precisely. In describing the core variable's complex process, the researcher clarifies the nature of the variable, its contexts, and the potential consequences by using theoretical codes. Glaser (1978, p. 74) wrote about what he calls "families of codes," such as The "six C's" (causes, contexts, contingencies, consequences, covariances, and conditions). If the nurse is skilled in visualizing thoughts and concepts, it may help to draw pictures about the data until a diagram is developed that depicts the processes. Simple analytical schemes, such as placing the data on a continuum, placing data within a table, or looking at phases in the action help the researcher blend the data into an integrated theoretical framework. After a suitable picture format is discovered, the researcher describes what the schema depicts.

Memoing. As the researcher gets ideas about the interrelationships of data, it is important to put these ideas on paper or they will be lost. Through constant comparison of data, the researcher notices patterns and themes. Early memos may be a few words, and they will be less than brilliantly written. The purpose of a memo is to capture the idea. Grounded theorists keep pencils and paper ready in the house, office, and car in order to keep track of breakthrough thoughts about the conceptual framework. Until the theorist reaches a final, presentable form, the theory tends to subsume the researcher's thoughts. By the time the research report is written, hundreds of memos need to be sorted and ordered. Sorting memos provides an opportunity to cluster concepts through a categorizing process. The researcher may place a memo in the wrong category but will soon recognize this and move it to another category.

Production of the Research Report

The research report gives a clear and precise picture of the theory, which is substantiated by the data and the existing relevant literature. Most first-time grounded theorists realize the importance of their discovery and how well it explains the scene. They expect what their readers, too, will quickly grasp what it has taken the researcher months to develop. The grounded theorist would do well to remember the example of describing walking to a visitor from a foreign planet, and, therefore, detail the theory with sufficient care that even someone unfamiliar with the research method can understand it.

Just as a proposal provides a poor fit for a grounded theory study, numbers also seem out of place in this type of research report. In the real world of publishable literature, editors and peer reviewers want statistics, a literature review, and a section describing methods to explain how the researcher obtained findings. The choice of reporting seems simple: Write what will get published. The researchers might wish to present a series of aspects of the study and at different levels of abstraction. It may be difficult to present the theory in a condensed form. Similarly, chances are the theory is too dense to present well in a single article limited to 16 pages.

Final Points on the Process

The process described may sound as if it occurs in a series of orderly steps, but it does not. The researcher may have dry spells (limited ideas) and may feel depressed. It seems that the deepest feelings of depression come before a creative breakthrough of ideas, or when the researcher feels most confused and begins to write. A high or optimistic mood often occurs when the ideas come together and take form.

If the researcher gets stuck in the research process, two things seem to help: (1) reading other people's work and seeing how they put things together, and (2) talking to colleagues. If no one seems to know the method in your local area, get in touch someone who is familiar with it. Most well-known researchers love to talk research, and in addition, nurses like to help others. Ergo, it may be hypothesized that a nurse researcher would be a helpful person to call.

Connections with Past and Future Studies

The variables discovered in a grounded theory tend to connect with or be related to other studies and with social realities. It seems that once the core variable is discovered, it can be seen everywhere. For example, when the author studied the experience of Filipino immigrants there was a realization of culture shock that these immigrants felt with health care customs (Stern, 1981). This could be compared with my feelings of culture shock as the author moved from the San Francisco Bay area to Louisiana (Stern & Cousins, 1982). The ideas seemed to connect. With the new information, the author looked back at the stepfather study, and realized that the individuals in stepfamilies feel a kind of culture shock with the strange family behavior of the new members. This is because every family interviewed had what the author called its own "individual family culture" (Stern, 1982b) made up of values and rules, which were usually unspoken, but rigidly adhered to. Stepfamilies, intact families, and couples to whom the author described this concept validated it.

SUMMARY

Grounded theory consists of collecting, examining, comparing, and hypothesizing qualitative data, then checking hypothesis with more data for verification. The aim of this method is to discover a central complex process (core variable) that explains and clarifies the interaction between individuals under study. This complex clarifying process is described, with careful attention to its supporting processes and the conditions under which it occurs. A grounded theory is a careful description of the central clarifying process, supporting processes, and modifying conditions. A grounded theory can be called a conceptual framework, from which testable hypotheses are drawn.

REFERENCES

Chater, S. Research Seminar, School of Nursing, University of California, San Francisco, October, 1974.

Durkhein, E. *Suicide.* New York: Free Press, 1966. (Originally published as *Le Suicide* in 1897.)

Glaser, B. G. *Theoretical sensitivity.* Mill Valley, Calif.: The Sociology Press, 1978.

Glaser, B. G., & Strauss, A. L. *The discovery of grounded theory.* Chicago: Aldine, 1967.

Glaser, B., & Strauss, A. *Status passage.* Chicago: Aldine, 1971.

Graham, H. *Social nutrition: Factors influencing dietary patterns in older citizens of Nova Scotia* (unpublished master's thesis). Halifax, Nova Scotia: Dalhousie University School of Nursing, 1983.

Harris, C. C. The cultural decision-making model: Focus—circumcision. In P. N. Stern, *Women, health and culture.* New York: Hemisphere, 1985.

Hutchinson, S. *Grounded theory* (unpublished manuscript). Jacksonville, Florida: Jacksonville Health Education Programs, Inc., 1983.

Notter, L. E. *Essentials of nursing research.* New York: Springer, 1974.

Pyles, N. S. H. *Assessments related to cardiogenic shock: Discovery of nursing gestalt* (unpublished master's thesis). Shreveport: Northwestern State University of Louisiana College of Nursing, 1981.

Pyles, S. H., & Stern, P. N. Discovery of nursing gestalt in critical care nursing: The importance of the "gray gorilla" syndrome. *Image: The Journal of Nursing Scholarship,* 1983, *15* (2), 51–57.

Schatzman, L., & Strauss, A. L. *Field research: Strategies for a natural sociology.* Englewood Cliffs, N.J.: Prentice-Hall, 1973.

Seyle, H. *Stress without distress.* Philadelphia, Pa.: J. B. Lippincott Co., 1974.

Stern, P. N. Stepfather families: Integration around child discipline. *Issues in Mental Health Nursing,* 1978, *1* (2), 50–56.

Stern, P. N. Grounded theory methodology: Its uses and processes. *Image,* 1980, *12* (1), 20–23.

Stern, P. N. Solving problems of cross-cultural health teaching: The Filipino childbearing family. *Image,* 1981, *13* (2), 47–50.

Stern, P. N. Affiliating in stepfather families: Teachable strategies leading to integration. *Western Journal of Nursing Research,* 1982a, *4* (1), 75–89.

Stern, P. N. Conflicting family culture: An impediment to integration in stepfather families. *Journal of Psychosocial Nursing and Mental Health Services,* 1982b, *20* (10), 27–33.

Stern, P. N. Stepfamilies. An Overview for Therapists. *Issues in Mental Health Nursing,* 1984, 6 (1–2), 89–104.

Stern, P. N., Allen, L. M., & Moxley, P. A. The nurse as grounded theorist: History process and uses. *Review Journal of Philosophy and Social Science,* 1982, 7 (142), 200–215.

Stern, P. N., & Cousins, M. E. B. Culture shock as a positive force: Surviving West Coast to Northern Louisiana relocation. In C. N. Uhl and J. Uhl (Eds.), *Published proceedings of the Seventh Annual Transcultural Nursing Conference,* Salk Lake City, Utah: University of Utah, 1982.

Stern, P. N. & Pyles, S. H. Grounded theory: Its uses in the study of women's culturally-based decisions about health care. In P. N. Stern, *Women, health and culture:* New York: Hemisphere, 1985.

Strauss, A. L. Research Seminar, University of California, San Francisco, School of Nursing, 1975.

11

Ethnographic Nursing Research in a Black Community: Body Function and Sex Education Classes

Molly C. Dougherty
Myrna M. Courage
Lynne S. Schilling

Ethnographic nursing research permits the discovery of attitudes and beliefs underlying cultural patterns. The explication of attitudes and beliefs of identifiable cultural groups is an integral component of culturally relevant nursing care. Culturally appropriate nursing care involves providing information and skills which may be used to promote self-care in a variety of contexts. Ethnographic nursing research applied within a community setting permits observation, ongoing analysis, and further observation and analysis of health beliefs and practices. This research method permits refinement of interpretation within the research setting and is ideally suited to situations in which testable hypotheses are premature or inappropriate.

The information presented here is an example of community-based investigation in which ethnographic nursing research is used to fulfill the purposes of the study. The purposes of this research were to (1) provide culturally relevant information on body function and sexuality to preadolescent and early adolescent girls, and (2) gather information on the knowledge, attitudes, and values of preadolescent and early adolescent girls regarding body function, sexuality, and relationships with peers, family, and community members. The particular aim of the project was to gain systematic and in-depth knowledge of the Afro-American Southern black girls' beliefs, values, and behaviors regarding body functions and sexuality by the use of the ethnographic field method. The sensitive nature of sex education and body function

QUALITATIVE RESEARCH METHODS IN NURSING   Copyright © 1985 by Grune & Stratton, Inc.
ISBN 0-8089-1676-9   All rights of reproduction in any form reserved.

161

content in most settings was a further indication of the need for the ethnographic exploratory method for this study. It was also important to have systematic and regular field observations, and to analyze carefully the field data in order to determine the effect of the investigator's classes with the goals in the community. Field notes were taken carefully, were recorded, and were analyzed periodically as part of the ethnographic research method.

The sample, best described as convenience sample, was selected by resident women and further reduced by voluntary participation of the subjects. Three sets of classes were held; each subject attended only one set of classes, but some subjects were absent from one or two class meetings. Table 11-1 shows the number of girls, their ages, and the length of the class sets. The classes formed the basis of data collection.

REVIEW OF THE LITERATURE

Pertinent themes in the literature indicate that ethnographic nursing research techniques have not been used to study the sexuality-related interests of preadolescent and early adolescent girls in a community setting. It is clear that more and more adolescents are engaging in sexual intercourse and are initiating sex at younger ages. Zelnick and Kantner (1977) present data from two national surveys indicating that the prevalence of sexual intercourse among never-married teenage women between the ages of 15 and 19 is on the rise. Additionally, there has been a decline in the median age at which first intercourse occurs.

The consequences of this for the adolescents are only partially known. Zelnick and Kantner (1977) have shown that few adolescents begin using contraception at the time they initiate sexual intercourse. The factors contributing to the initiation or non-initiation of sexual activity during adolescence have received little research attention. However, some literature is available on the nature of sexual experiences (Arnold, 1974; Schoof-Tams, Schlaegel, & Walczak, 1976), sexual interests (Rubenstein, Watson, Drolette, & Rubenstein, 1976), sexual values (Schoof-Tams et al., 1976), and sexual attitudes (Antonovsky, 1980; Carton & Carton, 1971; McNab, 1981) prior to or during adolescence.

Some attempt has been made to study the effects of sex education programs on adolescents' subsequent sexual knowledge and attitudes (Carton & Carton, 1971) and sexual behavior (Brody, Ottey, & Lagranade, 1976; Spanier, 1976). Considerable attention has focused on sex education in school settings, which has usually fol-

Table 11-1 *Composition of Three Sets of Body Function and Sex Education Classes*

Set	Number of Girls	Ages of Girls	Number of Meetings
1	4–6	9–14	8
2	8–13	11–15	8
3	5–7	7-10	6

lowed a predetermined format and has maintained sensitivity to potential parental opposition. Concern for the high incidence of sexually transmitted diseases and teen parenthood has been evident in the literature (Kroger & Wiesner, 1981; Polley, 1979). It is acknowledged that parents and society have a major responsibility for sex education (Brick, 1981; Hacker, 1981). Several authors however, address the programatic aspects of sex education (Chethik, 1981; Eberst, 1981; McNab, 1981) and teaching methods in formal programs (Chesler, 1980; Vacalis et al., 1979). These contributions provide needed information on the social norms and constraints affecting sex education efforts.

The nursing literature provides more diverse offerings. Leppink's literature review (1979) summarized research findings and presented psychological factors that influence adolescent sexual behavior. Roesel (1980), who stated that what is considered sexually normal and healthy is culture bound, described culturally recognized normative developments relative to sexuality. Workshops to prepare grade school teachers to teach family life education (Seybold & Klisch, 1982) and individual counseling with very young adolescents in a clinical setting (Peach, 1980) were among approaches used by nurses in teaching sex-related content. Sapala and Strokosch (1981) employed a questionnaire in a clinic setting to assess the knowledge and attitudes of adolescent girls. The findings were used to individualize care for clients.

Although neither the assessing of needs for sexual information using qualitative methods nor the providing of sexual information in community settings has received much attention from nurses, approaches to community-based instructional programs have been addressed in a number of publications. Understanding the needs of clients or communities before intervention is initiated is a common concern of nurses and social scientists. In community-based projects and in client-centered relationships, the interests and needs of clients should be identified. It has been recommended by transcultural nurse researchers that program recipients be included in the planning of programs and that close communication be maintained at all times (Leininger, 1978).

To ensure optimal acceptance of sex education programs, it has been suggested that adolescents be included in the planning of these courses and that securing parent participation is both advisable and feasible. Research on sexual activity is recognized as a sensitive area of inquiry (Spanier, 1976), as is the introduction of sex education programs (Reichelt, 1977).

Many anthropologists report the efficacy of developing reciprocal relationships with subjects and the value attached to the services rendered by the anthropologist. Close interpersonal relationships are seen as important in obtaining high quality, accurate, and complete information on the subject of inquiry (Agar, 1980; Dougherty, 1978; Lenocker & Dougherty, 1976; Liebow, 1967; Stack, 1974). The relationships between preadolescent or early adolescent sexual values, knowledge, attitudes, and social relationships are infrequently addressed in the literature. This small study explored these factors in a sample of Black,* low socioeconomic status, preadolescent and early adolescent girls.

---

*The Black cultural identity of the community was an important contextual variable, but the research focus was chiefly related to the age and sex of the students. No effort was made to evaluate the community in reference to its cultural identification. The authors do not recommend generalization of these findings to other Black communities in the United States.

SETTING FOR THE INVESTIGATION

The research was carried out at a federally funded apartment complex in a north-central Florida city with a population of approximately 100,000. The apartment complex housed about 650 persons, of whom approximately 70 percent were under 18 years of age. In 136 of 172 households it was reported that no adult males were in residence. Most of the residents are Blacks who were born in the United States and who moved to the community from rural areas in hope of obtaining better jobs, schools, and housing (Harris & Dougherty, 1976).

Public health nursing students at the local state university provided care to families and conducted a clinic in the complex. It was through the community's concern about pregnancy among adolescents that the request for body function and sex education classes was communicated to the investigators by a public health nursing professor and the apartment manager. The contacts with community members are discussed later.

The apartment complex included a community center that housed a day-care center. Two small rooms at the center were used as nursing clinics on a scheduled basis. The two clinic rooms were available on a specific schedule for the body function and sex education classes.

The classes were shaped (content, approach, conceptualization, and interpretation of events) by the investigators' backgrounds. A commonality was that all investigators were nurses and had expertise in women's health and anthropology, in primary pediatric nursing and child and family development, or in psychiatric and mental health nursing.

INVESTIGATORS' ASSUMPTIONS OF THE STUDY

While no single theoretical framework guided the project, the investigators were sensitive to their own assumptions about communities, human development, and education, which influenced their approach to the research. Several assumptions in each area were made.

Assumptions about the Community

Bonds of friendship and kinship existed in the community. Lines of communication within the community were more direct and clear than from the investigators to community members. Despite bonds among community members, there was cross-cutting competition and rivalry, which potentially could affect the project. Mothers were the primary providers of body function and sex knowledge to preadolescent and early adolescent girls. Parental consent was an important part of gaining community acceptance for the project. The cultural milieu, principally relationships based on kinship and friendship, was the source of values and attitudes regarding body function and sex knowledge. Obtaining information about the cultural milieu was needed to provide culturally relevant learning experiences.

Assumptions About Human Development

The attention span of students in the 9 to 14 year age range is approximately 20 minutes. The girls came to class after a full day in school, necessitating a class format that would hold their attention. An open, accepting environment in class would result in the girls' expressing their feelings and perceptions of themselves and their relationships with others. The girls would not necessarily be alike in their interests and aptitudes for informational content or in their conceptual abilities.

Between the ages of 8 and 12 years girls experience many physiological changes consistent with physical maturation. Physical changes are accompanied by intense psychological and emotional signals, a dual development that causes the girl to change the way she thinks of herself as her body changes. In the classes the girls would be able to verbalize about and express interest in the changes in their bodies and body images. Self-respect, self-esteem, and self-knowledge are valuable and are important in developing healthful behaviors.

Assumptions About Education

Loosely structured classes and open acceptance and respect for the students would facilitate the expression of values and feelings. To achieve openness from students, it would be necessary for investigators to also be open with them. To maintain the interest of the girls, it would be necessary to employ a number of teaching modalities.

It was assumed that attitudes are formed and changed by knowledge and experiences, and that attitude formation depends on available knowledge. Parents, peers, community, and school are probable sources of knowledge and attitudes. This knowledge is not always uniform or always accurate; nor is the transfer of knowledge and attitudes always complete. Trusted investigators could share body function and sex knowledge, which could potentially influence attitude formation concerning health and sexual behaviors.

Many of the younger girls (primarily but not exclusively those under age 11) would need a concrete teaching approach (visualization through pictures, manipulation of objects, direct experience of ideas or situations through films or field experiences) to understand the information. Additionally, the ability to reflect on their thoughts or to hypothesize about future behavior would be expected only of the older girls.

ETHNOGRAPHIC METHOD AND STRATEGIES USED IN THE STUDY

At the beginning of the project, it was agreed that the project had a dual purpose: (1) to provide a service, and (2) to collect data through the ethnographic nursing research method. The approach to the community required open-mindedness and directed observation. Observation and data collection were essential to identify domains and broad categories of cultural behavior. Domains represent aspects of social behavior which are culturally relevant to residents and subjects. Implementation of the research method involved several steps, some of which were repeated after each class and each set of classes. The following research steps and activities were carried out:

1. A consistent format for recording field notes.
2. A format for observations during all contacts with community members and classes.

3. Independent chronological field notes were written by each investigator.
4. Field notes were reviewed weekly, to compare observations and identify culturally relevant domains for concentrated observation and analysis.
5. Tentative interpretations of behaviors were discussed.
6. Intensified observations were made in domains revealed by tentative interpretations.
7. Field notes about culturally relevant domains were further discussed and analyzed.
8. Domains appropriate to the final analysis and project report were selected. The five domains selected for intensive investigation were (1) the informational needs of the girls, (2) group dynamics, (3) teaching materials and methods, (4) the formation of the girls' attitudes, and (5) community relations.
9. Illustrative examples in each domain were selected for inclusion in final report.
10. Outlines and content of papers were discussed and manuscripts were written based on the project.

Qualitative research methods depend on flexibility and creativity. They require returning to research findings when new insights are uncovered. This project also required communication with community residents and clarification of the needs of the community before the research was initiated.

The aim of preliminary contacts in the community was to ensure that the community leaders and parents of potential students supported the classes, had input on topics to be covered, and consented to their daughters' participation.

Our initial contact was with Ms. Leader,† the apartment manager, who said that she saw our role as presenting accurate information but without moralizing, i.e., telling the girls what is right and wrong about sexual matters. Topics that might be included in classes were discussed. The topics Ms. Leader mentioned as being important were (1) protection against pregnancy, (2) protection against disease (sexually transmitted diseases), (3) the appropriate time and place for sexual activity, (4) changes that accompany menstruation, and (5) masturbation as an alternative to sexual activity until a person is old enough to be married.

Ms. Leader had listed the names of 14 girls aged 9 to 16 years. She thought that they would benefit from the classes and introduced the investigator to the girls mothers. When their daughters' participation in the classes was discussed, the mothers expressed the desire for their daughters to take part in the classes and their pleasure that they would be getting information from someone "who knows how to talk about it."

In discussions with the mothers, the following points were made by the investigators: (1) the classes would meet one afternoon each week in the day-care center, (2) the teachers would not be stressing right and wrong, (3) talk with their daughters about the classes would be helpful, (4) the mothers' permission was required for the girls to attend, and (5) the mothers were welcome to discuss the classes with us at any time.

After meeting with the mothers, a list of topics was developed that reflected their preferences for class content. The list of words or concepts understandable to the girls was: (1) what our bodies are like and how we feel about them, (2) what

---

†All names of all individuals have been changed to protect their anonymity.

happens in the body as it grows and develops, (3) how feelings change as growth occurs, (4) menstruation, changes in the body, and feelings, (5) how to care for yourself during menstruation, (6) responsibilities that go along with sexual activity, (7) understanding sexual feelings, (8) how to deal with sexual feelings, and (9) what to do about boys or men who want to have sex when you do not. A variety of teaching methods and materials were to be used, which included films, books, pamphlets, models, and diagrams. During the classes the investigators attended to the responses of the girls and focused on methods and materials which caught and held their attention.

The investigators were prepared to help students who were not practiced at three-dimensional representations of the body to understand the models, and expected that diagrams would confuse those who lacked familiarity with them. A visit to a women's health clinic was planned as a field experience. The plan was to elicit a topic from the girls and then present information for 5 to 10 minutes; open discussion, examination of materials, or a film would follow. The intent was to encourage discussions and questions to clarify the information, and to understand better the thoughts, feelings, and values of the girls. Refreshments at the end of class were intended to encourage an informal atmosphere and communication.

ETHNOGRAPHIC FINDINGS

From the teenage classes, several insights were discovered about the girls, the community, conducting classes in a community setting, presenting information in culturally relevant ways, and eliciting feedback from the girls. In this section, data and findings are presented. Each quotation from field notes is followed by a notation identifying the set of classes from which the notes were taken. All classes were one to two hours in duration. Set 1 met for eight weeks and included four to six girls 9 to 14 years of age. The second and third set; met during the same period of time in different rooms and were divided on the basis of age. Set 2 met for eight weeks and included 8 to 13 girls 11 to 15 years of age. Set 3 met for six weeks and included 5 to 7 girls 7 to 10 years of age (Table 11-1).

Articulation of the Girls' Needs

The investigators had planned to present factual information and to provide opportunities for the girls to explore feelings about themselves and the class content. It was believed that the girls would be able to express their needs and the investigators were prepared to listen closely and to encourage their verbalizations.

At the first meeting the investigators presented the tentative list of topics mentioned earlier to the girls and stated that they would like them to tell us about any other topics in which they were interested. They verbalized none, and, as our field notes revealed:

We tried to get them to tell us what topic they wanted to start with. It took them a while to get it out. Finally, someone in the back, Susie I think, made a pronounced 's' sound, and someone else finished the 'ex' sound. So then we had it. They wanted to know about sex first. (Set 1)‡

---

‡The set number in parentheses indicates the set in which that particular field note was written. All extracts in this paper were taken from the researchers' ethnographic field notes.

Although it appeared difficult for them to verbalize their priority interest, it did come out, and when queried it was shared by all.

Generally, specific informational needs were more easily shared by the girls than more abstract ideas or feelings. On several occasions we provided opportunities to share feelings, but often the girls would talk among themselves about unrelated material or redirect the focus to more concrete material. For example, one in-class activity was to read a comic book format presentation on various topics, of which one was sexual thoughts and fantasies. This topic evoked no comment. A later section was on birth control.

> Birth control provoked the most interest and a lot of questions, including: What is the discharge from the vagina? Can a girl get pregnant if she hasn't had a period? What is a douche? What is an IUD? Where does it go? How does it work? What is a hymen? Do you take a diaphragm out right after intercourse? (Set 2)

As a result of the needs expressed by the girls, the original list of topics underwent alteration. Originally a number of affective topics were included, but the content was redirected by the girls toward more factual, informational topics.

The plan had been to avoid imposing normative, middle-class values on the girls, but rather to explore and possibly validate the norms and values expressed by the Afro-American girls. Our affective behavior, however, did seem to be an important part of the learning process and may have reflected the girls' affective needs. The younger girls seemed to need body contact with their teachers.

> The little girls seemed to want a lot of physical contact with me. . . . One after another they would walk up close to me, touch my arm and put my arm around them, then go off and come back, Brenda more so than the rest. (Set 1)

In later classes similar behavior was observed.

> I find the contact with most of the girls rewarding and warm. They are demonstrating some of the nuzzling and touching behaviors that we saw from the younger girls from the first group. Several of them seem to be saying that they want me "to be involved" with them in a caring way if I am going to teach them. (Set 3)

Set 3 was composed of younger girls because our experiences with Set 1 indicated that age was related to interest and class behavior. When Set 2 and Set 3 were initiated, we tested whether greater age homogeneity contributed to group cohesion by dividing Set 2 and Set 3 on the basis of age. We were satisfied that age stratification was helpful. The older girls seemed less retrained in their questioning and interpretation of questions, and informational answers were not needed as often with older girls. Among younger girls, less conflict among group members and less attention-getting behavior were observed. Age stratification by class grouping provided some insight into group dynamics.

Group Dynamics

It was assumed that the girls were volunteers, and that they would be attentive if the content met their needs. In Set 1 it appeared that friendship was a criterion for membership. At the urging of group members, one girl was added to the group late, and one girl who sought membership late was not. In the second instance, the group members made it very clear to the investigators that they did not want the girl added. The investigators handled the situation by telling the girl that we would be doing another group later and that she could join a later group. Similarly, in Set 1, there was an apparent attempt to exclude the younger girls. In Set 1 the quasi-group leader was definitely the oldest girl, and she was supported in her role by the next to oldest girl. Ginger demonstrated her leadership role by telling others to be quiet, telling them where to sit, and, in one class, assigning dialogues in a reading selection.

Set 2 was a large group owing to the recruitment procedure (see Analysis of Community Relations later in this chapter). The size seemed to affect the presentation of information and to offset some of the advantages of greater age homogeneity. In Set 2, classes of 10 to 15 persons (including the investigators) were in a room approximately 8 feet by 11 feet. Although the students did not seem to mind sitting closely together and on a variety of seats, the investigators were aware of the students' reactions to the size of the group and geographical space. One noted:

> The group is a little discouraging to me. I am having a lot of trouble learning names. . . . Because there are so many and the noise level is high, I feel all I can accomplish is information giving and do not receive adequate feedback. (Set 2)

A more ideal situation would have been to have fewer students in order to increase the opportunity to verbalize on each subject, but even in Set 1, our notes reflect that the girls interact with each other rather than as a group to the topic.

> Theresa was sitting beside Ginger interjecting questions and comments. This is very distracting. Everyone interjects just when they feel like it. By the time I've zeroed in on the question or the direction of their comment, someone else has a meaty question or comment. I feel overstimulated all of the time. (Set 1)

In Set 2 these problems were compounded until group cohesiveness was demonstrated by members.

> Stephanie told the others to be quiet, in particular, she told Joan to speak less loudly, not to interrupt and the others modified their behavior accordingly. She stood beside the investigator, gave information, had the facts, wrote "Emko" on the board when Sally asked for clarification on its use . . . and asked about age of onset of menstruation. (Set 2)

The merit of supporting group interaction until peer leaders emerge to control disruptive behavior was demonstrated in a later class. When the investigator told directly Jill to be quiet, she responded, but indicated that her feelings were hurt. The group also responded by becoming more quiet and less responsive. The next week attendance was at its lowest, and Jill was absent. Having fewer group members permitted more responsiveness to what group members were saying. However, it also appeared that the group felt that authoritarian behavior by the investigator directed at one member was an indirect assault on all of them. Members of a cohesive group will defend the group against internal and external threats (Yalom, 1975); the defense of group standards was important to the cohesiveness of the group.

Analysis of Teaching Materials and Methods with the Black Girls

In Set 1 classes, the format which seemed to work well was the following: (1) at the end of one class, establish the next topic, (2) briefly present the topic at the beginning of the next class, (3) invite questions, (4) use visual and manual teaching materials to elaborate on the topic, and (5) encourage free discussion and questions. Films were the overwhelming favorite of all the groups. Books and pamphlets were also helpful. During the first session of Set 1, sex was the topic.

> M. started by defining sexual intercourse. Ginny said she didn't understand what M. said, so M. repeated her definition. M. elaborated a bit and began finding pictures in books she had brought along. The pictures certainly captivated them! In fact, all at once they were up on the somewhat shaky table, all trying to see at once. M. suggested we move to a more comfortable (safer) place. The books were grabbed up and we all moved to another area. (Set 1)

When using books and pamphlets, questions and discussion flowed easily. During films, however, spontaneous questions were disruptive to the investigators because the questions seemed to interfere with hearing the dialogue. Differences between the girls' and the investigators' patterns of communication were often noted.

During a film on birth it seemed to the investigators that the relationships between film characters that were intended to be obvious were not always clear to the girls. In a film in which a man and woman in the hospital were kissing, signaling love or a marital relationship to middle-class people, the girls asked if the man and woman were doctor and patient. We took this to be an indication that nonverbal communication that would be obvious to middle-class adult viewers could be misinterpreted by the girls. Apparent differences in perceptions of events on film between the girls and investigators were frequent. When perceptual differences became apparent, we explored them with the girls. Later we tried stopping the film every five minutes or so to clarify with them their understanding of what was happening. Another technique was writing words or phrases that merited further description on the chalkboard. After a film on birth, the field notes reflected:

> The film was well received. There were interruptions with questions. I tried to respond to some of them, but most of the time I wrote a key word on the board so that I could talk about it later. The words on the board at the end of the film were: anesthesia, analgesia, natural childbirth, controlled breathing, transition, ice chips, and a couple of others. After the film we talked about each of them. (Set 2)

Another technique to deal with comprehension of content and questions is illustrated below.

> Without too much ado, we went right into the VD film. All watched rather intently. After the film, in order to generate discussion I gave several of the children pens and asked them to write their thoughts and questions on the easel. This turned out to be an effective maneuver for this group. While some wrote their questions, I addressed the comments of the others—interrupting at times to answer written questions. (Set 3)

Having the opportunity to manipulate objects that illustrated a topic seemed to be important to learning. This was demonstrated first in the class on menstruation. Trying on sanitary belts and pads over their clothes seemed to reinforce understanding for the girls. In a later class, the field notes revealed:

> As the group had expressed a desire for information on douching, I started out by discussing this—passed around a disposable douche, etc.
>   Once again it was evident how much this group needs to "handle" the objects we discuss to truly *understand* them. (Set 3)

At times the girls would suggest a learning method. Not surprisingly the methods they suggested were well received by the group.

> L. asked if they had a chance to look at the book we gave out last week. Betty and Ginger said, "Yes." Ginny said, "No." They didn't have questions but suggested reading some of the dialogues in the book. This they really seemed to enjoy—taking charge of finding dialogues in the book, assigning parts, etc. We did this for about 30 minutes. Then, things started deteriorating and L. suggested we quit. (Set 1)

Consistent with the observation that manipulating objects was important to learning, we found that a visit to a women's health clinic was well received.

> M. said she would walk them through the clinic, just like they had come for an appointment. The girls seemed attentive. When we got past the waiting room area they quickly latched onto M.'s statement about BP measurement with Ginger asking that hers be taken. Ginny followed suit but Brenda declined. We went to an examining room and M. proceeded to explain the examination. The girls seemed more easily distracted here, breaking up the flow of the explanation several times with extraneous joking. Ginny indicated that she had had a vaginal examination before and that it had been scary for her. The girls seem particulary interested in the Pap test. Once again they showed their preference for directly manipulating things—fingering the slides, swabs, speculums, etc. Despite the joking and bantering it was clear that they were "taking in" M.'s explanations with interest. (Set 1)

It appeared that many learning experiences were punctuated by laughing, joking, talking, and touching. The investigators interpreted some of this behavior as tension release. It also seemed necessary to provide a focus before a discussion could begin. Modifications in our approach resulted in the following strategy: (1) have the group select the focal topic, (2) use models, materials, films, and pictures to supplement the focus, (3) allow tension-relieving activities, (4) encourage questions, and (5) terminate when attention waned.

Analysis of Attitudes and Relationships Among the Group

When male-female relationships were the focus, more tension-relief behavior was observed. It seemed that relationships were more abstract and therefore more difficult for the girls, and it seemed very difficult for them to discuss their own relationships in the group. We tried to provide distance between the girls and the content by using hypothetical cases or situations. The girls' statements reflected various attitudes, but the variation was consistent with the experiences of girls and women they knew. Their reluctance is reflected in these field notes.

When we tried to initiate a discussion of relationships with boys the group did not seem to respond, even when we couched it in terms of the readings in the booklet. Ginger's suggestion that we do the readings out loud seemed to confirm that the information was important to them, but that they did not want a free discussion. They undertook the readings with zest. The aside comments during the readings seemed to reflect that they had given the boy-girl issues some thought and that they had experiences that were related to the readings.

This approach was their suggestion. It seemed to give time and importance to the topic in a pretty unthreatening way. This alternative was a comfortable one that allowed the material to be revealed. (Set 1)

Films seemed to be a quite successful way to present hypothetical examples. One film included boys and girls talking about their bodies, changes in them, seeing the bodies of the opposite sex, masturbation, sexual relations, responsibility for parenthood, and other topics. The discussion that followed provided insight into attitudes toward pregnancy and community and group norms, as well as an opportunity for values clarification.

During discussion about the film the girls expressed impatience and rejection of a "guy" who would not accept his responsibility for a pregnancy. The expectation that women and men assume total responsibility was strongly expressed. It was generally agreed that if a man loved or cared for a girl he would immediately offer to take care of her. We asked if that was true even if he was young, say 15 years old. They responded, "Yes, if she can have the baby, he can take care of her and the baby." They felt that he was responsible even if he had to quit school, or attend school and work. Their expectations of the man were almost matched by their expectations of girls (or themselves); one said, "If you're old enough to have a baby, you're old enough to work."

They agreed that if they were pregnant, they probably would not tell the baby's father first. A man, they seemed to feel, would "know" about the pregnancy from little signs *if he cared*. One suggested that she might tell the "guy" and see what he *did*. Most girls said they would tell their mothers if they were pregnant.

Consistent with this, they indicated that their mothers would probably not be pleased. They might have to "tell her and run," or she may even "put them out" of the house. Yet all the girls were sure they would be able to work something out; some said that their mothers would help care for the baby. Abortion was mentioned on the film as an option, but not one of the girls brought it up for discussion as an option or had questions about it. The subject of pregnancy was one about which all of them had ideas. One researcher wrote:

> It was amazing to me that they internalized ideal and real norms about marriage and parenthood at an early age. (There was consensus that 18 years of age was an ideal age.) The ideal (and a fairly unattainable one they seemed to feel) is that they will be married before pregnancy. More realistically, they indicated they would like to be old enough to have a job and be able to provide financially for their baby. But, from a here-and-now perspective, if they became pregnant, they would find a way to care for the baby.
> At one point, the film discussed how difficult it is for a child, to be unwanted. . . . The girls seemed to appreciate this, but put their own twist to it. If they had a baby they would definitely want it. So, this issue did not really apply to them. Their empathy for unwanted babies and children came through clearly. (Set 1)

While they seemed to see responsibilities for themselves lying ahead, they were uncertain what role men might play in their lives. They seemed secure in their feelings that mothers, kin, and friends would be helpful. Each seemed to feel that she would need to be able to support herself and her children. We were intrigued by the attitudes the girls expressed and thought that experience and maturation would probably nudge them to see some of the issues differently. At this time their ideas seemed to be based on the experiences they had seen mothers, sisters, and community members experience and were consistent with the ideals they expressed. Throughout the classes, the action researchers were sensitive to the interaction between community as represented by mothers, community leaders, and the classes.

Analysis of Community Relations

The approach to the community was to maintain constant sensitivity to community attitudes by eliciting feedback whenever possible. The investigators talked with mothers who came to pick up other children at the day-care center and others who worked at the center. At times a willingness to modify our behavior based on feedback resulted in considerable inconvenience. For example, the original plan was to use the day-care center after hours (around 5:50 P.M.). However, the day-care center director did not want to leave the day-care center key with us, and she feared that the girls would leave the building in disorder. In short, she did not welcome having classes in the center after hours. The compromise was that the classes meet in the nursing clinic rooms in the center during regular day-care hours. However, high noise levels in the class were disrupting to napping day-care children, adding a constraint to class activities. In addition, the rooms were too small, and although the investigators had a key to the rooms, we did not have a key to the center and it was mandatory that we be out of the center by 5:30 P.M. Thus, the investigators' willingness to work within the constraints created inconveniences.

Working through and with community members is usually regarded as central to the acceptance of a project like this. When the investigators were ready for the second set of classes, Ms. Leader asked a resident to select girls for the classes. She was reported to have good relationships with the girls and indeed must have had influence with them. It was through her efforts that Set 2 had a large membership, actually much too large for the room. But after the class had been identified, it was not feasible to ask half the girls to leave the class and wait several weeks for it to be offered again.

The investigators were concerned about whether the class content was acceptable to the girls' mothers. Feedback was solicited from mothers, and on occasion, mothers came to the investigators. Their comments seemed to indicate that the content was acceptable, but that they needed to confirm their perceptions about the classes.

The investigators were concerned at times about how the girls might use the information they received in class. They were cautioned not to share the information with younger children or girls whose mothers did not want them to attend the classes. As it turned out, our concerns were well founded. On one occasion:

> She [Brenda and Theresa's mother] volunteered that Theresa was enamoured with the book she got last week—was taking it outside the apartment, showing it to *everyone* who came over, etc. I shared with her our initial concern that the "younger girls" might not know how to use the book wisely. I mentioned that we had cautioned them to keep the books inside, and that we would remind the "little girls" again. I said I hoped it hadn't been a problem for her [Brenda and Theresa's mother]. She said "No." (Set 1)

On more than one occasion we were impressed with the willingness of mothers to communicate with their daughters about sexual matters, even though others expressed the feeling that they did not know how to talk with them. The most dramatic example of how communication between mother and daughter reinforced the classes was provided by a girl nine years of age.

> Peggy seems to have had a lot of high quality sex education from her mother. She said that each night when she and her sister came home from this class they talk about what they have discussed. Peggy said that after we talked about masturbation she was confused about just where her clitoris was. Her mother encouraged her to look and feel the next time she took a bath, and to just see what it felt like to touch that area. (Set 3)

In class Peggy encouraged Flora to do this when Flora expressed difficulty understanding the reality of the clitoris.

The investigators were prepared to present as little or as much material as the girls and their mothers wanted. It was relatively easy to identify and address the needs expressed by the girls; understanding and responding to community needs were more uneven. The experiences with the classes and community members suggest that the project functioned within acceptable parameters.

DISCUSSION AND IMPLICATIONS OF THE FINDINGS

The ethnographic nursing research method was a natural choice as a research methodology. The fact that two investigators were present at most classes provided an opportunity for one to observe the group while the other led the class. One aim of the project was to gain a systematic understanding of the girls' beliefs, values and behaviors with regard to body function and sexuality. The findings of this project demonstrate the value of the ethnographic field method focused on direct input and planning with community members. Implications for community nursing and nursing research include the following:

Blacks are usually considered a subculture in the United States; fieldwork among United States populations is a growing component of transcultural nursing and anthropology using the ethnographic field method in such settings as this one to provide a systematic method of observing, recording, interpreting, analyzing, and presenting field note findings.

Age categories are a viable subdivision within a cultural group. Preadolescence and early adolescence is a developmental period during which group members are usually being socialized. Therefore, this sample would not be expected to be key informants for the total subculture, but the members were general informants for the ways preadolescent and early adolescent girls think, perceive, and behave.

The analysis of sex and gender differences has become an important component of transcultural nursing and anthropological research studies. Findings from this study partially describe the ethos of maturing girls; another project involving boys would provide an important comparison.

The focus of the project, body function and sex education, is usually considered sensitive among United States populations. These types are rarely investigated in a community context, and research usually conducted among youth older than the girls who participated in this study. Therefore, these findings would appear to be of interest to a broad range of scholars and practitioners as well as to those interested in conducting a research study in the Afro-American natural and familiar environment.

The findings from this study related to adolescent pregnancy. This topic domain has been of much interest to many health professionals, politicians, and religious leaders in the past few years. Much has been written about adolescent pregnancy and its effects. Resistance to providing sexual knowledge to adolescents and preadolescents persists. This research method of tailoring content to the cultural setting and to the needs of girls within a community might be transferred to other settings, regardless of political or religious affiliation. The teaching materials and methods are applicable to body function and sex education programs for preadolescent and early adolescent girls.

These findings suggest that girls are able to communicate about their needs, and that loosely structured classes are an effective model to use. The high interest of the girls in sexual matters may alarm some, but it is reassuring that the girls seemed to understand, adhere to, and espouse community values regarding the family. The presentation of content is facilitated when cultural values are known. The results of this project indicate that a knowledge of cultural domains can be obtained while at the same time providing knowledge to the group being studied. Perhaps these findings, which should be regarded as preliminary, may be built upon by others to better target sex education content, and to refine and to further examine the use of the ethnographic nursing research method to study cultural groups.

STRENGTHS AND LIMITATIONS OF THE ETHNOGRAPHIC METHOD FOR NURSING RESEARCH

The ethnographic nursing research method as employed in this research had both strengths and limitations. Strengths of the method were the following: (1) the girls participated in planning the classes on a weekly basis, (2) the ethnographic approach permitted the investigators to respond to verbal and behavioral cues of the girls, (3) the investigators were able to utilize and assess various teaching materials and techniques, and (4) the setting permitted careful observation and the discovery of attitudes and beliefs underlying cultural patterns. Limitations of the method involved the lack of control in the research situation. Constraints of space and time had an unquantifiable effect on the classes. The reliability of the findings is open to question, and it is unlikely that the study could be replicated; therefore, validity of the findings cannot be verified. These limitations restrict the generalizibility of the findings. Nonetheless, a strength of the ethnographic method is the discovery of cultural patterns and the generation of questions or hypotheses that can be tested in further research; the research was successful in describing behavior and providing direction to future inquiry.

REFERENCES

Agar, M. H. *The professional stranger: An informal introduction to ethnography.* New York: Academic Press, 1980.

Antonovsky, H. F. *Adolescent sexuality: A study of attitudes and behavior.* Lexington, Mass.: Lexington Books, 1980.

Arnold, S. Chicago Planned Parenthood's teen scene: A sociological study for participants. *Adolescence,* 1974, *9,* 371–389.

Brick, P. Sex and society: Teaching the connection. *Journal of School Health,* 1981, *51,* 226–230.

Brody, E. B., Ottey, F., & Lagranade, J. Early sex education in relationship to later coital and reproductive behavior: Evidence from Jamaican women. *American Journal of Psychiatry,* 1976, *133,* 969–972.

Carton, J., & Carton, J. Evaluation of a sex education program for children and their parents: Attitude and interactional changes. *The Family Coordinator,* 1971, *20,* 377–386.

Chesler, J. J. Twenty-seven strategies for teaching contraception to adolescents. *Journal of School Health,* 1980, *50,* 18–21.

Chethik, B. B. Developing community sup-

port: A first step toward a school education program. *Journal of School Health,* 1981, *51,* 266–270.

Dougherty, M. C. *Becoming a woman in rural black culture.* New York: Holt, Rinehart and Winston, 1978.

Eberst, R. M. Health educator's notebook: Proclaiming sexuality education. *Journal of School Health,* 1981, *51,* 625.

Hacker, S. S. It isn't sex education unless. . . . *Journal of School Health,* 1981, *51,* 207–210.

Harris, F. G., & Dougherty, M. C. The space intruders: The interpretation of space use in a housing development. Paper presented at the 104th Annual Meeting of the American Public Health Association, Miami, Florida, October 1976.

Kroger, F., & Wiesner, P. J. STD education: Challenge for the 80's. *Journal of School Health,* 1981, *51,* 242–246.

Leininger, M. *Transcultural nursing: Concepts, theories and practices.* New York: John Wiley and Sons, 1978.

Lenocker, J., & Dougherty, M. C. Adolescent

mothers' social and health related interests: Report of a project for rural black mothers. *Journal of Gynecological Nursing,* 1976, *5,* 9–15.

Leppink, M. A. Adolescent sexuality. *Maternal–Child Nursing Journal,* 1979, *8,* 153–161.

Leibow, E. *Talley's corner: A study of Negro street-corner men.* Boston: Little, Brown and Company, 1967.

McNab, W. L. Difficulties in implementing sex education: The Nevada experience. *Journal of School Health,* 1981, *46,* 537–542.

Paul, B. D. Understanding the community. In B. D. Paul (Ed.), *Health, culture and community: Case studies of public reactions to health programs.* New York: Russell Sage Foundation, 1955.

Peach, E. H. Counseling sexually active very young adolescent girls. *Maternal–Child Nursing,* 1980, *5* (3), 191–195.

Polley, M. J. Teen mothers: A status report. *Journal of School Health,* 1979, *49,* 466–469.

Reichelt, P. A. The desirability of involving adolescents in sex education planning. *Journal of School Health,* 1977, *47,* 99–103.

Roesel, R. The nurse's role in primary prevention in sexual health. *Imprint,* 1980, *27,* 27–28.

Rubenstein, J. S., Watson, F. G., Drolette, M. E., & Rubenstein, M. D. Young adolescents' sexual interests. *Adolescence,* 1976, *11,* 487–496.

Sapala, S., & Strokosch, G. Adolescent sexuality: Use of a questionnaire for health teaching and counseling. *Pediatric Nursing,* 1981, *7,* 33–34, 52.

Seybold, S. A., & Klisch, M. L. Preparing grade school faculty to teach family life education. *Maternal–Child Nursing Journal,* 1982, *7,* 50–54.

Schoof-Tams, K., Schlaegel, J., & Walczak, L. Differentiation of sexual morality between 11 and 16 years. *Archives of Sexual Behavior,* 1976, *5,* 39–67.

Spanier, G. B. Formal and informal sex education as determinants of premarital sexual behavior. *Archives of Sexual Behavior,* 1976, *5,* 39–67.

Stack, C. B. *All our kin: Strategies for survival in a black community.* New York: Harper & Row, 1974.

Vacalis, T. D., et al. The effect of two methods of teaching sex education on the behaviors of students. *Journal of School Health,* 1979, *49,* 404–409.

Yalom, I. D. *The theory and practice of group psychiatry* (2nd ed.). New York: Basic Books, 1975.

Zelnik, M., & Kantner, J. F. Sexual and contraceptive experience of young unmarried women in the United States, 1976 and 1971. *Family Planning Perspectives,* 1977, *9,* 44–71.

12

Combining Qualitative and Quantitative Methodologies

Toni Tripp-Reimer

Despite current arguments, qualitative and quantitative research may not be opposing methodologies. They, in fact, may provide complementary data sets which together give a more complete picture than can be obtained using either method singly. Each has advantages and limitations; when fused, the positive aspects of both may been seen.

Qualitative studies tend to be exploratory in nature, providing rich descriptive and documentary information about a topic or phenemenon. Because of this feature, they tend to be hypothesis-generating, rather than hypothesis-testing. Qualitative research is used appropriately when an investigator does not have a comprehensive understanding of the topic at hand. It is particularly useful when investigators do not know the way important questions should be asked or the range of responses likely to be elicited. Qualitative studies produce information about background features of the topic that will ultimately influence the nature of the questions that need to be studied by quantitative methods.

In addition to providing new information on a topic, qualitative studies can offer a fresh perspective on an area already well investigated. Qualitative data facilitate serendipitous findings, raise unexpected questions, and identify topics the investigator might not otherwise have considered. On the other hand, quantitative methods are needed when the researcher wishes to know how much, how often, be used to or

Copyright © 1983; Permission obtained from American Journal of Nursing Company, 1983. Rewritten from the article entitled "Retention of a folk-healing practice (Matiasma) among four generations of urban Greek immigrants." In *Nursing Research,* March/April, Vol. 32, No. 2, pp. 97–101.

to what extent a phenomenon is present. Quantitative studies tend to be used to test hypotheses with the goal of explaining or predicting.

For a variety of reasons, qualitative study may be used as an important precursor to quantitative studies. The use of qualitative data generally means that the investigator has developed close personal relationships with subjects. This intimate association with the target population will often result in the opportunity to achieve more reliable results when quantitative questions are asked. Generally this intimacy increases the willingness of subjects of participate (resulting in a higher response rate) in subsequent studies involving quantitative questions. Qualitative data also provide a generalized background for interpreting later statistical results. The statistical results should be compared with the qualitative data to discern if there is a "fit" between the two data sets. To obtain a comprehensive understanding of a topic, qualitative and quantitative data sets should be combined.

The following chapter presents the results of an investigation that combined qualitative and quantitative methods. Qualitative methods (participant observation and the use of guided [informal] interviews) produced a qualitative data set that resulted in rich descriptive information regarding belief in the evil eye among Greek immigrants. The qualitative data enable the investigator to delineate specific facets of *matiasma*, the configuration surrounding the evil eye.

Quantitative data came from structured interview questions and resulted in information concerning the distribution pattern of this health belief system among the Greek immigrant population. The quantitative data allowed the investigator to trace the retention of knowledge and use of this configuration over four-generations, thus demonstrating the importance of generation depth as a variable in transcultural nursing research.

Practicing in a pluralistic society, American nurses in most clinical settings work with clients from a variety of cultural groups. Because client values, beliefs, and customs have a direct influence on health and health behaviors, consideration of these traditional beliefs and practices is an essential element in delivering effective nursing care to minority clients.

In planning health care for a minority or subcultural group, the first step is the identification of traditional (folk) beliefs and practices used by members of that group. The second step is the determination of the extent of the practice of these folk traditions within the group. Subsequently, this information can be used to deliver culturally sensitive health care. As part of a larger research project, this phase of the research was undertaken to obtain a description of a specific Greek-American ethnomedical configuration, the *matiasma* (evil eye). In addition, the distribution of this configuration was ascertained by tracing its retention over four generations of Greek immigrants.

GREEK IMMIGRANTS

The first Greek settlement in the United States dates from 1785, when a Scottish physician founded the Greek colony of New Smyrna, Florida (Polites, 1945). The first Greek Orthodox religious community established in the Western Hemisphere was the Holy Trinity Church of New Orleans, Louisiana, founded in 1864. Major Greek immigration to the United States was chiefly a product of the late nineteenth and early twentieth centuries. During this period, migration depleted the population of Greece by about one fifth. Greek migration was contemporaneous with that of other Eastern and Southern European groups. The most prominant factors accounting for this mass exodus were economic hardship, relative overpopulation, and political and religious oppression (Fairchild, 1922; Saloutos, 1964; Xenides, 1922).

Immigration to the United States decreased considerably in 1921 and 1924 with the passage of immigration restrictions in the form of the National Quota Acts. A second major wave of immigrants came to the United States in the 1960s and 1970s after the restrictions on immigration were modified by the Immigration and Nationality Act of 1965 (Saloutos, 1980).

The 1970 Federal census (which counts first and second generations) places the Greek-American population at 434,000. However, Greek-Americans contest this number, noting that it considers only two generations in a cohesive ethnic group, and that it does not count Greeks who were born in other countries (especially Turkey, Rumania, and Egypt). Although political and religious leaders contend that there are nearly three million Americans of Greek descent in the United States, Greek-American scholars place the figure closer to 1.5 million (Saloutos, 1980). Even using the more conservative figure, Greek-Americans at present constitute the largest Greek community outside Greece itself.

SETTING

The target site for this project was Columbus, Ohio. Greek immigrants in this community came chiefly from the Peloponnesus. The first Greek settler in Franklin County, Ohio, arrived in 1898, and the community grew rapidly over the following 25 years. During that time, the majority of Greek settlers lived in a geographically circumscribed area of Columbus. After World War II, members of the Greek community moved away from that central location and are now geographically dispersed over the entire greater Columbus metropolitan area (Tripp-Reimer, 1980).

Although confronted by continuing acculturation pressures and a growing population, the Greek community of central Ohio is attempting to preserve many facets of the traditional way of life. Through fraternal organizations, church groups, sports clubs, and informal associations, these Greek-Americans retain a strong ethnic identify. In addition, a majority of the population appears to have a deep commitment to the Greek Orthodox Church. The combination of this commitment, a church doctrine that strongly promotes endogamous marriage, and a high degree of ethnic cohesion within the population results in a high rate of ingroup marriages. The historical and cultural characteristics of the Columbus Greek community showed that although it is geographically, economically, and politically well integrated into the larger Columbus population, the Greek community constitutes a viable ethnic group with distinct aspects of a continuing cultural tradition.

Members of the Columbus Greek population reported that the community had a history of seeking good medical care. Early in the century, a Greek immigrant graduated from the Ohio State University College of Medicine. Greek immigrants, unable to speak English, sought out this physician for formal medical care. Prior to the arrival of this physician, the community used the services of an Albanian doctor fluent in Greek. Thus, in seeking medical care, the population did not experience the significant language barriers of many immigrant groups. In addition, education and professional status are highly valued among the Greek people. As a result, patients' fear of the professional was not as great as that reported by M. Clark (1970) among other immigrant groups. Finally, the rapid upward mobility of the members of the community allowed them to afford formal medical care.

While orthodox Western health care is well utilized by this population, the Greek community has also retained ethnomedical beliefs and practices that differ dramatically from those of Western health care. This paper is concerned with one of these configurations: the *matiasma* (beliefs and practices surrounding the evil eye).

STUDY QUESTIONS AND HYPOTHESES

There were two major aims of this phase of the larger study. The first was to provide baseline qualitative data concerning the description of *matiasma* as practiced by a specific Greek immigrant community. The second was to quantify the distribution of these beliefs and practices within the population. Two hypotheses were developed with regard to the second study aim:

H1:   There is no difference between males and females in the retention of beliefs and practices concerning *matiasma*.

H2:   There is a positive correlation between members' generation of immigration and retention of beliefs and practices concerning *matiasma*.

DEFINITION OF TERMS

Terms were defined as follows:

Matiasma: The configuration of beliefs and practices surrounding the prevention, diagnosis, and treatment of the evil eye.

Greek immigrant: A person living in the United States who has at least one parent of full Greek ancestry and who self-affiliates with the Columbus, Ohio, Greek community

Generation of immigration: The number of successive filial stages since the first lineal Greek ancestor arrived in the United States (immigrant group = first generation).

DESIGN AND METHODOLOGY

This research was conducted in the greater Columbus, Ohio, metropolitan area from July 1976 to March 1977. Data were secured from personal interviews and participant observation.

Access and Preparation Strategies

Following approval of the research plan by The Ohio State University Human Subject Review Committee A, a lengthy period of preparation was essential for full access to the community. The locations of Greek churches, businesses, organizations, schools, and residential areas were ascertained. Greek community leaders, including the priests, business leaders, and presidents of Greek ethnic organizations, were identified. Initial contact with the community was made through a Greek Orthodox priest. Entry into the community was facilitated by an announcement briefly describing the study, which was placed in the Greek Orthodox Church bulletin on three consecutive Sundays. Access was further facilitated by an article which appeared in the Greek community news bulletin. This article presented the investigator's personal history, the purpose of the study, and an endorsement by a lay leader of the Greek community.

During this preparation period, a relatively complete list of Greek community members was made. The membership rosters from the Greek Orthodox church, Greek ethnic organizations, fraternal and social organizations, student associations, and athletic (soccer) clubs were consolidated to form a master list. This master list was considered to be comprehensive in that it identified most Greek-Americans (n = 3000) who affiliated with the Greek community in Columbus.

Methods of Data Collection

Data for this study were conducted using two major methods: (1) intensive semi-structured interviews with 328 individuals from 102 extended family units, and (2) participant-observation. Strategies for collection and analysis of the data varied with each method of data collection.

Instrument

A questionnaire was devised to elicit information in the following areas: demographic social and cultural characteristics of the population, and Greek ethnomedical beliefs and practices concerning *matiasma*.

Face and content validity were ascertained for the demographic questions by a physical anthropologist on the faculty of Ohio State University. Content and face validity for social questions were obtained from three sources: an anthropologist who had conducted field work in Greece, a doctoral student from Greece, and a Columbus Greek Orthodox priest. All were asked to check on these aspects:

1. The content of the questions would elicit the data required to answer the study questions.
2. The questions were socially and culturally valid.
3. The wording was appropriate.
4. Other questions needed to be asked.

Although the substantive areas remained the same, the reviewers made several suggestions concerning the rewording of questions for clarity and appropriateness.

Pilot Study

A pilot study was conducted prior to the actual investigation. Five individuals from the Greek community who were already well known to the researcher were asked to participate in the pilot study. As a result of the pilot test, changes were made in the sequencing of topical areas. However, no substantive changes were made and the conceptual nature of the questionnaire was not altered. The pilot test indicated that the semi-structured questionnaire was clear, was usable, and would elicit the desired information.

Interviews

Semi-structured interviews with members of the Greek community were conducted over a four-month period (December 1976 to March 1977). Scheduling the interviews after the researcher had become familiar with the members of the Greek community increased the probability that individuals would be willing to be interviewed. Data concerning retention of folk beliefs and behaviors were elicited from 328 individuals during the 102 semi-structured interviews with extended family units. The informants spanned four generations and represented chiefly Greek immigrants or their descendants from the Peloponnesus.

Individuals to be interviewed were generally selected randomly from the consolidated Greek community membership roster. The exception was the purposeful inclusion of eleven families who had resided in the Columbus area for the longest period of time. Nonparticipation in the study was exceptionally low: 110 families were asked to participate and only seven declined (one later withdrew information). This relatively high rate of voluntary participation can be attributed to several factors, including extensive access and preparation strategies. Another important factor influencing the high rate of participation, however, seemed to be the community members' profound interest in the history and trends in their community.

Appointments for the interviews were made by telephone. When phoning, the investigator stated her name and mentioned that the person being questioned might be familiar with the study either from the Sunday church bulletin or from the Greek community newsletter. If the individual did not recognize the investigator, the name of a member of the Greek community was given as a reference. The purpose of the larger study were then explained: to determine demographic characteristics and social history of the Columbus Greek community, to study the maintenance of traditional values and customs, and to detect changes in family patterns over the generations. Each individual was informed that all information would be confidential and that consenting to an interview did not obligate the subject to answer any questions considered too personal. After the subject agreed, an interview time was established.

Interviews were usually conducted in the subject's home, but occasionally (6 percent) in a business office at the request of the subject. After amenities were exchanged upon entering the home, informed written consent was obtained prior to asking pertinent questions. Interviews were generally conducted in English with a few words or phrases in Greek. No interview was conducted wholly in Greek.

Demographic questions were administered in a standard manner. Social, cultural, and historical data were obtained from open-ended questions and promptings. Interview notes for social and cultural data were tape-recorded or taken in shorthand and later transcribed onto note cards for reference to particular subjects. Interviews averaged about three hours each. The longest single interviews were one seven-hour and two six-hour interviews; the shortest was 40 minutes.

Participant-Observation

Participant-observation was used to obtain descriptive data concerning the practice of *matiasma*. The period of participant-observation lasted from July 1976 to May 1977. Information was obtained during such activities as attending church services, meetings of organizations, community festivals, and memorial services, and frequenting local restaurants and family-centered taverns.

Participant-observation data also were derived from a few strategic or key informants who were willing to allow close scrutiny of their personal lives. However, the most important data obtained by this method were gathered during informal socialization with community members. Particularly informative periods were the days spent with members of the Greek community with whom the investigator developed close personal relationships.

Bruyn (1966) suggests that the accuracy of participant-observation data can be assessed by the following criteria:

1. Time: How long has the observer participated in the setting?
2. Place: Where has the observer participated in the physical setting?
3. Circumstance: In what social groups and social roles has the observer participated?
4. Language: How well does the observer know the language?
5. Intimacy: In what private social arrangements does the observer participate?
6. Consensus: How does the observer confirm what meanings he or she finds existing in the culture?

These criteria are addressed consecutively below.

Time.   Participant-observation was conducted daily over an 11-month period. This is a customary period of time for conducting substantive ethnographic studies. Less time (such as studies reporting that a community was visited twice a week for three months) generally indicates that the investigator might not have sufficient contact with the population to be able to accurately judge what is occurring.

Place.   Data were collected at the following locations: informants' homes, churches, community festivals in the "old neighborhood," restaurants and taverns, Greek businesses, schools, hospitals, and clinic offices. These locations provided a variety of physical situations so that contacts with community members were maximized.

Circumstance.   The investigator participated in the following social groups: informal social gatherings, congregational church services, meetings of Greek ethnic organizations, women's church groups, community festivals, memorial services for deceased Greek persons, christenings, meals at local Greek restaurants, and entertainment nights at family-centered taverns. For some of these activities, the investigator acted strictly as an observer (as when initially attending women's organizations). At other times, the investigator acted more as a participant in the (church member, customer at restaurant, dancer at tavern). The investigator participated in roles other than researcher, including teacher at a state university, nurse, anthropologist, wife, woman, friend, and student. Roles varied according to self-presentation, manner of introduction by other, and nature of the circumstance. Again, this variation permitted data to be gathered in a wide variety of groups, with the investigator participating in a wide variety of roles. Generally, accuracy is increased as the investigator is more integrated into the community.

Language.   While not wholly bilingual, the investigator had taken Greek language (Demotic) courses and was sufficiently fluent to be able to follow conversations in Greek when community members chose to do so. In this study, considerable data were generated from informal conversations in Greek that were initiated in the "background."

Intimacy. Initially, the investigator was introduced to the community and endorsed by lay and professional leaders of the community. Approximately three weeks after initial contact with the religious leader and entry into the community, the investigator was first invited to a family's home for lunch. Later, invitations were made for other meals (breakfast, brunch, dinner, and special holiday meals). Developing close personal relationships with four extended family units enabled the researcher to learn about intimate and personal life patterns. This information was primarily derived during informal (often late night) and extended visits. Because a member of one family was a folk practitioner, the investigator was able to obtain more detailed information concerning healing practices than might otherwise have been possible.

Consensus. One way consensus was achieved was by asking a variety of individuals about the same topic. By doing this, obtaining a group consensus was possible. In general, then, information was not reported if it was derived from only one person. Corroborating evidence was obtained. Thus, purely idiosyncratic beliefs and practices are not reported.

These criteria serve as standards for judging accuracy of the data. The length of time, variety of locations and circumstances, language fluency, and degrees of intimacy, and consensus indicate that these data are probably accurate.

Data Analysis

Analysis of qualitative data from open-ended interview questions and participant-observation was conducted independently from analysis of quantitative and demographic data derived from structured questions. The qualitative and quantitative data sets were subsequently combined as complementary sets.

Qualitative Data

In recording data from the semi-structured interviews, as well as from participant-observation, Murdock's (1971) number-topic system was used as specified in his "Outline of Cultural Materials." Additional numerical codes were developed as necessary. This part of the data coding is similar to the grounded theory method described by Stern (1980). As data were transcribed, the investigator applied Mu dock's system of open coding. This means examining the data line by line and ident fying topics. These topic areas are then given a numerical code. An excerpt fro one interview provides a coding example.

> The *evil eye?* Oh yes, many Greeks believe in that. We call it *matiasma.* Well, to get rid of the eye my grandma used to say some words. I don't know what they were; she never told me, because—well, she told me that you have to get those words from a man if you are a woman, and from a woman if you are a man, so I do not know those words. It has something to do with Jesus and Mary, and something like that. I think she begs Jesus to take care of that person and to relieve him of the bad eye. [755] Oh, I know a nun, and she's doing another trick to get rid of the bad eye: she takes a small glass of water, and she

says some magic words and after she takes olive oil and she puts one or two drops on the water. If the oil spreads around, it means that you do not have bad eye, but if it stays like a drop—and it is unusual to stay like a drop—that means that you have the bad eye.[787] And after she takes the whole thing and puts water and oil on you (making the sign of the cross), and if you start going like that (blinking and yawning), that means that you have the bad eye. And she keeps watch on you until the oil spoils, or stains your clothes. She believes it works.[755] For newborns and the young children—we used to put the *blue eye* on them. I have one. It's a blue stone, like an eye, with silver or gold. And we used to put it somewhere where everybody can see. They believe— the villagers and all the people—they believe that the eye can protect you because blue is the color against the bad eye.[751]

As indicated above, portions of this excerpt were given the following three numerical codes taken from Murdock (1971):

751   Preventive Medicine

755   Magical Therapy

787   Divination (diagnosis)

Because this particular observation was coded for three distinct topics, this description was then reproduced on three 5 x 7 inch sheets of paper, one per topic code. The papers were then filed by number, making all observations on a single topic (e.g., 751: methods of prevention) easily retrievable.

During the analysis phase, the data were studied topic by topic. Descriptions of each topic were then written. At no time was purely idiosyncratic behavior reported; data needed to be reported by at least two family groups to be included.

Quantitative Data

Quantitative data concerning demographic and social characteristics and knowledge and use of *matiasma* were coded and transferred onto computer cards. Responses concerning *matiasma* were coded according to the greater use or knowledge. The following criteria were used for coding:

Category 1.   Subject knew and had used practices concerning *matiasma.*
Category 2.   Subject did not use practices concerning *matiasma;* could detail knowledge having to do with at least two of the following: diagnosis, prevention, or treatment of *matiasma.*
Category 3.   Subject did not use practices concerning *matiasma;* could detail knowledge of only one of the following: prevention, diagnosis, or treatment of *matiasma.*
Category 4.   Subject did not use practices concerning *matiasma;* could not detail any knowledge concerning diagnosis, prevention, or treatment of *matiasma.*

Reliability of this categorization was established through the use of inter-rater reliability. Data from a random sample of 30 subjects (9.3 per cent) were independently coded by a doctoral candidate at Ohio State University. Coding scorer reliability was established with 97 per cent agreement with that of the investigator. These data were then analyzed with computer assistance using the Statistical Package for the Social Sciences (SPSS).

RESULTS

Matiasma

The evil eye is a pervasive folk illness known throughout Mediterranean and Spanish-speaking cultures. Among Greeks, this configuration is called *matiasma*, or more commonly simply *mati* (the eye). A configuration of beliefs was found to surround the *matiasma* or evil eye, and more than half of the Columbus Greek population were quite familiar with these beliefs. The following is an ethnographic description of *matiasma* gleaned from participant-observation and semi-structured interviews.

Agent of Matiasma

The evil eye was generally considered to be an unintentional result of envy or admiration, although a few informants felt that the sender needed to have a desire to inflict harm in order for the eye to be effective. Occasionally, gossip ("the whisperings of an old lady") was also thought to cause *matiasma*.

Blue-eyed people were thought to be particularly capable in casting the eye, as were old women (especially spinsters). The following were also singled out as having special *mati* power: red-haired women, those born on the wrong day of the week (Tuesday), or a mother who "did wrong during her pregnancy."

Subjects Prone to Attack

While children are particularly susceptible to attack from the eye, it was clear that anyone could be the recipient. The eye was thought to be able to harm a very wide range of things, including inanimate objects (a beautiful vase), plants (grapevines), animals, or humans. One may be susceptible to the eye because of beauty, happiness, or personal excellence.

Symptoms of Matiasma

The following were common symptoms noted to be the result of the casting of the eye: lethargy, headache, fever, chills, and stomach ache. There was, however no consensus on the seriousness of the problems resulting from the *mati*. Nearly half of the informants considered the eye to be very threatening ("it can kill"); but more felt that if a illness resulted from the eye, it would not be too serious.

Prevention of Matiasma

A variety of strategies are used to protect against the eye. Four categories of prevention were known in the Columbus population:

1. Protective charms were the most widely known methods of avoiding the eye. These included, in decreasing order of priority, (a) Blue beads or blue stones (occasionally with a black spot), these were called eye beads; and were thought to reflect the evil eye; (b) *Phylactos* or amulets, which primarily consisted of wood from a saint's statue or monastery and/or incense from the church; (c) Religious

medals (particularly crosses) made of gold; (d) Garlic (worn on the person or placed in the kitchen); (e) Teeth from a dead individual.

2. Positive or action behaviors included delicately spitting three times after complimenting someone, and making the sign of the cross.

3. Avoidance behaviors included not flaunting wealth or children ("don't make over a child"). As one informant stated, "People will try to give you the eye if they envy you. The less they know about you, the better. The fewer people that can curse you, the better luck you have."

4. Three sayings were commonly used to deflect a compliment: "Spit in the eye of the Devil," "Your eyes." Invocations to the *Panaghia* (Virgin Mary).

Detection of Evil Eye

The most common method of detecting *matiasma* consisted of placing olive oil in a glass of water. Generally, if the oil dispersed, the evil eye had not been cast. However, a few informants thought that if the oil came *together*, the eye had been cast.

An alternate method of detection was to drop a wooden cross into the oil-water mixture. If the oil then bubbled, it signified that the eye had been cast. Further, oil attaching to the cross indicated a severe or strong case of the eye.

One Columbus woman was considered to have the power simply to look at a child and detect if the eye had been cast. Another woman's eyes would puff and tear, or she would yawn when she concentrated on a child who had been "matiased."

Counteracting Matiasma

Although a few informants believed that *matiasma* would disappear after it had been detected, most felt that additional ritual acts needed to be performed. These acts fall into two general categories:

1. Physical acts, such as taking three sips of the oil-water mixture; making three crosses over the glass, then washing up the face with the water; or making the sign of the cross over the affected part of the body.

2. Ritual prayers or sayings that have the power to remove the evil eye. A few informants believed that general prayers could be made for removal of the evil eye but more believed that praying to the *Panaghia* was most effective. However, the majority held that there are special prayers to remove the evil eye. These prayers were called *koupas* by one informant and *vaskania* by another; however, neither of these terms could be validated with other informants.

It was commonly believed that these prayers or "the words" are effective when said aloud. They may be transmitted to members of the opposite sex, but not to members of the same sex; thus, a woman can pass on the words to a male, but not to another female. If a female curer told the words to another woman, her healing ability would lessen. However, the majority of women claiming to know the words insisted that they would not lose their curing ability if they wrote the words down and gave them to another woman. Two sayings were written for me; they are roughly translated as "Jesus Christ wins and sends away all the bad things," which is repeated as the healer makes the sign of the cross and, "So all bad eye goes on cats," which is repeated as one throws the oil-water mixture on a house cat.

Most informants agreed that the Greek Orthodox priest knew an exorcist prayer that could remove the evil eye. The prayer is reported to "call upon angels to come and help, to ask God to help take away the sickness, and to remove from the patient every attack of the evil and every bad spirit that might come to him." Two informants held that only the priest was qualified to ask God to remove the evil eye, as one stated, "Some women ask the Holy Spirit to come and help, and they don't have the right to ask this because of their sins."

Distribution of Beliefs and Practices

The majority of the total sample interviewed were knowledgeable about beliefs and practices surrounding the *matiasma*. These beliefs and practices have just been described as they are known in the Columbus Greek population. However, quantitative data are crucial for ascertaining the distribution of these beliefs and practices.

Data were collected from 328 individuals in the Columbus Greek population. The demographic characteristics of this population are presented in Table 12-1. Following the demographic pattern in the greater Columbus population, Generation I was represented by most subjects, followed in order by Generations II, III, and IV. The slight preponderance of males in all generations accurately reflects the larger numbers of males in the entire Greek Columbus population (Tripp-Reimer, 1980).

As expected in an immigrant population, the earlier generations comprise generally older subjects. The mean age for Generation I was 64.9 years (range, 21–93); for Generation II, 43.7 years (range, 16–75); for Generation III, 26.9 years (range, 16–54); and for Generation IV, 22.6 years (range, 16–29).

To determine the distribution of beliefs and practice of *matiasma* in the Columbus Greek population, two hypotheses were tested. The first, "There is no difference between males and females in the retention of beliefs and practices concerning *matiasma*" was tested using $X^2 = .81096$; df = 3).

Table 2-2 depicts the retention of folk beliefs and practices concerning *matiasma* over four generations of immigrants. As hypothesized, there was a positive correlation between generation of immigration and retention of these folk medical beliefs and practices.

From inspection of the table, it is apparent that the more recent the generation of the subject, the less likely the subject was to retain *matiasma* knowledge and practice. The second hypothesis, "There is a positive correlation between members' generation of immigration and retention of beliefs and practices concerning *matiasma*" (H2), was tested. These data were subjected to Kendall's Tau (B) test, resulting in a corre-

Table 12-1   *Demographic Characteristics of Greek Immigrant Subjects*

Generation	n	Male	Female	Mean Age (years)
Generation I	143	79	64	64.9
Generation II	111	58	53	43.7
Generation III	52	32	20	26.9
Generation IV	22	12	10	22.6
	328	181	147	

Table 12-2 *Knowledge and Use of* **Matiasma** *Among Four Generations of Urban Greek Immigrants*

| Knowledge and Use | Generation of Immigration | | | |
	I	II	III	IV
I. Knew and practiced	124	35	5	0
II. Did not practice; knew details of at least two (prevention, detection, cure)	12	50	27	4
III. Did not practice; knew details of only one (prevention, detection, cure)	7	98	9	6
IV. Did not practice; did not know	0	7	11	12
	n = 143	n = 111	n = 52	n = 22
			TOTAL	n = 328

lation of +0.61. This correlation is significant (α = .05) and indicates a strong association between the individual's generation and retention of traditional healing beliefs and practices. This pattern is further clarified in Table 12-3.

In Generation I, the majority (86.7%) both knew and had used practices concerning the evil eye. In Generation II, only about one third (31.5%) knew and used these practices. By Generation IV, no subject reported knowing and using practices the evil eye. Correspondingly, no individual in Generation I lacked knowledge of the evil eye. This was true of less than one tenth of Generation II, and about one fifth of Generation III. However, the majority (54.5%) of Generation IV were not knowledgeable about beliefs and practices surrounding the evil eye.

DISCUSSION

Nursing's claim as a holistic discipline mandates inclusion of the cultural dimension, for as Clark (1978, p. vii) points out, "Ignorance of cultural differences can indeed pose serious problems in diagnosis and treatment, for without such knowledge we will alienate the individual and run the risk of making recommendations which will be ignored. Only if the cultural dimensions are considered, can we claim that we are practicing holistic or comprehensive health care."

Table 12-3 *Proportion of Each Generation Knowing and Practicing* **Matiasma**

Generation	Practicing	Knowledgeable
Generation I	87.4%	100%
Generation II	31.4%	93.7%
Generation III	7.8%	79.4%
Generation IV	0	45.5%

The combination of a rapidly expanding interest in health anthropology with a heightened concern for American minority groups has resulted in a profusion of studies reporting extant American folk health practices. A problem resulting from this increase has been the sometimes indiscriminant characterization of minority populations as traditionalists. That is, all members of a cultural group are portrayed as maintaining traditional ethnic values, beliefs, and customs. Patterson (1979) contends that this literature suggests a continuing ethnicity among the groups in question, although considerable data indicate the contrary. A decade ago, Ragucci (1972) pointed out that most comparative studies dealing with traditional ethnic responses to illness disregard or minimize the differences which may be present between generations. She indicated that valid generalizations concerning cultural differences and their persistence require an adequate sampling of at least three generations (with the immigrant group as the first or baseline).

Some nurse researchers have been the sometimes indiscriminate characterization of all members of minority populations as traditionalists, with subcultural groups portrayed as maintaining traditional ethnic values and beliefs.

Since consideration of traditional beliefs and practices is essential in delivering effective nursing care to multiethnic clients, the first step in planning health care for minority or subcultural groups is the identification of traditional (folk) beliefs held by members of the specific group. The second step is the assessment of the extent of practice of these folk traditions. Then, on the basis of data gathered in the first two steps, the researcher may anticipate which individuals are most likely to use traditional folk practices prior to or in conjunction with scientific (Western) health care practices.

This paper has presented the ethnomedical beliefs and practices of Greek immigrants surrounding the *matiasma*. It has also demonstrated the importance of the second step (determining the distribution pattern of these folk practices). While it is crucial to be sensitive to cultural beliefs and practices, it is just as essential not to overgeneralize and assume that all members of the subculture hold to a particular belief or practice. This paper proposes that the cultural background can serve only as a cue to the health professional. To make appropriate assessments and plan appropriate interventions, the nurse must also have additional information regarding the distribution pattern of these beliefs and behaviors in the client population.

This study in addition to showing the importance of not assuming that traditional health behaviors will be retained in individuals with high ethnic affiliation, also demonstrates the importance of combining quantitative with qualitative data sets for full understanding of the situation with multiethnic clients.

Viewing the Columbus Greek community as a statistical whole, we found that while orthodox medicine is well practiced by this population, the Greek community has also retained traditional folk healing practices which differ dramatically from those of Western medicine. One of these *(matiasma)* is particularly notable. However, when the Greek community is divided into four generational cohorts, distinct differences appear among the generations in the retention of folk medical beliefs and practices.

As health practitioners, the researcher must be careful not to overgeneralize ethnographic data. Knowing that a majority of members of the Greek-American community know and practice *matiasma* does not indicate that this behavior can be expected in all members. In this particular population, the individual's generation of immigration was highly predictive of both knowledge and use of ethnomedicine.

For those Greek community members who retain *matiasma* practices, there are a number of implications for clinical nursing. Zola (1972) estimates that 70 to 90 per cent of all self-recognized episodes of sickness are managed exclusively outside formal health care systems. This is particularly true when the episode is a folk illness. Greeks generally do not seek professional health care for diagnosis or treatment of *matiasma*.

However, nurses in a variety of care settings may encounter clients who hold to a parallel folk system prior to, or in conjunction with, use of scientific health care services. For example, nurses in a newborn nursery or pediatrics unit may encounter parents who wish to keep a protective blue stone or *phylacto* on their child throughout hospitalization. School nurses may also encounter these protective charms in young (grade school) children. Mental health nurses and others in counseling should also be aware that belief in evil eye need not indicate paranoia. *Matiasma* is a culturally sanctioned belief system which does not, by itself, indicate pathology. Finally, when belief in *matiasma* is strongly held (as among many first- and second-generation immigrants) we need to understand that treatment by orthodox health care services may be delayed because of this parallel folk care system.

Limitations and Implications for Future Research

Probably the greatest limitation of this study is its lack of generalizability. That is, these data cannot be taken to be representative of ethnic groups in general, or even of Greek immigrant groups in the United States. Further, these results cannot be generalized to the retention of other ethnic practices, including even other folk health beliefs and practices among Greek immigrants in Columbus, Ohio. From these limitations, however, important implications for future research can be derived. This study suggests that the following research questions merit attention:

1. What is the distribution pattern of folk healing beliefs and practices in other ethnic groups?
2. How does the retention of this folk configuration (*matiasma*) compare with other Greek immigrant groups? In other Mediterranean groups?
3. What is the distribution pattern of other folk health beliefs and practices in the Columbus Greek population? Do they parallel the pattern for *matiasma*? Areas for investigation here may focus on other folk medical beliefs, such as use of herbal remedies (*praktika*), the practice of cupping (*vendousas*), or retention of ethnic foodways.

Another limitation of this study results from the differences in mean ages of the generational cohorts. The earlier generations (I and II) were considerably older than generations III and IV. This age discrepancy (typical of new immigrant populations) may introduce a confounding variable. Because children are considered particularly susceptible to the evil eye, it is possible that individuals do not learn or use practices surrounding the *matiasma* until they have their own children who become ill. Future research could follow these individuals after they have passed the child-bearing years. However, this could only be accomplished through longitudinal study, because only a few community members are currently of the fourth generation.

Other study questions that emerge from these results are the following:

1. What factors contribute to the retention of folk healing practices?
2. Does the retention of folk beliefs and practices influence the choice of seeking orthodox health care?

CONCLUSION

This study has delineated specific facets of the configuration surrounding the evil eye and has traced its retention over a four-generation period. It also demonstrates the importance of specifying the generation depth and controlling adequately for the generation variable.

Finally, this chapter indicates the importance of combining qualitative-ethnographic method with quantitative methodologies. This fusion results in rich and complementary data sets and ultimately gives a more complete picture than could be obtained using either method singly.

REFERENCES

Bruyn, S. *The human perspective in sociology: The methodology of participant observation.* Englewood Cliffs, N.J.: Prentice-Hall, 1966.

Clark, A. *Culture, childbearing and health professionals.* Philadelphia: F. A. Davis, 1978.

Clark, M. *Health in the Mexican American culture.* Los Angeles: University of California Press, 1970.

Fairchild, H. *Greek immigration to the United States.* New Haven: Yale University Press, 1922.

Murdock, G. *Outline of cultural materials.* New Haven, Conn.: Human Relations Area Files Press, 1971.

Patterson, G. J. A critique of the "new ethnicity." *American Anthropologist,* 1979, *81,* 103–105.

Polites, M. Greek Americans. In F. Brown & J. Roucek (Eds.), *One America.* New York: Prentice-Hall, 1945.

Ragucci, A. The ethnographic approach and nursing research. *Nursing Research,* 1972, *21,* 485–490.

Saloutos, T. *The Greeks in the United States.* Cambridge: Harvard University Press, 1964.

Saloutos, T. Greeks. In S. Thernstrom (Ed.), *Harvard Encyclopedia of American Ethnic Groups.* Cambridge: Harvard University Press, 1980.

Stern, P. Grounded theory methodology: its uses and processes. *Image,* 1980, *12*:20–23.

Tripp-Reimer, T. Genetic demography of an urban Greek immigrant community. *Human Biology,* 1980, *52,* 255–267.

Xenides, J. *The Greeks in America.* New York: George H. Doran, 1922.

Zola, I. Studying the decision to see a doctor. In Z. Lipowski (Ed.), *Advances in psychosomatic medicine.* Basel: S. Karger, 1972.

13

Southern Rural Black and White American Lifeways With Focus on Care and Health Phenomena

Madeleine Leininger

"If the bottom of your foot itches, you will walk on strange land"; "Crowing hens will bring bad luck"; "You will have good luck if you throw a penny out the car window when passing a cemetery"; "Haste makes waste"; "Time and tide wait for no one"; "Beauty is only skin-deep—ugly goes to the bones"; "Aging can be beautiful and something to enjoy"; "If you care for people, you like this friendly place."

These folk statements provided the researcher with several clues about a different culture, namely, the southern rural Afro- and Anglo-American culture in the deep South. The author gradually discovered that if one cares for people, one will indeed like this friendly community in the South.

As a nurse-researcher interested in the systematic study and documentation of care and health values, beliefs, and attitudes of cultural groups, the author developed many new insights into the rural Afro-Americans (Blacks*) and Anglo-Americans

---

Reprinted from Leininger, M. *Care: The essence of nursing and health.* Thorofare, N. J.: Charles B. Slack, 1984, pp. 133–160. With permission.

*Throughout the chapter the term "Black" will be used as a shorthand expression for Afro-Americans and "White" for Anglo-Americans or Caucasians. These terms are used with the realization of their general limitations.

QUALITATIVE RESEARCH METHODS IN NURSING
ISBN 0-8089-1676-9

(Whites) in south central Alabama. Their constructs of care, health, and ethnonursing practices were discovered.

The purpose of this chapter is to present some of the research findings from the investigator's study of southern rural Black and White cultures, with a focus on care and health values, beliefs, and practices, as well as on the general lifeways of the people. A full research report is being prepared on the cultures. Only major themes and findings are reported here.

Besides studying the general lifeways of the people, the author investigated and analyzed several research questions in reference to her theory of the diversity and universality of transcultural care. (Leininger, 1978, 1985). Some of the major research questions under investigation were:

1. What *ethnohealth (emic)* values, beliefs, and practices can be identified with the people?
2. What *ethnocare (emic)* values, beliefs, and practices can be identified with the people?
3. What are the perceived differences and similarities between the rural folk and the urban professional health care practices?
4. What is the general lifeway of the Black and White villagers, especially related to care and health cultural expressions?
5. What are the implications for therapeutic ethnocaring and ethnonursing care practices, based upon the research findings?

In this chapter, these questions are addressed in a general manner, with recognition that much more could be presented about the villagers.

DEFINITION OF TERMS

1. *Care:* refers to those assistive, facilitative, and/or enabling decisions or acts that aid another individual(s), group, or community in a beneficial way (Leininger, 1981a).
2. *Health:* refers to beliefs, values, and action-patterns that are culturally known and are used to preserve and maintain personal or group well-being, and to perform daily role activities.
3. *Emic:* refers to the language expressions, perceptions, beliefs, and practices of individuals or groups of a particular culture in regard to certain phenomena.
4. *Etic:* refers to the *universal* language expressions, beliefs, and practices in regard to certain phenomena that pertain to several cultures or groups.
5. *Ethnocaring:* refers to the *emic* cognitive, assistive, facilitative, or enabling acts or decisions that are valued and practiced to help individuals, families, or groups (Leininger, 1978).
6. *Ethnohealth:* refers to those *emic* cognitive beliefs and actions used to preserve or maintain personal or group well-being, and to perform daily role activities.
7. *Ethnonursing:* refers to *emic* learned knowledge, values, and practices of caretakers used to provide assistive, facilitative, and/or enabling actions or discussions beneficial to care recipients.
8. *Cultural care accommodation:* refers to cognitive-assistive actions and decisions or to plans to facilitate client-specific care that take into account the cultural beliefs, values, and practices of the client(s).

9. *Cultural care preservation or maintenance:* refers to those deliberative-assistive or facilitative actions or decisions that take into account ways to preserve or maintain cultural values and lifeways viewed as beneficial to care recipients.

10. *Cultural care repatterning:* refers to those deliberate actions that are assistive or facilitative to the client(s) and that combine several different aspects of a client's beliefs, values, or practices in a meaningful or beneficial manner.

11. *New cultural care practices:* refers to the cognitive action of incorporating different or new assistive or facilitative actions designed to be beneficial to the client.

THEORETIC AND CONCEPTUAL FRAMEWORK

The theory of "transcultural diversity and universality of care" and health was used for this study to describe, explain, and predict the lifeways of the southern villagers (Leininger, 1985). Essentially, the theorist holds that care and health differ with cultural cognitions, values, and practices among cultures, with some identifiable universal features. Social structure features (i.e., religion, kinship, economic, and cultural values) are closely related to health and care values and practices, and they influence or account for health care differences and similarities.

Culturally meaningful and efficacious nursing care is contingent upon the use of culturally derived ethnographic data on health and care. Ethnonursing is a culturally cognitive approach designed to be assistive and facilitative to individuals, families, and cultural groups in order to provide care that is *congruent* with clients' values, norms, and practices (Leininger, 1985). Ethnographic, ethnologic, and ethnonursing data on cultures provide the bases for facts and principles of ethnonursing care practices. There are three major types of ethnonursing care and actions in therapeutic health practices: (1) care accommodations; (2) care preservation and/or maintenance; and (3) care repatterning. (See abovementioned definitions.) The theoretic and conceptual model that depicts these transcultural dimensions is found in Figure 13-1—the Leininger Sunrise Model—and has been discussed in other publications (Leininger, 1978, 1981b). Other transcultural nursing care concepts, facts, and principles are available in other of the author's works.

Some major theoretic premises related to transcultural nursing theory are as follows:

1. Culturally based care values, beliefs, and practices are essential to human growth, living, and survival.

2. Care is the essence and the central, dominant, and unifying focus of nursing.

3. Health values, beliefs, and practices are derived from the culture, and vary between and within cultures.

4. Health and care concepts are identifiable by cultural groups and are linked together by cultural values and action patterns.

5. Features of social structure are powerful forces influencing health and care in any culture.

6. Folk *(emic)* and professional *(etic)* care and health values and action patterns are identifiable in a given culture.

7. Ethnocaring and ethnohealth concepts are essential for therapeutic ethnonursing care practices.

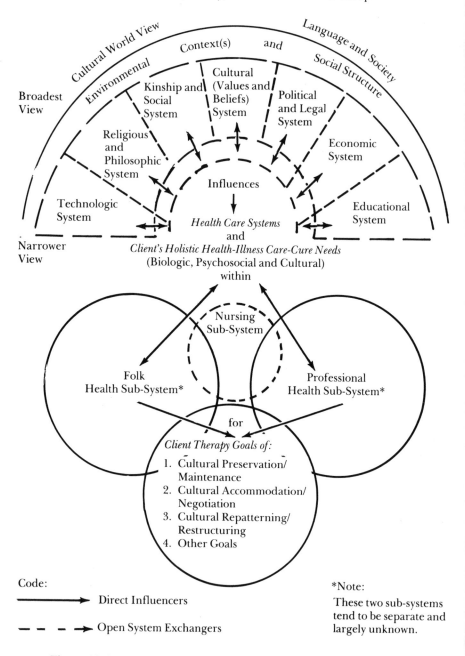

Figure 13-1. Leininger's "Sunrise" Conceptual Model For Culturologic Interviews, Assessments, and Therapy Goals

8. Care accommodations, preservation or maintenance of health, and repatterning are creative modes of providing ethnonursing care to achieve therapeutic outcomes, and are mainly based upon *emic* data of particular cultures.
9. Culture-specific and universal care practices can be identified and used as a sound basis for nursing care practices (Leininger, 1978, 1980).

The major hypotheses under consideration for this ethnonursing study are:

1. There is a close relationship between the social structure—including cultural values, practices, and beliefs—and ethnohealth and ethnocaring practices of cultural groups.
2. Rural folk and urban professional care practices reflect differences among people due to value differences regarding care and health.
3. The greater the differences between rural folk and urban professional care practices, the greater the need for nursing care accommodations and repatterning.
4. Therapeutic ethnonursing care is dependent upon the cognitive use of ethnocare and ethnohealth concepts, and ethnographic data (Leininger, 1980).

REVIEW OF THE LITERATURE

A review of the literature revealed that this was the first investigation focused on ethnocaring and ethnohealth lifeways of southern rural Afro-Americans (Blacks) and Anglo-Americans (Whites) in the United States. There are, however, many general reference books about the Black and White cultures from historic and contemporary perspectives. Billingsley's book (1968), *Black Families in White America*, provides information about the interrelationships between Black and White families. Lerner's work (1970), *Black Women in White America: A Documentary History*, is another source of valuable data about Black women's lifeways and some of the social structures and historic factors influencing their lives (1970). Another publication that offers valuable cultural insights into Afro-American families is Stack's work (1980), entitled *All Our Kin: Strategies and Survival in a Black Community.*

Most recently, Kennedy's anthropologic research investigation, entitled *You Gotta Deal With It*, has provided a vivid description of many of the social, political, economic, and environmental factors influencing the health and illness status of southern Black Americans. Kennedy cogently describes Black-White relationships influencing the general welfare and well-being of the people. The ethnographic findings are invaluable in grasping the Black-White cultural relationships in one area in the South.

Another study that focuses indirectly on ethnocaring and ethnohealth in the rural southern community is a work entitled *Becoming a Woman in Rural Black Culture* (Dougherty, 1978). This investigation, completed in 1977, provides rich ethnographic and ethnologic data about adolescent maturation and the day-to-day lifeways of young Black women. The relationship between social structure and the process of becoming a woman is well presented. The study, however, does not focus on care and health, even though the author is a nurse and an anthropologist.

Although a number of other studies might be cited about the Black and White cultures, none pertains directly to the phenomena of care and health in the southern rural Black-White communities, or to the rural folk and the urban professional health beliefs and practices.

RESEARCH DESIGN AND METHOD

The research was designed as an ethnographic, ethnologic, and ethnonursing study to describe and explain the health and care lifeways of a rural community in the southern United States. The design was for a 10-month field study of Afro-American (Black) and Anglo-American (White) villagers. In-depth interviews, participant-observations (with structured and unstructured interviews), life histories, daily living accounts, health care assessments, photographs, drawings, and other anthropologic and ethnonursing care methods and field techniques were used to study one community in an intensive manner. Qualitative and quantitative research methods were used as corroborative means to discover, describe, and validate the lifeways of the villagers. In the second village, a cursory study was done to obtain reflective comparative data to determine the "typical" aspects of the main community being studied. The ethnonursing and anthropologic research methods used in this study have been described in other literature sources and are not discussed here (Leininger, unpublished data, 1981c; Pelto, 1970; Spradley, 1979, 1980).

VILLAGE DESCRIPTIONS AND SAMPLE

Two villages were chosen for the study. One village was chosen for an in-depth study and analysis, and is referred to by the fictive name of the Friendly Village. A second village was chosen to provide a *reflective comparison* with the Friendly Village to determine if the latter was highly unique. The second village was called Pecan Village. Friendly Village is the focus of this report, since it was the principal village studied intensively for approximately 10 months. Pecan Village is referred to occasionally for contrast. The researcher made regular visits to Pecan Village, but no in-depth ethnographic and ethnonursing study was done.

Both villages met the following criteria: (1) a southern village in a rural southwest central part of Alabama; (2) a small rural farm and town community linked to a moderately sized city (over 25,000 and under 50,000) within a 20- to 30-mile area, (3) a village with Afro-American (Black) and Anglo-American (White) people living together; and (4) a village perceived to be a typical rural southern village by indigenous people of the geographic area.

Friendly Village: The Major Research Focus

Friendly Village was a small town of approximately 2500 people located in south central Alabama. It was a town-farm community with about 300 people living in a 10-mile radius of the town. Most villagers saw the town and farms as contiguous. Approximately 60% of the villagers were Black (Afro-Americans) and 40% were White (Anglo-Americans)—approximately 1500 Blacks and 1000 Whites.

Historically, the town was established in the mid-nineteenth century by an interested White businessman. The town has always been dependent upon the rural crops, wood pulp, and small business enterprises. During the nineteenth century, cotton was the major crop until the boll weevil destroyed the plants. Today, peanut growing is the principal livelihood, along with the wood pulp industry and small businesses.

There are two schools: an elementary and a high school. There are two banks, 22 small stores, a police station, a small library, a fire and rescue station, approximately six gas stations, several auto repair shops, and about nine churches in the town and rural community. Unquestionably, the nine churches (two White-Baptist, two Presbyterian, and five Black-Baptist) were of central importance to the villagers. There is no hospital and only a small clinic, with one physician providing all professional health services. Three mortuaries (two used primarily for White people, and one for the Black villagers) and a home for the elderly are located in the village.

Black and White people tend to live in different geographic areas in the town, and they are interspersed in the rural community. Black and White villagers attend separate churches. The small businesses on the main street are mainly operated by White businessmen and women with assistance from Black villagers. The schools in the town are integrated; however, some White parents send their children to a nearby all-White urban School. Both Black and White people participate in business affairs and selected political, social, and religious activities.

In regard to economics, the yearly income for the average Black family (or household) was estimated by key informants (and from other data sources) to be approximately $5000-$7000 per year. There was great variability in Black and White incomes, in that 30% of the Black families and 5% of the White families had incomes of less than $5000 per year. There were no Black families known to have an income of more than $20,000 per year. Some White widows in the village were said to be both "wealthy and generous." The wide range of differences in family or household income made the lifeways of the people different, but cultural values seemed to play an even more significant role. Political, kinship, and religious aspects were major forces affecting the villagers' lives.

Sociocultural activities for White and Black villagers were largely influenced by religious beliefs and practices. Village activities that were initiated through the church seemed to be more acceptable and valued than nonchurch-based activities. Religious values were evident in business and social affairs. Many lifecycle ceremonial activities such as marriages, births, funerals, and teenage events reflected the sociocultural rhythm and daily patterning of the villagers' lives.

Pecan Village: A Reflective Contrast

Pecan Village, a reflective contrast, is a town-farm community with a population of 3000 people located in south central Alabama.

The Black to White population ratio in Pecan Village was similar to that of Friendly Village, ie, 60:40. Blacks and Whites lived in different geographic locations in the town and country, similar to Friendly Village.

Pecan Villagers mainly depend upon raising pecans, peanuts, and small grain crops. Wood pulp, general farm equipment, and several small-town commercial enterprises were other livelihoods. There were approximately 12 Baptist and Presbyterian churches in the town and rural community—again similar to the Friendly Village in that they had nonintegrated church practices.

This village had a wide main street with several small clothing, grocery, drug, and appliance stores. The farm equipment and auto repair shops, along with the gas stations, were slightly greater in number than in the Friendly Village. Other businesses and community service shops found in Pecan Village were also found in the Friendly Village.

Religious activities were a dominant activity in Pecan Village, and were closely linked to social, economic, and political affairs—all features similar to the Friendly Village. The village's political council meetings with a mayor were held regularly. Church weddings were frequently held on weekends in the churches.

In general, the Pecan Villagers did not seem quite as friendly and ready to meet and accept strangers as the researcher found initially in the Friendly Village. Pecan and Friendly Villages had essentially the same social structure, and they knew the systems by which they functioned. Religious, kinship, and social aspects were slightly different in cultural expression and history, but the cultural values were similar.

Interestingly, both villages felt that they had a unique cultural history that made them different from other nearby rural and urban communities. However, the researcher found similar historic and migration patterns in the two villages. Slightly different lifestyles were identified, but common behavior patterns prevailed. When the researcher asked: "Do you have ways similar to or different from X village?" these statements were heard from the Friendly Villagers, who knew or had heard about Pecan Village: "They are not as friendly as our folks. We care for our people in lots more ways than they do. We raise more peanuts, fruits, and vegetables than they do and really care for each other around here." The Pecan Villagers said: "We have always been a friendly place. We raise more pecans, do more farming, and go to the 'big city' more than those folks."

Pecan Village was proud to have a 50-bed hospital serving the community, with approximately 22 nurses and 10 regular physicians. In addition, there was a 45-bed nursing home with adequate staffing.

As for location, Friendly Village was 10 miles from the nearby city with 30,000 people; Pecan Village was about 32 miles from this city. The villagers seldom interact with one another, and there is limited economic and social exchange. They know of each other only in name and in limited ways.

INFORMANT SELECTION

During the 10 months that the researcher interacted with many of the Friendly Villagers, she also met with a small number of the people in the Pecan Village. The researcher interviewed approximately 90 Friendly Villagers and selected 60 for in-depth study. The telephone directory was used to select every tenth villager for in-depth observations, interviews, and other research data. Two villagers informed the author whether the ones she had selected were Black or White so that she could get a 50% sample of the two cultural groups. The selection criteria for the Friendly Village were:

1.   Adults and children who had lived in the village three years.
2.   Southern Afro-Americans (Blacks) and Anglo-Americans (Whites).
3.   Male or female villagers (approximately 50% of each).
4.   Members of a family living in the community.

For the Pecan Village, the researcher did not use a random sample; instead, spontaneous "walk-up-to" or casual visits were made randomly. The researcher visited Pecan Village approximately three times each month for comparative reasons.

The researcher had no prior knowledge of either village, and there were no known formal anthropologic or ethnographic studies done in Friendly or Pecan Villages prior to this time.

ENTRY TO AND RESEARCH IN FRIENDLY VILLAGE

The researcher drove into Friendly Village and parked on a side street. Then she walked around to meet and visit with the people. As she drove into the village, she saw beautiful rolling hills, many forested areas, several small lakes, and plots of farmland. In one part of the village, there were painted and attractive large homes with well-kept yards. (She later found that these belong to Whites.) There were also unpainted, very small homes with fairly clean yards that belonged to the Blacks and poor Whites in the village. On one side of town, there were only a few White people seen working outside their homes, and very few children playing in the yards. In contrast, there were many children playing in the streets and yards where the Black people lived. During the day, about 10 to 20 people were usually found visiting or watching for someone, or both. Cars were driven down the highway or street in a slow and orderly way. Seldom were there teenage racers on the main or side streets.

A nursing student who attended the urban university about 10 miles away had recently moved into the Friendly Village with her husband and family. She suggested that the researcher might want to visit with a few persons who were leaders of the community. Among these persons was a man who was a leader of the Town Rescue Squad in Friendly Village. The researcher walked to his place of business and identified herself as a nurse and anthropologist who was interested in learning about the lifeways of this village, and especially how he thought the people kept well and prevented illnesses. She indicated to him (and others she met later) that she would like to visit and study the people during the next 10 months. He responded in a friendly way and said: "I think it would be good to study the villagers, since there has never been a study here." He then suggested other informants the researcher might visit to tell her about the people and their lifeways. He invited her back for a visit "any time."

From that initial visit and entry into the Friendly community, the author began to interact, observe, and participate in the community. Unfortunately, these rich experiences cannot be presented here, but will be reported later in another publication. In general, the ethnography and study of the people went well, with no major or serious problems. The author's previous studies of four other cultures enabled her to use her ethnographic and ethnonursing skills favorably, with considerable confidence and sensitivity to the people.

GENERAL REPORT OF FINDINGS

In this next section are reported some of the major findings and themes derived from study of the Friendly Village. The findings are of necessity briefly reported in relation to the research questions posed for this study.

Ethnohealth Findings

What ethnohealth (emic) values, beliefs, and practices can be identified with the people?

From the unstructured and structured ethnonursing interview guide, direct observations, and participatory experiences, several ethnohealth themes, values, beliefs, and practices were identified and discussed with the villagers.

1. Health had similar meanings for the Black and White villagers in that both viewed health as being "able to be up and around the place and able to do what is expected of you—that is, your business, garden, and house or job duties." This was manifested in their daily life practices by the "healthy man, woman, and child being able to work." The ability to be active in one's church activities was most important, and was most talked about in their daily work. The dominant theme abstracted from both Black and White villagers was the concept that *health means being able to do your work in the home, church, and community.* The villagers said that to be healthy, "one had to think about one's neighbors and friends and how one cared for or helped them." The criterion of being able to be *active* and to carry forth one's daily activities or role functions was stressed as being a desired value and norm of the villagers. For Blacks, the daily activities were mainly work in the garden and fields, and church activities. For Whites, being able to conduct one's daily business affairs at the store or on the farm was a determining factor of whether one was healthy. Hence, health was an objective reality, a practice, and of high value to the people, varying in degrees between Black and White villagers.

2. The *second* dominant meaning associated with health was *to live by the Bible and do what Jesus (or God) teaches."* Ninety-two percent of the White and Black villagers would say: "If you follow what is in the Bible, you will be well and stay well." Practically all Black adults older than age 40 held firmly to the idea that religious beliefs and action patterns keep you well (98%). Many examples from the Bible were cited by Black villagers to substantiate that health and religion are tightly linked together, and that one cannot speak of health without considering the idea of spiritual health as a total way of living and acting. Black elderly people would say: "The Bible teaches you how to keep well and avoid evil thoughts and actions that could make you ill." One elderly man (age 93) said: "I don't think a lot of White (nonvillage) people understand health and the Bible. If they did, they wouldn't be running into that hospital (referring to the nearby city) for their children and themselves. One has to let Jesus be the healer. I have always let Jesus heal me when I get upset. I have never spent a day in the hospital, nor will I go there. Jesus can heal and keep you healthy. People who are not working with Jesus have to use other people to heal them." (This man was physically very healthy.)

   The majority of the White villagers (85%) felt that religion was essential to remain well and "have presence." Many White Baptist and Presbyterian active church attendees frequently replied to the investigator's question "What makes you healthy?" with this reply: "I believe God keeps me well if I listen and pray to him. He knows how to get me well and keep us healthy in this community. I know this to be true." An older White woman (about age 91) said: "I rely on my friend or Jesus to keep me well. I have never been in the hospital. I read about those places." At church services, both Black and White villagers would often identify a list of 20 to 30 parishioners who needed Jesus (or God) to make them well. They would state each name and actively pray for keeping them well or for recovery from illness. White folks used the word "God" more frequently than "Jesus"; whereas the Blacks always used the word "Jesus" and the expression "Jesus heals and saves us—and always has."

Nearly 98% of all Black villagers belonged to the Southern Baptist fundamental religion. Adults and small children were regular church attendees; however, some of the young male teenagers (ages 14 to 30) did not always attend church on Sunday. Several told me that they "had work to do and Jesus did not do everything." Most White villagers (72%) attended the Southern Baptist churches, and the others attended the Baptist and Presbyterian churches. Salvation was with God or Jesus through *fellowship with others,* and by living together in the community in a concerned (caring) way. Doing what is right and avoiding evil can keep one healthy and well. These were themes from the White villagers.

The values of health, wellness, healing, and religion were inextricably linked together for both Black and White villagers. The concept of concern for others and self was often expressed as a healthy act, as well as visiting others when they were ill. While the villagers recognized sickness, it was more of a deviation from health (as described previously) and was not an isolated concept. *Sickness* meant the lack of a fully healthy person—a *wholeness* concept in fulfilling one's role and involvement expectations with others, i.e., with families, individuals, community groups, and strangers.

3.   The *third* idea associated with health was the means to *preserve* it: eating foods grown in one's own garden or raising foods that were viewed as good for them. They did not like to eat foods contaminated "by commercial solutions that the big city folks made, and put in tin cans." Many Black women and men proudly showed their canned (glass) food goods. Foods such as collards, peas (of 10 varieties), and turnips were particularly viewed as healthy for the Black villagers; whereas the White villagers saw lettuce, tomatoes, carrots, onions, sweet peas, and potatoes as *preserving* one's health. The concept of health preservation was linked with the caring value of concern. The villagers believed that if you are concerned about *others* (first) and then yourself (second), you will *preserve* good community health and your own health. The concept of focusing on others for self and community health was interesting.

Other concepts associated with health and the absence of health were expressed in response to this question: "What do you believe is unhealthy or not related to a good healthy lifeway?" The majority (94%) of responses were these: (1) "You are not being concerned about others" (Black or White villagers); (2) "You are not doing your work or job to keep healthy"; (3) "You are not understanding what Jesus tells us, and listening to and praying to Jesus, as he can make us well"; and (4) "You are unwilling to 'pitch in' and work or help others in this community."

ETHNOCARING FINDINGS

Turning to the villagers' responses to the question, "What ethnocare *(emic)* values, beliefs, and practices are identifiable with the people?", the following themes were revealed (Table 13-1). The villagers' responses were obtained by use of open-ended

Table 13-1   *Comparison of Care Meanings and Actions Among Black and White Friendly Villagers (60 Participants)*

Black Villagers	Percentage	White Villagers	Percentage
1. *Concern for Others as Caring* (A) Providing for own "brothers" and "sisters'" needs; (B) Being aware of others' needs; (C) Helping others to receive.	90	1. *Concern for Others as Caring* (Some self-care expressed) (A) Being aware of "friends" needs; (B) Providing for "friends" and self's needs; (C) Help/aiding others as a Christian	93
2. *Presence as Caring* (A) "Being there" in need; (B) Being around the place or seen.	94	2. *Presence as Caring* (A) "Being seen around" here; (B) Being around village, church, job.	89
3. *Involvement as Caring* (A) Participate in family and neighborhood affairs; (B) Concern about one's "brother" or "sister."	76	3. *Involvement as Caring* (A) Participate in community affairs; (B) Talk and know happenings; (C) Participate in "fellowship" church activities.	92
4. *Touching One's Own "Brother"* (A) In time of sorrow and losses; (B) To know reality as it is; (C) To elicit true family feelings.	97	4. *Selective Touching as Caring* (A) On special occasions; (B) As act of affection or to help others.	48
5. *Sharing as Caring* (A) Sharing food among family; (B) Sharing through religious experiences; (C) Sharing to survive; (D) Sharing as a family responsibility.	89	5. *Sharing as Caring* (A) Sharing food, goods, information, and money with others; (B) Sharing through religious fellowship activities; (C) Sharing social and religious experiences.	92
6. *Caring with Sex Role Differences* (A) Mother as main caregiver and provider in home; (B) Father as providing care through external resources; (C) Religion ascribes sex roles and care practices.	76	6. *Caring with Sex Role Differences* (A) Mother as child caregiver; (B) Father as "material goods" provider; (C) Religion ascribes sex role differences.	84

questions such as: (1) Tell me about your ideas of daily care; (2) Describe a caring person; (3) What does care mean to you and the people? and (4) What ideas seem most important about care?

The responses from 60 participants obtained through several in-depth interviews and recurrent sequenced daily observations by the investigator in the village are presented in Table 13-1. The comparative qualitative and quantitative data on the ethnocare values and meanings clearly show the domains of similarities and differences between the village cultural groups. Of interest is the fact that the *emic* care values could be identified and described by the villagers once this area of inquiry was made known to them. Hence, *cognitions of care were identifiable and could be explained by the people.* Some of the domains of similarities and differences in care are discussed next with their meanings and beliefs.

First, care meant *concern for others* for the Black (90%) and for the White villagers (93%). Both saw concern for others as most important, but some White villagers would also include concern for self. Repeatedly the Black and White villagers said: "We have always been concerned for one another since we first came here over one hundred years ago." "Concern" translated to the villagers as being interested in others and being helpful to people in the community. One woman villager (age 32) had gone to live in California and returned to visit her family. When I asked her about similarities and differences in living and health maintaining, she quickly replied: "Oh, it is so good to be back home in this community. These folks really care for you and are concerned about you. In California, they don't care one bit for you and everyone is for themselves. I also miss these Friendly Villagers. Here, everyone is concerned about each other and helps one another." A Black woman in the group said, "I have always lived here and I'm fixin' not to leave. We folks know how to care for one another. I depend on the White folks and they depend on me. If I needed help, I would go to my close Black and White friends, and they would help me." Many Black women and men made similar statements. Concern was also expressed by 90% of Black villagers in these ideas: Concern means (1) being aware of friend or community needs; (2) providing for one's own "brothers" and "sisters" in a religious and cultural way in order to help them survive; and (3) helping others who need care to accept and receive it. With respect to the latter, several Black villagers told the investigator that it is difficult for some Whites to receive care (or help because of their pride. The Blacks said that they teach their families how to receive care in order to survive.

The White villagers spoke about concern for others in a way similar to the Black villagers; however, subtle differences from the Blacks existed. For Whites, care means concern for others, especially as Christian friends and friends in need. They explained that care is a human need, for often there are limited human and material resources, and one must care for friends. Other ideas associated with care and validated by practice were: (1) Providing *direct* help to "friends" in need under stressful conditions when they are helpless or feel helpless (note that White villagers use the term "friend," which is different from the more common Black term of "brother" or "sister"); (2) being helpful toward others as an expectation of Christian fellowship; and (3) showing concern by getting actively *involved* in assistance for others in need.

Interestingly, both Blacks and Whites view care as an *activity* and a *necessity* for health. Care as healthy concern is closely linked with being active and helping others. The idea of "watching out for" or "pitching in" to help someone in need was frequently stated by the Black and White villagers. Historically, the villagers gave many examples of the Blacks helping the Whites with their work for many decades on the farms and in town. Reciprocally, the Whites said that they often helped the Blacks with money, food, equipment, and so forth. Both types of villagers are afraid, with forced integration and outside influences, that this reciprocal helping process, value, and lifeway between Blacks and Whites will be lost. They firmly stated that "we knew how to care for each other as a decent White family and Black individual or family" through the years.

Through ethnoscientific analysis, other differences regarding care were identified. Care for the Black villagers was unequivocally related to survival, whereas the Whites saw care as preservation and as always being attentive to friends' or others' needs or losses. Furthermore, for the White Baptists, care was a "Christian act" (ethical) that should be valued and continued.

Two White bank managers (who have been in the villages many years) spoke about care as concern for others. They said that they always cared for Blacks by lending them money or credit in times of need. They knew Black families, and trusted and worked with them. For nonvillagers, it was much more difficult to get quick bank credit or money unless they were linked to the Church through family or friends. Anticipating needs of Black or White villagers was important and a desired cultural value to be preserved. Exploitation between Blacks and Whites was denied when this topic was pursued.

The *second* major ethnocare concept identified through ethnographic study was *presence* as *caring*. Both the Black (94%) and White (89%) villagers in the Friendly town and farms identified presence as caring. The people defined *presence* as *making a direct personal appearance or remaining with another villager as a sign of care*. Several villagers said: "If you care for others you will be with them. You will come and see others in person. You will show your concern by your presence. This means a lot to us." One Black man said: "If you are concerned and care for people, you come around here. We see them. They know they can get help from us—and we help them. If they don't come, then we aren't caring—we can't do too well without their being here."

Presence was more important for the Black than the White villagers. Presence is validated by "seeing you at church, seeing you at business, seeing you at the home place," said Black women. Many Black teenagers and grown adults held that being present at the annual church homecoming is extremely important to being a caring family and church. Hence, presence at the Annual Baptist Homecoming was imperative and a test of *presence as caring*. Black villagers save money and make great sacrifices to come home each year for this church and family homecoming. The Blacks repeatedly said that when there's sickness or death, it is important that a family member *be present*. Then one is a caring and concerned person.

For the White Friendly Villagers, *presence as caring means "being seen around" the home and community or at one's place of work*. It also means "being around" so villagers can see that one is all right or needs help. One cares for and prevents illness problems. Presence at church social gatherings or fellowship nights is an important means of validating presence as caring. As several villagers said: "If you are not present at these church meetings, or not seen around, we are concerned." Presence for Black and White villagers was an extremely important component of care, with ethnical implications for Black families, and socioreligious expectations for White villagers.

The *third* dominant ethnocaring component of the Friendly Village was *involvement as caring*. Seventy-six percent of the Black villagers and 92% of the White villagers held that involvement was important to caring. For the Black villagers, involvement meant *participating directly in activities to assist others*. The major indicators that validated involvement as caring were: (1) participating in Black extended-family affairs for a variety of reasons, i.e., getting food, clothing, or information, or doing general work activities for survival; (2) actively discussing affairs affecting one's Black "brother" or "sister"; and (3) using one's religious beliefs and kinship values to help Black and White people. Several detailed ideas about involvement were abstracted from the raw ethnographic and ethnologic data. This reflects the emphasis and the variety of ways that one can, and should, be involved as a Black villager.

Ninety-two percent of the White villagers identified involvement as caring and defined it fairly similarly to the Black villagers. There were, however, differences in the ways one becomes involved in the various kinds of activities. For example, ethnoscientific analysis of data revealed that these forms of involvement were important: (1) participating in community affairs; (2) being involved in different church and work activities; (3) participating as a caring person by talking about village happenings with others; and (4) being a Christian in its sense of involvement with others.

The *fourth* concept of caring was physical and psychosocial *touching*. Touch was culturally perceived and experienced as part of caring, but showed cultural variations among the villagers. Ninety-five percent of the Black villagers held that "touch" means placing one's hands on another person with different degrees of firmness or lightness depending on the occasion or need of the person. The form and variation of touch as body-to-body contact varied. Several Black villagers said: "We have always used touch to care for our 'brothers' and 'sisters,' in times of sadness and happiness." Touching to them was an important cultural expectation from birth through death. It was viewed as "a way of feeling and knowing how things really are. it is to let our family know that we are fully there in a real way." The researcher observed Black mothers stroking the newly born infant by rubbing the soles of the infant and touching every part of the body. The touching was done gently and with a smile on the mother's face. Black women and girls say they do much more touching of one another in crisis and noncrisis situations than do men and Whites. The researcher observed women and girls putting their arms around each other, rubbing arms, or engaging in spontaneous body (torso) embraces. Black people touch on joyous and sad occasions. They give upper-body hugs and firmly clasp hands on the death of a loved one or on a happy occasion. With the loss of homes, cars, or money, touching by a shoulder embrace was often seen in the Village. At funerals, the investigator witnessed much body touching, hand clutching, and mouth and cheek kissing. The dead person was touched at the mortuary and at the church services by Black family members and friends.

In marked contrast, White villagers did not touch one another as often as Blacks (only 18%). There were more cultural taboos about the unspoken "proper" time, place, and occasion to touch. Their touches were much less spontaneous, more formal, and more reserved. Occasionally, the researcher observed some handshakes between White adults, but only on special occasions or when they had not seen each other for a period of time. Strangers (nonvillager) usually offered their hand before the White villagers offered it. Handshakes as ritual greetings were acceptable on the streets, at the farm home, and at ceremonial events. Occasionally, kisses on the mouth and body embraces were observed among Whites, but they were much more reserved than among Blacks.

The amount of touching between Whites and Blacks was interesting in both the Friendly and the Pecan Villages. In the past, there was an unspoken cultural *taboo* for Blacks and Whites *not to kiss*, hug, or intimately touch one another except on vary rare occasions, and then it was not in public. Today, this cultural norm generally prevails, but not entirely, since some Black and White adults were observed to give hugs on a few occasions. Black informants said: "We just don't touch or give a handshake unless the White person offers his (her) hand first. While we feel close to some, we would like to touch them, but don't." One middle-aged Black said, "It will take time, but I hope it happens some day, as true brothers and sisters." Several villagers were pleased and surprised that the researcher "offered your hand so quickly and were not afraid to sit on our porches and in our houses." They continued, "Most Whites seem afraid to touch us and visit with us in our homes. They are good to talk with us in the banks, business, and their homes. We get along fine and respect each other, but don't touch much." White villagers did not seem aware of the value of touching Black villagers, but they were aware of the cultural norms.

Several older Black women who raised and cared for children expressed concern that "young girls do not spend as much time touching the infants as they did in the past." The Black women believe that "touching (stroking) the infant a lot, from birth until they can run about, is an important part of caring for the child. It helps them grow healthy." They added, "We want this good child care practice to continue into the future and are trying to teach them how to touch infants when they have children."

White nurses working in Pecan Village were aware that Blacks, while in the hospital, touch their infants and clients more often. The nurses said, "This was hard for us to do, as we White nurses have not seen that need in the past." Several said it was easier to touch the Black children than teenagers and adults. As the researcher explored the idea, the White nurses became more cognizant of touching Blacks and of their feelings about psychocultural and physical touching.

These ethnocaring components of concern, presence, involvement, and touch were discovered from direct observations and interviews. Differential features were noted in the ethnonursing and domain analysis. Several additional features were noted which appeared important between Whites and Blacks, and which were areas generally not heretofore documented and talked about by the villagers. Each care construct was extremely relevant to care and cure processes.

RURAL AND URBAN FOLK PROFESSIONAL
HEALTH CARE

With respect to the question, "What are the perceived differences and similarities between the rural folk and urban professional health care practices?" several findings became evident. They are briefly highlighted here. Rural folk and urban professional lifeways could be markedly contrasted by direct observation and through the viewpoints of the Black and White Friendly Villagers. Table 13-2 shows some of the major areas of comparative differences among the Friendly villagers as well as

Table 13-2 *Cognitive Differences Between Rural Folk and Urban Professional Health Care of the Friendly Villagers (60 Participants)*

Rural Folk Health Care Lifeways	Urban Professional Health Care Lifeways
1. The best and most secure lifeway (96% of both Black and White villagers).	1. A frightening experience with potential dangers and "evils" for rural folks (94% Black and White villagers).
2. A friendly and healthy way of living: (A) Friends and families care for each other; (B) Friends care for and heal each other.	2. Friendly in hospitals with: (A) A few family and friends; (B) No support and alone; (C) Confusing the further away from home.
3. Rural home remedies are helpful (Blacks 95%; Whites 56%).	3. White doctors spend all their time diagnosing and doing treatments of bones and body. Personnel do not see villagers as "whole persons" (Blacks 90%; Whites 62%).
4. Religion helps heal and is used in rural lifeway (95% of both Black and White Villagers).	4. Religion is limitedly practiced in the city.
5. Local caretakers and healers.	5. Strangers attempt to give care in ways strange to rural folks.
6. Know foods and activities that keep rural people well and healthy.	6. Urban people eat canned foods in tins, which are artificially preserved and not good for them.
7. Can get immediate care and help, if needed.	7. Have to sit for hours in hospital waiting room for help when really ill.
8. Cost is known, modest, and reasonable.	8. Cost of hospital services is very high.
9. Like to stay at home, and be with folks rather than with strangers in unknown and strange place.	9. Tend to get frightened when leaving the rural area. ("People unknown are impersonal and cold.")
10. Talk the same way and understand each other.	10. Talk different with lots of strange words and strange actions.
11. More signs of being well if live at home (rural) environment.	11. More signs of illness, crime, and social problems in the city.
12. Quiet and peaceful in rural area.	12. Noisy and dirty in the city.

their first-hand experience with the nearby urban community. Oral legends and folk tales also were heard concerning these differences.

1. The rural folk lifeway was viewed by 96% of the Black and White villagers as "the best and most secure lifeway." They saw the urban lifeway with health professionals as less desirable, and they feared going to the urban hospital because there were "potential dangers and evils." The rural villagers on the farm and in the town could quickly identify why they preferred staying in their own location. Several villagers had gone to moderate (over 25,000) and large cities (over 100,000), but they soon returned. More than 72% said they were very frightened while in these cities and got confused and disoriented. It was clear that the larger the city and the further away from home they went, the greater the tendency to become confused and disoriented. Several teenagers and adults (20 to 30 years of age) had "tried" going to large cities to visit relatives or friends, and told the researcher, "I am glad to be back home where it is safe and secure. Those people are not friendly like we are here. They don't trust anyone; they stare at you, take your money, and never say 'thank you.' "

   Several Black and White adult men and women of the village frequently mentioned many accounts and legends about going to a nearby urban hospital to get professional help. They said, "The further I got away from here, the more frightened I became. While the hospital staff is nice, you still are in a strange and frightening place. You are a number. They quickly get information and your money from you, but we don't know them." Another man said, "I signed more papers than I ever did my whole life—and I was confused the whole time I was there. Do tests show confusion as expected behavior?" Several were frightened as they were told to go from one place to another and to follow lines on the floor and signs. Several disliked waiting in the hallway for hours.

   Several Black villagers (of all ages and both sexes) were frightened by the urban experience, and said they hoped they would not become ill. It was too frightening to them because "those folks [urban doctors and nurses] don't know our talk and ways." They concluded, "It's best to stay at home and live with your aches, broken bones, or internals that don't work, rather than go to that strange place [hospital]." Most of the Black villagers older than 50 years said they preferred to have local women care for them, or to have care "from our own known physician in this town." The Black villagers use a number of local folk medications and healing practices that have long been used by the Black southern folk healers and carers—most of the care administered by mothers and grandmothers. Their practices are passed on through oral traditions and demonstrations to younger female adults. The use of kerosene for injuries and dermatitis and the use of a variety of local salves and massage treatments are common for Black folk carers and curers.

   Both the Black and White villagers are pleased with the local male physician. He is a native to the community and listens to the people, and he does not demean their local treatments. The researcher found the villagers (over 90%) thought of the White physician as helpful and one who could be trusted. The physician told the researcher, "They know what helps them, and some things tend to work, so I let them go ahead and use them." Because of his good rapport with and trust of the Friendly Villagers, this physician has been giving medical services to the people nearly 50 years. In general, the villagers trust and value the physician and how he helps them. The author found that none of the villagers disliked this physician's services, and that he has integrated folk and professional services in an effective and sensitive way.

2. Several villagers said they disliked most professional ways in the urban hospitals and clinics because they are not treated as "whole people" and because of the "unfriendly folks." The emphasis on physical problems is different in that their view of being a whole person involves their religious, family, and other beliefs and values. When they are in the urban area, they often have no one near to support them because their family and friends cannot remain with or near them while in the hospital. This leaves them insecure and at risk with the urban professional staff. They also said that when they had to go to the "big hospital" and the "big city," they had to leave their family and friends behind—people that knew them and how to care for them. The Blacks disliked waiting around for hours because they had to leave their children and elderly family members at home alone. One Black man summarized the hospital experience as, "You are without your family and friends. There is no one to care for you like we do in this community. We like our small doctor's office here in this community. He's safe and he knows us."

3. The majority of the Black (95%) and of the White villagers (56%) perceived that the rural life was best because they knew that home remedies were effective and because they had direct control over the use of these home remedies. In the urban hospital and community, these home remedies seemed to be unknown, and cure was totally controlled by the health personnel. Several feared the power of professional medicines compared with their home remedies. Ninety percent of the Black villagers and 62% of the White villagers found that the professional physician seemed mainly interested in diagnosing an illness, but did not help one keep well. Nurses did more in this area.

   White villagers were much more tolerant of medical diagnostic and treatment regimens than the Black villagers. Some White villagers wanted to try new medicines and treatments, but would trust only a few. The Whites and middle- and upper-class villagers viewed going to the "big city" and to specialists as prestigious, and they were willing to pay for such services. They did, however, note the absence of a warm and friendly attitude on the part of the health professional toward them. Dependency on and control by the "big city" physician was evident. At the same time, many White villagers valued the use of modern technology such as cardiac resuscitation and the latest heart revival equipment. The Village Rescue Squad was mainly a team of White villagers who valued modern equipment and perfecting their skills.

4. Rural lifeways incorporate and allow for their religious and kinship beliefs and practices, whereas in the big city, these are absent. They perceive this as a major lack in urban professional services that needs to become part of healing, diagnoses, treatment, and care practices. Practically all villagers (more than 95%) wanted religion to be used in healing, curing, and caring for the people, and the Blacks wanted the extended family to be active participants in health care.

5. The Friendly Villagers said, "I know who can help me get well at home, but I am not sure who can help me when I go to that big [more than 60 beds] urban hospital." They acknowledged that lots of special equipment and experts are

used, but they still do not know what works and why. The "magic" or urban practices were part of the perception of health care—and a disturbing factor. The adolescents were, however, curious about the "city hospital things and ways." The Black villagers didn't know if they could trust White strangers that they don't know. Adolescent boys had several "weird stories" about what folks do in the big city. In general, the urban professionals are strangers, as is the environment in which they work. It is a risk of great concern to the Black villagers, but of considerably less concern to the White villagers.

6.   The Black villagers were concerned that the nearby hospital did not provide the foods that they believed were healthy for them. While hospitalized, they may or may not receive foods such as chicken and bean soups, collards, and other southern foods. The older Black villagers would request their families to bring these foods to them (if they could sneak them in). The White villagers were not as concerned, but did value their beans to help them get well. Naturally raised garden foods were much preferred to the canned foods, as the latter are often perceived as "poisonous" by the Black villagers.

Other points of contrast can be noted in Table 13-2; several of these contrasts between rural and urban perceptions are comparable to other cultures studied (Leininger,1981d). Blacks communicating with Whites was of major importance, as was assessing attitudes of Whites in urban environments regarding their friendliness or hostility. Rural Blacks find that White people talk "strange," and Whites may find it difficult to understand them, since southern Black language is different from Anglo-American. A major finding was that the greater the distance away from the village, the greater the signs of fear, anxiety, and confusion in rural adult Blacks, especially in regard to what might happen to them in an urban hospital. For them, an urban hospital poses greater risks. The implications of this predominant finding must be given consideration by nurses, physicians, and other health care providers.

IMPLICATIONS FOR ETHNONURSING CARE

To address the question, "What are the implications for ethnocaring and ethnonursing care practices?", several points can be made in this last section. One of the most important implications is the realization that meaningful and therapeutic nursing care judgments, decisions, and actions should be based upon cultural data derived from cultural values and social structural knowledge. The social structural framework provides the most comprehensive and holistic perspective for knowing and understanding human health and caring behavior. A second important principle derived from this research is the realization that care and health can be cognitively identified and documented by ethnonursing research methods and techniques. Ethnocaring and ethnohealth data derived from the client, family, or cultural group provide essentially new data (emic) for understanding and helping clients from their viewpoint and from the world view rather than relying so heavily upon professional (etic) assessments, judgments, and knowledge.

From the research findings of this study, the following implications for therapeutic ethnonursing can be offered:

1. Ethnocare and ethnohealth constructs of *concern, presence, involvement,* and *touch* were dominant values and practices of the southern rural Black and White villagers in the United States. These values are facts to guide therapeutic care.

2. Health and care for the Black and White rural villagers had similar meanings and values, but there were also differences in the cultural and psychosocial forms of expression. Hence, cultural similarities and variabilities were identified.

3. Cognitions, perceptions, and experiences related to rural folk and urban health professional views about health care services and experiences reflected marked differences from rural folk Blacks' concerns, fears, and confusions about urban health professional attitudes and practices in a city hospital. White rural villagers had more favorable perceptions and experiences. Black and White male teenagers revealed mixed acculturation, with an attitude of curiosity toward the city hospital.

4. Several areas of cultural conflict and stress exist between Black rural folk and the predominantly Anglo-White urban·professional health system, which necessitated cultural care accommodations or repatterning of urban health services, or both, to fit the cultural needs, values, and concerns of the people.

5. The concept of touch as a caring value, belief, and practice reflected differences between the Black and White rural villagers. It requires specific nursing care accommodations.

6. Specific care practices need to be developed to provide *culture-specific* care for the Friendly Villagers, with slight variations in the nursing interventions related to *presence, involvement,* and *concern.*

7. Use of other specific care and health findings from this study need to be explicated for greater precision and for provision of meaningful care to the villagers.

The interrelationships between care and health in the Friendly Village social structure and values are under full analysis, but are not reported here.

In summary, this was an ethnographic, ethnologic, and ethnonursing investigation of southern rural Afro-American (Black) and Anglo-American (White) villagers over a 10-month period. It focused on ethnocare, ethnohealth, and general lifeways of the people. The partial findings reported in this chapter indicate the importance of identifying care and health values of cultures from an *emic* perspective. This research study is part of a larger transcultural care study of a number of Western and non-Western cultures. Cultural differences prevail among most of the 30 cultures studied, and only a few common care constructs were universal *(etic)* among the cultures studied (Leininger, 1981a). More systematic and in-depth investigations of specific cultures are needed to verify and validate caring and health cross-culturally. Moreover, similar ethnomethodologies need to be considered for their reliability and validity factors.

From this study, however, health personnel could initiate specific nursing care interventions to help the community maintain favorable health care practices. Most important, the study points to the need to base health and care practices upon the clients' perceptions, cognitions, and experiences, rather than impose health professional practices and ideologies on representatives of different cultures, so that meaningful and satisfying health services can be realized.

REFERENCES

Billingsley, A. *Black families in white America.* Englewood Cliffs, N.J.: Prentice-Hall, 1968.

Dougherty, M. C. *Becoming a woman in rural black culture.* New York: Holt, Rinehart, and Winston, 1978.

Kennedy, T. R. *You gotta deal with it: Black family relations in a southern community.* New York: Oxford Press, 1980.

Leininger, M. *Transcultural nursing: Concepts, theories and practices.* New York: John Wiley & Sons, 1978.

Leininger, M. Caring: a central focus for nursing and health care services. *Nursing and Health Care* 1980, *1* (3): 135–143, 176.

Leininger, M. *Caring: An essential human need. Proceedings of Three National Caring Conferences.* Thorofare, N.J. Charles B. Slack, 1981a, p. 9.

Leininger, M. Intercultural interviews, assessment and therapy implications. In P. Pederson (Ed.): *Interviews and assessments.* Beverly Hills, Calif., Sage Publishers, 1981b.

Leininger, M. Ethnonursing research field methods: a different approach to traditional research in nursing. (Unpublished paper, 1981c)

Leininger, M. Transcultural nursing: its progress and its future. *Nursing and Health Care.* New York: September, 1981d, Vol. H, No. 7, pp. 365–371.

Leininger, M. Transcultural care diversity and universality: A Theory of nursing. *Nursing and Health Care* 1985, 6 (4): 209–212.

Lerner, G. (Ed): *Black women in white America: A documentary history.* New York: Random House, 1970.

Pelto, R. J. *Anthropological research: The structure of inquiry. Intentions and theory of anthropology.* New York: Harper and Row, 1970.

Spradley, J. *The ethnographic interview.* New York: Holt, Rinehart, and Winston, 1979.

Spradley, J. *Participant-observation.* New York: Holt, Rinehart, and Winston, 1980.

Stack, C. *All our kin: Strategies for survival in a black community.* New York: Harper and Row, 1970.

14

Use of the Family Health Calendar and Interview Schedules to Study Health and Illness

Joyceen S. Boyle

An understanding of how individuals and families experience health-illness situations can be the basis for understanding and planning for nursing and health care needs within a defined context. Knowledge of the client's cultural context, lifestyle, health beliefs, and behaviors can enhance nursing judgments and decisions (Leininger, 1978). With such information, nurses will be able to understand when or how to intervene to prevent or alter untoward client experiences. In addition, this cultural knowledge will help nurses develop a sensitivity to the cultural group and to recognize and intervene in areas of potential stress, misunderstanding, or incongruence for both clients and professionals. How cultural groups perceive care and illness and the social structure factors that influence sickness and health are basic knowledge for health professionals in order to provide efficacious health care services.

In this chapter, the primary focus is on the use of two research tools to study the health beliefs and illness behavior of a particular cultural group in a defined geographical setting. The two research tools are the Health Beliefs Interview Schedule and a Family Health Calendar Recording. The use of these tools will be discussed as they relate to the purpose of the study, the type of data collected, and the analysis of the findings. The information is presented as an example of a qualitative descriptive type of nursing study in which the researchers used these two tools with several ethnographic methods and other techniques to achieve the desired research goals.

SAMPLE SELECTION

The site chosen for this study was a small *colonia** of 218 households in a city located in the central highlands of western Guatemala. A convenient sample of 22 households (134 individuals), whose head of household was Cakchiquel Indian and born within the city boundaries, was selected from the households within the *colonia*. The research project began with a census of all residents in the *colonia*. Data were obtained from each household regarding number and ages of persons living within each household, and the place of birth and ethnic identity of the head of household. Fifteen families volunteered to participate in the research at the initial contact made with the investigator during the census survey. The remainder of the sample population was selected by referrals from sample families to their kin or neighbors or through chance encounters in the *colonia*. To ensure heterogeneity within the sample, households were selected that showed variation in household composition, age and sex, lifestyle, and living conditions.

METHODS USED

The traditional anthropological method of participant-observation was used during this 13-month fieldwork experience. The use of participant-observation required direct contact with research subjects over a long period of time and provided an opportunity to observe and record daily life and routine experiences in the *colonia*. The continuous collection of data over time was basic to the use of other short-term research techniques. Data from participant-observations provided insights and clues necessary for developing interview questions and other research instruments. The interplay between participant-observation and other methods of data collection enhanced validity of the study in that collaborative and comparable data findings were obtained from a number of sources. The use of relatively unstructured, long-term observations and key informant interviews, in conjunction with structured interviews and more formal procedures, such as the Family Health Calendar, helped to support reliability aspects of the study.

The Health Beliefs Interview Schedule

An initial goal of this investigation was to explore with those in the sample which illnesses were perceived as being "frequent and common" and the health beliefs that were associated with the causation, treatment, and prevention of these illnesses. For the purposes of this study, the term "health beliefs" refers to propositions accepted as true about the causes, symptoms, and remedies related to wellness and sickness (Goodenough, 1963).

The Health Beliefs Interview Schedule was a research tool developed to differentiate among illnesses, ideas of causation, appropriate treatment actions, and culturally prescribed behaviors to promote health and prevent illness. A copy of the Health Beliefs Interview Schedule appears in Figure 14-1.

---

*A *colonia* in Guatemala is a politically defined urban settlement.

Figure 14-1. Health Beliefs Interview Schedule

Part A: *Common Illnesses*
Directions: Describe the causes, treatment, or prevention of these common illnesses.

Illness Conditions

1. Headache	5. Lack of appetite	9. Chills
2. Weakness	6. Fever	10. Stomach ache
3. Vomiting	7. Leg pain	11. Crying
4. Cough	8. Throat pain	12. Sadness
		13. Chest pain

1. What do you believe causes _____?

2. What would you do if you had _____? Why? _____
_____

3. Describe what you can do so that you won't suffer from _____
_____

4. Rank order these illnesses beginning with the most serious condition to the least
serious condition.

5. Why are _____, _____, and _____ the
most serious?

6. Why are _____, _____, and _____ the
least serious?

Part B: *Folk Illnesses*
Directions: Respond to the question below by providing descriptions of the illnesses.

1. There are some illness which people sometimes have that physicians do not believe
in—for example, *el ojo, empacho,* and *susto.* Have you or any member of your family
ever had one of these diseases or other diseases that physicians do not believe in?
Can you describe the illnesses for me?

2. What is the best thing to do when you or a member of your family has one of
these illnesses? _____

A pretest sample of five households who met sample criteria but who lived outside the boundaries of the *colonia* was selected to assist in the development of the
Health Beliefs Interview Schedule. This pretest sample was chosen to avoid pretest
effects that might have occurred had regular sample households been used to develop
the interview schedule.

An important contribution made by the pretest sample subjects was their ability to
rephrase questions which had originally been written in English and then translated
into Spanish. The pretest sample members were helpful in assisting in the construction of the interview schedule and in phrasing questions which elicited relevant information. The pretest efforts thus contributed to the internal validity of the instrument.

Persons in the pretest sample were asked to list common illness conditions, by
which a list of 22 illnesses was obtained. The pretest sample members then were
asked to sort the illness conditions into two categories—"frequent or common," and
"not as frequent or common." A list of ten common and frequent illness conditions
was obtained in this manner.

Two additional items were added to the ten common illness conditions which had been identified by the pretest sample. All of the original ten illness conditions had a physiological basis. The pretest sample members agreed that these items were "frequent" and "common" conditions often experienced by themselves or their family members. Other illness conditions were excluded because the informants indicated they were infrequent and occurred only on rare occasions. However, the pretest sample members reported that it was possible for an illness to result from psychological disturbances; therefore, item 11, "sadness and crying," was added to the list because I wanted to explore health beliefs surrounding psychological conditions. Item number 12, "chest pain," had been eliminated by the pretest sample members in the sorting process. Because I believed it was important to learn if the illness manifestation of chest pain reflected beliefs related to concepts of pain or danger, it was included on the final draft of the Health Belief Interview Schedule. The final list of twelve illness conditions included headache, weakness, vomiting, cough, lack of appetite, colds, leg pain, sore throat, fever, stomach ache, sadness and crying, and chest pain.

During the interview with sample subjects, questions were asked to elicit their beliefs regarding causes of each illness condition, actions taken to obtain relief, and prevention of each condition. Then respondents to the Health Beliefs Interview Schedule were asked to rank order the illness conditions from most serious to least serious and to explain their rankings. Respondents were asked to sort the illnesses according to whether they were "serious" or "not serious," and through a process of elimination the "serious" illnesses were ranked according to the level of perceived seriousness of each condition. The same procedure was used with those illnesses which had been identified as "not serious," beginning with the question: "Which of these conditions [read aloud to respondent] is the least serious?" The ranking process was carried out verbally between the respondent and myself. The respondents had no difficulty in making distinction among illnesses according to perceived seriousness. The use of flash cards would have been an ideal method to use for this type of ranking; however, because many respondents were unable to read or write, the task was accomplished by verbal ranking. I was careful not to impose a particular structure or response on the respondents.

Reasons and comments provided by sample subjects in the course of their rankings were a valuable source of additional data. When the administration of the Health Beliefs Interview Schedule was completed, median rank scores were calculated for each illness condition. While there were interesting differences among the rankings given by the respondents, the results indicated a high degree of consensus among sample members. The ranking procedure yielded a native hierarchy of illness. Content analysis of the respondents' comments and their responses to the interview questions about the ranking process identified important concepts and criteria that informants used to differentiate among illness conditions.

In addition, I was interested in obtaining information about indigenous or folk illnesses and the traditional care modalities maintained by Guatemalan Indians who lived in an urban setting. Thus, questions were included in the Health Beliefs Interview Schedule to elicit responses about common folk illnesses.

The Health Belief Interview Schedule was administered to adult members of the sample. Interviews were obtained from 70 of the 72 persons in the sample age 18 years and older. The intent of this method was to provide a general framework for differentiating among illnesses, ideas of causation, appropriate treatment actions, and culturally prescribed behaviors and strategies to promote and maintain health.

The Family Health Calendar

A Family Health Calendar (FHC) was used for a one-month period to identify those persons who experienced illness and to identify the symptoms, remedies used, person(s) suggesting therapy, and person(s) consulted for health advice, including contact with health practitioners. The FHC (Fig. 14-2) is a form of health diary that yields information about how each family or household unit shows specific characteristics in maintaining health, preventing illness, experiencing morbidity and treating illness.

A structured family health calendar was used in studies by Alpert, Kosa, and Haggerty (1967). Ailinger (1977) also used a modified FHC in a study of illness referrals. Litman (1974), in a review of family health care research, suggested that although the FHC provides a source of comprehensive health information about the family, there are problems with insufficient compliance and normative influences as to what is, or is not, deemed important enough to be recorded. Litman suggested that such instruments are best used in conjunction with other data collection techniques, such as focused interviews and subsequent home visits to assist with recording.

For the purposes of this study, modifications were made in the instrument in order to improve qualitative reliability and validity factors with the cultural group under study. The major modification was that, in this study, family members were asked to describe the symptoms in their own words to obtain their meanings and viewpoints; whereas in other studies, families were asked only to record illnesses, based on a provided list.

The purposes and procedures of the FHC were carefully explained to those in the sample prior to its use, and cooperation was solicited. A contact person was identified in each household who would provide information about illnesses of household members. Usually, mothers in the households were chosen to provide data for FHC, as they proved to be informative about the health status of all family members, and household members recognized them as being knowledgeable about health matters. I visited each household every other day to ensure that as complete and accurate data as possible were obtained. Data collection would have been enhanced if daily contacts had been made with each household; however, there was a total of 22 households in the sample and so daily visits to each household were not possible.

The investigator made all recordings on the FHC because of literacy variability among members studied. Several of the women, for example, were unable to read or write, and others had only minimal skills in these areas. Another important factor contributing to success in administering the FHC was the use of the instrument toward the end of the field work experience after I had developed a positive relationship with the study group. Since the FHC requires active participation by those in the study over a period of time, close cooperation between the investigator and respondents was necessary to ensure success. (A copy of the Family Health Calendar is shown in Figure 14-2.)

During the four-week period in which the FHC was used, each household in the sample was asked the name of the person who experienced illness, the symptoms encountered (described in their own words), remedies used, and the person who suggested the therapy. Questions related to persons sought for advice and assistance and the past relationships and experiences with such persons were asked in order to identify the existence of the lay referral network subscribed to by the

Person experiencing illness	Symptoms: Client will describe in own words	What was done for the symptoms? Suggested by?	With whom did you talk to about the symptoms?
Date			
Date			
Date			
Date			
Date			

Figure 14-2. Family Health Calendar Recording

respondents. Data were sought on choices of health specialists and health care facilities, and why they were chosen, in order to identify the type of practitioner and facility, as well as attitudes toward the care that was received.

Twenty-five persons identified by the FHC as having been ill with the same symptom for three consecutive days or more were asked to respond to the Illness Episodes Interview Schedule (shown in Fig. 14-3). This instrument elicited beliefs regarding causation of illness and the interpretation of symptoms, along with changes in daily life routines. Questions were asked regarding the kinds of care and assistance that ill persons believed they needed and why. Activities and practices believed necessary to restore health were also elicited. The Illness Episodes Interview Schedule was an important adjunct to the FHC, as it facilitated the collection of data related to specific illness events.

FINDINGS OF THE STUDY

The data obtained from the Health Beliefs Interview Schedule can be viewed within the context of what constitutes a typical occurrence of illness in the *colonia*. Examination of the data provided many insights about causation, treatment and pre-

Figure 14-3. Illness Episodes Interview Schedule

1. What symptoms did you have during your recent illness?
2. What do you believe caused these symptoms?
3. What remedies and/or treatments did you use?
4. Who suggested these remedies and/or treatments?
5. In what ways did these remedies or treatments help you?
6. What else did you do that made you feel better or aided in your recovery?
7. What activities were you unable to do?
8. What activities did you continue to do even though you were ill?
9. What effect did your illness have on other members of your household?
10. Who did you consult about your illness? Family? Friends? Neighbors? Others? Why this particular person(s)?
11. Describe your past and present relationship with the person(s) whom you consulted for help and advice.
12. Did you seek help from a health car specialist? If so, who? Why did you choose this particular health specialist?
13. Who made the decision to seek this help?
14. Were you satisfied with the care you received from the health care specialist? If not, why not? If so, why?
15. What things did you like about this particular health care specialist?
16. What things did you not like about this health care specialist?
17. Where did you see the health care specialist?
18. What advice, help, or treatment was given to you by the health care specialist?

ventions related to the general categories the subjects used. The data from the FHC and focused illness interviews provided similar data. In addition, these two instruments provided documentation not only of what the persons in the sample believe about illness, but also what they actually do in response to illness. In addition, the FHC and Illness Episodes Interview Schedule provided data about attitudes, beliefs, and experiences of the sample subjects with health care systems. All data obtained by use of the Health Beliefs Interview Schedule and the FHA cannot be shown here because of space limitations; however, examples of data will be provided to demonstrate the value of these instruments and to support data analysis and conclusions.

Health Beliefs

Data from the Health Beliefs Interview Schedule provided considerable information about health beliefs associated with common illness conditions. Table 14-1 shows beliefs about causes of headache and fever. A preliminary analysis indicated that data related to causation of illness conditions could be divided into two categories, external and internal causation. External causation included factors which were related to the environment and to events that were external to the individual. Internal causation were factors that involved the individual's own actions or behaviors, or reflected notions of susceptibility or vulnerability on the part of the ill individual. The data related to illness causation were coded, classified and analyzed according to external and internal ascription, and this provided a way to organize information and delineate data trends.

Table 14-1   *Selected Illness Conditions and Ascribed Causations*

Illness Condition	External Ascribed Causes*	Internal Ascribed Causes*
Headache	Heat Cold Changes in climate	Other sickness, such as colds, flu, upset stomach, eye strain, pregnancy, fever
		Intense emotions, such as anger, anxiety, worry, thinking, sadness or depression, nervousness
		Individual behavior, such as being sleep, tired, working too hard, drinking too much
Fever	Heat Changes in climate	Being warm and then getting chilled
		Not taking care of yourself, especially not taking proper care of colds and influenza
		Getting wet or going out in the cold when you have a cold
		Other illnesses, such as stomach infections, bronchities, pneumonia, measles, typhoid fever, inflammation, or infections Immunizations

*In order of frequency reported.

Two kinds of conditions related to individual characteristics or states were explored to interpret the causation ascribed to the illness conditions. The first condition was that of the individual's psychological state or the condition of being strong-weak or hot-cold. A person who became ill for any reason was said by sample subjects to have been too hot, too cold, chilled, or weakened by a variety of causes. External agents, such as cold air, rain, sun, and wind, were believed to be sources of excess heat, cold, or a "force" that may enter the body, upset its normal balance, and cause illness. Hot and cold qualities, which historically have been attributed to Spanish cultural beliefs, were the most common factors believed to influence health and illness. Illnesses tended to be attributed to cold more frequently than to heat.

The second condition necessary to understand disease causation was associated with extreme or intense emotional states. Extreme anger, passion, grief, fright, or sadness could render a person susceptible to illness. This population believed that extreme emotional states could affect the strength or weakness of individuals. A person who was very angry could become *muy fuerte* (very strong) and cause illness in others by his strong state, or he might become weakened by his state of anger and become susceptible to certain illnesses.

Content analysis of the data obtained from the Health Beliefs Interview Schedule indicated that illnesses such as headaches, crying and sadness, weakness, lack of appetite, and stomach pain were associated with strong emotional experiences. Chest pain, cough, colds, sore throat, and fever were related to both external and internal conditions of hot and cold and to external climatic conditions, such as wind or dust. Only three persons in the sample associated chest pain with the heart. Vomiting was associated with eating contaminated foods, eating or drinking too much, or other internally ascribed factors, such as pregnancy and motion sickness. Leg pain was associated with cold but was more commonly attributed to walking or running in excess or to trauma.

Data from the Health Beliefs Interview Schedule indicated that folk illnesses still occur, but that they are not a major health concern. Older women and children suffer more frequently from folk illnesses than do men. Analysis of data indicated that animation beliefs are uncommon, and that external causation was related to social environmental conditions or circumstances which could directly cause illness; while internal causation rendered the individual susceptible to illness.

The respondents to the Health Belief Interview Schedule reported a wide variety of actions that could be taken for the illness conditions of fever and headache. As can be seen in Table 14-2, reported health practices depended, in part, upon the integration of a given set of actions with an understanding of the significance of those acts.

Data relating to prescribed treatment for the common illness conditions indicated that the concepts of hot-cold and strong-weak that underlie causation beliefs were important considerations. Illnesses believed to be caused by becoming either too hot or too cold were treated with home remedies that were believed to contain the opposite qualities. Pharmaceutical preparations were purchased frequently to aid in the treatment of illness; however, their efficacy, rather than innate qualities of hot and cold, seemed to be more important to sample members. Psychological states of illness, such as sadness and crying, were thought to be outside the realm of medical treatment. Most respondents indicated that if the illness condition were painful or incapacitating, or if the condition persisted for a long period of time, they

Table 14-2   *Reported Treatment Actions and Preventive Practices of Selected Illness Conditions*

Illness Conditions	Treatment Actions*	Prevention*
Headache	• Analgesics were cited most frequently, with aspirin being reported as the most frequently taken • Home remedies such as slices of lemon soaked in coffee and then applied to the temples, herbal teas • Alka Seltzer and lemon in hot water • Prayer • Only natural treatments or herbs are used during pregnancy to prevent damage to the unborn child	• Not getting angry, taking things calmly • Trying to solve problems • Avoiding worry • Being tranquil and at peace with one's self and family • Being content and serene • Taking care of one's self, such as not getting wet, dressing properly for the cold, not standing in the sun for long periods of time
Fever	• Seek professional advice from physician • Medications from the pharmacy; aspirins and oral antibiotics • Injections of antibiotics • For children: suppositories and herbal baths • Herbal teas • Alcohol rubs • Cold cloth on forehead • Laxatives	• Taking care of yourself when you have other illness is most important; then complications like fever won't develop • Treat colds and flu with medicine; not getting chilled • Treatment of other conditions that might cause fever, such as stomach infections, bronchitis, and other infections • General good health • Avoid cold drinks • Avoid getting wet in the rain • Good personal hygiene • Don't bathe when it's cold

*In order of frequency reported.

would seek advice from a physician. The possibility existed that symptoms which did not appear critical because of cultural interpretation could in fact be indicative of serious illness and might be handled by folk treatments. The illness manifestation of chest pain represents such an example, with the majority of respondents failing to associate chest pain with cardiac function.

Table 14-2 also lists the preventive practices that were reported by respondents for the manifestations of fever and headache. Preventive practices were based on ascribed causes of the illness. The respondents to the Health Beliefs Interview Schedule reported that preventive measures were indicated when the individual was thought to be able to manage his/her conduct or condition. When the individual had no control over external factors, preventive measures could still be taken by individual to lessen susceptibility or the impact of the illness.

Data indicated that the respondents maintained an awareness of external environmental hazards as they went about their daily activities, and that they avoided such agents as rain, cold, heat, night air, and wind, if possible. Strong emotional states were to be avoided, and such personal behaviors as avoiding the consumption of too many hot or cold foods, wearing protective clothing, and not getting chilled or wet were reported to be important preventive measures. Good nutrition, fresh air, exercise, and proper amounts of sleep were also believed to be important.

When respondents to the Health Beliefs Interview Schedule were asked to rank order the illness manifestations from the most serious to the least serious, fever, stomach pain, and weakness were perceived as the most serious. These conditions were believed to be fatal on occasion and could lead to other serious conditions. These illness conditions did not always respond to home remedies and therefore needed medical intervention for recovery. Colds and leg pain were viewed as the least serious illnesses because they lasted only a few days, usually did not lead to more serious illnesses, and could be adequately treated by family members in the home environment.

The Health Beliefs Interview Schedule facilitated an accurate description of a body of culturally relevant knowledge regarding illness beliefs and reported health practices. The data illustrated beliefs and actions that reportedly occurred during typical illness experiences. Content analysis of the data suggested that beliefs about the causation of illness influenced actions that were related to the treatment and prevention of illness. The recognition of illness, its definition, and the responses associated with it were variable, highly complex, and interrelated. The data analysis suggested that the evaluation of any illness was subject to personal interpretations, which were influenced by cultural traditions and social reality. These interpretations formed the basis for reported actions that influenced health-illness states.

The Family Health Calendar

The Family Health Calendar facilitated the collection of data about how sample members actually managed illness episodes, including contacts with health care systems.

All 22 households, or 100 per cent of the households in the sample, reported illness incidents during the month of the FHC. Table 14-3 shows that 135 incidents were reported, and the average per household had 6.2 illnesses. Three fourths of the women (77.4 per cent), one fourth of the men (24.3 per cent), and fewer than half (43.3 per cent) of the children reported illness incidents. In the study by Alpert and colleagues (1967) of 78 low-income families (selected at random from a case pool of 500 families in the Boston area), 93 per cent of the families reported illnesses over a four week period. Ailinger (1977) followed 19 families of Latin-American descent living in an eastern city of the United States; her study revealed that 89 per cent of the families experienced illness over a one-month period. Fewer males reported

Table 14-3 *Frequency and Distribution of Family Members (n = 132)*
Reporting Illness Incidents (n = 135)

| | Sample Members | | | | | |
| | Women | | Men | | Children* | |
Number	n	%	n	%	n	%
Total respondents	31	23.5	41	31.1	60	45.4
Persons reporting illness	24	77.4	10	24.3	26	43.3
Incidents of illness	54	40.0	14	10.4	67	49.6

*All persons below the age of 18 years.

illness symptoms than females in all three studies. Ailinger reported that 50 per cent of the males in her research experienced illness; 34.9 per cent of males reported illness in the study by Alpert and others, compared with only 24.3 per cent of the men reporting illness incidents in the study. The percentage of females reporting incidents is higher in this study of Guatemalan Indians (77.4 per cent) than in the Alpert and Ailinger studies, both of which reported 50 per cent of females reporting illnesses.

A more detailed view of illness experiences was obtained by analyzing the reported symptoms by category. The symptoms as described by informants in general symptomatic terms were classified into broad categories. Respiratory and gastrointestinal symptoms and problems of the lower extremities were easily categorized on the basis of the information supplied by the informants. The category of "other" was added to include miscellaneous symptoms that could not be included in other categories. Examples of illness symptoms placed in this category were low back pain, fever, allergies, eye infections, nose bleeds, lack of appetite, and trauma from spouse abuse. The category of emotional problems presented some difficulty as a number of symptoms shown in this category could be included in other categories. Illness symptoms were classified as emotionally based on the information provided by the ill persons or family members. In particular, care was taken to classify emotionally related illnesses according to causation beliefs, which were elicited from the individuals experiencing the illness symptoms. Conditions such as "stomach ache," "headache," and "anger" were classified as emotionally related illnesses when the ill informant or a family member reported the illness incidents were caused by "nerves" *(por los nervios)*. Additional questions explored the precipitating factors or events which were perceived by informants as triggering the emotionally related illness symptom.

Table 14-4 shows that respondents using the FHC reported 135 identifiable symptoms during this four-week period. The most frequent symptoms were related to respiratory ailments (36.3 per cent) and gastrointestinal complaints (23.0 per cent), which together accounted for nearly 60 percent of all symptoms reported. These findings were basically the same as those reported in urban populations in the United States by Ailinger (1977) and Alpert and co-workers (1967). Children experienced more incidents of both respiratory and gastrointestinal symptoms than did adults. Women experienced more problems of the lower extremities, more headaches, more respiratory and gastrointestinal symptoms, and more emotionally related symptoms

Table 14-4 *Illness Incidents as Reported by the Sample (n = 132)*

Symptoms by Category	Frequency Reported	
	n	%
Respiratory	49	36.3
Gastrointestinal	31	23.0
Emotional	14	10.3
Problems of lower extremities	9	6.6
Headaches	5	3.7
Other	27	20.1
Total	135	100.0

than did men. One family reported one chronically ill member who was hospitalized with diabetes during the month of the FHC. Two rather serious gastrointestinal illnesses occurred during the four-week period. Only one individual reported a folk illness: a middle-aged woman complained of *colera*, an illness believed caused by anger and anxiety that results in headache and stomach pain. This illness was classified as an emotionally related illness on the basis of the reported beliefs about causation. Duration of the illness symptoms varied somewhat, depending on the severity and chronicity of the compliant.

A primary concern during the use of the FHC was not so much "what the people think" as "what they do," and how actions were explained by the respondents during the actual illness occurrence. To find the answers to such questions, follow-up interviews were conducted using the Illness Episodes Interview Schedule with each of the 25 persons who experienced an illness symptom for three consecutive days or more. The use of the Illness Episodes Interview Schedule facilitated the collection of in-depth and comprehensive data about specific illness events and was a valuable component of the FHC.

Table 14-5 represents a reconstruction of one illness episode experienced by a male sample member during the FHC. This table provides case study information derived from the FHC and the follow-up interview using the Illness Episodes Interview Schedule. The left column of Table 14-5 indicates symptoms, problems, and diagnoses identified by the ill person, a family member, or a health care specialist. These are frequently multiple and reflect different levels of conceptualization and labeling as well as alternative sources of information. Direct quotations have been used whenever possible. The middle column describes the therapeutic action that was taken by the patient, family, or health care specialist. The right side of the column indicates the rationale for the therapeutic action and at the top an explanation for the illness.

The organization of qualitative data in this manner facilitates an understanding of how individuals recognized and interpreted illness conditions or symptoms. The recognition of illness always involved reliance on commonsense notions of what was normal and what was not. The meaning of events of illness and the prescribed behaviors were not identical for everyone because interpretations, decisions, and actions differed; however, a general pattern of evaluation, decision making, and treat-

Table 14-5   An Example of an Illness Episode: Jose, age 58 years

Day	Symptoms	Therapeutic Action	Rationale
1	Pain in lower back	Liniments and massage	To help the pain
		Massage with alcohol	Is a "cold" substance
2	Pain in lower back	Went to pharmacy and explained symptoms. They gave him medicine for "kidneys"	Does ot have money for a physician and does not like the public clinics because "you have to wait too long"
			The medicine will *disinflamar* (decrease the infection) in the kidneys
		"Cold" food and liquids: a drink made from corn silk and vanilla. "Cold" foods such as vegetables and salads.	Inflammation is a "hot" condition
		Avoid foods with grease	Greasy foods are "hot"
		Avoid foods with sugar and salt	They affect the kidneys
3		Contine to go to work despite wife's objections	Will lose job if he does not go to work
		Liniments and massage	For the pain
4–5	Pain	Medicine	Will cure the inflammation
		Massage	For the pain
6–7	Pain in lower back	Medicine	Will work against inflammation
		Massage	For the pain
		Special "cold" foods	Will help the inflammation

ment was evident in the multi-episodic character of the illness events which occurred during the one-month period of the FHC.

The data from the FHC and focused illness interviews revealed that the nature of a person's daily activities, life style, and role performance could change during an illness episode. Decisions about what to do when ill tended to be based on beliefs and understanding of illness symptoms, the nature of the social environment, the perceived cause, and alternative resources that were available for care. Behavioral changes that occurred in response to illness revealed the organized actions taken by the ill person and family to couteract an illness.

Additional data collected by the use of the FHC revealed that a considerable number of individuals may be involved in the management of any one illness episode. In addition, the majority of persons who identified themselves as ill utilized multiple sources of care outside of the family. The informal or community sources of care appeared to have greater importance to the respondents than did the professional or institutional resources for the management of illness. Table 14-6 shows that 32 per cent of the 135 reported illness incidents were self-treated or managed

Table 14-6 *Management of Illness Conditions (n = 135) During a One-Month Period in the Sample*

Sources of Care	Modalities of Care	Common Illness Conditions
Self and family care (32%)	Home and herbal remedies	Respiratory conditions
Self-addressed (7%)	Home treatment, simple medications	Minor health problems
Family (25%)	Advice, information sharing	Beginning illness conditions
	Consultation, comfort measures	
Community care (60%)	Home and herbal remedies	Gastrointestinal problems
Social network (19%)	Home treatments	Emotionally related illness
Pharmacies (32%)	Advice, information sharing	Muscular aches
Indigenous caregivers (5%)	Simple and pharmaceutical medications	Severe colds, cough, flu
		Headaches
Religious systems (5%)	Injections	Fever
Professional care (7%)	Prescribed herbal remedies and medicines	Chronic problems
Curanderos (1%)		Infections
Spiritualists (1.5%)	Advice and special instructions	Severe and/or chronic gastrointestinal symptoms
Public health care facilities (3%)	Pharmaceutical medications	
	Prayer	
Private physicians (1.5%)	Assistance from supernatural	
	Prescribed rituals	

within the family or household constellation. Respiratory conditions and minor maladies were treated by herbal remedies, simple medications such as aspirin, comfort measures, advice, and information sharing.

The second mode of illness management utilized sources of informal care within the community. The FHC revealed that 61 per cent of illnesses were referred to nonprofessional sources of assistance outside of the family household. Nineteen per cent were referred to a social network of kin, neighbors, or friends. Thirty-two per cent of ill persons sought assistance in the form of advice and medications from pharmacies. It should be noted that in Guatemala it is possible to purchase a variety of medications without a physician's prescription, and it is possible to self-medicate using what would ordinarily be considered "prescription" medication. Five per cent of the sample sought help from indigenous care givers, who are usually women who sold herbal medicines or give injections. These women's services were used between family care and care offered by health professionals. Five per cent of the ill respondents (all members of Protestant religions) requested religious intercession for illness in the form of prayer and faith healing.

Table 14-6 also shows that during the one month with the FHC, nine illnesses or (7 per cent of all symptoms reported by respondents) were seen by some type of health care specialist. A professional health specialist was defined as an individual who was recognized in the community as having the ability to heal and who practiced his or her profession on a full-time basis. Visits were made to health specialists for infections, chronic diseases, and gastrointestinal complaints. Sources of Western medical care were private physicians and public and charitable hospitals or clinics. Indigenous health specialists, or folk healers, were spiritualists and *curanderos*, known locally as *curas*. All health specialists used pharmaceutical medicines in their treatment modalities; *curas* also used herbal remedies and traditional treatments reflecting hot-cold and strong-weak concepts. Spiritualists used their occult abilities to serve as mediums between the spirit world and the client.

From this investigation, data from the FHC revealed that professional medical care was obtained in public facilities or from private physicians on a fee-for-service basis in 4.5 per cent of the 135 illness conditions that occurred. Traditional practitioners were consulted for 2.5 per cent of all illnesses. Alpert and co-workers (1967) found that in low-income families in Boston during a one-month period 4.7 per cent of all illnesses were treated by a physician. Ailinger (1977) reported that, in families of Latin-American descent followed for one month with a FHC, 30 per cent of the illnesses reported were treated a physician, which was a high percentage of physician referrals. In the study of Demers and associates (1980) of illness behavior of 107 adults belonging to a prepaid health care system in the Seattle area, utilization of physicians' services occurred in 5.4 per cent of illness episodes during a three-week period. A more precise method of comparison, however, is to examine the annual visit rate; Demers and colleagues found it to be 3.06 per cent whereas 2.7 per cent is the national average for the United States (National Ambulatory Medical Care Survey, 1980). The results of this research showed that physician visits numbered six during the four-week period, which is equivalent to an annual visit rate of only 0.58 per cent for the respondents.

Overall, respondents to the FHC reported that they preferred to obtain health care services from physicians because they believed their services were most effective. However, data from the FHC revealed that the respondents actually consulted physicians less frequently than they consulted folk practitioners. The data obtained with the use of the Health Belief Interview Schedule and from participant-observation suggested that sample members occasionally sought care from folk practitioners, but the data from the FHC revealed that the respondents regularly and consistently sought out a variety of traditional forms of health care during the four-week period. In addition, the FHC revealed the extent to which over-the-counter pharmaceuticals were used by respondents without consultation with a physician. Other practices, such as religious intercessions, were documented by the FHC, indicating that a variety of folk care sources were sought during this four-week period, each of which reflected a different healing tradition.

The respondents to the FHC reported that the cost of health care was of much concern. The cost of services provided by *curas* equaled or sometimes exceeded the cost of private medical care. Care given at public institutions at a reduced rate was believed by the informants to be of inferior quality, but it was utilized because of cost factors. The reasons sample members sought care from indigenous practitioners could not be determined definitively. However, some tentative suggestions can be offered from the analysis of the data collected through the FHC and interviews with persons experiencing illness during this study period. Choices made by the respondents to obtain treatment for illnesses were based on the knowledge of the relative effectiveness of the alternatives. These choices were influenced by assumptions about the cause of illnesses and their appropriate treatment. The data analysis indicated that when alleviation of illness symptoms did not occur, individuals sought the services of other types of health care practitioners, who offered different kinds of care modalities. Finally, respondents indicated that relative costs and access were important considerations in seeking health care.

Folk health practitioners imitated the professional medical care system in the use of pharmaceuticals, thus attesting to their belief in the efficacy of pharmaceutical medications in the treatment of disease. The folk practitioners included traditional beliefs and practices in their services, which were undoubtedly compatible with traditional beliefs and values of the sample.

Data collected through the use of the FHC revealed that the family was the most frequent locus of health decision and action in the search for and provision of health care. In the long run, it was most often the household unit, not the individual and not the health professional, that decided whether or not to seek or use another source of care. The skill and confidence of a family household operating in unison facilitated the treatment and care of the ill member. It was usually members of the household, rather than the ill person, who exerted the energy necessary to attain health goals. The families studied integrated many aspects of the care received from outside sources into their own modalities of care. Advice was rejected or complied with, medications were purchased and given according to directions, and other special regimens were carried out by the family to augment outside health care. The ability of the family unit to provide home care for the ill family member was a very important factor in the overall scope of health care, as families implemented much of the care and advice that was dispensed through other sources within the larger system.

STRENGTHS AND LIMITATIONS OF THE INSTRUMENTS

The Health Beliefs Interview Schedule facilitated the collection of a considerable amount of data regarding the causation, treatment, and prevention of specific illness conditions. Content analysis of the data obtained by the use of this tool was difficult because of the amount of information and the number of interviews (70). Asking respondents to rank each illness condition was time-consuming and difficult for many respondents. As mentioned previously, the use of flash cards would have provided more structure and taken less time if all respondents could read the terms. Assignment of mean scores to rank the illness conditions was a tedious procedure; however, it was a means to quantify and order qualitative data.

The major problem in constructing the Health Beliefs Interview Schedule was in phrasing questions that elicited the information being sought. The use of a pretest sample to assist in construction of interview questions was vital to the development of a useful instrument. A mix of relatively closed and open-ended questions also contributed to the quality of the data obtained. The open-ended questions permitted a wide variety of responses from the respondents. These responses were shaped by what respondents considered important rather than categories provided by the researcher. The relatively closed interview questions were easier to tabulate and analyze.

The FHC provided a rich source of comprehensive health information about each household. Problems of compliance were to some extent avoided by home visits to assist with the recording. It is probable that recall would have been improved by daily visits. Long-standing relationships with each household facilitated cooperation and participation in the use of the FHC. If I were to use this instrument again, I would train an assistant to help with data collection; conducting 11 home visits each day in addition to the focused illness interviews required precise scheduling and occasional 15-hour days. Having a research assistant available would have been reassuring had illness or other unforeseen problems problems occurred and would have alleviated interviewer fatigue.

The use of a FHC raises questions regarding normative influences on what persons believe is important enough to be reported. It might be alleged that simply keeping a record of illness symptoms altered the level of sensitivity to symptoms and increased the reporting of symptoms. Since a household member was the identified contact person, the data reported might be different from a self-report method. Moreover, sensitive material might not be reported, thus decreasing the number of problems recorded. The strengths and limitations of the FHC need to be studied further.

The FHC can best be used with other instruments such as the Illness Episodes Interview Schedule for more in-depth corroborative data. The latter interview schedule also focuses on a specific illness event and behavior related to it. Although subject to constraints inherent in all interviews, this interview schedule tool with open-ended and semi-closed questions helped to elicit beliefs regarding causation of illness and the interpretation of symptoms in addition to changes in daily life styles. The Illness Episodes Interview Schedule was, therefore, an important adjunct to the FHC.

Similar data were obtained regarding health-illness beliefs and practices from the three instruments used. The collection of data over time through participant-observation method reinforced the validity and reliability of data from these three instruments. The use of a defined sample population contributed to the effectiveness of the instruments, and although the unique population makes the results difficult to generalize, they are nonetheless an accurate data base and provide valuable information to understand the people studied. Knowledge about common illness conditions provides insights and directions for the provision of primary health care to this population. Concepts of disease prevention, along with treatment and preventive practices, provide important clues that will help prevent misunderstandings between health professionals and the people studied. The research instruments provided data that indicate how a particular cultural group perceives and cares for illness and how cultural factors influence the behaviors related to illness and health.

REFERENCES

Ailinger, R. A study of illness referral in a Spanish speaking community. *Nursing Research*, 1977, *26*(1), 53–56.

Alpert, J., Kosa, J., & Haggerty, R. A month of illness and health care among low-income families. *Public Health Reports*, 1967, *82*(8), 705–713.

Demers, R. Y., Altamore, R., Mustim, H.,

Kleinman, A., & Leonardi, D. An exploration of the dimensions of illness behavior. *Journal of Family Practice*, 1980, *11*(7), 1086–1096.

Goodenough, W. H. *Cooperation in change*. New York: Russell Sage Foundation, 1963.

Leininger, M. *Transcultural nursing: Concepts, theories and practices*. New York: John Wiley and Sons, 1978.

Litman, T. J. The family as a basic unit in health and medical care: A social-behavior overview. *Social Science and Medicine*, 1974, *8*(9), 495–519.

National Ambulatory Medical Care Survey: 1977 Summary. In National Center for Health Statistics (Hyattsville, MD): *Vital and Health Statistics*, Series 13, No. 44. Health, Education and Welfare Publication No. (PHS) 80-1795. Washington, D.C.: U.S. Government Printing Office, 1980, p. 20.

15

Ethnoscience Method and Componential Analysis

Madeleine Leininger

The ethnoscience method is becoming of increased interest to nurse researchers who value cognitive meanings, world views, and precise ways to analyze language use and meanings. Since the first work on ethnoscience was published in 1970 (Leininger, 1970), many nurses have requested more information. This chapter fits well with discussions of qualitative types of research and leads the researcher further into the use of this method.

DEFINITION AND FOCUS OF ETHNOSCIENCE

The word *ethnoscience* is derived from the Greek term *ethos*, "nation," and from the Latin term, *scientia*, referring to knowledge (Werner and Fenton, 1973, p. 537). Ethnoscience is a linguistic and anthropological method with the goals to obtain culturally based knowledge that is derived from language use of the people and ultimately to establish universal laws of knowledge (Werner and Fenton, 1973, pp. 538–539).

Ethnoscience refers to a *formalized and systematic study of people from their viewpoint (the emic view) in order to obtain an accurate account of how the people know, classify, and interpret their lifeways and the universe* (Leininger, 1970, p. 168). The goal of ethnoscience is to discover, document, and make explicit cognitive knowledge from the people's viewpoint, the "inside view" *(emic* perspective) rather than "outsider viewpoints." Ethnoscience is known to some as the "new ethnography." However, principles and characteristics of this approach have been in existence since the beginning of the 20 Century with Boas and Malinowski, as both of these ethnographers emphasized in their ethnographies the importance of collecting data from the native's cognitive perspective (Pelto, 1970, p. 68). Sapir, an ethnographic linguist, was also a firm advocate of the importance of obtaining the local people's behavior by language as an accurate way to know and understand the people's lifeways. Getting "inside people's thoughts and actions" by means of their languages and experiences was viewed as essential to support the ethnoscience method.

The terms *emic* and *etic* were used by Pike to contrast two different ways to know people (Pike, 1954, p. 8). *Emic* refers to the local or native view derived directly from the people's language, beliefs, and experiences; the *etic* view was the external, more universal, and generalized view. The *emic* view is grounded in language use and expressions, whereas the *etic* view may be the researcher's or an outsider's views and interpretation of some phenomenon under investigation.

The ethnoscience method is the formal and explicit way to study culture based on language use and emic data of the people. It is a systematized methodology for obtaining cultural, biological, physical other kinds of knowledge of a local group and their environment using a formal process to arrive at the meaning, classification, and principles of knowledge obtained. Ethnoscience relies heavily upon knowing people through *their* written and spoken values, norms, and lifeways, but it also includes observations of action patterns.

Ethnoscience differs from general ethnography and ethonursing (even though some principles apply to these methods) in that ethnoscience is a more rigorous, formal, and systematized way of documenting, describing, and analyzing data by language expressions than ethnonursing (see definition of each in Chapter 3). Ethnonursing focuses mainly on observing and documenting interactions with people of how these daily life conditions and patterns are influencing human care, health, and nursing care practices. The nurse researcher is interested in the beliefs and values of people and how social structure factors impact upon health nursing care from an action and experimental viewpoint. Some concepts and principles are used from ethnoscience, but with less rigor and systematization of written and spoken client data. Nurses need to be aware of the differences between the two methods of ethnonursing and ethnoscience and not assume the focus and methods are the same.

The aim of ethnoscience is to systematically document, classify, and interpret the people's cognitions and experiences so that they accurately reflect their lifeways and knowledge (Goodenough, 1964, 1967). The ethnoscientist must carefully observe, record, and validate information from the people so that it is congruent with their reality and makes sense to them. The ultimate goal of ethnoscience is to discover the culturally relevant domains of knowledge and experiences that reveal the people's views in a reliable and accurate way (Leininger, 1970, p. 169). From this people-based knowledge (the epistemological roots), the researcher formulates principles and makes abstractions to arrive at specific and general (or universal) laws about a certain phenomenon. Originally, ethnoscience took into account only semantics (word use and meaning); however, since the early 1960's the author has included action patterns of people to reaffirm their language statements and behaviors. Hence what people say and do are both important to understand people. This is especially important in developing meaningful and accurate nursing knowledge through language and actions.

BASIC ASSUMPTIONS AND PREMISES
OF ETHNOSCIENCE

There are several basic assumptions and premises of the ethnoscience method that should be understood at the outset (Leininger, 1970, 1978):

1. Humans are able to perceive and *know* (cognitions) their world and to *communicate* it to others.
2. Humans are able to *classify* and *order* their knowledge into meaningful relationships, which are generally shared knowledges in communities.
3. The *emic* or "inside view" using language and actions can provide "truths" or a fairly accurate account of the people.
4. There are culturally relevant domains of knowledge that have both *emic* and *etic* referents.
5. Language is an essential way to know people, but actions as experiences are equally as important and help to verify what is said.
6. Rules, values, and language terms derived directly from people are rich sources of data.
7. Ethnoscience rests on the belief that culture is shared in that groups hold similar emic world views and experiences, which provide for some degree of generality of knowledge until proven otherwise.
8. The emic or people's inside views, lifeways, values, meanings, and experiences can be obtained if the researcher remains an active listener, observer, and systematic recorder of information, and if he or she believes that people can and do make sense out of their world of knowledge and experiences.
9. The ethnoscience method provides data on what people believe in to function in an acceptable way as members of a group or society (Goodenough, 1964).

IMPORTANCE OF ETHNOSCIENCE METHOD
TO NURSING

In view of nurses' desire to establish a distinct body of nursing knowledge that is accurate, reliable and relevant to society and the world, the ethnoscience method with the researcher's goal to establish cognitive knowledge of people from diverse cultures holds much hope for nursing. Moreover, nurses are in a special and unique position to have direct, intimate, and continuous contact with people to obtain first-hand ethnoscience data. Conducting ethnoscience research means obtaining information concerning the language expressions, meanings, and actions of people and analyzing the data by the methods proper to ethnoscience. Using the ethnoscience method in nursing often leads to new knowledge with an indepth study of nursing phenomena using language and action expressions. The phenomena of human care, health experiences, rehabilitation, chronicity, child and adult health modes, wellness, and many other areas are yet to be fully studied using the ethnoscience method. Indeed, some different perspectives of old nursing problems and care patterns could be forthcoming with the use of this method.

Further benefits to clinical nursing lie in the fact that the research findings would be derived directly from the client or family; these viewpoints could then be used to guide nursing decisions and interventions. Such client-derived data could reduce speculations and false assumptions about clients' needs and concerns. It could reduce culture imposition practices whereby professional staff impose their values and beliefs unduly upon client or family. Nurses and other health professionals who use such primary or client-derived data could give more thought to "what is best for the patient," rather than "what is best for the system or professional group needs." Now and in the future, it is important that nursing and medical care be based largely upon the client's world view, values, life styles, and care patterns; in addition, nurses should utilize professional advice and practices that are congruent to the client's views. Indeed, perceptual and cognitive differences in care and treatment give rise to problems in communication and therapeutic outcomes (Leininger, 1970, 1978). People from different cultural backgrounds are especially vulnerable to cultural conflicts and incongruities in care. Cognitive values, beliefs, and lifeways of clients may be virtually unknown to health professionals because of present-day trends in which the professional staff has so limited time in which to listen and talk with clients, families, and friends of the client. Findings from the ethnoscience method provide personalized and intimate data of the client and his or her family cognitive beliefs, values, and practices about health and human care.

Some examples of nursing studies that have used the ethnoscience method are the research studies by Bush; Ullom, & Osborne (1975); Horn (1976); Leininger (1965, 1969, 1970; 1981a); Smith (1971); and Thompson (1979). Other ethnographic studies have used a modified approach, but only a few studies reflect a systematic and rigorous use of the ethnoscience method and analysis process. Using *emic* and *etic* data alone does not, however, by itself make the study an ethnoscience investigation. Instead, it is the epistemological premises and linguistic and action analysis methods used that support the ethnoscience method per se. Thus some ethnographic studies may be labeled ethnoscience when actually they are not. While the "new" ethnography includes *emic* data, it is how the data are collected and analyzed that distinguishes ethnographic, ethnonursing, or ethnoscience studies. Such methodological distinctions should be recognized in nursing to prevent future ambiguous research studies and classification of them. Knowing the nature, purposes and epistemological assumptions of the ethnoscience method can help the nurse to be cognizant of subtle and patent differences among research methods used in nursing.

GUIDELINES FOR THE ETHNOSCIENCE METHOD

In conducting ethnoscience research, the following guidelines and epistemological premises are important to know:

1. The ethnoscience method focuses on *eliciting* and *classifying emic* data that comes from the people's thinking, cognitions, language use and experiences. Getting figuratively "inside the world or the mind view of the people" (not the researcher's point of view) is important to document for the people's cognitive structure of knowledge.

2. The researcher works for an understanding of the words, perceptions, cognitions, and interpretations of the *meaning* of whatever is presented or observed in the

context of the informant. Asking the informant to explain or interpret meanings or experiences is essential. Starting from the informant's interpretations helps to understand the behavior, and provides a basis for going beyond this knowledge to make abstractions and generalizations. Ethnoscience is kept foremost in mind as "the systematic study . . . to obtain an accurate account of the people's behavior and how they perceive and know their universe" (Leininger, 1970, p. 168)

3. The informant's statements and categories have meanings and are analyzed individually and collectively to determine similarities and variations in group-shared cognitive knowledge (semantic analysis).

4. Observations of the informants in their natural or familiar settings are made to ascertain the congruence of what is said with what is done.

5. Initially, the researcher selects a domain of inquiry or general category of study and its boundaries. For example, the author's research on the *domain of care* includes a large number of Western and non-Western cultures, but it is limited to human care, not animal care (Leininger, 1981b, 1984).

6. The number of informants is small because of the focus on obtaining in-depth knowledge about the domain. The researcher seeks to know the domain as fully as possible and from virtually every perspective. This requires studying a domain exhaustively and from different viewpoints. Ethnoscience supports the qualitative research method because it's researchers deal with meanings, attributes, and characteristics of a particular domain of inquiry. While some quantitative data are obtained, this is not the primary focus of ethnoscience.

7. Different eliciting techniques are used at different phases of the research in order to explore fully the informant's ideas and to confirm (or validate) ideas or experiences. The eliciting techniques generally follow the Spradley (1979) and Leininger interview methods (1969, 1978).

8. The data are classified and ordered into categories of knowledge (taxonomies) in order to obtain relationships among the linguistic terms and other information collected. The ordering of knowledge helps the researcher to know how individuals or groups order their world and the principles that guide their cognitive knowledge and experiences. The informants' way of ordering or classifying ideas generally makes sense to them, but it may take awhile for the researcher to grasp their classification scheme. Some data may not instantly fit together, but the researcher should be patient and allow time for the ideas to sort out. Different sorting techniques are used to order, classify and establish accurate taxonomies of the domain of study under investigation.

Definition of Terms

1. A *taxonomy* refers to a *system of different contrastive sets about a given phenomenon*, such as "ways to care for people" (Frake, 1962, p. 80).

2. A *domain of inquiry* refers to a *particular area of study to be investigated and which has a boundary such as caring phenomenon.* A domain is generally a broad knowledge area in which smaller units of knowledge and their attributes can be discovered. (The terms domain and category will be used interchangeably by the author as they are similar to each other.)

3. A *segregate* is a *distinctive bundle of attributes which contrasts with other bundles of attri-*

butes (Frake, 1962, p. 83). A segregate is a part of a domain and can be differentiated from other features. Segregates share exclusively in *at least one defining feature*, i.e., setting in which they are found, or characteristics, or attributes. Segregates have contrast sets.

4. A *contrast set* refers to a *class of mutually exclusive segregates, which tend to occur in the same domain*. These contrast sets of data are distinguishable from others. The contrasts have rules that govern their meaning and existence, such as sick and well behavior, two kinds of care (i.e., supportive and non-supportive). Hence segregates have attributes that distinguish sets of items from each other (Leininger, 1970, p. 172). After identifying the segregates with their contrast set, the researcher finds the relevant attributes which distinguish the item (or terms) from one another.

5. *Paradigm* refers to a *set of segregates which can be distinguished by their meaning* (Leininger, 1970, p. 172). Only two segregates can be viewed as a paradigm, e.g., wellness and illness, but there may be a number of subsets within the paradigm.

6. *Componential analysis* refers to the *final step of the ethnoscience method in which high level abstractions are made to establish a generalized meaning of the domain. Principles, rules, laws, hypotheses, or theories usually result from a componential analysis of a domain.* The detailed study and analysis of a domain with its segregates and contrasting sets (their meaning and attributes) leads to this last summative and most important step of the analysis. The phase of *componential analysis* of the data is characterized by the researcher formulating integrated principle(s), law(s), and making high-level abstract statements from the taxonomized data. It is a most difficult intellectual task, but an essential one to achieve the purpose and goals of the ethnoscience method. From such an analysis, new, recurrent, or different meanings related to the domain under study are discovered. Doing a componential analysis and discovering new relationships among knowledge areas is one of the most exciting and rewarding experiences for a researcher. Lately, componential analysis has been used in a general way to analyze large units of data into smaller units of knowledge, but this use is a particularized mode of analysis, rather than a generalized process of high level abstraction that characterizes the original and true intent of this last phase of analysis in ethnoscience.

AN EXAMPLE OF THE ETHNOSCIENCE RESEARCH PROCESS

Since the ethnoscience method is a complex sequential process, the author will give a partial example and a simple diagram of how to conduct an ethnoscience investigation. Data from the author's transcultural nursing research of care phenomenon with Anglo- and Afro-Americans will be used, including the ethnonursing method of in-depth interviews, observations, and direct participatory experiences during a nine-month field study (Leininger, 1981b). Sixty key informants were chosen from a small community of Southern Afro-Americans and Anglo-Americans with these criteria in mind: (1) a willingness of the informants to participate in the study; (2) informant's interest in the phenomena of care; (3) male and female subjects about equally represented; (4) life span age distribution from 16 to 70 years;

and (5) the informants had lived in the community ten or more years (the latter to assure shared cognitive data).

The following ethnoscience methodological steps were taken to derive Table 15-1.

Step I   Identify the *domain* of inquiry such as human care.

Step II   Identify and classify the *segregates* with their *contrasting sets* about care through the process of interviews with question frames.

Step III   Develop the *paradigm* by discovering the major *contrasting segregates* such as "concern for" and "involvement" as distinguishable care units (mutually contrasting terms).

Step IV   *Identify and classify subsets and sub-subsets related to each major segregate*, e.g., "friends" (whites) and "brothers and sisters" (blacks).

Step V   Formulate the informants' principles, rules and/or laws by which the people know their world of living and experiencing.

When these steps were completed, a partial taxonomy in Table 15-1 was discovered.

Through the process of systematic recording of in-depth interviews and observing what happened with 60 informants in their familiar living environment, the taxonomy of care in Table 15-1 was derived. This is a partial analysis to show some of the total segregates about the domain of human care as identified, known, and confirmed by the people. Other care segregates were discovered, e.g., presence, touch, helping, and watching for. These segregates had contrasting sets that were distinguishable from each other by language and cultural beliefs and daily action patterns. From these data, the author formulated statements of principles and rules that guide human care behaviors in the village. Recording phrases or words as the informants expressed them was done systematically and conscientiously. The language statements had to be clarified by open-ended interview techniques, and their responses were kept separate from the researcher's observations of the people's actions. The researcher must stay close to the informant's language uses, their interventions, and specific meanings of terms. In addition, the two sets of data are studied for areas of *similarities* or *differences*. The researcher found the verbal *emic* statements of the people were repeatedly supported by their daily patterns of living, and contrasted with *etic* statements that did not allow their action modes. For example, the Afro-Americans expressed human care as being "concerned for" their own "brothers and sisters" (emic statements) especially those who lived closely related to them or were linked by kinship and survival ties. Their actions revealed "concerned for" their "brothers and sisters" by giving them food and clothes and sharing whatever they could share in material and human resources. Human care was "concern for" their "brothers and sisters" both fictive and kin related.

Getting to the meaning and attributes of care was important; the author used a variety of interview techniques (several described in Chapter 3) and some of Spradley's interview strategies (Spradley, 1979, pp. 78–79, 85–87, 155–172) such as the following:

1. *Using broad inquiry or "Tell me about" or "I would like to learn about" exploratory statements* such as: "I am interested to learn about your ideas of human care/caring. Could you tell me about your beliefs or ideas about care as you know them?"

Table 15-1 *Example of ethnoscience data analysis.*

	Partial Analysis of Ethnocare as Example of the Ethnoscience Method					
	Ethonocare Study of Southern Blacks and Whites in the United States*					
Domain of Inquiry →	Human Care					
Caring Segregate →	Paradigm Segregates					
	"Concern For"			"Involvement With"		
Subsets →	Blacks		Whites	Blacks		Whites
Sub-subsets →	1. "Brothers and sisters" • blood brothers • close brothers		1. Friends • store • around here	1. "Brothers and sisters" • "gotta be there" • happening		1. Friends • "around" • "gone"
	2. Church folks • see on Sunday • see rest of week		2. Community folks	2. Church folks • pitch in and help • know what they need		2. Community things • town affairs • other affairs
	3. Others around me		3. Strangers • within town • outside town	3. All others • big town • little town		3. Strangers • within • outside

Note: Principles and rules for living were formulated from the total data of the domain of care.
*Terms "Black" and "White" were shorthand terms for Afro-Americans and Anglo-Americans respectively.

2. Asking general *descriptive questions:* "Could you describe human caring acts from your daily ways of living here? What are your general thoughts and experiences about human caring as practiced here?

3. Using *"lead-in" statements* to be completed by the informants such as, "Caring for people means _____."

4. Using *"focused-in" or specific statements:* Tell me specifically about the care as you know it to be "concerned for your brothers and sisters." "Could you give me some specific examples?" I would like to focus in on the meaning of 'light and hard touch' as caring to you."

5. *Using experience queries:* "What experiences have you had with caring for your brothers and sisters in the community or neighborhood?" "When you spoke of your family gatherings, how did you experience family care?" "Tell me whatever you would like to about care as you saw or experienced it in your growing up in this community."

During the interview and observation sessions, the researcher used the informant's language phrases, terms, or descriptive experiences in order to get into their world and encourage ideas familiar and known to them. Using their own language expressions made the informant more comfortable or at home with his or her ideas rather than struggling with the researcher's language. One also noted in this way unfamiliar terms that are not otherwise meaningful nor understood.

Another helpful technique was to ask if the informants would tell the researcher what a typical day, night or situation was like in their caring lifeways. Listening to and recording a typical day helped to show use of terms, patterns, and lifeways related to care and non-caring attributes, plus getting insights about general experience "around the clock." Obtaining contrasts of daily or special event experiences of the informants helped to identify the subcategories of each segregate and subset with explanations for any differences. For example, differences in being "concerned for" whites and blacks became clear by the examples of social and family care activities, and the informants were able to identify, explain, and interpret such differences.

Obtaining the contrasts in experiences in different environmental situations generally led to identifying principles or *rules that guided the actions* for human care or caring patterns. For example, in church services, the Afro-Americans expressed *deep concern* for one's brother (or sister) by wailing or crying aloud when a dead brother (or sister) was presented to the community. (Touching the dead body while crying loudly was expected; whereas Anglo-Americans expressed care by controlling one's emotions and offering many verbal statements of sympathy.)

Open-ended or incomplete phrases were used to obtain the informant's explicit statements or to prevent the researcher from introducing his or her ideas. Opening framed statements such as "You define care as _____." were used to develop a class inclusion or specific ideas about aspect of a domain. "The term for care is _____." Letting the informant complete the statement permits him or her to express ideas as they know them—their cognitive knowledge of the domain. It is also most useful in establishing contrasting data responses and to validate ideas among informants regarding the segregate and subsets.

Especially important is the need to use contrasting questions to gain in-depth responses about the domain. Questions such as "What do you see are the differences between caring for a black brother and sister and a white friend?" Or, under what circumstances can a black brother or sister touch a white woman?" What do you see are the differences between a caring and noncaring brother? The latter usually brings forth many contrasting views. Requesting examples of whatever you are talking about helps to understand the true meaning and use of language and action modes.

Throughout ethnoscience investigations, the author has found that the phrase, "Tell me about," "Could you tell me about _____?" or "I would like to learn about _____" yielded much rich and meaningful data. Asking tightly formulated questions tends to yield less productive and meaningful responses. However, some specific questions may be in order in trying to get precise definitions, statements, or contrasts later.

In defining, refining, and classifying data, some other techniques are used such as the following:

Card sort for similarities or differences. This is a valuable means to clarify terms or phrases, sort differences and similarities, and to arrive at the informants' cognitive way of ordering ideas, experiences, symbols, actions, and material items. After obtaining the informants' language terms or phrases, the informant is asked to sort the card terms that are: (a) alike or different; (b) belong together; or (c) belong in different categories. The informant is asked to clarify *why* he sorted the piles in the way he did. The process of sorting the differences and similarities of any phenomenon under refinement is often repeated to examine the strength of the decision, or to obtain further verification about the specific knowledge.

Use of material objects. to explain or demonstrate cultural or social usage. This includes cultural objects as symbols of specific meanings and usage. For example, several informants revealed that the symbol of the Afro-Americans who wore a small sassafras bag was a caring act to protect them from illness. Another practice was to wear a string with thirteen knots around the waist to protect the woman from harm in while in the strange hospital environment.

Use of drawings, pictures, and personal documents. to explicate the meaning of terms or phrases.

Use of examples of experiences. related to the domain, such as home care, hospital care, or what happens in settings where noncaring occurs.

Use of role playing. sketches done by adults and children to clarify or verify the meanings or expression of the domain being studied. Checking and rechecking of verbal statements and actions should continue at every phase of the research process to validate and increase reliability of findings.

ORDERING THE TAXONOMY

Ordering the taxonomy is a major challenge and task for the ethnoscience researcher. During the process of eliciting data about the domain and segregates, the researcher constantly tries to order different *taxons* (the smallest units of categorizing data) so that smallest and largest units of data are placed in proper categories according to the informants' world view. All these techniques and strategies help with the process, but the final "big picture" or the completed taxonomy has to be brought together or synthesized so that all parts fit reasonably, logically, and meaningfully together. This is major task, but an exciting challenge for the ethnoscience researcher. If the previous steps have been systematically and conscientiously followed, the overall taxonomy should begin to fall together, using an experienced ethnoscientist, however, is most valuable to the new researcher to achieve a final statement and synthesize large categories of knowledge.

ARRIVING AT COMPONENTIAL STATEMENTS, PRINCIPLES, OR LAWS REGARDING THE DOMAIN

The final step of ethnoscience research is to formulate componential statements from the data. In continuing with the example of the domain and taxonomy of care (Table 15-1), the four steps can be next demonstrated. Formulations about care are made by the researcher from spoken words and actions at the lowest level of abstraction (the specific *descriptive statements)* to the highest level of abstraction *(general principles, generalizations, correlational statements and occasional laws about the domain).* The highest level of abstraction requires an intellectual synthesis the categories of knowledge and the ability to formulate abstract statements. (This is frequently a problem for nurse researchers who are so firmly committed to use only empirical or factual data.) However, as the researcher becomes skilled in doing abstractions from categories of empirical data, high level abstractions become easier to do. The following steps are used to arrive at a componential statement of some phenomenon.

First step: Formulation of a specific statement. This refers to making *descriptive* statements from the informants' emic data. For example, the following specific statements of care were made from the Afro-American data: (a) My Black "brothers and sisters" care for each other in this town. (b) We care for each other for our survival. These descriptive statements portray common and recurrent statements and action patterns of the informants.

Second step: Formulation of a general statement. This refers to making a *broad statement* about the domain to show related general categories or segregates of knowledge or experiences. For example, (a) There are two contrasting categories of human care known to the people, which are "good caring" and "bad caring." (b) "Concern for" is a dominant care construct for Southern Afro-American "brothers and sisters" in the community studied.

Third step: Formulation of an abstract statement. At this point the researcher reflects upon the taxonomy and *formulates an abstract statement of the underlying meaning and usage practices of the domain.* For example, care has different meanings between Black and White people in the South village which are related to historical survival experiences and reciprocal relationships between Whites and Blacks to be protected and helpful in crisis situations.

Fourth step: Formulating a componential or correlational statement as a principle, rule, theory, or to guide actions or establish laws. This is the difficult task of the analysis. Abstracting data at a high level from the total taxonomy and the empirical data produced by the previous three steps is challenging. The correlational statement covers the essence, attributes, and deepest meaning of the domain under study with its segregates and contrasting sets of data. Continuing with the Afro-American example, the following componential formulations were made in an attempt to establish a theory, principle, or law to guide nursing interventions.

Theory statements: There is a positive relationship between "concern for" someone and healthy survival. Or, the greater the signs of "concern for" another "brother and sister," the greater the evidence of healthy survival and well-being.

Principle: "Concern for" Black and White villagers requires different care modes to give effective and satisfying nursing care to the people.

Law: Caring as "concern for" is inversely related to Black well-being and group survival. The statements will continue to be studied with other Afro-Americans and Anglo-Americans in Southern communities. But the ethnoscience data met qualitative validity and reliability criteria presented in this book (Chapter 3). Similar research investigations of different populations or cultures in the world will gradually lead to knowing human care as nursing's distinct knowledge and practice. The ethnoscience method is the most precise and valid means to get *emic* (or people-derived data) to assure this goal.

The ethnoscience method is one of the most challenging, stimulating, and rewarding ways to obtain the people's cognitive and experiential knowledge. It is a formal and rigorous method that requires systematic documentation and observations with repeated verifications. It is a method that is highly congruent with nursing's desire to intimately know the client's lifestyle and intimate care and health behaviors as a basis to guide nursing decisions and actions. Moreover, this is the new trend and "period of discoveries of lifestyles, patterns, world view, and meanings" of health and care to people; the ethnoscience method shows much hope to identify and know these differences. Sharing the informant's knowledge of these areas should increase the quality of healing, care, and treatment, of clients especially with people of different cultures. To get inside the people's frame of reference and understand their cultural values, meanings, and experiences of health, illness, and care is critical to ensure therapeutic or effective care to people. Many new insights and large areas of previously unknown information are being discovered by the use of the ethnoscience method. It is hoped, however, that more nurses will know how to use the ethnoscience method so that in-depth studies can be made of nursing phenomena.

REFERENCES

Adair, S. A. An ethnoscientific approach to identify the perceptions and experiences as perceived by an urban Mexican-American group in relation to medical and nursing care. Unpublished master's thesis. Seattle: School of Nursing, University of Washington, 1975.

Bush, M. T., Ullom, J. A., & Osborne, O. H. The meaning of mental health: A report of two ethnoscientific studies. *Nursing Research*, 1975, *24*(2), 130–138.

Frake, C. The ethnographic study of cognitive systems. In T. Gladwin & W. G. Sturtevant (Eds.), *Anthropology and human behavior*. Washington, D. C.: Anthropological Society of Washington, 1962.

Gladwin, T., & Sturtevant, W. G. Introduction to paper by Frake, C. In *Anthropology and human behavior.* Washington, D. C.: Anthropological Society of Washington, 1962, pp. 72–73.

Goodenough, W., Cultural anthropology and linguistics. In D. Hymes (Ed.), *Language in culture and society.* New York: Harper and Row, 1964.

Goodenough, W. Componential analysis. *Science,* 1967, *156,* 1203–1209.

Horn, B. An ethnoscientific study to determine social and cultural factors affecting native American mothers during pregnancy (doctoral dissertation). Seattle: University of Washington, 1976.

Johnson, A. W. The cognitive/structural orientation. In *Quantification in cultural anthropology.* Stanford, Calif.: Stanford University Press, 1978, 158–184.

Kay, M. A., & Evaneshko, V. The ethnoscience research technique. *Western Journal of Nursing Research,* 1982, *4*(1), 49–64.

Leininger, M. Convergence and divergence of human behavior: An ethnopsychological comparative study of two Gadsup villages in the Eastern Highlands of New Guinea (unpublished doctoral dissertation). Seattle: University of Washington, 1965.

Leininger, M. Ethnoscience: A new and promising research approach for the health sciences. *Image,* (Sigma Theta Tau Magazine), 1969, *3*(1), 2–8.

Leininger, M. Ethnoscience: A new and promising research approach for the health sciences. In *Nursing and anthropology: Two worlds to blend.* New York: John Wiley & Sons, 1970, pp. 167–178.

Leininger, M. *Transcultural nursing: Concepts, theories and practices.* New York: John Wiley & Sons, 1978.

Leininger, M. *Caring: An essential human need.* Thorofare, N.J.: Charles B. Slack, 1981b.

Leininger, M. Ethnocaring, ethnohealth and social structure of rural Southern Afro-American and Anglo-American cultures. In *care: The essence of nursing and health.* Thorofare, N.J.: Charles B. Slack, 1984.

Leininger, M. *Care: The essence of nursing and health.* Thorofare, N.J.: Charles B. Slack, 1984.

Metzger, D., & Williams, G. A formal ethnographic analysis of Tenejapa Ladino weddings. *American Anthropologist,* 1963, *65,* 1076–1101.

Pelto, P. *Anthropological research: The structure of inquiry.* New York: Harper & Row, 1970, pp. 67–84.

Pelto, P., & Pelto, G. *Anthropological research: The structure of inquiry,* (2nd. ed.). New York: Cambridge University Press, 1979.

Pike, K. *Language in relation to a unified theory of the structure of human behavior.* (Vol. 1.). Glendale, Calif.: Summer Institute of Linguistics, 1954.

Smith, D. L. Aspects of the ethnoscience approach to study of values and needs as perceived by the North American Indian women in relation to prenatal care (unpublished master's thesis). Seattle: University of Washington, 1971.

Spradley, J. P. *The ethnographic interview.* New York: Holt, Rinehart and Winston, 1979.

Spradley, J. P. *You owe yourself a drunk: Ethnography of urban nomads.* Boston: Little, Brown & Company, 1970.

Sturtevant, W. C. Studies in ethnoscience. *American Anthropologist,* 1964, *66*(2), 99–131.

Thompson, J. Ethnoscientific study of Mormon health beliefs and values, unpublished paper. Salt Lake City: University of Utah, 1979.

Werner, O., & Fenton, J. Method and theory in ethnoscience or ethnoepistemology. In *A handbook of method in cultural anthropology.* New York: Columbia University Press, 1973.

16

Ethnographic Research Method: A Qualitative Example to Discover the Role of "Granny" Midwives in Health Services

Rita A. Kroska

Childbirth in the United States has not always been physician-centered nor taken place in a hospital. As late as 1910, conservative estimates indicated that 50 per cent of all births in the United States were attended by midwives (Litoff, 1982). In these early years, of the 20th century, there were large numbers of European immigrants entering this country, many of whom employed a midwife. European and African immigrants, and other poor people, could not afford to pay a physician's fee, nor were they eager to enter a hospital, which they viewed as a place in which to end life, and not to bring forth new life. Moreover, some people were morally opposed to having men serve as birth attendants (Litoff, 1982) and still others preferred the midwife, or "granny" as she was affectionately called, for childbirth.

Nurse researchers need to be aware of such historical factors and the diverse lifeway factors of mother-infant health care in order to understand, plan for, and work with a large Afro-American (Black) population in the South.* This chapter, therefore, uses a focused and mini-ethnographic field research method as an example of an important type of qualitative research to discover past and present lifeways of the "granny" midwives. The purpose is to obtain knowledge to guide professional nurses in their work and to understand the role that granny midwives

---

*In this paper, the term "Black" will be used as a shorthand reference to the Afro-Americans living in the southern part of the United States.

QUALITATIVE RESEARCH METHODS IN NURSING
ISBN 0-8089-1676-9

played in the health care services in the South. The ethnographic field study method was chosen because of the researcher's interest in, preparation in, and familiarity with the research method and professional midwifery. This method is viewed as one of the best research methods to understand contextual factors regarding the life-ways of human groups. Most importantly, the ethnographic approach can provide a holistic view of human groups in their natural settings. This chapter will, therefore, describe a focused ethnographic method with participant-observation to study granny midwives by the process of describing, analyzing, and presenting data about these midwives and factors affecting the birth and health of infants. Some historical contextual factors that led to the granny midwives' role in American health care practices will be provided through the autobiographic method, another important method often used within the broad ethnographic research approach. An ethnographic emic questionnaire was used to elicit specific and general data about factors affecting the birth weight and health of infants. A description of the geographic area and life-ways of the people will help the reader obtain a holistic view of the granny midwives and their past and current role in health care services to mothers and infants. As a certified professional nurse-midwife and nurse-anthropologist, I have used these combined research methods to know and understand mothers and infants of different cultures and subcultures.

THE RESEARCHER'S INTEREST DOMAIN

From the perspective of professional nursing, there is much to be learned from historical and current aspects of a maternity and infant professional health care systems that retain the supervisory responsibility of the granny midwife. This cultural phenomenon of supervision by county health center personnel of granny midwives will undoubtedly disappear from the American way of life, but the cultural, social, and economic factors that supported this system of health care for many years need to be recognized and understood, as new or alternative forms of professional nursing care come into existence. The critical and important nursing problem is how does a professional nurse integrate her or his knowledge and skills with those of folk health practitioners, i.e., the large granny-midwife system that has for nearly a century served the people? The ethnographic research approach, with a culture history that focuses on understanding the traditional and current health services, appeared to be the appropriate method to provide a meaningful account of the complex phenomenon. Thus, the domain of interest was focused on granny midwives using an ethnographic qualitative research method to obtain an accurate account of the midwives. This method has been used by nurse-anthropologists or those prepared in transcultural nursing since the early 1960s, and is now being introduced to nurses as a valuable method in nursing research.

In thinking about this interest area and the question posed, some preliminary facts about the granny midwife help identify the problem or inquiry area of interest to the researcher. For many years granny midwives were the principal birth attendants for nonhospital deliveries for both poor Blacks and Whites throughout many rural areas in the United States. At the turn of the century, high infant and maternal mortality rates triggered alarm, and medical opposition to the granny midwives arose. Anti-immigrant and anti-Black prejudices, and the increase in hospital construction were other factors that led to the gradual decline in the number of granny midwives in the United States (Litoff, 1982).

Because many of the granny midwives were not educated through formal programs of study, they had to depend upon public health nurses, health officials, sympathetic physicians, and others to support or speak for them. Hence, much of the support for the midwife came from public health officials who believed that maternal and fetal mortality would be considerably reduced if granny midwives were trained and regulated by professionals (Litoff, 1982).

In the state of Alabama, as late as 1940 there were 2600 granny midwives. The Alabama Department of Public Health therefore has had long and continuous contact with these indigenous workers and their role in health services (Houde, Humphrey, Boyd, & Goldenberg, 1982). Since 1940 there has been a steady decline in both the number of granny midwives and the number of home deliveries attended by them. Although granny midwives are no longer practicing in large numbers, there are, nevertheless, 70 midwives attending home births in 1983 in the state of Alabama. In Houston County, the county with the largest number of granny midwives, there were 70 home births in 1982, attended by a total of five "grannies." The need to explore and document the caregiver role of the granny midwives by the ethnographic method as they provide health services to people in the South became apparent.

ETHNOGRAPHIC METHOD: A QUALITATIVE RESEARCH APPROACH

Since the major goal of nursing research is the improvement of nursing practice, qualitative research, by its very nature, is important and essential to help nurses understand the world in which clients live and express their health needs (Leininger, 1978a; Swanson & Chenitz, 1982). Ideally, the ethnoscience approach as described and used by Leininger lends itself to fresh insights into a particular culture's health-illness universe (Leininger, 1970, 1978a). She states that ethnoscience "refers to the systematic study of the way of life of a designated cultural group with the purpose of obtaining an accurate account of the people's behavior and how they perceive and interpret their universe." The ethnoscience method is important to discover qualitative life factors in a systematic way. This study draws upon selected ideas, but it is not an ethnoscience method per se.

Because I wished to study a group of caregivers, the granny midwives of the southern United States, I used a combination of research methods known today as the ethnonursing research approach (Leininger, 1970; 1978a). Several elements and features of the well-known general ethnographic research method employed by anthropologists were used, such as systematic observations, direct participant experiences, informal interviews, autobiographic studies, and others (Spradley, 1979, 1980; Leininger, 1970; 1978a). For the development of rapport, I relied heavily upon my past years of clinical nursing experiences in assisting with home deliveries as a certified nurse-midwife. The ethnonursing method, using several combined approaches and clinical nursing experiences, helped me to develop trust with the midwives and get the world view of the granny midwives (See Sunrise Model, Ch. 3, p. 45).

I also used a tape recorder (with the midwives' written permission) in order to record data verbatim. I used this tool to get the feeling tones and specific experiential content from the midwives, and to study and analyze their expressions. With the tape recorder and interviews, I documented some historical aspects to show how each midwife perceived herself as a person and as a functioning midwife for a number of years in a southern community. Autobiographic techniques, keeping the focus on the midwives and their cultural ways, were also important in documenting historical factors. I wanted to get their responses and viewpoints as they perceived and knew their role through the years.

In the process of the interview, each participant was asked how she came to be a granny midwife and what her beliefs were concerning weight of the newborn infant. The experiential questions or inquiry area were chosen because I was involved in obtaining both quantitative and qualitative anthropometric data of the birth weight determinants of pregnant adolescents and their general cultural lifeways. Each structured inquiry (Fig. 16-1) was preceded with the phrase, "Based on your experience. . . ." The last question was, "Is there anything else you can think of that causes a big baby or a small baby?" Tapes were made of the interviews with each of the key informants and were later transcribed onto paper.

Content from the responses were listed as cultural domains; sketch maps of activities, friends, and clients; and comparative analysis of cultural domains. By comparing, contrasting, and analyzing cultural domains—such as kinds of clients,

---

Figure 16-1 Experiential Questionnaire

From your experiences:

1. Can you tell me what you think makes a small baby?

2. Can you tell me what makes a big baby?

3. Do you think height and wieght of the parents of a baby affect birth weight?
   yes _____   no _____   Give me an example _____

4. Do you think height and weight of the grandparents of a baby affect birth weight?
   yes _____   no _____   Give me an example _____

5. Do you ever have pregnant women ask you what they should eat (during pregnancy)? yes _____   no _____

6. What do you tell them are the good things to eat?

7. Do the pregnant mothers have any unusual eating habits, such as eating starch, clay, or dirt?

8. With those pregnant mothers who were serious (conscientious) about food intake, do you believe they had babies weighing seven pounds and over?

9. With the pregnant mothers who smoke cigarettes, do you notice any difference in the size (weight) of the baby?

10. With the pregnant mother who drinks too much (alcohol), do you notice any difference in the size (weight) of the baby?

11. With the pregnant mothers who do (use) drugs, do you notice any difference in the size (weight) of the baby?

12. Do you think having worries or having a bad scare can affect the size of the baby?

13. Is there anything else that you can think of that causes a big or a small baby?

ways of talking, things to eat—the ethnographer begins to identify relationships among domains through a careful content analysis of all data collected. Relationships among the cultural themes, such as maintaining status, cultural contradictions, and mobility of the granny midwife, provide new or reaffirmed insights about the people under study. This intensive thematic content analysis is a powerful and accurate means to learn about, document, and understand the totality of the granny midwives' subculture, and it provides an important knowledge for future professional nursing care practices—i.e., cultural content and context data of human behavior.

THE CULTURAL AND HISTORICAL SETTING

The cultural setting for this study is Houston County, which is located in the far southeastern portion of Alabama. It is bordered on the south by Florida and on the east by Georgia, by Dale and Geneva (Alabama) Counties on the west, and by Henry County on the north. Total population for 1981 was 74,632, and 35 per cent were living in rural areas; the average per capita income was $6,432 for the same year (Dalzell, 1981). Approximately 22 per cent of the people living in the county are non-White. Twenty thousand of the total population are eligible for social or welfare services (food stamps, Aid to Families with Dependent Children [AFDC], and so forth) (Dalzell, 1981). The greatest number of the population is employed in wholesale and retail sales and in factories or manufacturing industries. The remainder of the population is involved in construction, government, and services (Dalzell, 1981). There are 92 physicians licensed to practice in the county, eight of whom provide routine prenatal care and six pediatric care. Although there are a total of five granny midwives attending childbirth, there are no certified nurse-midwives practicing at present in the county. There are two hospitals, offering prenatal classes and labor and delivery service. It has been suggested that better medical care and better access to this care through regionalization programs that emphasize improving the survival of low-birth-weight infants account for the rapid decline in neonatal mortality in Alabama (from 17 to 9 per 1000 live births) from 1970 to 1980 (Goldenberg et al, 1982). It should be noted that 18.4 per cent of births in the county in 1982 were to mothers aged 10 to 19 years (Alabama Department of Public Health, Bureau of Vital Statistics, 1983).

GRANNY MIDWIVES AND THE HOUSTON COUNTY
HEALTH DEPARTMENT

In the following arrangement for the continued phasing out of the granny midwife in Alabama and in anticipation of the certified nurse-midwife, there is much to be learned about the blending of two different health care systems, the professional and the traditional folk ways:

Title 22 of the Alabama Code, Chapter 19, predominantly regulates the practice of nurse-midwifery and also allows for the continuation of practice by lay-midwives holding current permits from the county board of health. It is the interpretation of the law by the Alabama Department of Public Health that no new lay-midwife permits will be issued. Only those lay-midwives previously issued permits to practice will be issued annual renewal applications. It is the responsibility of the county board of health wherein the lay-midwife practices to issue a permit annually upon the recommendation of the public health nursing supervisor or senior nurse. Because the lay-midwife program requires ongoing nursing supervision, it is recommended by the Alabama Department of Public Health that the county board of health delegate the authority and responsibility for providing such supervision to the county health department. (Division of Public Health Nursing, 1980)

In 1958, serious efforts to teach granny midwives were made by the Alabama Health Department. The Maternal-Child Nursing Consultant for Alabama held a two-week training program for midwives in Houston County. This program was attended by three of the five currently practicing midwives; the remaining two gained their permits to practice three years later. Requirements for receiving a permit were (1) to attend the two-week training session: (2) to be knowledgeable about the policies governing their practice; (3) to observe six home births; and (4) to have a satisfactory physical examination. Renewal of permits are based upon the results of an annual physical examination and the verification of attendance at monthly meetings conducted by the county public health nurses (only two unexcused absences in one year are allowed).

No midwife may practice in Houston County without a permit, which must be renewed before April 10 of each year. The permit is to be kept in the midwife bag at all times. Midwives from other counties are not permitted to deliver babies in Houston County except in an emergency. An important regulation states that a midwife must not accept a case unless the client has a clinic card or a permit signed by a physician. The maternity client is given an appointment to attend the registration clinic, held once a month, and the maternity return-visit clinic, held twice a month. Clients who wish a home delivery with a granny midwife attending must have a maternity clinic card indicating physician approval for midwifery delivery. Also on the card are reports of the Rh factor, VDRL (Venereal Disease Research Laboratory, a serological test for syphilis), gonorrhea culture, and Papanicolaou smear.

Further built-in protection for the granny midwife clients include the following: the midwife may carry only four maternity clients at a time and she may not give any medicine other than the prophylactic silver nitrate solution (furnished by the Health Department), which is instilled into each eye of the newborn within two hours after birth. She must take and record and Apgar score on the birth certificate in the home. The granny midwife is to report each delivery within 24 hours to the nursing supervisor or senior nurse at the county health department. The birth certificate is to be filed with the county registrar at the county health department within five days. To do this, the midwife presents the signed physician information letter when she files the birth certificate. Failure to do so may be grounds for revocation of the midwife permit.

According to state regulations, the midwife is never permitted to perform an internal examination (vaginal or rectal) on the client for any purpose either before or after the baby is born. She is not allowed to wear gloves or even carry gloves in the midwife bag, which must be checked by the nursing supervisor after each delivery and at least once a month. Her hands are to be scrubbed with brush, soap, and water, and fingernails cleaned with a fingernail stick before caring for the client. She wears a clean gown and cap during a delivery. Inside her midwife bag she carries the autoclaved scissors and cord clamps (Hollister) from the Health Department.

Should a premature (5 ½ pounds or less) baby be born or any abnormal condition be present, the midwife must report this to the Health Department immediately. She carries a small scale in her midwife bag to weigh the infant soon after birth, and she remains with the new mother and infant for two hours after the placenta has been delivered. Should any client require longer than 12 hours to deliver after the midwife arrives, she is to be taken to the Emergency Room at the Southeast Alabama Medical Center. This practice is upheld if there is "too much bleeding before or after delivery," if the client has dizzy spells or faints, if the delivery is premature, or if there is any difficulty with the delivery. Consultation for these situations are made with the nursing supervisor in the county health department.

It is the nursing supervisor at the County Health Center who is responsible for the coordination and supervision of the granny midwife program. It is she or her alternate who is, literally, on 24 hour call to the five midwives. Her relationship with them is obviously one of sincere caring and close supervision. They, in turn, respect and admire her. For the past 20 years, the nursing supervisor has held a monthly class with the five midwives for purposes of continuing education and checking the preparation of their midwife bags (Farmer, 1983). During this one-to-one relationship, the maternity nurse supervisor questions them and instructs them, particularly if there was a hospital transfer of a mother or infant or if the mother complained about the midwife's care.

The maternity nurse supervisor keeps a list of those mothers anticipating a home birth and those already attended by a midwife. These clients are given an initial physical examination by one of five obstetricians who staff the County Health Center. Thereafter, the registered nurses check the client during the months preceding delivery. During the last month of pregnancy, the obstetrician assesses the suitability of the client for a home birth and gives the mother a signed card denoting his approval. The client may select a hospital delivery and pay the physician $250 to $500 or slightly more, or to have a home birth and pay the granny midwife $100.

For follow-up care of mother and infant, registered nurses from the County Health Center make a home visit to the new mother and infant within 24 hours after delivery. If the district nurse cannot make the home visit, one of the two maternity program supervisors visits the home. Follow-up visits continue to be made by district registered nurses.

AUTOBIOGRAPHICAL VIGNETTES OF THE FIVE GRANNY MIDWIVES

To understand the granny midwives, the researcher interviewed five of them, and some autobiographical vignettes are presented here to reveal these midwives as they presented themselves.

Typically, the Alabamian granny midwife is an older Black woman possessing little formal education. She came into her occupation of midwifery by a variety of ways, among them hereditary claim, aptitude, or encouragement of sympathetic physicians or family kinfolk. Her knowledge base of human anatomy and physiology is minimal; she does not take blood pressure nor does she listen to the fetal heart tones. She does not test urine for the presence of glucose and protein, nor does she measure fundal height for uterine growth. Without these fundamentals to guide her, she is unable to detect fetal distress or potential maternal complications. She functions as a comforter to the woman in labor and is a recognized quasi-leader in her community. She is sought out and accepted by some, but most of all, she is always available to people in her community.

As a group, the five remaining practicing granny midwives in Houston County are Black and range in age from 50 to 68 years. All have been delivering infants and helping mothers in birthing process for at least 20 years, and one for 50 years. All have been given permits to practice beginning in 1958. Two live in Dothan, the largest city in the county; one lives in Cottonwood, another in Ashford, and the fifth in Pansy. All responses were gathered by individual, private tape recordings with written permission from each midwife.

When asked how they became midwives, each responded with different answers.†

My great-grandmother was midwife for the slaves. She had only two children. Her daughter was a midwife just after slavery. And she had Sarah, my mother, who was also a midwife in her lifetime. So I began following grandmother when I was about 12 years old. Grandmother was old and I'd go with her, and she'd always let me tend to the baby while she see after the mother. Then I began to go along with my mother. And if grandmother and my mother were gone I would go to be with her (the woman in labor). I'd always fill out the birth certificates for grandmother and mama and send them off . . . but I was 18 years old before I delivered one by myself.

Her daughter, also a midwife, had this to say:

I've been a midwife for 25 years. My mother, my grandmother, my great-grandmother, and my great-great-grandmother were midwives. My mother is still practicing. She and I got our licenses [permits] at the same time. My mother delivered three of my four children. The last one I had was born in the hospital because it was a breech.

The youngest midwife married into a midwife family:

My mother-in-law delivered babies and when I married into the family, she asked me to come along. But I would also go with the doctor when he would deliver babies in the home, and after a while I would do the work and he would just look on.

The fourth midwife who is licensed (by permit) in Dale County and in Houston County stated:

I began workin' as assistant to a doctor in 1959 when his nurse took time out to have a baby. He delivered babies at his office and in homes. He felt I was

---

†These are verbatim statements made by the lay midwives from the tape recorder, and are presented to give the local language.

real good at it. One day he said, "Have you considered being a midwife?" I said, "Oh, no doctor." "Well, I think you should." He came back at me weeks and months later, saying I should take it up, saying why don't you check with the Health Department. He was more or less lettin' me make up my own mind. Think about having a self-employing job instead of working for someone else, and now I've been 23 years at it. I married at 14 years of age. I wanted to finish school. I had finished 8th grade. They started givin' adult general education to finish high school. The doctor said I should go back to school. So I went, three nights a week at school and two nights a week learnin' seamstressing. I had six kids at that time and I was 24 years old. I stayed at home until all my children got into school. So I accepted the job with the doctor and went to school and seamstressin' at 6 o'clock in the evenin'. I was 38 years old when I completed high school. I'm 53 now.

Another midwife who lives in a rural area about eight miles from the County Health Department related that it was her husband who encouraged her to become a midwife:

My husband was "takin' up the trains" and asked me one day if I didn't want to be a midwife. At first I told him "no," and then he wanted to know why not. I said, 'cause I'd be so scared . . . if the baby died and I'd be scared, they'd think I did it." So I came on in and took the trainin' course right here in the auditorium [Houston County Health Department] in 1965, five days a week for two weeks. Mrs. Kirsh was our teacher [Maternal-Child Health nurse consultant with the Alabama State Health Department] . . . I delivered my first baby in 1966 and I was so scared. When I go to deliver babies I pray. I ask the Lord to help me.

At least one of the five midwives interviewed speaks of asking for divine assistance:

When they come to me to deliver babies I start prayin' and I sing my song. I starts to hum my prayer and all the time I'm away 'till I get to the house I hum my prayer. I say, "Thank you, Jesus." My song is this:

Down through the years,
I know the Lord did good to me.
Oh, down through the years,
I know the Lord sure did good to me.
I know the Lord sure did good to me.
Oh, he took my feet made outa clay,
And he did good to me.
Oh, he took my feet made outa clay,
And he did good to me.

One midwife's beliefs and values are apparent in her response to the question of payment for services ($100):

Some of them meet me on the street, and I have forgotten them or if it was a boy or a girl, but they know me and they'll buy me somethin' or give me a dollar or two . . . but still I often think this . . . Supposin' I'd been here long, long ago and Joseph and the Mother Mary came by and wanted me to deliver her and because he didn't have no money, would I turn the Baby Jesus down? And I think about all the babies. . . . I don't know who they are or what they'll be. And so I don't hold it against the babies because the mommy and daddy don't pay up or because the mommy and daddy wasn't married or 'cause the mommy and daddy wan't white or what not. It doesn't matter. I don't hold that against the babies. I keep foster children 'cause they are human beings. I help get 'em up to where they can ask for bread.

GRANNY MIDWIVES BELIEFS ABOUT BIRTH WEIGHT DETERMINANTS

One of the uses of ethnographic and qualitative research is to improve professionals' understanding of the knowledge and beliefs held by health workers, and to translate these into health care objectives. To increase knowledge content of a transcultural nature, a tape recorder was used. During a one-to-one interview, each participant in the investigation willingly told how she became a granny midwife and about the folk practice of midwifery. Each were then asked a series of loosely structured questions related to determinants of birth weight (Fig. 16-1). These responses were also tape recorded for later analysis. The inquiry questions were broadly stated and prefaced with "Based on your experience. . . ." the author was especially curious to learn about how midwives perceived factors affecting birth weight. Thus the interview and questions covered such topics as what makes a small or big baby (term), does height and weight of parents and grandparents of the newborn affect birth weight, what are the good things to eat during pregnancy, what are the unusual eating habits some mothers have, and is there any difference in the size at birth of the baby of a mother who smokes cigarettes, drinks alcohol, uses drugs, or has a bad scare during her pregnancy.

The responses to these questions were recorded on tape and then transcribed onto paper. These responses lent themselves to comparative analysis, with similarities and differences noted and recurring themes emerging. Since these granny midwives made approximately three antepartal home visits to the client (in the sixth, seventh, and ninth months "to see if she has all of her supplies, has everything fixed" for the delivery), it was believed that they had sufficient contact with their clients over the years to respond to questions about factors which may influence birth weight. The responses to the questions reveal one aspect of the cultural context in which these five granny midwives function.

Question 1: From your experiences, can you tell me what makes a small baby (at term)? Their verbatim responses were:

Midwife A. In my opinion, the mother wasn't eatin the right foods. She needs to do a lot of exercising in pregnancy—no beer, no whiskey, and no smokin' when pregnant.

Midwife B. Exercisin' and eatin' properly prevents a small baby being born.

Midwife C.   Maybe smokin' cigarettes, I believe, has somethin' to do with it . . . and eatin' the right foods, not junk foods.

Midwife D.   A mother not eatin' proper food, smokin' too much and drinkin'. Maybe baby comin' from small parent will make a small baby. If she drinks soda water and won't take the proper food, that makes a small baby.

Midwife E.   Family trait, the makeup of the family.

Question 2:   Can you tell me what makes a big baby (term)?

Midwife A.   Eats too much. Eats fattenin' foods, sweets, lot of bread, rice. Starchy food makes a big baby.

Midwife B.   Eating lots of pork.

Midwife C.   Eatin' a lot of fatty foods and not enough dark and yellow vegetables. And eatin' cookies, pies, and drinks that have sodium in it; also too much starchy food.

Midwife D.   Coming from a big-stock family. Diabetes. Overeating just because grandma says you have to eat it.

Midwife E.   If not from the parents' build, then somewhere in the family background.

Question 3:   Do you think height and weight of the parents affect birth weight?

Midwife A.   Don't see any relationship of height and weight of parents to size of baby.

Midwife B.   No response.

Midwife C.   I think back about this eleven-pound baby I delivered. Its mother was real tall but not broad. That has lots to do with it—the height—'cause the baby has more room to grow. And if the mother is fat and broad . . . I've had them like that . . . it seems like to me it takes somethin' from the baby expandin' that helps to make them little. I really do believe that height has a lot to do with that baby expandin' and being' tall.

Midwife D.   Sometimes.

Midwife E.   The family makeup (build).

Question 4:   Do you think height and weight of the grandparents of a baby affect birth weight?

Midwife A.   Don't see any relationship of height or weight of grandparents to birth weight of baby.

Midwife B.:   All of my (own) babies were small. And I say, look at their grandparents—they are all small. So it seems to go back to heredity. So if the grandparents are small, the babies are small.

Midwife C.   Yes, ma'am, in some ways I really do. I just don't know how to hardly answer that question. My mother weighed 265 pounds and I have a sister who you'd think I'm her daughter as far as size is concerned. And I'm the one who has had bigger babies. Mine were bigger than hers and she weighed more than I ever did and she's taller than I. So maybe height and weight of grandparents do affect the weight of the baby.

Midwife D.   I'm not sure about that.

Midwife E.   The family makeup (build) includes grandparents.

Question 5:   *What do you tell women are the good things to eat during pregnancy?*

Midwife A.   Milk, lots of fruit and turnips. Don't eat too much pork. Mothers make their own cornbread and biscuits, chicken, fish, and eggs.

Midwife B.   Lots of lean meat, vegetables, plenty of milk, butter . . . most of my patients are on the WIC program.

Midwife C.   Try to eat plenty of vegetables, green beans, spinach, lean meat, stay away from fatty meat like pork. For fish, we have catfish, white fish, mullet, flounder, perch, snapper comin' in.

Midwife D.   Yes, encourage vegetables, lean meats, milk, lay off onions and cabbage greens when nursin' cause it causes the milk to smell. Yellow and green vegetables. Fish.

Midwife E.   Lots of vegetables, drink milk. The WIC program is one of the biggest things that ever happened. I know the lower-income people eat better when they're pregnant.

Question 6:   *Do the pregnant mothers have any unusual eating habits, such as eating starch, clay, or dirt?*

Midwife A.   Mothers eat chalk [like dirt with no grit in it] that they get from the sides of ditches. And a lot to them eat starch and flour. Eat it all through pregnancy, every day. I craved the chalk [dirt] with my oldest child. I'd put it in the stove and bake it hard and then I'd crunch it. Mothers take a laxative and this works it [clay] out.

Midwife B.   Some have cravin'. Older patients I have crave starch, dry sand, or clay.

Midwife C.   Yes, ma'am, they do. Only one or two.

Midwife D.   No response.

Midwife E.   Some of them will eat starch and clay. If they all get WIC food, they wouldn't have all the cravin'. They eat dirt. You tell em if they get constipated, they'll have a harder delivery. The dirt smells good to em. A lot of people don't have food to eat.

Question 7.   *With the pregnant mothers who smoke cigarettes, do you notice any difference in the size (weight) of the baby at birth?*

Midwife A.   I have some that smoke and their babies are smaller [than average].

Midwife B.   Chain-smokin' mother [White] had a baby who was small, under-weight.

Midwife C.   I notice that the babies at birth—and this might seem strange—are just not as lively. They don't get the color as quick as those of the mothers who are concerned about themselves while they're carryin' them. The babies are more sluggish in picking up its color real good. I really haven't had too many sluggish ones.

Midwife D.   Yes, ma'am. A mother of foster kids who comes to me smokes a lot. Hers is small and cries a lot. Yes, if the mother blows smoke over the baby's crib, he's crying because of the smoke.

Midwife E.   No, I haven't noticed any difference in the size of the baby if the mother smokes or doesn't smoke.

Question 8:   With the pregnant mother who drinks too much (alcohol), do you notice any difference in the size (weight) of the baby?

Midwife A.   I never knowed about the drinkin' part. I never smelled it on them.

Midwife B.   Drinkin' strong drinks makes underweight babies.

Midwife C.   This girl had been drinkin' liquor all during the day she was in labor and he [her husband] had been in jail. I took that baby to the hospital and they checked it out and said it was alright. I try to do things before they happen.

Midwife D.   Yes, I do notice they have small-sized babies. The reason is the mother won't eat.

Midwife E.   Yes, the baby would be smaller. I know about a lot of my patients, and drinkin' has a lot to do with small babies.

Question 9:   With pregnant mothers who do (use) drugs, do you notice any differences in the size (weight) of the baby?

Midwife A.   I know nothin' about that.

Midwife B.   No response.

Midwife C.   When I find out that her and her husband been smokin' that stuff, the baby is small and not as lively.

Midwife D.   The foster babies I get from mothers on drugs are smaller sized. It is so pitiful, the baby will have to withdraw on its own. I have walked the floor many a night pettin' and lovin' the baby.

Midwife E.   In drugs, I believe she would have a miscarriage—either born dead or premature.

Question 10:   Do you think having worries or having a bad scare can affect the size of the baby?

Midwife A.   No response.

Midwife B.   I don't think a scare could affect the size of the baby. I remember back in the 50s they said don't go to the movies or shows with animals, lions, tigers 'cause those animals are afraid of pregnant ladies and they might break loose or something. And I remember I went to a show once and a man asked if there was any woman pregnant and if so would they please leave. A lady had to leave. And I wondered because they say people can mark their babies by seein' an animal. I would tell them, if they asked me, to stay away from animals the first three months cause that's when the baby is being formed.

Midwife C.   Probably worries do. Yes, ma'am, worries do. Something like a death in close family or bills and don't have money to pay. It can stop appetite, too. But I don't think a scare can affect the size of the baby.

Midwife D.   I don't think havin' a bad scare would affect the size of the baby. If she will eat, it will be OK.

Midwife E.   A real bad scare, I think, would affect the nervous system. A mother [who] is calm during her pregnancy determines the attitude of that child as it grows.

Question 11: **Is there anything else that you can think of that causes a big baby or a small baby?"**

Midwife B.   I go by the size of the lady's husband, especially the size of his head. I was 92 pound when my first baby was to be born (I was 15) and the doctor wanted to see my husband. He measured his head and told him: Don't get frightened, your wife is so tiny and the baby has a really huge head—not water head—but we might want to take this baby a few weeks early. I goes by that a whole lot.

CONTENT ANALYSIS

After the verbatim responses are transcribed from tape to paper, a comparative analysis of the transcription can begin. Cultural domains are identified and compared. Out of the comparative analysis themes begin to emerge, such as cultural conflict, mechanisms of social control over clients, and maintaining midwife status. Based on identified themes, inferences can be made that provide fresh insights into the life styles of these key informants and their clients. From this intensive analysis of the subculture of granny midwives, the ethnographer gains a clearer understanding of one specific subculture. With the study of more granny midwife groups, hypotheses to test a theory of a subculture can be developed.

In most of the United States today, traditions of childbearing are changing rapidly in response to larger cultural forces. It is noteworthy to view those areas where folk practices still remain visible. The presence of granny midwives in Alabama and their gradual phasing out under the watchful eye of the State and County Health Department has revealed mutual respect and concern for mothers and infants. These midwives function within a network of neighbors and friends. They take care of Black and White clients. The supervisor of nursing at Houston County Health Center, Bobbie Stough, states that "We definitely recognize their function and until we can get something to replace them and on another level of care, we know the family has supervised prenatal care, all of which boosts the quality of life for the newborn"

(Stough, 1983). If the role of granny midwives had been terminated suddenly, one wonders what would have been the alternatives for pregnant women who could not afford a hospital delivery. Mention has been made that if the granny midwife option were not available, there would be a black market on deliveries, with unlicensed people delivering and charging fees. The clients of the five practicing granny midwives in Houston County are closely monitored for risk factors. If a pregnant client of the midwife is deemed unacceptable for an out-of-hospital birth by the physician, potential complications are prevented for the mother as well as infant. Dr. Robert L. Goldenberg states, "There is substantial risk of neonatal mortality from out-of-hospital birth if the mother is white. . . . In the past ten years, as much as ten to fifteen-fold increase is noted, as compared to 1.5 increase in infant mortality for the Blacks" (Goldenberg, personal communication, 1983). This evidence permits the hypothesis that lack pregnant women are culturally motivated to seek help, and they seek the granny midwife who is culturally acceptable and accepted. On the other hand, White pregnant women are breaking a 40-year tradition of hospital-birthing by having a home birth and a lay-midwife in attendence. These White women frequently lack a cultural motivation pattern to seek prenatal care and are often without any previous care until they are in labor. By comparison, the Black mother-to-be in Alabama today is familiar with the traditional figure who has been identified and accepted by Blacks through the years as the person to whom one turns when pregnant, particularly when there is no other option but a home delivery because of insufficient income, lack of medical insurance, high unemployment, and inability to qualify for Medicaid. With the security, protection, and close medical and professional nursing supervision provided to the granny midwife, there is no reason for her to step out of line for health care services to the Southern Black mothers. If granny midwife program is in existence, this is one illustration of how it can be made to work.

SUMMARY

In summary, this chapter presented the use of various ethnographic methods and tools to help elicit information that would give a picture of Alabama granny midwives. Methodologies used were participant-observation and tape-recorded, verbatim interviews with each key informant. Some historical and autobiographical components were included in the content for comparative analysis and extraction of themes, which can provide a way to construct meaning that is more reflective of the world of practice and more suitable to the study of the domain of professional nursing.

ACKNOWLEDGEMENT

Grateful recognition is given to the Houston County Health Center personnel, who have provided valuable information for this chapter: Marilyn Crumptom, M.D., Health Office; Bobbie Stough, R.N., Supervisor of Nursing, and especially Annette Farmer, R.N., and Barbara Thomlinson, R.N., Maternity Program Supervisors. Lastly, gratitude is extended to the five gracious and valiant granny midwives, without whom this chapter could never have been written nor so much learned.

REFERENCES

Alabama Department of Vital Statistics, Alabama State Department of Public Health. Information obtained by telephone interview, February 9, 1983.

Dalzell, S. *Houston county profile*. Dolthan, Alabama, March 1981.

Division of Public Health Nursing, Bureau of Maternal and Child Health and Family Planning. *The Alabama midwife* (2nd ed.) Montgomery, Alabama: 1980.

Farmer, A. Personal communication, January 10, 1983.

Goldenberg, R. L. Personal communication, February 7, 1983.

Goldenberg, R. L. Humphrey, J. L., Hale, C. B., Wayne, J. B., & Boyd, B. Neonatal mortality in Alabama 1970–1980. *Journal of Medical Association of State of Alabama*, August 1982, 6–13.

Houde, J., Humphrey, J. L., Boyd, B., & Goldenberg, R. L. Out of hospital deliveries in Alabama 1970–1980. *Journal of Medi-*

cal Association of State of Alabama, August 1982, 20–25.

Leininger, M. *Nursing and anthropology: Two worlds to blend*. New York: John Wiley & Sons, 1970.

Leininger, M. *Transcultural nursing: Concepts, theories, and practices*. New York: John Wiley & Sons, 1978a.

Leininger, M. Futurology in nursing: Goals and challenges for tomorrow. In N. Chaska (Ed.), *The nursing profession*. New York: McGraw-Hill Book Company, 1978b, pp. 329–396.

Litoff, J. B. The midwife throughout history. *Journal of Nurse-Midwifery*, November-December, 1982, 27, 9.

Stough, B. Personal communication, January 17, 1983.

Swanson, J. M. & Chenitz, W. C. Why qualitative research in nursing? *Nursing Outlook*, April 1982, 241–245.

17

A Qualitative Clinical Account and Analysis of a Care Situation

Blythe Hudgens Peterson

Jane (pseudonym) came into the hospital for the delivery of her third child. Nothing indicated that Jane's labor and delivery would be extraordinary, but problems occurred. Staff members who had cared for Jane more than a year ago still recalled how angry and frustrated they were about Jane and her family's religious beliefs, which seemed to jeopardize her health. These thoughts and feelings about Jane remained with the nurses and they had several unresolved questions of how best to work with her if she returned in the future. One nurse expressed her feelings and the situation in this way:

> We were literally watching her [the client] bleed to death. Staff feelings ranged from rage to helplessness. Basically it went against everything we had been taught as nurses. Our job is to save lives, not watch them die. For a long time afterward, I questioned whether I wanted to continue to be a nurse. I still ask myself that question. I don't think I could go through it again.

The purpose of this chapter is to describe, document, and analyze a client-staff study situation involving conflict and care in order to demonstrate a qualitative method of data collection and analysis from a clinical setting. A sequence of clinical events lead to the identification of client-staff conflicts and the way the conflicts were met. The importance of carefully observing and documenting nurse-client situations cannot be underestimated if the nurse is to identify care themes or patterns of behavior in clinical nursing and health care situations.

The author also focuses on value conflicts, coping, and care to show the interrelationships among these concepts and to help future nurse researchers understand ways to study such concepts. From the observations and mini units of analysis, a final analysis of the clinical situation and a model are presented to depict salient themes. This method might be viewed as a mini ethnographic account of particular critical incidents in which *meaningful patterns* and themes of behavior are identified over a span of time (Leininger, 1978). It is a method that combines gestalts of patterns of behavior with critical incidents so that the nurse researcher can see both specific and larger perspectives of human interaction, attitudes, and general behavior. Essentially, I used three steps: (1) a description and documentation of a clinical situation over a span of time; (2) identification of themes of conflicts and patterns of care; and (3) development of a summary statement with a model to depict what transpired. This was a real situation, but the names of people were changed to protect their identity.

DESCRIPTION AND DOCUMENTATION OF THE SITUATION

The Overall Situation: Background Factors

Jane was admitted in labor to the obstetrical unit of a large general hospital. Her admission examination revealed no abnormal findings. Her husband, John, accompanied her to the labor room and assisted her during the labor and delivery, which proceeded normally.

Following delivery of the placenta, Jane began to have excessive vaginal bleeding. Despite the administration of several emergency medications and uterine massage, her uterus failed to contract due to uterine fibroids. She was transferred into the obstetrical recovery room for close observation. John remained with her.

The obstetrician consulted an internist and an anesthesiologist, who recommended a blood transfusion for Jane. However, the blood transfusion was rejected by the family because Jane was a Jehovah's Witness. Jane continued to lose blood. Her hemoglobin dropped from 12.3 to 1.7 mgm and her hematocrit fell from 35.9 to 4.5 mgm. Blood volume expanders were given. The anesthesiologist tried to insert a subclavian catheter but was unable to do so. The family continued to refuse a blood transfusion for Jane. As Jane's blood pressure decreased, she began to have grand mal seizures, and then she lapsed into unconsciousness. Her urine output diminished markedly to 10 cc per hour. Her heartbeat became irregular.

The obstetrician agreed to move Jane to the intensive care unit where she could be monitored more closely and could receive several intravenous medications, plasma expanders, and other treatments deemed necessary to maintain minimal function of vital organs. Supportive nursing care was given in the intensive care unit.

The internist, Dr. C., told the family members that without blood, Jane would die. John, the husband, refused the transfusion. After suggesting several alternatives that were unacceptable to the family, Dr. C. realized that the only way to stabilize Jane's condition was to stop the source of her bleeding by a surgical procedure. He arranged for Jane to be placed under the care of another surgeon in another state—a surgeon who had treated Jehovah's Witness patients without giving blood. John agreed to transfer Jane and she was flown to a hospital in another state.

Jane's Hospitalization: Feelings and Impact

Jane and her husband, John, reached a decision about not accepting blood because of their cultural values and beliefs. The nurses knew that the usual medical treatment for a falling hemoglobin level is to replace the blood in order to ensure adequate oxygenation of vital organs. Hemoglobin is replaced by giving blood, but John and Jane could not accept this remedy. They clung to their religious belief as tenaciously as the hospital staff advocated their solution to Jane's problem.

Hospitals have rules and norms of behavior, which tend to be imposed upon clients admitted to the hospital, and Jane's care exemplified these norms (Brink & Saunders, 1976; Leininger, 1978). Health professionals who rigidly enforce their rules and norms of behavior upon seriously ill persons often limit the client's choices and ways of dealing with value conflicts. If decisions are made for the client without his or her consultation and input, conflicts may develop. Strangers may assume responsibility for the client's welfare, survival, or vital life processes, but the client frequently has his or her own values, and this was evident in this situation.

The obstetrician and nurses initially focused on Jane's physical need for blood as part of the immediate postpartum therapy, for they knew that hemoglobin is important for health maintenance. The hospital staff were trying to support their values of optimum health (Rogers, 1970) by insisting on blood transfusions for Jane. The staff insisted on Jane's accepting a transfusion because of her rapid loss of blood and the fear that death would occur if she did not get a blood transfusion. The obstetrician kept John informed of his wife's deteriorating condition and reiterated that she would improve if she were given a blood transfusion. Once the obstetrician and the medical internist realized that Jane and John would not yield, Dr. C. insisted that Jane be transferred to the intensive care unit where her physiological condition could be closely monitored. Routines in the intensive care unit were rigorously maintained, but the family was limited in being able to visit Jane. The intensive care unit was, indeed, more easily controlled by the physician and nurses than the ward.

The nurses interpreted Jane's and John's refusal of a blood transfusion as rejection of medical and nursing care and as an unwillingness to get well. Since nurses and other hospital staff generally expect clients to desire wellness, this was a value conflict in care for the staff, especially for the nurses. As Leininger states: "If patients show signs of behavior contrary to staff norms, the staff may subtly reject the patient, avoid him, or give him an early discharge under the aegis of various kinds of rationalized staff explanations" (Leininger, 1970, p. 162). Physicians and nurses may also respond to value conflicts by taking decisions away from the client.

The staff nurses who worked with Jane recalled an earlier incident in which a hospital official obtained a court order to give blood to a Jehovah's Witness client, who subsequently survived. They also recalled that the client was ostracized by the church and the family. Hence, the staff nurses and physicians were aware of this conflict situation and they wanted to prevent such anguish, but still save Jane's life.

Unquestionably, when Jane refused to accept a blood transfusion because of her religious beliefs, this decision meant to the health professionals that she could die under their care. Physicians and nurses felt confident that they could save her life and prevent further injury if only the client would have a blood transfusion. Jane's choice seemed to sabotage the health professionals' goals and desires in care and treatment. Indeed, the physician's treatment goals were contrary to those of the client and family. The physician might override the family's objection to the blood transfusion and order that it be given. But if the physician respected Jane's decision to refuse blood, then he felt certain she would continue to lose blood and die. This value conflict and ethical dilemma was also felt by the nursing staff. Interestingly, the physicians who were unable to persuade Jane to have a blood transfusion considered using a hyperbaric chamber in another hospital. They were also unsuccessful in obtaining administrative permission to use an experimental synthetic blood product. The staff continued to explore many types of treatment to save Jane's life but her condition became grave. The physician's and staff's frustration with the client's decision led to the client's being moved to a hospital in another state, which was a sizable professional risk. It was a risk, however, that was accepted by the client and her husband. John, aware that Jane might die whether she received blood or not, persevered in upholding the cultural values of Jane and her desire for eternal salvation (Mead, 1970).

Family Responses

After Jane entered the hospital, John insisted on being with Jane almost continuously. He insisted on being in the obstetrical recovery room, a place ordinarily restricted to clients and hospital personnel. John's concern for Jane meant a disregard for some hospital rules, for he believed that his wife's critical condition preempted any regulation which restricted his contact with her. He sat at her bedside and held her hand while talking to her. He seemed to gather strength from Jane's mother, who remained in the hospital. He sat for hours with little rest or food. The nurses recognized that John's attention focused on Jane and excluded extraneous events or personal comfort needs.

For a while, Jane knew that John was with her. They discussed their new son, a robust, healthy boy, who was placed in the nursery. As Jane's hemorrhage continued, she felt weaker and less able to sustain a conversation with John and the family. John encouraged Jane to rest while he remained at her bedside holding her hand. He began to phone relatives and friends as her condition grew worse. Several people came to the hospital late at night. The hallway beside the recovery room was filled with friends who were members of Jane's culture, who wished to see and help her. The nurses requested that each person limit their visit to a few minutes and that only two visitors be with Jane at any one time. When they were not with Jane, friends and family members talked quietly among themselves, offering prayers or words of comfort to John.

It was evident that John's religious faith sustained him as Jane's condition became critical. When Jane was transferred to the intensive care unit, John stayed with her. He asked for extended visiting privileges so that he could sit at her side during the night. He saw the nurses begin cardiac monitoring, with frequent measurement of pulse, respiration, and blood pressure. He observed Jane's convulsions and tried to help her in many ways. Several hospital staff would come to see Jane; people were coming and going at a regular pace, each bringing either a piece of equipment, supplies, intravenous solution, or medication to her. Despite the activity of people in the hospital environment and some harsh admonitions by the staff, John remained with Jane. He continued to decline a blood transfusion. This sequence of events was observed and carefully recorded by the author.

Caregiver Responses

Caregivers responded to Jane when she began to hemorrhage after the delivery of the child. A skilled obstetrical staff group responded with medications and manual massage to try to stop the bleeding. However, the treatments and most care measures seemed to be of limited help. The obstetrician suspected that uterine fibroids were the cause of the difficulty and recommended close observation, intravenous fluids, and a blood transfusion; if Jane continued to bleed, he wanted to perform a hysterectomy. But John and Jane rejected the blood transfusion.

Jane kept bleeding, with her blood pressure falling rapidly. The obstetrician then consulted an internist, and the two physicians debated their course of action. Both anticipated Jane would soon die. Jane did lose consciousness as her blood pressure and hemoglobin level dropped.

Nurses in the obstetrical recovery room monitored Jane's vital signs. They gave intravenous fluids, comforted her with tepid baths, and moistened her dry mouth with cool compresses. Jane's first convulsion prompted the nurses to pad the bed rails with cloth in order to protect her. Her seizure indicated to them that she was getting worse. Although the nurses knew that Jane and John had objected to a blood transfusion, they still felt that with her critical condition, the religious beliefs would be relinquished. This did not occur. The nurses thought that Jane would die, or that if she lived, she would have permanent brain damage from the diminished oxygen supply to her brain. They felt frustrated because they could not change the circumstances. They were not in control. They suppressed their anger toward John, for they saw him as the "villain" because he was in control of the decisions for his wife. Seldom had the nurses experienced such frustration and hopelessness. They had helped to deliver Jane's baby, and they did not want her to die.

Jane's transfer to the intensive care unit relieved some of the anxiety and fear of the obstetrical nursing staff. While nurses in intensive care managed complex physiological monitoring and titrated medication dosage, the nurses in the nursery arranged for Jane to have her new infant son with her for short periods of time in the intensive care unit. Maternal-infant interaction early in the postpartum period, or bonding, was practiced to enhance family relationships (Klaus & Kennell, 1976). Nurses arranged for the baby's visits by notifying the nursery when Jane was ready for the child.

As Jane's level of awareness declined, she became weaker and the nurses expressed the fear that she might inadvertently harm the baby if she held him. Hence, they discouraged the baby's visits, which also limited the physician's management practices.

IDENTIFICATION OF THEMES OF CONFLICT AND NURSING CARE PATTERNS

Value Conflicts and Care Acts

From the foregoing descriptive and abbreviated ethnographic account of this critical incident, it can be seen that Jane's hospitalization led to many conflicts between the values held by health professionals and those of the client and her family. Hospital personnel considered the value of sustaining life to preclude all other values, whereas Jane and her family valued the adherence to the law of God as they saw it. Jane's critical condition brought these two major areas clearly into conflict. As a result, there were tensions and disagreements among health professionals and between them and Jane about the method for treatment and care. Conflicts in care acts were apparent, and will next be discussed, using Leininger's identified theoretical care constructs (Leininger, 1981; 1982; 1984) and ethnographic data derived from this study. Specific care constructs could be identified and considered by the nursing staff.

Caring Acts

Realizing the importance of Jane's religion and her physical care needs, the nurses designed Jane's care in relation to her physical condition and spiritual needs. Jane's nursing care plan included several methods for achieving this goal: providing rest, giving oxygen and medications, supporting the family, and respecting Jane's beliefs and choices. Care planning conferences strengthened the nurses' ability to work with Jane toward fulfilling the client's goals and to reduce care conflicts.

Support as Care

Weiss (1976) suggested that "almost the only useful form of help to people in crisis is support" (p. 215). Support will be considered to be "behaviors aimed at helping the patient to maintain, restore, or increase his strength in order to enhance his ability to interact and adapt" (Gardner & Wheeler, 1981, p. 71). Weiss identified behaviors characteristic of persons in a crisis and noted that individuals exhibiting such distress symptoms benefited from a helper or ally who could assist in reestablishing the client's equilibrium. The helper interprets the individual's experiences and responses. He or she may provide information about others who have undergone similar crises.

Jane's health crisis placed her in a position of needing supportive care. Certain forms of medical treatment, such as the blood transfusion, were prohibited because of Jane's religious beliefs. This posed problems for Jane, given the potential for being rejected by her religious congregation, the Jehovah's Witnesses. John realized that Jane's physical condition threatened her ability to make decisions and choices. John therefore gathered family members and friends of the Jehovah's Witness church to come and see Jane or be present with her in the hospital. Jane relied on John's supportive care actions to provide comfort and meet her religious needs. John and Jane's family and friends were the client's support group.

The hospital staff were a support group for their professional peers. The obstetrician consulted two other physicians in the hospital and at least one surgeon in another state. The nursing supervisor came to the hospital from her home the evening that Jane was in critical condition. "I didn't need to take care of the patient. My staff could do that. I needed to be there for the staff." In this crisis situation, professionals contacted colleagues by way of the usual communication lines of consultation. They sought the help of peers who would understand the physiological and ethical-religious aspects of the client. Physicians and nurses worked closely together. The gravity of Jane's condition directed physicians and nurses to a common and urgent goal of support to preserve Jane's body functions, by supporting her physiological responses in a manner that was acceptable to Jane and her family. The staff relied on supportive care acts functioning as a team to help the client.

Comfort as Care (With Spiritual Care)

The nurses created a plan of comfort care that addressed the physical and psychological needs of the client. Physical comfort care measures were given by cleaning, feeding, and protecting Jane from injury. Psychological comfort care needs were met by nurses by touching Jane, offering her support and understanding, and providing for her family concerns. Nurses provided comfort by holding Jane's hand during painful procedures, and Jane responded to these comforting care actions. This was evident by her becoming more relaxed and resting quietly and sleeping. Jane's responses made the nursing staff "feel like we were doing something."

The nurses took turns caring for Jane's physical needs. They bathed her, offered her liquids, changed her linens, spoke to her, and touched her. They wanted to do more, but her husband would not always permit this. The disappointment of not being able to cure her with blood transfusions became too stressful for one nurse to provide continued comfort care. Interestingly, I observed that not one nurse relieved another in the client's room without touching her peer. The symbolic comfort of the nurse touching another nurse continued throughout the time that Jane was a client on the obstetrical ward. Touching was a means for the nurses to share feelings and a comfort measure to each other. Some additional care acts besides comfort were expressed among nurses, namely, compassion, empathy, support, touching, and nurturing. Nurses confirmed these care acts during and beyond the eight-hour shift. For example, nurses who witnessed the onset of Jane's excessive bleeding stayed at the hospital for an hour or two after their shift ended and discussed Jane's condition and the implications. Nurses also shared their feelings of anger toward John for refusing the blood transfusion. Several considered him to be the "villain."

Jane relied upon John's support, and he in turn sought comfort and reassurance from friends and family members who responded to his summons to the hospital. His goal was to sustain his wife's religious belief in the face of adversity. He insisted on remaining with Jane, even in hospital areas where this practice had not been permitted. John encouraged other family members to come to the bedside to minister to Jane's spiritual needs and to reaffirm his own belief that in refusing blood, he strengthened his religious group affiliation and beliefs. While John realized that Jane might die, he prepared Jane to accept this reality by prayers and inspiration from members of their religious congregation. The latter believed that if Jane lived, she could assure others of a life after death—a belief by Jehovah's Witnesses of exceeding the glory and majesty of earthly existence. But Jane was told by the family to look forward to death through her faith. Her family and friends rejoiced that Jane's salvation would be her triumph over death (Mead, 1970).

Protective Care

Nurses who worked in the nursery showed a protective attitude toward the newborn child. This care attitude was different from that of the obstetrical nurses and their attitude to Jane. The nurses in the nursery assumed the role of mother for the infant and protected the newborn baby in many ways. Their protective care reflected that the nurses feared Jane would die and leave the infant motherless. Hence, protective and nurturing care acts were needed to sustain and help the infant survive. Interestingly, the nursery nurses did not carry out their usual role of acquainting a new mother with her baby and of caring for the family as a unit. These nurses felt somewhat distant and detached from the client and her husband, but they gave the infant much affection, protection, and attention. They spent time feeding, cleansing, comforting, and cuddling the infant. Their actions showed concern for the newborn's need for nourishment, safety, and closeness. The baby in his dependent state accepted and responded to his caregivers' protective and nurturing acts.

Presence as Care

To John, presence meant staying close to Jane while she was gravely ill. He would touch her body to assure continued contact even though her level of consciousness decreased. John kept a persistent vigil at Jane's bedside, and he summoned the family members to the hospital as her condition changed. The family waited in her room or in the hallway just outside the door of the obstetrical recovery room in order to have physical proximity to Jane. John relied on presence more than verbal comments. He did, however, affirm his affection for his wife on several occasions.

Jane looked to her husband to support her decision to refuse blood when her will wavered. She asked his opinion about taking blood. He refused the blood and continued to refuse each staff member's offer. He protected her from violation of her religious beliefs. His persistence was reinforced by Jane's mother, who assured John that refusal was the right thing to do. His mother-in-law's support sustained John and helped him to cope with the conflict. The family provided presence as care for the client and for family members. The family's presence seemed to serve as a most sustaining force for Jane and John. Although the nursing staff used presence to care for Jane, it did not seem as direct and meaningful to the client and family.

Nurturance as Care

The obstetrical and intensive care nurses met informally in groups of three or four nurses to establish a plan for nursing care that included nurturant acts and which was consistent with their professional values. Through their collaboration, they arranged for the baby to be taken from the nursery to Jane in the intensive care unit so that maternal-infant bonding might progress. Intensive care nurses closely observed Jane's responses and evaluated her level of consciousness during these contacts in order to ensure infant safety. In the event of a seizure, intensive care nurses phoned the nurses in the nursery to inform the staff of the need to delay or interrupt family visits. Nurses in the nursery responded by arranging alternative hours to take the baby to the unit or, if the seizure began once the baby was already with the mother, by going to the intensive care unit and returning the baby to the nursery.

Jane's illness and nurturant caring needs united nurses from normally two separate and specialized nursing groups, namely, the obstetrical and intensive care nursing staff. Their shared goals of promoting optimum function and of maintaining the integrity of the family decreased departmental and geographical obstacles. Caring by nurturant acts of growth-promoting relationships with the client and among the nursing group was evident in the analysis of the ethnographic patterns.

Restorative Care Behaviors

The nurses gave restorative care and promoted healing by helping Jane as much as possible and by improving existing conditions of the client. The nurses collaborated with the client toward the goal of restoring maximal function. Nurses tried to delay death for Jane or to change the situation by participating in aggressive intervention. Nurses gave restorative care that reflected their professional values and actions, in that they insisted on providing oxygen to the client; they explained why replacing Jane's blood by a transfusion was necessary; and they protected her by closely monitoring her physicial condition. They decreased Jane's metabolic demand for oxygen by encouraging rest and by assisting her in personal care.

Medical Curing Regimes

Nurses began to advocate medical practices for the purpose of sustaining optimum health as a life action. The focus of Jane's care gradually shifted from supportive caring attitudes and acts to aggressive medical curing acts. Physicians reinforced curing actions through such means as blood therapy, surgical interventions, and intravenous medication. Caring activities were largely subjugated to curing medical regimes.

As Jane's bleeding continued, the physicians demanded that certain curing actions be carried out by the nurses. Priority for specific nursing care intervention gave way to assisting the physician in collecting equipment, such as arterial catheter lines, or in medical activities, such as drawing blood for determination of blood gases or setting up machinery to record an electrocardiogram. In meeting the physician demands, the nurses gave more time and attention to the physician and equipment than to the client. Attention to curing methods precluded caring and generated an attitude of estrangement (Boyle, 1981) toward Jane and John. Client resistance to blood therapy produced frustration for the hospital staff, who limited their definition of optimum health mainly to Jane's physical condition. As the shift from care to cure became clearly evident, care acts, at the same time, decreased to the client. Interestingly, Jane's psychological need to sustain family and religious ties seemed to be temporarily suspended or less visible during this time.

Estrangement Behaviors

An interesting phenomenon of estrangement behavior occurred as a result of conflict between client and professional staff. When Jane began to hemorrhage and efforts to stop the bleeding were unsuccessful, a polarization of the family and the hospital staff occurred with the critical decision of the family not to allow Jane to receive a blood transfusion. The refusal of the blood transfusion caused each side to assert its position uncompromisingly. The professional staff felt frustrated with trying to compromise in what they saw as a nonnegotiable situation. Biophysical findings confirmed that the only way for the professional staff to solve the critical problem was to give Jane blood, but this treatment was unacceptable to the patient and the family. An uncompromising attitude on both sides led to intense conflict, anxiety, and helplessness for the professional staff. "Feelings of anxiety and inadequacy are often expressed through depression, withdrawal, or eruptions of anger . . . or by seeking out peers to the exclusion of others" (Brink, 1976, p. 130).

Both client and professional staff realized the value conflict and concommitant stresses related to the conflict. The client and family sought support from family members; the hospital staff gave support to each other by their beliefs and practices. Staying at the hospital for several hours after their shift ended and talking about the ordeal became ways the professional staff dealt with the conflict. Each side excluded contact with the other for periods of time. Estrangement, or separation of self from concern for the other, characterized the behavior of the professional staff toward the client and family and interfered with caring acts (Boyle, 1981).

As the client's husband, John, continued to refuse a blood transfusion for his wife, the nurses became angry. They watched as John stood by Jane's bedside, stroking her hair and holding her hand as she slipped from consciousness. He kept repeating softly to her, "I love you." Later, one nurse remarked, "I hope no one ever loves me enough to let me die." At the same time, nurses noticed an "uncanny electricity" in the client's room, for "we felt the energy that was bonding that couple together even when Jane was not responsive. It was spooky," as one nurse said. Indeed, John's caring, touching, and presence were caring acts to his wife. One nurse said, "We could sense a wall between the husband and the nursing staff."

The shift in activity from supportive caring to medical curing acts also estranged the staff from the client and family. Preparing complex equipment and carrying out procedures consumed time that was previously devoted to attending to the client's reaction to her physical and religious needs. Staff members initiated a schedule for monitoring Jane's physiological responses: hourly measurement of urinary output, 15-minute determination of vital signs and central venous pressure, and continuous assessment for cardiac arrhythmias. The nurses administered treatments, medications, and plasma volume expanders. The nursing personnel focused on the medical regimen for cure. They were concerned about Jane's physical condition, for they feared that if she were not able to respond from a very low hemoglobin level, she would probably sustain permanent damage to the brain owing to decreased oxygen. When John continued to refuse a life-sustaining blood transfusion, the staff verbally lashed back with anger and incomprehension of his resistance of treatment. By immersing themselves in activity and routine over which they had control, nurses dissipated some of their emotional energy. Perhaps the staff's detached or estranged demeanor and hostility represented the first step in anticipatory grief for Jane's death, an event the staff presumed certain to occur under the circumstances.

SUMMARY OF QUALITATIVE DATA ANALYSIS WITH CONFLICT MODEL

This mini ethnography of a real-life client, nurse, and physician provides much qualitative data to understand patterns of behavior. Given an analysis of the situation over time, it was evident that the hospital personnel, physicians, and client had different cultural values and ways of dealing with Jane. As differences became evident, each group and the client tried to establish ways to cope with the situation so that personal integrity and their respective values would be preserved. Some recruited support from helpers and excluded people with different viewpoints and values.

Professional peers and the client's family affirmed their respective group values. When such factions reestablished contact, each side asserted its position supported by its helper or value supporters. Confrontation forced the development of alternative approaches to the problem, which were often not accepted by family members, physicians, and nurses. Some resolution of the conflict occurred as participants selected some available decisions and gave group comfort among the limited choices.

Dr. C. ultimately responded to the family's resistance by transferring Jane to a hospital in another state for help. The referral prevented the staff from resolving their emotionally charged conflict with the family, an eventuality marked by the nurses' persistent feelings of bitterness. Rejection, avoidance, and early discharge decreased liability and responsibility for care, but left unresolved feelings and thoughts. The nursing staff failed to identify fully the nature of the value conflicts, especially concerning the physician's expectation of them. Consequently, they experienced an internal struggle between their desire to express professional nursing values and simultaneously to reject the impact those professional values had on the client. A few nurses, including the supervisor, still questioned whether they wanted to remain in nursing after this critical incident, which made them feel helpless and at times incompetent.

Once Jane was transferred from the intensive care unit to another hospital, the staff had no chance to continue resolving their conflicts about the quality of nursing care.

Nurses remained dissatisfied with their contacts with Jane and John while Jane was in the hospital. When Jane returned to the obstetrical unit for a visit one month following her surgery and recovery, the nursing staff did not choose to respond to Jane as they often had to other recovery patients returning to the hospital. Instead, the nurses remained cool and nonengaged with Jane. They offered little time to greet Jane and to learn the details about her hospitalization and how she actually did recover. The nurses did not ask about the newborn son and her mothering acts. It was as though Jane's presence reminded them of their inability to resolve their conflicts, fears, hopes, and care expectations with Jane. The nursing staff expressed disappointment in their ability to help Jane. They commented about Jane's slow responsiveness to questions and her reduced ability to care for her three children during the return visit. Nurses blamed themselves as a part of the cause of Jane's current and possibly permanent disabilities. Some nurses considered themselves to be responsible for Jane's mental impairment (slow response behavior), and so they questioned whether they deserved to retain the title of nurse. Verbal statements and nonverbal ethnographic data affirmed the above behaviors and themes.

A model for coping with conflict arose from the analysis of the clinical situation. As individuals interacted with each other, conflict occurred. Coping with conflict is perceived as a process that proceeds through time in a series of events, which may either coincide or occur sequentially. The self and the existence of other events bring unique contributions and experiences to a conflict situation, which are often revealed in the process of coping with conflict. Coping with conflict represents one mode of self and other interactions. If no conflict occurred, other interactive modes prevailed. Conflict precludes using other modes of the self as well as precluding others from investing in different and incongruous values (Fig. 17-1).

Jane's values conflicted with those of health professionals caring for her, which led to a conflict situation. Jane and her caregivers acknowledged the existence of a

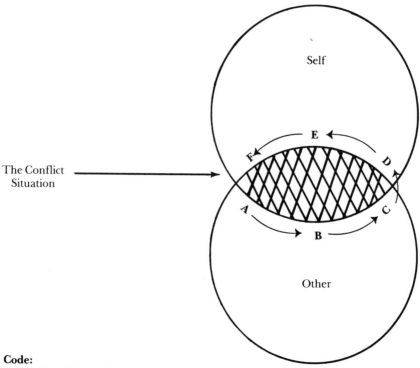

The Conflict
Situation

Code:
A = Identify conflict
B = Recruit support
C = Affirm group values
D = Confrontation
E = Negotiation
F = Resolution

Figure 17-1. Coping with conflict: a model. The model represents a process of coping with conflict in which a conflict situation activates the elements of conflict in self and others in the situation. Each individual verifies that his or her thoughts or beliefs conflict with those of at least one other participant; otherwise, no coping or change in behavior occurs. If the individual realizes that conflict exists, he or she becomes involved in the circular process of coping with conflict depicted in the diagram. Data from the clinical situation will be used to explicate the model.

value discrepancy as the source of the conflict, but because each participant affiliated closely with his or her own value and because Jane's life potential weighed in the balance, the resolution of the situation carried some urgency. Each participant gravitated toward other people who shared similar values and outlook on the problem. Jane and John's values were supported by their Jehovah's Witness friends, and hospital personnel dealt with their value conflicts with their professional colleagues. A confrontation occurred when Dr. C. refused ongoing care for Jane unless she accepted his decisions for medical care. John knew he could not take Jane home with her severe bleeding and convulsions, and so he entered into negotiation with Dr. C. The treatment options were limited, but with the help of a social worker, John learned of a physician in another state who performed surgery on Jehovah's Witnesses without using blood. This conflict was partially resolved when Dr. C. arranged for this surgeon to accept responsibility for Jane's care by transferring her to another hospital, yet the conflict with the staff remained.

Figure 17-1 represents an individual's interaction with one other person in the social and cultural value sphere. A more complex scheme would include interacting with several others, with overlapping portions representing other–other interchange. The areas of overlap suggest that conflict may occur within those relationships as well as between the self and other (Fig. 17-2).

Dissatisfaction with the outcome of Jane's care might be conceptualized as a lack of awareness of the effect of overlapping self–other conflicts in different value systems. Figure 17-2 represents Jane's care, and each participant could examine the situation with the self having contact and potential value discrepancies with self and others. This helps one to recognize that values may clash within the profession, between two professional groups, or between health professional and the client.

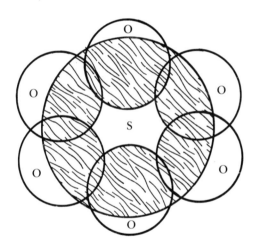

Code:
S = Self
O = Other
■ = Overlap of self and other conflict areas

Figure 17-2. Self and others: interaction conflict model. Overlapping self–other conflicts in different value systems are illustrated in this diagram, which represents Jane's care. Each participant examines the situation, with the self having contact and potential value discrepancies with self and others. This diagram illustrates that values may clash within the profession, between two professional groups, or between health professional and the client.

CONCLUSION

This qualitative mini ethnographic study of a critical clinical situation helps the reader to discover themes and patterns of behavior. This study revealed that a conflict arose between the goals of physician-managed treatment, the values of the client and family, and the values of the nursing staff. The conflict was often covertly expressed, yet real and of concern. An unresolved disagreement between the nurses and the physician occurred due to the requirement that the nurses meet medical goals of cure and reduce care acts. Whether nurses ascribed to medical values or identified more closely with nursing care needs was a subtle and unspoken conflict between the two major professional groups. A close identification with the physician's objectives for cure led the nurses to evaluate the outcome of nursing care on the basis of the client's acceptance of medical treatment of the physiological problem. Tension rose as Jane's condition became critical. Some nurses accepted responsibility for persuading Jane to accept blood transfusion, but when Jane rejected the idea, the nurses interpreted this as personal and professional failure.

Some nurses in this situation felt responsible for Jane's life. How could they betray her? They retreated from her presence and immersed themselves in ritual and hospital routines as their way of expressing their estrangement. On the other hand, nursing peer groups helped other nurses to recognize the contribution of empathy, acceptance, and caring. These nurses evaluated the process rather than the outcome of Jane's care. They identified that Jane's personal attitudes opposed a medical treatment, but realized that nursing care offered several options for intervening in preserving her optimum level of function. Jane challenged them. The staff persisted in involving themselves with Jane and her family, but with much conflict and often angry feelings. At no time did the nurses and physicians identify and discuss their conflicts and the value differences that prevailed.

In general, the nursing staff could not relate to Jane effectively and therapeutically when she rejected medical treatment. They tended to withdraw from her and yet they carried on some care activities that were helpful but not fully recognized. The disparity between reality and what the nurses expected of themselves caused frustration and anger among nurses, who misinterpreted the sources and nature of the conflict. Some staff who observed and identified differences in medical and nursing approaches to the client did not estrange themselves from the client. Some nurses recognized that they could not provide Jane with the medical cure that she so adamantly refused, but their nursing orientation allowed them to approach Jane from her frame of reference. They respected her right to refuse treatment and they suggested alternatives. Some comforted Jane and tried to encourage her to rest and conserve her body's strength. These nurses believed that their interventions promoted Jane's optimal health and growth. Genuine concern for Jane fostered acceptance of her right to choose, even if she chose to die. Their caring respected that choice for the client.

The qualitative data presented here were both empirically and inductively derived from a nursing situation. Systematic observation and participation were essential to document and record what transpired each day. This mini clinical ethnographic study could be used by other nurse researcher's. It is a method that focuses on quality attributes and on identifying sequences of events to determine behavior patterns and nursing care needs of clients. This method, which involves getting into the *world of the client,* of the family, and of the professional staff, was a method the author learned from transcultural nurse specialists through shared learning at local and national conferences. It was a method that supported the author's view of quality research and nursing care practice. It highlighted the importance of comparative viewpoints, and clarified the nature of value conflicts derived from cultural differences. This method also helped to value the qualitative method of looking at themes and patterns of behavior, and of analyzing care and cure behaviors from a broad gestalt viewpoint. The other strength of this clinical qualitative method and analysis is as an application in the use of inductive documentation and problem-solving skills to know and understand nursing situations.

REFERENCES

Boyle, J. S. An application of the structural-funtional method to the phenomenon of caring. In M. Leininger (Ed.), *Caring: An essential human need.* Thorofare, N.J.: Charles B. Slack, 1981, pp. 37–47.

Brink, P., & Saunders, J. M. Cultural shock: Theoretical and applied. In P. Brink (Ed.), *Transcultural nursing, a book of readings.* Englewood Cliffs, N.J.: Prentice-Hall, 1976, pp. 126–137.

Gardener, K. G., & Wheeler, E. The meaning of caring in the context of nursing. In M. Leininger (Ed.), *Caring: An essential human need.* Thorofare, N.J.: Charles B. Slack, 1981, pp. 69–79.

Klaus, M., & Kennell, J. H. *Maternal-infant bonding.* St. Louis: C. V. Mosby, 1976.

Leininger, M. M. *Nursing and anthropology: Two worlds to blend.* New York: John Wiley & Sons, 1970.

Leininger, M. M. Transcultural nursing methods. Oral presentation at Transcultural Nursing Conference, Salt Lake City, Utah, 1977.

Leininger, M. M. *Transcultural nursing: Concepts, theories and practices.* New York: John Wiley & Sons, 1978.

Leininger, M. M. *Caring: An essential human need.* Thorofare, N.J.: Charles B. Slack, 1981.

Leininger, M. M. Caring: A central focus for nursing and health care services. *Nursing and Health Care,* 1982, *1*(3), 135–143, 1976.

Leininger, M. M. *Care: The essence of nursing and health.* Thorofare, N.J.: Charles B. Slack, 1984.

Mead, F. S. *Handbook of denominations in the United States* (5th ed.). Nashville: Abbington Press, 1970.

Norris, C. *Concept clarification in nursing.* Rockville, Md.: Aspen Systems Corporation, 1982.

Quinn, J. F. Client care and nurse involvement in a holistic framework. In D. Krieger (Ed.), *Renaissance nurse.* Philadelphia: J. B. Lippincott, 1981, pp. 197–210.

Rogers, M. E. *An introduction to the theoretical basis of nursing.* Philadelphia: F. A. Davis, 1970.

Weiss, R. S. Transition states and other stressful situations: Their nature and programs for their management. In G. Caplan & M. Killilea (Eds.), *Support systems and mutual help.* New York: Grune & Stratton, 1976.

18

Learning To Do a Mini Ethnonursing Research Study: A Doctoral Student's Experience

Anna Frances Z. Wenger

THE LEARNING OPPORTUNITY AND PURPOSE

Learning how to do an ethnography or an ethnonursing research study is a new experience for most nurses because of the limited number of nurse educators prepared in anthropology and transcultural nursing. Even today there are only a few graduate nursing master's and doctoral programs with faculty prepared to teach and demonstrate qualitative types of nursing research, such as ethnography, ethnonursing, or ethnoscience methods. The need for such qualitative research studies is clearly apparent, however, and this was one of my major reasons for choosing a particular doctoral program in transcultural nursing. I recognized the need to learn about qualitative types of research, especially ethnographic and ethnonursing methods, for my future nursing research interests.

Although I had had some transcultural nursing experiences, the doctoral program provided an opportunity to learn ethnographic and ethnonursing research methods from an experienced transcultural nursing researcher and theorist who had studied health, care, and general lifeways of several cultures. Shortly after my arrival, my mentor told me, "It will be important for you to learn ethnographic and ethnonursing research methods and, at the same time, learn about the people." I was challenged with these questions: How do I begin? How do I get into the world of another culture? What basic knowledge do I need to conduct a successful ethnography or ethnonursing research study?

Through several graduate courses, I learned there were distinct ethnographic types of research and different methods of data collection and analysis that differed from quantitative types of research. It was essential to conceptualize this difference before I began ethnographic research. I also learned that ethnonursing research methods were being developed so that nurses could use this method to focus on specific phenomena of nursing. Ethnonursing research focuses on nursing theories, methods, and practices unique to nursing and as a means to explicate nursing data. I discovered that learning about a cultural group was stimulating and an invaluable experience in my doctoral education. I realized that nurse researchers now and in the future need to study people in their natural, familiar setting and over a period of time, in order to learn from them and to understand cultural and nursing data.

After completing courses on the methods and theory of anthropology and transcultural nursing, I selected for study a Soviet-Jewish immigrant community in an urban area. I was interested in these people and in their health, care, and acculturation processes. My domain of inquiry was, therefore, on cultural health, care, and lifeways of these people. I chose my mentor's theory of transcultural care diversity and universality as a guide to my field research.

The purpose of this chapter is to highlight these aspects, but most importantly, it will focus on the learning process, including entering the field, remaining among, and leaving the people, and on some of my methods of data collection and analysis. The reader will realize that ethnographic and ethnonursing research is not a rigid method, but rather there is some flexibility to conduct field research according to the researcher's interest or goals and the people under study. I discovered that the more experienced the nursing field researcher is, the more skillful will be the conduct and analysis of a field study. The content presented has been abstracted from my larger field study of the Soviet-Jewish immigrant people because space limited a full exposé of the research (Wenger, 1983).

Preparing for the Field Research

In order for the nurse researcher to do an effective research study of a culture and the people's health and care practices, it is essential to learn as much as possible about the people, the research method, and modes of collecting and analyzing data. The researcher should learn about the culture over a period of time. Such knowledge helps the nurse researcher to envision and anticipate some features of the culture and how to proceed with fieldwork. There were many aspects to learn about entering and remaining in a culture. There was a large body of knowledge I had to grasp, quite different from quantitative types of research. In fact, many ideas on purposes, methods, and linguistic terms were quite different from quantitative research. These will not be identified here but are found in other sections of the book and elsewhere in the literature (Aamodt, 1976; Glittenberg, 1981; Leininger, 1978, 1981, 1983; Ragucci, 1972; Spradley, 1979, 1980).

Fortunately, some ethnographic data are now available on practically all cultures in the world. These cultural data serve an important purpose to help the researcher learn about the cultural group in their life context. Only a few ethnographic themes and cultural situations will be presented here.

The Culture Under Study and Situation

In 1973, a wave of Jewish people immigrated from the Soviet Union to the United States as a result of a special law passed by the United States Congress. Between 1975 and 1980, 66,480 Jews emigrated to the United States (Schiff, 1979). Fifty percent settled in New York City, and most of the remainder in Chicago, Los Angeles, and Philadelphia. One hundred and fifty-four went to other Jewish communities in the country. Nearly 5000 Soviet Jewish immigrants came to the Detroit area between 1973 and 1981 to join family and friends or to seek employment in several large industrial organizations. With this immigration, there were many sociocultural changes to consider, such as language and the health care, political, economic, and other systems or social structural changes. The immigrants were also faced with acculturation and adaptation to a new country with many different values and lifeways from those of their homeland.

A few health care professionals were aware of stresses and conflicts in providing health care services to Soviet-Jewish immigrants, but most health professionals in the city were not aware of the real-life stresses of the people, except for marked language differences and problems in communicating with them. A Jewish community service agency and hospital had been responsive to the immigrants and since their arrival had instituted social, vocational, and health care services. Most immigrants, however, continued to find that obtaining health care services was a major problem for them due to language problems, finances, transportation difficulties, and differences in the way our health services were organized and offered to them. Decisions about health care services posed many problems to the Soviet-Jewish immigrants in different health care settings. Hence, an ethnographic study was needed to understand the people's viewpoints, problems, adjustments, and general lifeways about health, care and services to this group in a new and different culture for them.

Domain of Inquiry

One of my early learnings was to focus on a domain of inquiry for study of a culture rather than necessarily a problem, question, or series of hypotheses. This domain of inquiry is essential when knowledge is unexplored or unavailable about a cultural group (Leininger, 1978–1983). This approach also permits openness to discover the unknown.

At the same time, I learned that the research goals or purposes should be stated to guide the research. It is also possible that some researchers may use questions or hypotheses depending on the state of knowledge attained about the culture (Leininger, 1978–1983; Pelto & Pelto, 1978).

I did a focused ethnographic and ethnonursing research study, with my major purpose to describe, analyze, and explain selected cultural domains regarding Soviet Jewish immigrants' health and care experiences or needs. I decided to use four research questions to guide my work:

1. What is the meaning of health care for Soviet-Jewish immigrants?
2. What constitutes health in the acculturation process for Soviet-Jewish immigrants?
3. What constitutes caring in the acculturation process for Soviet-Jewish immigrants?
4. What are the ethnonursing implications of the Soviet-Jewish immigrants' perceptions of health, caring, and health care?

These questions helped to guide the direction of my study, but they did not limit or close my exploration of learning about the people. The questions helped me focus on my major domains of study.

Why is it necessary to describe, document and use questions? Description with documentation often leads to more specific questions to be asked, in order to formulate theories, propositions, or future research areas. It is a means to pursue an accurate account of a cultural situation or any area under study that is of interest to the nurse researcher. Most importantly, qualitative research helps to generate new knowledge and to provide empirical or inductively derived, accurate knowledge about health, care, and the people under study.

THEORETICAL FRAMEWORK

Health

Health and care from a transcultural perspective were two major domains of inquiry for this ethnographic investigation. In recent years, health has been the focus of an increasing number of nursing and health-based research studies as well as theoretical models (Antonovsky, 1979; Becker, 1974; Chrisman, 1977; Kasl & Cobb, 1966; Newman, 1979, Parse, 1981). Most of these theorists and researchers have defined health care to promote research strategies which will test hypotheses regarding health behaviors. The major problem in these studies has been the ethnocentrism of looking at health from a unicultural perspective. Culture must be included to understand health, because health is culturally defined (Chrisman, 1977; Landy, 1977; Leininger, 1978, 1983, 1984; Polgar, 1962). An increasing cadre of transcultural nurse researchers are reporting studies on the transcultural aspects of health perceptions, health care, and nursing care accommodations (Aamodt, 1976, 1978; Bauwens, 1978; Boyle, 1982; Glittenberg, 1981; Leininger, 1978, 1984, Ragucci, 1977). Some cultures may not consider health attainable in their physical lifetimes. Others place great emphasis on monitoring their health indices, as in the Anglo-American culture. The concept of health varies among cultures and as Leininger states, "health is culturally defined and expressed." Culture must be considered in health care research to know and understand people in an accurate way.

Care

The concept of care has received more attention in recent years by nurse theorists and researchers. Leininger initiated in 1960's the humanistic and scientific study of care or caring phenomena among nurse researchers by engaging in ethnographic research herself and encouraging others to do so (Leininger, 1978; 1981; 1984). One of the major tenets in the study of care or caring has been the recognition of the cultural attributes and meanings to people. A key assumption posited by Leininger is that "human caring is a universal phenomenon, but expressions, processes and patterns vary among cultures" (Leininger, 1981, p. 11). These emic expressions, processes, and patterns must be investigated through exploratory ethnographic studies, eliciting data from the specific cultural group's point of view before the universality of the caring phenomenon can be tested.

Acculturation

In this study, health and care concepts are considered in relation to acculturation. Acculturation refers to the process whereby previous lifeways undergo some changes because of cultural contacts (Teske & Nelson, 1974). Since degrees of change take place in one or both of the groups who have cultural contact, this usually means that one group dominates the other and contributes more to the flow of cultural elements. Padillo (1980) suggests that there may be a characteristic three-phase course of acculturation: contact, conflict, and adaptation. "The first is necessary, the second is probable, and some form of the third is inevitable" (Padillo, 1980, p. 11). It is generally accepted that acculturation produces sociopsychological stress as people, especially migrants, adapt to cultural differences. This depends on the desirability of the migratory move and the permanency of the change. For immigrants, the change is usually permanent, and acculturation occurs in some form. Nevertheless, the degree and rate of acculturation depend on many factors.

Graves and Graves (1974) state that adaptation for the migrant has three sources of constraint: (1) the community which the migrant leaves, (2) the community of migrants, and (3) the host community. Each has its own pressures, which affect the migrant. The home community is still a part of the migrant's life through cherished values and often linkages with friends and relatives. The migrant community is created by linkages of crisis needs among people who in the home country or community may never have been associated. The host community is present to the degree that its members seek to assist in the acculturation process. Acculturation is a complex process, which continues to be studied by anthropologists and other scientists. Acculturation is important to this study because I was interested in what aspects of the past and new culture were adapted to or preserved in relation to health care and nursing care needs of Soviet-Jewish immigrants.

Nursing Theory Framework

Leininger's nursing theory of cultural care diversities and universalities, provides the framework for the study of health and caring in the acculturation process (Leininger, 1984). Positive and negative or neutral relationships may exist between health or illness status of the individual, family, or group and their care values, beliefs, and practices within social structure, health systems, and worldview perspectives that can be determined through *emic* and *etic* analyses. Cultural care values, beliefs, and practices must be identified in order that efficacious nursing care can be provided. Culture-congruent nursing care is dependent on three principles: (1) cultural care preservation; (2) cultural care accommodation; and (3) cultural care repatterning. This nursing theory accommodates both inductive and deductive research approaches. In this study the inductive approach was used in order to explore the values, beliefs, and practices of a specific cultural group in relation to health and caring in the context and in relation to acculturation. The deductive approach is an abstraction from extant sources or innovations of knowledge sources (Leininger, 1983, 1984).

QUALITATIVE ETHNOGRAPHIC AND ETHNONURSING RESEARCH

With qualitative research, the explanatory principle is often described as being teleological rather than causal, as the latter is known with quantitative research (Bruyn, 1970). This means that in qualitative research the explanations are based on manifestations of design or pattern of the variables under study; in quantitative research, conversely, the ultimate goal is to establish cause-and-effect relationships, which can be unicausal or multicausal. I wanted to learn about the meanings, attributes, values, and patterns of behavior related to health and health care of Soviet-Jewish immigrants who are becoming acculturated in a new and very different social structural milieu for the purpose of establishing ethnonursing care practices. I was not interested in determining cause-and-effect relationships per se. I wanted to gain first-hand or primary source data from the people.

Ethnonursing is described by Leininger as "the systematic study and classification of nursing care beliefs, values, and practices as cognitively perceived by a designated culture through their local language, experiences, beliefs, and value system" (1978, p. 15). The ethnonursing method requires the nurse researcher to elicit a given culture's perceptions and knowledge about folk and professional health and caring values, beliefs, and practices. Ethnonursing research is based on the assumption that persons can define and know their cultural beliefs and practices about caring, nursing care, and health-illness beliefs and practices (Leininger, 1978). The goal of this research was to gain some understanding of Soviet-Jewish immigrant's perceptions of health, caring, and health care.

Rationale for the Ethnographic-Ethnonursing Study

This is a small-scale ethnonursing study using a modified ethnographic method and research design. I chose a mini-ethnographic study with an ethnonursing emic focus in order to get inside the world of the people being studied, which is important to obtain accurate or truthful insights about the people. Ethnographic and ethnonursing research emphasizes the *direct personal* involvement of the researcher in the community with the people (Agar, 1980; Leininger, 1982, 1983, 1984). In hypothesis-testing research, on the other hand, the researcher attempts to standardize the data collection and to minimize the effects of the relationship between the researcher and the subject in order to control for bias and reduce direct researcher and subject contacts.

The ethnographer assumes a learner role, attempting to learn in any way possible about the lifeways of the people (Agar, 1980; Leininger, 1982, 1983, 1984; Spradley, 1979). The goal of ethnographic research is to understand the cultural patterns and meaning of the domains of inquiry according to the people's world view. This requires the use of several methods as well as constant efforts to validate observations and interview data through careful selection of informants, who are bearers of the culture. Clarifying and reclarifying the researcher's perceptions and analysis of the observations and interview data are important to validate the informant's cognitions with other informants as a means to identify cultural diversities or universalities within the cultural group. The learner role of the researcher required that I focus on the complex process of grasping the culturally relevant aspects from the people's viewpoint. I used tools and methods of data collection and analysis that were closely related to the cultural group's values, beliefs, and perceptions. Finally, the findings and analysis of the study should be understandable and acceptable to the people being studied.

My study is referred to as a small-scale or mini study for several reasons. It is a mini study in that I wanted to use a small number of informants in order to obtain in-depth perceptions of health, caring, and health care. I held at least six hours of interviews with each informant over a minimum of three months. The focus was on quality data rather than quantity, as ethnonursing research seeks depth and breadth of knowledge discovery. The key informants represented some variation in age, sex, occupation, education, and geographical origin from the Soviet Union. If a large-scale ethnonursing study had been done, more global informants would have had more global representation. Because I was learning the process of qualitative ethnographic research, I was counseled to use only a small sample to develop my powers of observation and related research skills, and to develop a trusting relationship and rapport with the people. Developing my skills of observation, listening, and documenting holistic, social structure and cultural data was a big challenge. I soon discovered that this holistic perspective is much broader and a more intense study than any other type of nursing research. I had to look at the broadest and yet the smallest human expressions of care, health, and patterns of living in context and with strangers.

I used principally unstructured ethnographic interviews and observation-participation. There are many techniques and tools which can be used to increase validity and reliability and to increase the scope and complexity of large-scale ethnographic studies. Mini studies allow the researcher to focus on a comparatively limited domain of inquiry, using a minimal number of selected data collection methods with a small number of informants during a brief period of time in order to grasp the world of these people in-depth and to describe various aspects of relationships, meanings, and patterns. Mini studies are logical and meaningful preliminary studies for larger-scale ethnographic studies, which attend to intra-cultural and inter-cultural variations in particular domains of inquiry.

METHODOLOGICAL FEATURES FOR STUDENT LEARNING

In this study, I was learning the basic and essential process of becoming an ethnographic nurse researcher in which I assumed the learner role vis-à-vis the Soviet-Jewish immigrants. I prepared myself to enter the field by studying transcultural theory and methods, reviewing anthropological studies (including acculturation theory), and doing an extensive literature search on Soviet-Jewish immigration to the United States. I used Leininger's field model and principles for entering the field, such as driving through the community where many of these people lived to become familiar with the type of housing, shops, schools, parks, and synagogues (Leininger, 1982–1983). I visited social agencies and interviewed three health professionals who had responsibilities for Soviet-Jewish immigrants' health services in order to learn about such services and the professional's views of the immigrants' needs. I went to local supermarkets and shops to discover the foods and material goods the immigrants generally purchased.

Throughout this initial part of the ethnonursing study, I learned how to ask broad and specific ethnographic questions which encouraged my informants to describe and interpret health and care beliefs and practices (Spradley, 1979, 1980). According to Agar, sometimes "the ethnographer surrenders the control of situations, questions, and samples, apprentices himself to group members, and learns how they interpret their world" (1980, p. 194). I found myself involved in a major task of feeling, knowing, and understanding the immigrants' culture and world view, rather than mine—an important goal of ethnonursing research.

Natural Setting

This study was deliberately done in the natural setting rather than in a health care facility to decrease the number of influencing factors, such as informant role expectations or provider-client relationships, which could change or inhibit their freedom to discuss accurately perceptions or experiences of health care. In the natural setting, I was essentially their guest, but later I became a regular visitor and friend. They gave me clues concerning when and how they would let me enter their world. I was constantly looking for cues that would let me know what they wanted to share about their world view and perceptions of health and care. I knew that education was highly valued in the Jewish culture and, therefore, I noted their comments about wanting to be of help with my research project and to support my educational pursuits. I became increasingly aware of their readiness to discuss certain topics, such as caring and noncaring activities within the Soviet-Jewish community or negative perceptions of American nursing activities.

Timing, Trust, and Role-in-Context

I learned that timing and my role-in-context were important with this research method. Sometimes I waited to validate interinformant cognitions in order to have a context that would be acceptable or conducive to the topic to be explored. Trust and building a relationship with informants were important to obtain accurate and reliable data. Trust meant that is was safe for the informants to share their valued and intimate ideas, as well as their secrets, with me. For example, it was not until the sixth interview that my key informant discussed her personal reservations about leaving the Soviet Union. This became an important link in understanding her responses about stress, health, care, and conflicts. After I had established trust with an informant, and at a proper time during a discussion on the manifestations, causes, and culturally acceptable treatments for stress-induced physical symptoms, the following statement was made:

> You know, I didn't want to come to the United States. I didn't want to leave my relatives and friends in Russia. I had a good job and an apartment. My

husband had died there. But I knew my sons wouldn't come without me. I knew it would be better for them here. I didn't want to lose my sons! . . . I was here only two weeks when I was put in the hospital for those terrible stomach pains. We have stomach problems more in Russia. The doctors in Russia know what to do for your insides. I think it is because of the war. With the war there were so many stresses and tensions.

Prior to this discussion, in five previous interviews, this informant had always emphasized the positive aspects of her emigration from the Soviet Union. She validated her trust and confidence in me as she said she could tell me her real feelings, stresses, and conflicts. This was a rewarding experience and helped me to understand other ideas alluded to in previous visits. Hence, I learned it takes time to get "truths" from informants and I began to question the validity and reliability aspects of one-time questionnaires or interviews.

Although I had read and been taught that cultural context was important, the meaning of context as different aspects of holistic living now became meaningful to me. Context refers to the overall situation in which an event occurs. Contextual meanings and content must always be a part of ethnographic and ethnonursing research to increase validity and reliability of the study. This is, again, quite different from hypothesis-testing research in which the researcher attempts to do contextual stripping by isolating variables under study and controlling for confounding variables, which may contribute to or compete with the conclusion. In quantitative research elaborate procedures are developed to isolate variables from the personal and social contexts in which they operate (Mishler, 1979, p. 2). Contextual identification of meanings of human action is essential and valued in ethnonursing research in order to understand collected data. Meaning in context was emphasized by my research mentor.

The neophyte researcher needs opportunities to develop skills in attending to contextual elements which affect the researcher-informant relationship. Here is where my experienced research mentor was of help to me in discovering diverse covert and overt aspects of a particular context and the multiple or singular meanings linked with it. For example, I learned to observe space arrangements of the informants in group interviews and the place I was invited to take in social gatherings. I learned to note the chronology of the topics discussed. I learned to observe many symbolic referents in a room. The relationship of many human and nonhuman objects became meaningful to me.

I learned that it may be significant that the informant initiated the topic instead of my asking the question. Spradley (1980) gives practical guidelines on how to facilitate comments and questions, such as descriptive, structural, and contrast types. It was gratifying to use these skills and find the informants willing and able to describe and interpret their perceptions of health and care. My fieldwork was productive and meaningful. On each visit I learned much from my informants that I had not anticipated. Something new was discovered each time, or I found patterning of behavior being verified in the informants' natural setting and context of living.

Social structure factors are important, but it took some time to learn these broad and complex factors, which give contextual meaning to data. Informants do not usually organize their cognitions about domains of inquiry, such as health and caring, according to religious, political, economic, cultural, and other sociocultural factors which influence their perceptions. My informants would discuss their perceptions about government responsibilities for health care services, trust or lack of trust of health care providers, and the relationship of people to the bureaucracy of the health care system. The content and repetition of these perceptions indicated the importance of political factors in their perceptions of health care delivery. I attempted to learn about the social structure and cultural values which impact on health and care beliefs and practices of Soviet-Jewish immigrants. I used Leininger's "sunrise" conceptual model of transcultural care diversity and universality (Fig. 18-3) to give structure and focus for my data collection and analysis of contextural factors. This conceptual model kept me alert to diverse cultural and social system ethnonursing factors as I listened to and abstracted data from the people. I was unfamiliar with all aspects of social structure and had to study these important systems to provide the holistic view, and I discovered a wealth of new knowledge about health and care related to social structure and cultural values.

Continuing Creative Process

Ethnographic and ethnonursing methods gave me an opportunity to be intensely involved in all phases of the study. Throughout all phases, the researcher obtains, defines, and continues to refine data to validate findings. Because the researcher is a main instrument, she or he must constantly evaluate her or his role to reduce unfavorable observer bias and to be sensitive to data inputs. A heightened sensitivity of the researcher leads to the discovery of new insights throughout the study. The researcher begins to record themes or patterns while keeping extensive and systematic field notes. These themes change as they are validated. As the researcher records verbatim statements, he or she begins to note categories, which then lead to general statements and finally to abstractions. This creative thought process continues throughout the research study. I also learned that subjective ideas and inferences are acceptable and important in qualitative research, which makes this aspect quite different from quantitative research methods. Comparative data analysis also goes on continuously as part of the ethnographic research.

Role of Mentor

As nurses develop their own research methods, the role of research mentor becomes strategic. Mentorship is a relationship that requires a high degree of involvement between a novice in a discipline and a person who is knowledgeable and experienced in that area (May, Meleis, & Winstead-Fry, 1982, p. 23). As yet, little has been written on the process of conducting ethnographic or ethnonursing research. A few authors discuss some issues of validity, reliability, and the development of observation-participation skills (Agar, 1980; Leininger, 1978, 1982–1983, 1984; 1980; McCall 1969; Ragucci, 1972; Spradley, 1979,). Few textbooks provide detailed guidelines. Therefore, a mentor is highly recommended for the neophyte ethnonursing researcher. My mentor generously offered suggestions from her past experiences, reviewed my initial field notes, and assisted me in developing a recording and analysis format. One of her most valuable contributions was when she joined me in my field study observations. She observed my interactions and I learned from observing her techniques of getting into the natural context of the informants. We also validated our perceptions of the interactions, which served as checks on validity factors.

PHASES OF THE STUDY

During my study, I used the observation-participation process (Leininger, 1982). The sequence is for the researcher to focus first on observation (with active listening), and later having some participation. The Leininger field method follows four general phases; clarification of the primary focus for each phase is given in Figure 18-1.

According to Leininger, each phase reflects a dominant focus of the researcher's fieldwork goal and guides the process in a relatively systematic way. Phase I is primarily an observation phase with active listening. In Phase II the major focus is on observation but with some participation. Phase III reflects a time of active participation by the researcher, generally occurring in ceremonies and other life pattern activities. Phase IV reflects the time when the researcher is ready to leave the field and she or he focuses again mainly on observing, listening, and reflecting on the effects of the researcher and on validating previous observations and participation with the people. This sequential process I found to be true as one enters, remains in and leaves the field. This is a useful way to conceptualize fieldwork; and it places different emphasis on participant-observation, since participation occurs only to a limited extent in most field studies, and observation, listening, and reflection are the dominant researcher activities (Leininger, 1982–1983).

Table 18-1 illustrates the concept of observation-participation and gives examples of activities that occur during each phase.

The phases as presented in Table 18-1 are not discrete; some overlapping occurs. Phase IV preferably takes place after a period of time has elapsed and the researcher returns to the field or begins to analyze his or her effect on the community and to validate the findings. McCall states that "participant-observation is most sensibly regarded, operationally, as the blend of methods and techniques that is characteristically employed in studies of social situations or complex social organizations of all sorts" (1969, p. 3).

In my study, I used the observation-participation process and discovered that my activities fitted into the schema at least in a general way. Figure 18-2 illustrates my major activities within the four phases.

In a large-scale ethnographic study there would be more involvement of the researcher in diverse activities within the community than take place with this mini field research study. Attending marriages, religious events, and an array of political affairs helps the nurse to validate and document social structural factors related to health and care. Several of these community ceremonial activities were described to me. I was invited to one ceremony, which I was unable to attend, but I learned about

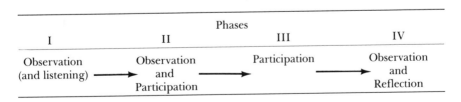

		Phases	
I	II	III	IV
Observation (and listening) ⟶	Observation and Participation ⟶	Participation ⟶	Observation and Reflection

Figure 18-1. Leininger's Phases of Observation-Participation

Table 18-1 *Leininger's Observation-Participation Focus and Process*

Phases	I	II	III	IV
	Observation	Observation and Participation	Participation	Observation and Reflection
Relative Time Period	20%	55%	20%	5%
Types of Activities	Primarily observation with focus on the whole context	Focus on the domain of inquiry while participating and observing directly with people	Become involved in health and care rituals and activities	Examine effect researcher has on the people
	Friendly exchanges	Mostly intense and active observation and interviews with some participation in daily life activities	Make general statements	Validate your conclusions of meanings and patterns
	Begin to identify the social structural elements		Observe interactions as researcher participates in an indirect or direct way	Deductions
	Identify representative informants			Abstractions
	Record data as seen, heard, and experienced	Observations and interviews continue		Statements
	Interviews with key and regular informants	Construct similarities and differences		

most of their community ceremonies from the informants' viewpoints, and descriptions. When I was preparing my informants for my "departure from the field," I began getting more invitations for participation in their ceremonies. Suggestions were also made that I interview more informants, reflecting their trust and confidence in me. I viewed these situations as indicators that I was accepted and trusted to work in their cultural context, and that they were concerned that I obtain an accurate and full picture of their world. My mentor had alerted me that this might happen and described it as a sign of effective field researcher.

Observation Phase

Two of my activities in Phase I, which require the development of skills used in qualitative research, will be discussed. These are the process of finding informants and recording and using field notes. Choosing informants is crucial in that persons should be bearers of the culture and who are capable of communicating cultural information verbally. Usually only a small number of individuals in any community are good key informants (Pelto & Pelto, 1978). These persons often have special

Figure 18-2. Observation-Participation Process With Soviet-Jewish Immigrants

Phases	I Observation	II Observation and Participation	III Participation	IV Observation and Reflection
Relative Period	May–June 1982	June–July 1982	July–September 1982	March 1983
Types of activities	Observing informants and contextual situations ⟶			
	Meetings with mentor ⟶			
	Visits to social service and health care facilities Literature review	Interviews with three health care professionals		Interviews and telephone conversations with key informants and two main informants
	Talking informally with researchers, American Jews, health care providers; walking and driving through community ⟶			
		Interviews with key informant ⟶		
		Group interviews with Soviet Jews in home of key informant	Interviews in homes of four main informants	Analyzing data
	Finding key informant			Writing report
		Selection of main informants		
	Development of a recording system for field notes			

Code: ⟶ = continued through the field study.

roles in the community and are recognized by others as having knowledge of the group as a whole. Validity is increased by choosing informants who are representative and knowledgeable of the culture. A historical perspective of the culture is valuable, and meaning in context remains important.

In this study I had five key informants. One key informant served as my contact to many other informants. Ms. A. had been an English teacher in Russia and was now assisting teaching English to other Soviet-Jewish immigrants in the community. She was also the secretary of the New World Club, an organization for the socialization of Soviet-Jewish immigrants. She was quick to grasp the intent of my research and invited a number of other informants to her home to interact with me. I used these occasions to learn from groups of informants. This process allowed me to have focused observations. I carefully observed their interactions and listened to their views on health and care. The major key informant had immigrated to this country two years ago. This was important in that she was here long enough to know the immigrant community, but was still becoming acculturated to American lifeways.

It was fairly easy to establish rapport with the major key informant. She spoke clear English and seemed eager to talk with me. She was open and eager to help me learn from her and others. Having myself lived for a brief time in Eastern Europe, I was familiar with some of the preferred social manners. I also spoke some German and could, therefore, understand some Yiddish and German used by a few of the informants. The key informant would sometimes introduce me to new informants with remarks such as "She knows about that (or us)." She became a linkage person to other informants.

Establishing rapport is a key factor in entering the field. It takes time to establish rapport and it is not easy to predict the outcome at the outset. Equally important is knowing the language of the informants and special phases related to the domain of inquiry. I would have been beneficial if I had known the Russian language, but my linguistic ability in German was a definite asset and helped me to establish rapport, trust, and exchange of ideas. I also discovered that focusing on cultural data was of much interest to the informants. Hence the importance of transcultural nursing data to focus on cultural phenomena became evident.

Observations and interview data need to be recorded in a manner that allows for sorting and easy retrieval. A recording format should be determined before beginning observations and interviews. Data can become voluminous and unwieldy in qualitative research unless the researcher finds an organized way to record and categorize the data. Ethical considerations are also important because the data usually involve sensitive information as people discuss their personal and intimate lifeways. Therefore, I established a system so that interviewees could remain anonymous in the public records and accounts of the research.

Unlike the case with quantitative research, the qualitative researcher does want to be aware of the identity of the informants through the data collection and analysis phases of the study. The researcher knows them as human beings, not as numbers or statistical data. A coding process was developed and kept close at hand throughout the study to protect informants. In my study, I used the letters SJ for Soviet-Jewish informants and identified each successive informant by letters A, B, C, and so forth. I found this a somewhat unwieldy system and would suggest using numbers instead (SJ1, SJ2, and so forth). In the written records the code should be used rather than any names to protect the informants' identities.

Spradley (1980) and Leininger (1978, 1982–1983) suggest a useful format for record keeping. Spradley uses as the condensed account, the expanded account, and a fieldwork journal. Leininger uses a similar approach, but with some refined differences, such as keeping a record of the researcher's feelings and reactions to events. The condensed account became the notebook which I used in the field to record direct quotes, specific words, and key ideas to jog my memory when doing an expanded account. I recorded ethnographic data on one side of the note paper, and my immediate reactions and questions on the other side, as used by Leininger and other ethnoresearchers in the past two decades of fieldwork.

The expanded account took the form of a loose-leaf notebook with lined paper that had a vertical line dividing the left third of the paper. I used the field notebook, which had the condensed account, to arouse my memory for the expanded account. On the left side, I wrote notes of my reactions, my beginning analysis, and categories. On the remaining two thirds of the page I wrote detailed accounts of recurrent and contrasting patterns. Whenever possible I used the linguistic terms of the informants and a number of verbatim comments which expressed a theme or pattern of behavior. It was extremely important to write the expanded notes within 24 hours of the interview or observation to ensure recall and accuracy. I found that within a short time I was learning to remember larger amounts of data and the details. I also noted increased sensitivity to contextural data and social structure features.

The fieldwork journal is a third kind of record. Spradley states that "like a diary, this journal will contain a record of experience, ideas, fears, mistakes, confusion, breakthroughs and problems that arise during fieldwork" (Spradley, 1980, p. 71). The journal serves as a source of data in ethnographic research. Since the ethnographer is the major research instrument, the personal biases and perceptions must be taken into account in the ongoing analysis.

Additional forms and charts can be designed as the researcher analyzes and interprets the data. I found this to be the most difficult part to learn. At this point, I relied on aid from my mentor, who had had much experience in developing categorizations of data. For my study, I used forms on which I recorded the ethnohealth and ethnocaring terms. I soon learned that the informants would speak of "here" (United States) and "there" (Soviet Union) when discussing health care and health care systems. I developed forms for recording their observations to fit their cognitions and linguistic categories.

Observation-Participation Phase

This phase refers to the period during which the ethnoresearcher continues to observe but increases her or his participation in the lifeways of the people (Leininger, 1982–1983). Before focusing specifically on the cultural group, I began by interviewing three informants who were members of the American health profession. These three informants held key positions in providing health care services to Soviet-Jewish immigrants after they arrived in this country. The rationale for focusing on them was twofold. First, I wanted to know how these American health professionals perceived and helped the immigrants as a basis to observe the immigrants' health care system. Second, I wondered how their views would compare with those of the immigrants themselves as they talked to me about health care services. In general, I wanted to learn what were the American health care personnels' perception of the Soviet-Jews' health problems and needs.

The interviews with these American professionals also gave me the opportunity to learn about their encounters with Soviet-Jewish immigrants since the early 1970s. It was helpful for me to learn about the community organizations and agencies which were involved in helping the Soviet-Jewish people from the time of their arrival. One of these informants gave me some excellent literature resources and information about the Detroit resettlement program. The insights and concerns of these American health professionals became background information to help me reflect upon how the Soviet-Jewish immigrants became introduced to the American health system from a comparative perspective—the immigrants and the health professionals.

Using the general ethnographic and ethnonursing method led me to discover similarities and differences in the patterns of health, care, and health care needs of the Soviet Jews under study. The similarities and differences were emphasized by my mentor as a means to examine her theory of transcultural care diversity and similarity as a theory of nursing (Leininger, 1983).

During this time I was taught that validity and reliability could be increased if the informants were observed and studied in their natural context. The natural context refers to the setting in which people live and establish their world view and roles and experience daily living with familiar people, i.e., family, friends, and community members. I was also desirous to have the immigrants see me as a nurse in the community rather than identifying me as a member of an agency or hospital, because I wanted to learn their community lifeway patterns directly from them. The naturalistic approach used in anthropology and transcultural nursing refers to the importance of humanistic and related contextual factors of the beliefs, specific beliefs, and behaviors within the context of other beliefs, values, attitudes, and behaviors of the people—all of which make up the lifeways of a particular community (Ragucci, 1972).

One of my key Soviet-Jewish informants chose to invite other immigrants to her home to meet me. She introduced me to the other nine informants by arranging for two or three to come to her home for group interviews with me. The group meetings at her house helped me to see collective and patterned behavior, and I was also able to continue with intensive interviews later in the informants homes. I observed the interactions of the Soviet Jewish immigrants together and alone. I wondered if they were accepted by others of their own cultural heritage. I chose four of these Soviet-Jewish persons with whom to work more intensively and worked with them for a three-month period.

With the in-depth interviews I learned the tremendous importance and value of obtaining first-hand data from the people in their familiar setting. I listened carefully to them and their perceptions of health, care, and illness. I learned the true meaning of holistic care as a broad and complex aspect of the participant's social structure. Patience, time, and a trusting relationship were important. As learned in class, one in-depth interview may be worth more than several questionnaires that have no meaningful items about the people. I learned that the linguistic expressions, subjective ideas, and contextural referents are important to obtain truths from people.

The Soviet Jewish informants were of both sexes, represented various occupations, and ranged in age from 20 to 68 years. They came from five cities in the Soviet Union. Gitelman (1978) makes a point in his study about the differences in the background of the Soviet-Jewish immigrants, which reflect their experiences with Jewish tradition and culture, acceptance of Jews by the local sociopolitical structures, and their occupations in the homeland. Fourteen of the 16 informants come from the Slavic "heartland." "Heartlanders" constitute 80 per cent of the Soviet Jewish population; they are further removed from Jewish tradition and culture than are the "Westerners" and Asian Jews. Many are third or fourth generation Jewish citizens in Russia who had lost many aspects of their Jewish culture before emigration. These immigrants experienced political alienation and had both economic motivations and a desire to escape Jewish restrictions, and as a result they constitute 85 per cent of those who emigrate to the United States and Canada, rather than to Israel

(Gitelman, 1978, p. 73). The informants who come from Moscow, Leningrad, Kiev, and Kharkov accurately reflected Gitelman's observations. Two of the informants came from Riga (that was formerly Latvia). Gitelman states that "Westerners" are more attached to Jewish identity than the other two groups, since they came under Soviet rule more recently. These informants remembered non-Soviet political systems, vibrant Jewish cultures, and active Zionist and other Jewish political movements (Gitelman, 1978, p. 73). Both informants from Riga spoke German and/or Yiddish in their homes. One woman stated that they seldom spoke Russian. She related many memories of pre-Soviet days and often reminded me that her responses were probably not like the other informants,' since she came from the Western region. Hence, patterns and themes of information were established.

Participation Phase

In ethnographic research, participants in a study function as "teachers" of the researcher. Because their role is to inform the researcher of the lifeways, values and rule of that culture (Spradley, 1979), they are called informants'. Good informant-researcher interaction is crucial to the study. Intense, broad, in-depth, yet focused relationships are sought as the researcher gains more understanding of the domains of inquiry from that culture's perspective. The type of interaction of the researcher with persons being studied differs significantly from that used in quantitative research. In quantitative research, the people being studied are termed subjects or respondents, controls are placed on the nature of the researcher-subject interaction in order to decrease bias and contextual influences. In ethnographic research, "the ethnographer seeks out ordinary people with ordinary knowledge and builds on their common experience. Slowly, through a series of interviews, by repeated explanations, and through the use of special questions, ordinary people become excellent informants" (Spradley, 1979, p. 25). Spradley is one of the few authors who has devoted a whole chapter of his book to the clarification of the differences and similarities in the social science roles of subject, respondent, and actors (the traditional roles of friend and employer), and the ethnographic role of informant. Ethnographic and ethnonurse researchers as well as persons who critique ethnographic research must be cognizant of the differences between qualitative and quantitative types of research.

In this study, I had two types of informants, namely, American health professionals and Soviet-Jewish informants. I observed, participated with, and interviewed a total of three American health professionals and 16 Soviet-Jewish informants (five of them being key informants) during a three-month period of time. One key informant was the secretary of the New World Club, a social and educational club organized by Soviet-Jewish immigrants. She assisted me in making contacts within the Soviet-Jewish community. I had four to six interviews and in-depth observation-participation with each of the informants in their homes. I interacted with the 11 additional informants, each for one or two times in group interviews. I met with the American health professionals for one or two times in order to gain a perspective of the health care of Soviet-Jewish immigrants from the American health professional point of view.

In learning about my informants, I needed to be aware of the differences and similarities in their views of health and care modes in relation to their age, sex, length of residence in the United States, present and past occupations, and the region of the Soviet Union from which they emigrated. I spent considerable time with the key informants, established effective rapport and trust, and obtained informative data. I observed the informants in their familiar setting to discuss concepts of health and care. Part of my time with the key informants was used to clarify and varify my perception of concepts discussed in the group interviews with the 11 other informants. In-depth interviews and observation-participation were used with the key informants and less intensive interviews and observations with the remaining 11 informants.

Both similarities or differences in the informants' themes occurred because the key informants restated, clarified, and verified some of the other informants' opinions as well as their own. I discovered this happening after several interviews with the major key informant when she would differentiate her views from other viewpoints of informants, thus providing a constant comparative perspective. For example, she said:

> J . . . is very political. He thinks things are too open here for everyone to know. He thinks prisoners are treated too well here and he thinks that bribes are used here to get what you want or need, just like in Russia, even for health care. That is his opinion, not mine. I want you to understand what he thinks.

She took her role as key informant very seriously and tried to make contacts for me with various kinds of people, and this helped me to learn about cultural variations.

All informants spoke understandable English to some extent, except for the three who were in their twenties, who spoke English with ease. The informants spoke of language difficulties in communicating with Americans. One man, who had been laid off from his job as a draftsman, recognized that in order to apply for jobs he needed to improve his language skills, but he found language learning tedious and difficult. In the Soviet Union, this man had been a recognized and accomplished violinist. In this country, he felt devalued and had much difficulty in expressing himself verbally. I was able to communicate in German with some of the informants who at times recalled German words, but could not think of the English equivalent terms. Although I spoke no Russian (which made it difficult to understand to some particular meanings and values of health and care), I was able to learn and validate a number of the important concepts and data the people wanted me to know and understand.

Job change or lack of employment was one of the major conflict areas for 50 per cent of the informants. Two of the men had been laid off owing to general unemployment in Detroit. The nurse, two physicians, dentist, and violinist were aware that before their emigration to the United States that jobs in their field would be difficult to get. The acculturation process becomes difficult when there is limited opportunity to use one's skills or to assume responsible work positions. Fisher states that employment has profound meaning for Russians (Fisher, 1975). It represents status and personal identity. Job mobility in the United States is often not understood by recent immigrants. Some have turned down jobs here in order to wait for that special niche which will be theirs.

Research students will note that the number of informants for qualitative research studies is small compared to the large numbers sought in most quantitative research.

Although a total of 16 informants were interviewed, the major part of the data came from the five key informants. Pelto and Pelto state that "sometimes the careful selection of four or five persons who are representative of significant intercommunity variations produces such high levels of interinformant reliability that it is unnecessary to add more individuals to the panel" (1978, p. 139). Satisfactory sample size continues to be an issue in qualitative research as researchers work toward increasing representativeness and reliability among informants when investigating multiple and complex patterns of beliefs and behaviors. Pelto and Pelto offer the general rule that "when addition of informants has little effect on the general structure of a complex pattern of data, then the present sample is satisfactory" (1978, p. 139). Agar comments that it is better to understand the interrelationship of many variables in a few cases than to misunderstand three in a population of 500 (Agar, 1980, p. 123). I learned, therefore, to value fewer numbers of informants, who provided large and rich amounts of qualitative data.

Informant interviewing using the Leininger observation-participation method was the primary focus of my ethnonursing field study. There were many techniques, tools, and methods to choose from in conjunction with the general observation-participation method. I wanted to focus on learning the basic techniques of the observation-participation and ethnonursing field study methods on a small-scale basis. Many supplementary tools of qualitative research can be used in a convergent or corroborative way to increase reliability and validity. It took a while for me to use these diverse research tools. I first focused on mastering the general ethnographic and ethnonursing field study methods.

With the ethnographic interviews and observation-participation in this study, I used topic and subtopic domains to guide my interviews and observations. I listened to the informants and used appropriate questions relevant to the ideas they were sharing with me. I would then ask elaboration and contrast questions within the informant's frame of reference to obtain further information. I gradually learned to let the informants tell me about health and care without asking questions. I listened carefully to their ways of constructing ideas and communicating these concepts to me. I learned to "probe" or clarify ideas in context and according to the informant's lifestyle—not mine. I learned how to keep ideas open for discussion. For instance, when I asked about the meaning of health, I soon saw that the pattern of their immediate responses focused on health care services and systems. All except two informants (ages 20 and 22) put their comments within the United States rather than Soviet Union comparative context. These two informants could be understood as exceptions, for they had immigrated to the United States at ages 15 and 17 years.

Using the ethnonursing interview approach, I asked broad, general questions or made statements in the first interview such as, "Tell me about what health means to you," or "I would like to learn from you about the meaning of health to you." The "tell me" statements allowed the informants to choose what was most significant or of interest to them. The lead-in phrases encouraged them to use their own terms—a strategy taught to me by my major mentor. I also relied on Spradley's two books, *The Ethnographic Interview* and *Participant Observation,* for specific ways to ask descriptive, structural, and contrast questions and to make descriptive, focused, and selected observations (Spradley, 1979, 1980). In addition I used ideas from the growing body of transcultural nursing field research methods (Aamodt, 1978; Bauwens,

1978; Leininger, 1978, 1981, 1982–1983; Ragucci, 1972 and others). I also learned how to do a culturological health interview assessment.

Observation Phase (With Reflective Validation)

After I completed the interviews and observations, I returned after six months to interview my key informants. I reviewed the themes which I had earlier collected, documented, and abstracted from them. I wanted to validate these cognitive statements to see if they were accurate and reliable. I checked areas that were unclear. The people were quick to affirm what was accurate or inaccurate. I was surprised to note the strength of their responses to be sure data were accurate and reliable. It was encouraging to hear them refer to information which they had discussed with me six months ago and to reaffirm the accuracy with firmness, pride and confidence. It also made me confident that the data I had obtained earlier were accurate. It was clear their responses were a part of their cultural lifeways. Thus, truth becomes sustained once identified and presented in a meaningful way to strangers, and it becomes the major criterion for internal and external validity for qualitative research.

I also wanted to formalize my departure and thank them for their participation. The manner of leaving the field is just as important as entering the field. These people allowed me to enter their world and that privilege must be handled tactfully and ethically within the cultural patterns of the group as well as the professional mores of the academic research community. I applied exit ethnonursing field techniques and principles as used in transcultural nursing, such as finalizing separation plans, checking concerns, clarifying use of data, and responding to any questions they may have had as well as to ways they wished to make the separation from me (Leininger, 1982–1983, 1984).

In sum, the processual steps of field study followed the Leininger model of the four phases with these dominant emphases during each phase from the beginning to the end of the field study: (1) mainly observation; (2) observation with selective participation; (3) participation and observation, and (4) observation, listening, and rechecking of data or general responses for accuracy and reliability of findings.

DATA ANALYSIS

Data analysis is an ongoing process throughout the field research. Each time observations and interviews are recorded, the investigator also records emerging themes and patterns as well as other, unanticipated behaviors. The use of the constant comparative analysis of ideas, themes, and patterns is an old and familiar method to anthropologists. I learned how to achieve this important technique as an integral part of ethnonursing field research. For instance, I noted how the word "politeness" was used among the informants. Three of the five key informants used the word to describe the behavior of nurses and physicians in the United States. I thought at first that it was associated with friendliness and concern. As the interviews continued, I learned that politeness also involved formality, respect, role, and status. In a group discussion with five informants, there was general agreement that in the Soviet Union, persons who serve are not polite. They used a hand gesture, as if pushing away, to emphasize what they meant to say. As data "loads on" an idea, the researcher reinforces or changes if the data do no fit the theme as known to the informants.

"Good" and "bad" were contrast sets used by the informants. Good and bad attributes were usually set in the context of "here" and "there," meaning the United States and the Soviet Union. "Good", "bad", "here," and "there" were words the informants chose to use. Examples of this usage include comments such as "Surgery here is good, but there it's bad. In Russia, therapy is better," or "In the Soviet Union there is no protection; you must take risks to get what you want. Here, you have protection; but you can't budge the government," or "Basic education requirements there are very good, but here it is bad to have too much choice."

In the ethnonursing data analysis, I categorized the data about health, care, and health care systems. Whenever possible, I separated them into contrast sets of differences between Russia and the United States and the preferences expressed by the informants. From these categorizations of descriptive statements I made second-level generalizations from the specific statements. These general statements formed the basis for the patterns that were identified. I found it difficult to analyze the data by identifying frequency of specific responses, since I did not use a structured interview guide and because this was qualitative type of study. Instead, I could identify themes and patterns which would be useful in the development of a structured interview guide or instrument that might be used for quantification of responses.

Patterns or themes were identified in the domains of health, care, and health care systems. Health care systems were not identified as a domain in the research questions, but every informant discussed health care services and systems when discussing health and care or caring. To identify the relevant sociocultural factors, I used Leininger's "sunrise" conceptual model on transcultural care diversity and universality (Fig. 18-3). The factors that impact on health-illness behaviors and health care include technological, religious, philosophical, kinship, social, cultural, political, legal, economic, and educational.

The process of data analysis included the following steps:

1. Documenting verbatim and observational domain data.
2. Describing data in extended accounts.
3. Identifying and categorizing the data themes.
4. Comparative analysis of themes.
5. Synthesizing themes into patterns of empirical and higher order statements as research findings.
6. Summarizing the findings.

These are some of the general steps of ethnonursing. They are logical steps that generally follow the research process with the informants in discovering their world and ideas. Data collection and processing of data for analysis are kept in mind throughout the qualitative research study.

REFLECTIONS ON LEARNING THE METHOD

Using the ethnographic/ethnonursing method broadened my view of research. Many of the interpersonal, observational and interview skills which I learned in previous nursing education and practice became relevant in a new way. I always knew

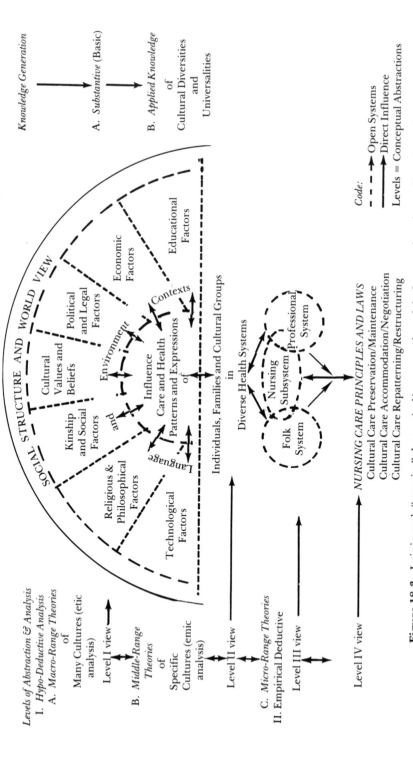

Figure 18-3. Leininger's "sunrise" theoretical/conceptual model of transcultural care diversity and university: a theory of nursing.

304

that human behavior was dependent on cultural and social context, but I had previously focused more on the interpretation of immediate transactions, often taken out of context. It was a difficult but exciting process for me to learn strategies to observe and elicit cultural data. It was even more difficult to use the massive volume of empirical data to deduce higher level abstractions in a systematized manner. I increased my cognitive ability to elicit, process, and analyze cultural data related to health and care, and the importance of cultural contexts.

Health and care constructs can be studied through a variety of methods in the development of nursing knowledge. My use of these constructs as domains of inquiry provided insights into the Soviet-Jewish immigrant culture. I learned about world views, family structure, role expectations, kinship relationships, educational values, religious values, group and family care expectations, and political ideologies. I learned about these factors by asking questions, listening, and observing behavior about health and care. My insights into the Soviet-Jewish culture should lead me to conceptualize other, more specific lines of inquiry and to propose hypotheses for testing concerning health care as well as other nursing domains of inquiry.

In analyzing the data I needed to constantly remind myself that my goal was to discern *meaning* and *pattern* of the informants' cognitive experience about health and care rather than measure degree and rate of occurrence. At first I wished for the convenience of responses that could be scaled into an orderly and precise numerical scheme. As I studied and reexamined my field notes, I tried several classifications which were based on the informants' own classification. For example, I noticed that the informants thought in terms of "here" and "there," meaning United States and Soviet Union. They categorized their perceptions of health care services, role of health care providers, self-care modalities, and traditional and professional health care into classifications of "before" and "after" immigration. Through this process I learned about the cognitive and linguistic meanings of informants' stresses of acculturation. There was a "fit" for the data which were cognitively known. It was enormously satisfying for me (as the researcher) and for the people as I discovered their world and what they were presenting and validating. My personal discomfort with the lack of order and precision in this rich massive amount of data gave way to my knowledge that I had valid insights with which I could make general statements about the research questions. I learned from the informants that they are the true bearers of knowledge if we listen very attentively and with thought to their frame of reference and world views.

Reinharz discusses the importance of the open research process which can yield new knowledge of the researcher as a "human being," the situation under investigation, and the process of research (Reinharz, 1979, p. 28). Learning ethnographic methods facilitated these three levels of knowledge acquisition for me. I was constantly reminded of my role as a sensitive research instrument and a human being genuinely interested in the people and the privileges of getting into their world. As I analyzed my data collecting techniques and reformulated my questions, the focus of the domain of inquiry was kept in center stage. Because of the continuing creative process of data collection and analysis, the process of the research became as important as the outcomes. Reinharz (1979) states that a student's intellectual growth is in part shaped by planned and unplanned research experiences. For me, this research experience has encouraged me to participate in the pursuit of nursing research methods that are logically consistent with holistic nursing and cultural phenomena.

RESEARCH FINDINGS WITH A QUALITATIVE PERSPECTIVE

Throughout the collection of data and analysis, the focus was on qualitative data analysis with appropriate quantitative ethnographic facts to support the qualitative findings. Three American health professionals and 16 Soviet-Jewish immigrants were interviewed using unstructured interview techniques. Tables 18-2 and 18-3 give the demographic data on the informants.

The total interview time per informant ranged from 12 hours to 30 minutes. The Soviet-Jewish immigrant sample consisted of two types of informants: five key informants and 11 general informants who took part in group interviews. The data collection and analysis process were described earlier. Only a brief report of cultural themes and patterns related to health and care are presented here in order to give the reader some appreciation of the kind of data that were discovered in this study.

Cultural Themes from American Health Professionals

The major theme that emerged in talking with the professionals was the difference in the Soviet and American political systems in relation to health care and care systems. Hence, the social structure factor was critical to understand health and care. In the Soviet Union, health care is free. Although the Soviet-Jewish clients like to have some choices as they find in the United States, they do not like or understand the cost involved. "They expect the state to provide", informant PB said. This causes the Soviet Jews to "have demands we can't fulfill." PA referred to a young couple who had given birth to a deformed baby. When she asked them how they planned to care for the baby, they said, *"You* [in United States] will put it in a institution." In the Soviet Union the government always take care of such ones. The cost of health and illness care in the United States seems to be a surprise to most of

Table 18-2 *Demographic Data on Informant's Health Professional*

Informant	Sex	Position	Number of Interviews	Interview Time	Place of Interview
PA	F	Hospital social worker	1	75 minutes	Hospital—private office
PB	F	Family counseling service—social worker	2	70 minutes	Agency—private office
PC	M	Hospital clinic administrator	1	40 minutes	Clinic—private office

the Soviet Jews. They expect decisions to made by authority figures about health care. The cost is handled by the government.

Dental problems as health and care concerns were mentioned by all three professionals. The informants saw Soviet Jews as having "a mouthful of awful teeth." Both PA and PB used the word "awful." The immigrants may have gold and stainless steel crowns, but "you don't know what is under that." PB stated that a lot of tooth loss occurs at an early age. There is a general belief among these American professionals that "dental care in the Soviet Union is behind ours, not as sophisticated." PA reported one dentist as saying that there is a fine line between dental emergencies and dental repair. If the main purpose for health maintenance work is to help them to become employable, then repair work becomes, in a sense, emergency work. This subject will be discussed later from the Soviet-Jewish immigrants' point of view.

Obesity, as a major health and care theme and concern, was identified by two health professionals. Both used terms like "major obesity" and "not just overweight." Young and middle-aged Soviet-Jewish immigrant women are reported to be extremely overweight. Obesity was seen as related to a high incidence of hypertension and diabetes among the immigrants. PB noted the relationship of obesity to diet; she stated that the immigrants eat lots of sugar and fatty cuts of meat. During the second interview I reported some observations I had made with a Soviet-Jewish informant that some Soviet Jews differentiate between heavily built Soviets and "fat" Americans. The American professional's first response was, "It is like the kettle calling the pot black." Then the health professional went on to observe that when she announced her engagement, a Soviet-Jewish immigrant man said, "Now you must put on some weight." She gestured with outstretched arms and said, "*Etwas zu anfass,*" meaning "something to hold on to."

Stress and anxiety were found to be the greatest health and care problems for Soviet-Jewish immigrants. According to the American health professionals, stress occurs because of several factors, such as language barriers, difficulty in job placement, and being faced with choices, but seldom with a cultural focus. Many times the choices in this country seem to be too numerous, stressful, and confounding. Anxiety was always found to be heightened with hospitalization, particularly when food was withheld. Stress about obtaining food was related to the effects of war. Two American health professionals associated the stress of hospitalization with food deprivation during the war as food was viewed as a symbol of life and when food is withheld, anxieties are noted.

Communication in relation to health and care was identified as a problem by the American health professionals. The American-Jewish community has responded by providing translators for many of the immigrants. PC stated that some immigrants do not think they need translators, and some translators do not get the proper training. Language acquisition is seen as the key to education and jobs, but it is still very difficult, especially for persons 45 years old and older. In addition, Soviets use a confrontationalist style, which is often not understood by American health professionals. Soviet Jewish immigrants make "demands" and attempt to go to superiors in the system. PB stated the immigrants also are apt to remain dependent on the agency and resist taking charge of their needs, such as housing, health care, transportation, and jobs. In order to gain access to health care and meet their perceived needs, they offer "bribes" in the form of money and gifts. PC and PB stated that there were many Russian dolls sitting around the hospital offices when the profes-

Table 18-3 *Demographic Data on Soviet-Jewish Informants*

No.	Informant Code	Age	Sex	Number of Interviews	Total Interview Time	Place of Interview	Years in United States	Reason for Immigration	Exit City or Region	Position in Russia	Position in United States
1	SJA	55	F	6	12 hr.	Own apartment	2+	Family and relatives	Kiev	English teacher	English teacher
2	SJB	48	F	1	1 hr. 45 min.	SJA's apartment	3+	Family and relatives	Kiev	Nurse	Unemployed
3	SJC	68	M	1	1 hr. 30 min.	SJA's apartment	3	—	Moscow	—	President of Russian Veterans
4	SJD	24	F	4	8 hr. 50 min.	SJA's apartment Own apartment	3	Anti-Semitism	Leningrad	Student	Computer student
5	SJE	57	F	2	4 hr.	Own apartment	2+	Anti-Semitism	Leningrad	Dentist	Unemployed
6	SJF	20	F	4	3 hr.	Parents' home	5	Parents' decision	Kharkov	Student	Student
7	SJG	22	M	1	45 min.	Fiancee's home	5	Parents' decision	Kharkov	Student	Student
8	SJH	57	M	1	20 min.	Own home	5	Better Opportunities	Kharkov	Civil Engineer	Civil engineer

(continued)

No.	Informant Code	Age	Sex	Number of Interviews	Total Interview Time	Place of Interview	Years in United States	Reason for Immigration	Exit City or Region	Position in Russia	Position in United States
9	SJI	61	F	2	2 hr. 40 min.	SJA's apartment Own apartment	4	Husband's decision	Riga	Seamstress	Seamstress
10	SJJ	66	F	1	1 hr. 10 min.	SJA's apartment	2+	Family and relatives	Kiev	Seamstress	Seamstress
11	SJK	65	F	1	30 min.	SJA's apartment	3+	—	Leningrad	Optics engineer	Retired
12	SJL	67	F	1	30 min.	SJA's apartment	3+	—	Leningrad	Physician	Retired
13	SJM	40	M	2	4 hr. 30 min.	Own apartment	4	Anti-Semitism	Kiev	Computer engineer	Electronic engineer
14	SJN	50	F	1	1 hr.	SJA's apartment	3	Husband's decision	Riga	Physician	Unemployed
15	SJO	59	M	4	5 hr. 20 min.	SJA's apartment Own home	3	Political ideologies and anti-Semitism	Leningrad	Violinist	Draftsman
16	SJP	55	F	2	2 hr.	Own home	3	Political ideologies and anti-Semitism	Leningrad	English teacher	Cleaning woman

sionals began to realize what was happening. This resulted in a hospital policy stating that gifts could no longer be accepted. Communication problems sometimes became evident when Soviet Jews failed to regard physicians with the respect the American physician is used to receiving. The role and status of physicians and clients seem to differ between the Soviet Union and the United States and Soviet Jews did not seem to be aware of these subtleties.

There are some medical and health care practices common in the Soviet Union which the Soviet Jews want to continue in the United States, according to the American health professionals. The major ones mentioned that have caused conflict have been abortions and the use of specific prescription drugs and folk medicines. In the Soviet Union, abortion is used as an alternative to contraception for unwanted pregnancies. Some American health professionals have difficulty with Soviet Jewish people, such as when caring "for a woman who has had nine abortions and would like another one." (informant PB) Many Soviet Jews brought herbs and drugs from the Soviet Union which they want to continue to use. Some physicians have had the drugs analyzed in an attempt to accommodate their wishes, but still many Soviet-Jewish immigrants are told they cannot use or obtain these medicines here. Attempts are made to accommodate the health care services to the needs and expectations of the immigrants who face many acculturation problems.

Cultural Health and Care Themes from Soviet-Jewish Informants

Although the domain of inquiry focused on health and care cognitives, most Soviet-Jewish informants chose to discuss their ideas with reference to personal health problems and health care services. A dominant theme became health care systems.

Health Care Systems. A major theme in relation to health and care was the cost of health care in the United States. All informants agreed that health care was expensive and that considerable money was needed to get adequate care. Soviet Jews come from a sociopolitical system in which health care, as well as housing and employment, are provided by the state. Six of the 16 informants mentioned that the health insurance system in the United States seems complicated and requires recipients to have a good job, which in turn requires education, and all of it costs money.

Technological care is considered to be superior in the United States. This was mentioned by 13 of the informants. Ten persons referred to conceptual differences between surgery and therapy. Therapy means medical and nursing acts, that include the use of herbs, drugs, treatments, manipulations, and alternative health services, such as health spas and recuperative centers. Surgery means the removal or repair of a body part done by surgeons within clinics or hospitals. Therapy was considered to be superior in the Soviet Union. Comments to support therapy were: "Stomach problems they know more about in Russia—maybe because of the war. You didn't have a war here." Various herbs and medicines were used in Russia which they have not been able to use or obtain in the United States. Two informants said, "The system here [United States] is geared more toward money than toward humans. Here they want to extract teeth, rather than repair them. And they want to do surgery rather than therapy." Four informants discussed alternative health care services that they had used and appreciated in the Soviet Union, such as health spas, homeopathic medicine, mineral baths, and mineral drinks. The informants all agreed that if you need high technology in health care, then the United Stated is the place to be.

Accessibility and availability of health care in the United States is another theme identified by all informants. In the Soviet Union, there are local clinics, and doctors and nurses come to the homes. One informant said, "When my baby had a fever, the doctor came immediately to my house in Russia." Here (in United States), she noted, people must often wait for health care services and they must travel long distances to the hospital. Transportation is a major problem for the immigrants in this metropolitan area. Most of them come from Soviet cities with excellent public transportation systems and few private automobiles. The themes of access to health care and its availability to the informants were of much concern.

Professional manner was another theme in the provision of health care services. In a group interview with four informants, they described American physicians and nurses as polite. This theme was picked up again by three informants in individual interviews. In the Soviet Union, people who provide services are not polite. They often treat clients gruffly, but people do get attention. Here in the United States, professional nurses and physicians are polite but often are not available.

Health. The meaning of health was a difficult concept to explicate with the informants in that they usually responded by talking about health care services. The key informants all defined health in functional and attributional terms. The functional terms included self-care, the ability to exercise and to walk outside, eat balanced diets, and work. People need fresh air and the opportunity to work to be healthy. Health was also defined in terms of being happy, being in control of one's thoughts and activities, and feeling good about oneself and others. Illness is present when people lose interest in their activities, have no work, are without friends, and lose trust in people.

It was evident that health and illness concepts include physical and mental attributes. Health involves personal and group relationships. Health can be discussed in concrete terms, but, as one informant said, "Health is like air. You don't think about it until you don't have it." Thus, health is a given expectation and if one does not have health, one becomes concerned.

Care or Caring. Care was most often discussed in terms of the family and community networks. The extended family was recognized for its past and present importance, even though people are geographically separated. In the Soviet setting, persons are addressed by their own first name and their father's first name. For instance, Natasha Schar, whose father is Mikhail Schar, would normally be addressed Natasha Mikhailova, a constant reminder of kinship. The emphasis is on the fact that she is Mikhail's daughter. Parents provide for their children because they "care," not as an obligation. Even after marriage, the sharing of time and resources continues. SJF stated that she and her fiancee will move in with her parents after they marry; her parents will not charge them rent. The children provide for their parents, and vice versa; throughout their lives. SJF stated that in the Soviet Union her mother stopped by her grandmother's house every day after work and her father also agreed with that practice. "Closeness in important." Her friends must accept her family, she said. "You cannot live separately from family." In the United States, marriage changes the parental role. Children tend to be more separated from their parents.

They do not share their thoughts, experiences, and money. In the United States, parents want their children to be self-sufficient. There seems to be concern mainly for the nuclear family. These are American family patterns which Soviet-Jewish immigrants view as not contributing to family caring.

Care is expressed by providing services for others. At the societal level, care is given when services are provided. If services are withheld, it is a sign of noncaring attitudes on the part of the government. Families care by providing unconditionally for their own children. Three informants discussed at length the way families continually provide for their children regardless of age. Children also return the care by providing for their parents in their old age. Professional nursing care also means "providing everything I need—doing things for *me*," was how one informant put it.

Trust was a dominant theme in caring. At the governmental level, trust was generally not expected, in that governments do not "care." However, one informant said that a person must be able to trust the government for jobs. This would be a sign of societal caring. The Soviet-Jewish immigrant community considers trust to be a major concern. Two informants discussed the lack of trust in the community in which they are living now and the need to keep relationships open. They thought this may be due to some problems in becoming acculturated. Four informants spoke of the trust and nurturance that was available and important to them through the various social organizations in the Soviet Jewish community as care.

Repeatedly, linguistic terms to describe care of caring included polite, attentive, nice, kind, being together, providing for, and helping others. If time had permitted, these terms would have been further contrasted and analyzed with the informants to derive a full explication and meaning of each care construct as analyzed in Leininger's ethnocaring studies (Leininger, 1978, p. 82).

FURTHER STUDY

This mini ethnonursing field allowed the investigator to the study Soviet-Jewish immigrants to know their lifeways and world. It provided many insights for further exploration of the domain of inquiry related to care, health, and an acculturated lifestyle of the people. From this study, I discovered data that was unknown in nursing, and I discovered the method of ethnography and aspects of ethnonursing research. As a consequence of this ministudy, I identified some patterns and themes of Soviet-Jewish immigrants in how they view health, care, and their needs as well as some indication of the meaning of health and caring. This study provided data to study further the needs and problems of the people, especially their care concerns of access to and availability of health care services that are congruent with Soviet-Jewish values. From this study, the following questions need to be studied using an ethnonursing approach:

1. What styles of communication would enhance better relationships between health care professionals and Soviet-Jewish immigrants?
2. How can acculturation be facilitated so that Soviet-Jewish immigrants' health care needs can be met without violating their sociocultural values?
3. What are the ideological differences in the sociopolitical systems of the Soviet Union and United States that are relevant in the provision of nursing care services?

A taxonomic analysis of the concept of care should also be done using the ethno-scientific method. Providing for others and trust were identified as care constructs on the societal, community, and family or individual level. These terms need to be further analyzed and differentiated to provide culture-specific care practices (Leininger, 1982–1983, 1984).

NURSING IMPLICATIONS: CULTURE SPECIFIC CARE

Many nursing care implications became apparent in this study, and the findings should be used for nursing care and care policies to help the immigrants at the present time. These intervention concepts could be used for culture specific care.

The major implication in nurse-client relationships with Soviet-Jewish immigrants is for the nurses to understand clients' perception of the health care system within their cultural framework. Nurses will be viewed as governmental representatives until the immigrants are able to become fully acculturated to our multidimensional system of agency sponsorship. Nurses need to understand that the confrontational style of communication is related to the development of trust. Trust seems to be a major care value and needs more exploration to determine how it is developed and maintained. The use of the care concepts of trust and being provided for are essential to help the Soviet Jewish people.

Since education is a high priority for the Soviet-Jewish clients, nurses should encourage health education. These efforts may work best in groups if the emphasis is information-giving and not therapy. Russians would not be accustomed to group therapy, but are open to informational sessions (Furchtgott, 1980).

Family relationships are very important, and inquiries should be made about availability of family members to assist with care. Even though they were not used to having families present in the hospitals in Russia, they value their presence and inclusion.

Soviet-Jewish immigrants express interest in humanistic care, yet may act as though they do not believe that physicians and nurses will be interested in or practice the humanistic aspects. There seems to be an underlying belief that "You [client] must give presents if you want good care." Although health care personnel are duty-bound to give humanistic care by virtue of their vocational position, the prevailing belief is that in the United States "nurses and doctors don't really care for the *person*." Having professionals accept gifts from clients is important to the Soviet-Jewish people. The art of receiving the gift graciously is the goal.

This study also indicates that schedule and order are important. Therefore, nurses should assess the clients' interest in schedules and facilitate whatever order is necessary for their welfare. One informant said, "The nurse was no help—she told me to breast-feed on demand, which was opposite the doctor said, and I know the baby needs a schedule." This same informant referred to what seems to be lack of order in the architecture of our cities and the way people arrange their furniture and wall hangings.

Nurses should also be aware that nurses are viewed in a subordinate role to physicians (mainly women) by Soviet Jewish immigrants. In Russia, nurses are known to give medications and to prescribe other therapies when physicians are not available. By contrast, the view of the American nurse is that she or he does only what the doctor tells her or him to do. What the nurses do, they do well and politely. However, nurses are also viewed as often being inaccessible.

CONCLUSION

This chapter was designed to lead the reader through the steps of doing a mini ethnonursing study. Selected data from a study on health and care among Soviet-Jewish immigrants were used to discuss the research method. The importance of an entirely different approach to obtain and analyze data from a quantitative research study was discussed. Entering the world of a distinct culture and focusing on the domain of inquiry (health and care) using the ethnonursing research approach were described as key elements in the research process. In doing this research, I learned to know and practice the ethnographic and ethnonursing research method as a major qualitative type of research. I also learned how to expand my thinking and areas of study to the broad and complex social structure features of health and care. I learned to value and use different research interview and observation skills and to use transcultural nursing and anthropological learnings in a meaningful way in nursing. I learned that qualitative research is complex, demanding, rigorous, and very different from quantitative research.

I discovered that the role of the research mentor is very important, especially when first doing this type of research. The researcher must continually evaluate his or her reactions as skills in interviewing and observation are developed. Data can become quite massive, complex, and detailed. The analysis methods need to be learned in order to sort and abstract generalizations that are derived from the data. A guided mentorship is ideal as the neophyte researcher works through the various steps in the research process and develops his or her own skills in qualitative research methods. This research experience was a different and new experience for me and is being used as essential knowledge and experience for my doctoral dissertation. I am now able to conceptualize and know some of the essential ingredients for qualitative research and specifically ethnonursing research. This field study was essential for me to learn the observation-participation process as used in ethnonursing research.

REFERENCES

Aamodt, A. M. Observations of a health and healing system in a Papago Community. In M. M. Leininger (Ed.), *Transcultural health care issues and conditions*. Philadelphia: F. A. Davis, 1976.

Aamodt, A. A. The care component in a health and healing system. In E. E. Bauwens (Ed.), *The anthropology of health*. St. Louis: C. V. Mosby, 1978.

Agar, M. H. *The professional stranger: An informal introduction to ethnography*. New York: Academic Press, 1980.

Antonovsky, A. *Health, Stress, and Coping*. San Francisco, Calif. Jossey-Bass. 1979.

Bauwens, E. E. *The anthropology of health*. St. Louis: C. V. Mosby, 1978.

Becker, M. H. The health belief model and personal health behavior. *Health Education Monographs*, 1974. 2, 2–30.

Boyle, J. S. The context of health and illness: Maya families in an urban setting. In C. N. Uhl and J. Uhl (Eds.), *Proceedings of the Seventh Annual Transcultural Nursing Conference*. Salt Lake City: University of Utah, College of Nursing and Transcultural Nursing Society, 1982.

Bruyn, S. T. The methodology of participant observation. In W. Filstead (Ed.), *Quali-*

tative methodology. Chicago: Markham Publishing Company, 1970, pp. 305–327.

Chrisman, N. The health seeking process: An approach to the natural history of illness. *Culture Medicine and Psychiatry,* 1977, 351–377.

Dublin, R. A. Some observations on resettling Jews. *Journal of Jewish Communal Service,* 1975–1977, 52–53, 278–280.

Fisher, L. D. Initial experiences in the resettlement of Soviet Jews in the United States. *Journal of Jewish Communal Service,* 1975, 51, 267–269.

Furchtgott, A. K. A support group for elderly Russian immigrants. *Journal of Jewish Communal Service,* 1980, 56–57, 231–238.

Gitelman, Z. Soviet immigrants and American absorption efforts: A case study in Detroit. *Journal of Jewish Communal Service,* 1978, 54–55, 72–82.

Glittenberg, J. E. An ethnographic approach to the problem of health assessment and program planning: Project Genesis. In P. Morley (Ed.), *Developing teaching and practicing transcultural nursing.* Salt Lake City: University of Utah College of Nursing and Transcultural Nursing Society, 1981.

Kasl, S. V., & Cobb, S. Health behavior, illness behavior and sick role behavior. *Archives of Environmental Health,* 1966, 12, 246–266, 531–541.

Landy, D. *Culture, disease and healing.* New York: Macmillan Publishing Company, 1977.

Leininger, M. M. *Transcultural nursing: Concepts, theories, and practices.* New York: John Wiley & Sons, 1978.

Leininger, M. M. *Caring: An essential human need.* Thorofare, N.J.: Charles B. Slack, 1981.

Leininger, M. M. Class notes and handouts from courses in Transcultural Nursing Theory and Research, Wayne State University, 1982–1983.

Leininger, M. M. *Care: The essence of nursing and health.* Thorofare, N.J.: Charles B. Slack, 1984.

MaCall, G. & Simmons, J. Eds. Issues in participant-observation. Reading, Mass. Addison-Wesley Publishing Co. 1969.

May, K. M., Meleis, A. I., & Winstead-Fry, P. Mentorship for scholarliness: Opportunities and dilemmas. *Nursing Outlook,* 1982, 30, 22–28.

Mishler, E. Meaning in context: Is there any other kind? *Education Review.* Mass: Harvard, 1979, 19, (1) 1–19.

Newman, M. *Theory development in nursing.* Philadelphia: F. A. Davis, 1979.

Padillo, A. M. (Ed.). *Acculturation: Theory, models and some findings.* Boulder, Colo.: Westview Press, 1980.

Parse, R. *Man-living-health: A theory of nursing.* New York: John Wiley & Sons, 1981.

Pelto, P. J. & Pelto, G. H. *Anthropological research: A structure of inquiry* (2nd ed.). Cambridge: Cambridge University Press, 1979.

Polgar, S. Health and human behavior: Areas of interest common to social and medical sciences. *Current Anthropology,* 1962, 3, 159–205.

Ragucci, A. T. *The ethnographic approach and nursing research. Nursing Research* 1972, 21, 485–490.

Ragucci, A. T. The urban context of health and illness beliefs and practices of elderly women in an Italian-American enclave. In M. M. Leininger (Ed.), *Transcultural nursing care of the elderly: Proceedings from the second national transcultural nursing conference.* Salt Lake City: University of Utah College of Nursing, 1977.

Reinharz, Shulamit. *On becoming a social scientist.* San Francisco: Jossey-Bass Publishers, 1979.

Schiff, A. Language, culture and Jewish acculturation of Soviet Jewish emmigres. *Journal of Jewish Communal Service,* 1979, 56–57, 44–49.

Schwartz, L. Soviet Jewish resettlement: Operationalizing Jewish consciousness raising. *Journal of Jewish Communal Service,* 1980, 56–57, 50–55.

Sidorsky, D. *The future of the Jewish community in America: A task force report.* New York: The American Jewish Committee Institute of Human Relations, 1972.

Spradley, J. P. *The ethnographic interview.* New York: Holt, Rinehart and Winston, 1979.

Spradley, J. P. *Participant observation.* New York: Holt, Rinehart and Winston, 1980.

Swanson, J. M., & Chenitz, W. C. Why qualitative research in nursing? *Nursing Outlook,* 1982, 30, 241–245.

Taft, E. The absorption of Soviet Jewish immigrants—their impact on Jewish communal institutions. *Journal of Jewish Communal Service.* 1977–1979, *54–55,* 166–177.

Teske, R. H. C., & Nelson, B. H. Acculturation and assimilation: A clarification.

American Ethnologist, 1974, *1,* 351–367.

Wenger, A. F. Z. *Health and care phenomena among Soviet Jewish immigrants in the acculturation process: A mini-ethnonursing study* (unpublished field study). Detroit: Wayne State University, College of Nursing, 1983.

19

A Qualitative Research Method to Study the Elderly in Two Residences

Mary Bailey

PURPOSE AND FOCUS

The focus of this chapter is on the ethnographic method and its use in studying the elderly, especially with respect to ideologies and support systems. The ethnographic field study method was used during the first year of this projected three-year study to describe, discover, and document in systematic detail the lifeways of the elderly and their support systems.

A central concept of the ethnographic method is that of culture. The word "culture" has various meanings, and I use Kottak's broadly based definition:

> That which is transmitted through learning—behavior patterns and modes of thought acquired by humans as members of society. Technology, language, patterns of group organizations, and ideology are aspects of culture. (1982, p. 10)

Culture also includes a host of other variables, all of which must be carefully studied in order to understand human conditions and lifeways.

Since ideology is part of culture, this research included investigation of the ideology of the elderly and the ideology underlying their support systems. Ideology includes many realms of human thought, such as values, norms, knowledge, themes, philosophies, religious beliefs, sentiments, ethical principles, world view, and ethos (Kottak, 1982, p. 11). Through ideological systems of thought, humans become aware of their identities and generally grow secure in relating to others because they share ideologies similar to those of others. With an ideology, a code is established that defines reality for oneself and for others within society. The code helps a person to attach meaning and value to his or her life. Thus, the concepts of culture and ideology as they relate to the elderly as a special cultural group within our society are essential to a full understanding of this group.

Ideology influences how older Americans define and utilize social support in their ongoing life situations. Social support is held to be a critical variable in maintaining health for all groups of people. There is a relationship between the individual's wellness experience and the support systems maintained throughout his life. Because of the growing population of elderly individuals, their health, and well-being especially need to be documented and studied. Recently some of the present concerns concerning the elderly were identified:

> The problem of care for the elderly is rapidly becoming a national crisis. Americans over 65 are probably the fastest growing age cohort in the country according to the United States Bureau of the Census. Between 1900 and 1980, when the population as a whole tripled, their number increased eightfold. The over-75 group, the segment with the most illness, has grown by more than 37 percent in the last decade alone. By 2030, when the baby boomers are well into their "golden years," the over-65 segment is expected to reach 55 million, nearly one quarter of the population. (Moore, 1983, p. 30)

Thus, with increasing numbers of people who especially need health care, ways to provide this care require special attention. Public health policies need to be developed that are sensitive to the elderly's needs. Future health policy in the United States should also be shaped by relevant research findings that include the elderly's viewpoints and their perceived health needs.

RATIONALE FOR THE STUDY AND RESEARCH QUESTIONS

This study was based on the assumptions that social support tends to increase coping ability for the elderly. Coping ability is thought to be the gate to health and well-being (Gore, 1978). Nurses and other health professionals generally recognize the role of social support in maintaining and gaining wholeness. Nurses have a commitment and a tradition of concern for the patient's environment and support system(s) to promote optimal health and function. Support has been a care concept of importance and is under study in clinical nursing (Gardner & Wheeler, 1981; Leininger, 1980, 1984). According to Norbeck (1981), systematic ways to assess environmental influences on the type of support the patient may need have unfortunately been limited. Social scientists, however, have studied social support and its impact on mortality rates (Berkman & Syme, 1979). Some studies indicate the relationship of social support to the facility with which people make major life transitions (Lowenthal & Haven, 1968; pp. 20–30). Especially worth noting is the relationship of social support to the beneficial effects of being able to talk out problems and concerns when anxious or worried (Vernoff, Kulka, & Douvan, 1981).

From all societal indications, the elderly need viable social support networks to deal with multiple stressful events (Philisuk & Minkler, 1980). These stressful events most often result in feelings of powerlessness and uselessness (Kuypers & Bengtson, 1973). To alleviate these feelings and enable the elderly individual to serve not only as a recipient but also a benefactor in a helping relationship, an adequate support system is necessary. According to Conner, Powers, and Bultena (1979), the elderly individual's sense of security, personal worth, and self-competence can be fostered by a supportive network.

For these reasons, it is essential for health care providers to understand fully the support systems of the elderly. Some of the research questions the author explored were: What is the nature of the support systems at the two residences? What factors or variables relate to maintaining current support systems? How might activity level of the two residences be influenced by support systems? What is the subjective view of health and well-being at both residences?

QUALITATIVE METHODOLOGICAL CONSIDERATIONS

Focusing on social support and the elderly, the author used Van Maanen's and Reinharz's qualitative research principles and methodological considerations. According to Van Maanen, Sabbs, and Faulkner, qualitative research involves five principles, which include the following:

1. *Analytic induction:* Qualitative work begins with close-up detailed observation. The specific and local are sought as a primary data base within which patterns may or may not be found. To the degree the investigator is initially uncommitted to a particular theoretical model, the more ideal the uncovered data. Generalizations are to be built from the ground up and only tentatively offered on the basis of their ability to fully contain the data in hand.

2. *Proximity:* Importance is placed on concrete occurrences and occasions, not on reports of such. The investigator should witness first-hand that which he or she proposes to understand. To the extent possible, people should be observed engaged in activities that matter to them, the performance of which is to them of more importance that their performance in front of the investigator.

3. *Ordinary behavior:* Topics for qualitative study are to be located within the natural world of those studied. Qualitative research is interested in everyday activity as defined, enacted, and made problematic by persons going about their normal routines. Whatever interrupts or otherwise alters and perhaps distorts ordinary lines of activity is to be minimized.

4. *Structure as ritual constraint:* Recurrent patterns of social activity are essentially arbitrary, a result of custom, present circumstance, and ongoing interaction. There is no primal social order or set of fundamental environmental conditions against which a "natural deviation" can be defined. Human actions are intentional, mediated by what people think they are accomplishing. To ignore these meanings and the contexts within which they are situationally relevant is to impose structure rather than discover it.

5. *Descriptive focus:* Qualitative work involves ontological inquiry. This is a fancy

way of saying merely that, at root, qualitative work seeks a description for what
is occurring in a given place and time. "What is going on here?" is the most
elementary qualitative research question yet the most difficult to adequately
answer. The aims of revelation and disclosure take precedence over explanation and prediction.*

I also found that Van Maanen's principles about qualitative research method
support Reinharz's comparative ideas about qualitative and quantitative research,
given in Table 19-1 (Reinharz, 1979, pp. 14–15). The center column represents the
more traditional concepts of science and quantification as applied to the research-
able universe. The right-hand column represents qualitative research with its emphasis on meaning and context. According to Reinharz (1979), qualitative research
includes the creation of gestalts and meaningful patterns. It also includes viewing
natural events in their ongoing context with theory emerging from research facts or
findings. These concepts guided the author in doing a qualitative research study of
the elderly.

Effective health care depends on nurses viewing and assessing the meaning that
certain concepts have for clients, in this case, the elderly. Thus, nurse researchers
using qualitative research methods can provide health care data that include the
meaning and description of lifeways of the elderly in order to develop a theory base
of practice. Researching social support of the elderly living in residences and its relationship to their well-being is an ongoing major focus of my study.

Another important methodological approach in this study was obtaining the
elderly's viewpoint from the *emic* perspective as well as the *etic* perspective—a focus
of transcultural nursing research since the early 1960s (Leininger 1960–1962, 1970,
1978). I used Kottak's definition of these terms:

> To study different cultures, anthropologists and most transcultural nurses have
> advocated two approaches, the *emic* (actor-oriented) and *etic* (observer-oriented).
> The *emic* approach views a culture as mental or ideational and assumes that it
> can be described only by getting into the heads of the people studied. . . . The
> anthropologist seeks the "native viewpoint" and relies on the culture-bearers,
> or actors, to judge whether something they do, say, or think is significant or not.
>
> The *etic* . . . approach implies different goals for the anthropologist. When
> describing, interpreting, and analyzing a culture, the anthropologist relies on
> his or her own extended observations and gives more weight to the trained
> scientist's criteria of significance than to those of the culture-bearers. Choice
> of the *etic* research strategy rests on the assumption that, as a trained and objec-
> tive scientist, he or she can take a less involved, more impartial, and larger
> view of what is going on.†

The emic approach is gained by spending time with a particular group to obtain
their view, whereas the etic or researcher's approach can be identified by compar-

---

*From Van Meanen, J., Sabbs, J., & Faulkner, R. *Varieties of qualitative research.* Beverly
Hills, Calif.: Sage Publications, 1982, p. 16. With permission.
†From Kottak, C. (Ed.). *Researching American culture.* Ann Arbor: University of Michigan
Press, 1982, p. 12. With permission.

ing the client's views against the observed societal views. Etic data often include the society's social structure, history, ecology, and religious beliefs. Both of these concepts were used to study the elderly, as complementary ways to view reality. The etic approach in this study involved viewing the elderly residents with regard to the historical place they occupy as "oldsters" in contemporary American culture. Their personal history within the context of past and current American values was also taken into account.

Yet another methodological consideration was to watch my own individual biases throughout the study. Fike's statement was kept in mind:

> Analysts must constantly remind themselves of the importance of being objective, and make a conscious and persistent effort to adopt a relativist's position. Cultural relativism is the attitude that a society's customs [must] be viewed in the context of that society's culture and environment. (Kottak, 1982:10)

GROUPS STUDIED: INFORMANT

Two groups of elderly are the informants of this three-year study. One group lives in a residence requiring them to pay from private resources under the auspices of a religious organization. The second group are residents within a federally subsidized housing unit. Both housing units are similar in size, consisting of 100 and 140 elderly residents, respectively, and both contain individual private apartments for each resident. Meals are provided three times a day at the private paying residence and five times a week at the subsidized residence. Both residences espouse a philosophy of offering housing for senior citizens who are independent and able to care for themselves. The private paying residence has a nursing home attached to the facility, but the independent living area of that residence is open only to individuals who are mobile and able to care for themselves.

THE FIELD DIARY: QUALITATIVE RESEARCH TOOL

An important qualitative research tool used during the study was the field diary, which requires the researcher to describe in detail the events, actions, interactions, and feelings of people as they occur naturally in a particular context or setting. The field diary is a systematic account of what happens to people over time; with it, the researcher can document and trace people's regular or divergent patterns and further understand the people's lifeways (Spradley, 1979, p. 76). One recurrent theme that in the field notes demonstrated, for example, relates to passivity-activity levels in both residences. As recorded in my field diary, for example, this theme of behavior, taken from conversations with residents and administrators as well as observed directly enabled the researchers to focus on the activity level of the elderly and to make inferences as to how activity was a key variable related to health, well-being, and social support.

The field diary was a tool used in both residences. The researcher recorded, interviewed and documented ongoing events or special occasions, and recorded her thoughts, observations, and general impressions related to the concept of aging. One

Table 19-1 *Research Models in Contemporary Society*

	Quantitative Research	Qualitative Research
Units of study	Predefined, operationalized concepts stated as hypotheses	Natural events encased in their ongoing contexts
Sharpness of focus	Limited, specialized, specific, exclusive	Broad, inclusive
Data type	Reports of attitudes and actions as in questionnaires, interviews and archives	Feelings, behavior, thoughts, insights, actions as witnessed or experienced
Topic of study	Manageable issue derived from scholarly literature, selected for potential scholarly contribution, sometimes socially significant	Socially significant problem sometimes related to issues discussed in scholarly literature
Role of researcher		
In relation to environment	Control of environment is desired, attempt to manage research conditions	Openness to environment, immersion, being subject to and shaped by it
In relation to subjects	Detached	Involved, sense of commitment, participation, sharing of fate
As a person	Irrelevant	Relevant, expected to change during process
Impact on researcher	Irrelevant	Anticipated, recorded, reported, valued
Implementation of method	As per design, decided a priori	Method determined by unique characteristics of field setting

(continued)

	Quantitative Research	Qualitative Research
Validity criteria	Proof, evidence, statistical significance; study must be replicable and yield same results to have valid findings	Completeness, plausibility, illustrativeness, understanding, responsiveness to readers' or subjects' experience; study cannot, however, be replicated
Role of theory	Crucial as determinant of research design	Emerges from research implementation
Data analysis	Arranged in advance relying of deductive logic, done when all data are "in"	Done during the study, relying on inductive logic
Manipulation of data	Utilization of statistical analyses	Creation of gestalts and meaningful patterns
Presentation format	Research report form; report of conclusions with regard to hypotheses stated in advance, or presentation of data obtained from instruments	Story, description with emergent concepts; including documentation of process of discovery
Values	Researcher's attitudes not revealed, recognized, or analyzed, attempts to be value-free, objective	Researcher's attitudes described and discussed, values acknowledged, revealed, labeled

*Reprinted from Reinharz, S. *On becoming a social scientist.* San Francisco: Jossly = Bass, 1979. With permission.

effect of the researcher's participant-observations and field notes was to change her views regarding the "best" living accommodation for the elderly, which was that the elderly in the United States need multiple options to meet their needs. This process of allowing observations made as a researcher to have an impact on one's thoughts is an essential aspect of qualitative research, and this influenced other changes in the researchers ideas as she reflected upon and observe the elderly in homes. The field diary will be a crucial tool in these reflections.

In maintaining the field diary, the researcher relied upon Van Maanen's first principle, namely, analytic induction, and his three principles concerning ordinary behavior. Following these principles, qualitative work begins with close-up, detailed observation, and the topics of every study are to be located within the natural world of those studied (Van Maanen, 1982, p. 16). Thus, the researcher's diary contains detailed observations of personal encounters with the elderly and administration staff of both residences, and verbatim statements with the researcher's own personal feelings.

THE OPEN-ENDED QUESTIONNAIRE RESEARCH TOOL

Since the researcher was interested in discovering gestalts of knowledge and meaningful patterns with the two groups of elderly persons, an open-ended questionnaire helped to identify social support networks, levels of health and well-being, activity level, income level, and related variables. A questionnaire that was originally constructed for a study conducted through the University of Michigan's Institute of Social Research; was used; however, it was modified to make the questions more open-ended. Items that provided data on the elderly's daily activities, views on federal and state policy issues, and definitions of recreation were included. The original University of Michigan questionnaire was developed for a national study conducted in 1978 on social support systems among various age groupings. The major purpose of this questionnaire was to obtain data on the nature of social support networks at different points in the life course, with particular focus on the elderly. This questionnaire was, in part, useful to this study as it was concerned with (1) the relationship between functional health and well-being of older men and women and their opportunities to give and receive social support; (2) the extent to which such needs and opportunities differ but persist throughout the life course; and (3) the distinctive form social support networks may assume within families and major social-demographic groups. Although this University of Michigan questionnaire had a focus on life span development across generations, this was not the researcher's primary focus. Nevertheless, items concerned with social support, level of health, wellness, and related variables concerning the elderly were of interest and could provide comparative data where possible.

As stated earlier, the original questionnaire had specific categories for respondents to answer, and they were used in an open-ended format. For example, the original questionnaire item was: "Taking all things together, how would you say things are these days; would you say you're *very happy, pretty happy* or *not too happy* these days?" The question was changed to: "Tell me about yourself and your life; how satisfied are you with your life at present?"

The questionnaire also aided continued interaction with the elderly. The questionnaire was not used in a rigid way, which limits the flow of ideas from the respondent, but rather in a way that encouraged them to share ideas about different aspects of their lives. As an instrument, it helped to elicit both qualitative and quantitative data. In addition, data from a portion of the questionnaire was used to compare responses with the findings of the 1978 national study conducted by the Michigan Institute of Social Research to determine how this small population of the elderly fit into a national pattern.

EMPLOYING THE QUALITATIVE METHOD AND FINDINGS

One purpose of this qualitative and longitudinal study has been to obtain an exploratory and meaningful descriptive account of the elderly in two different types of residences. The investigator closely followed the Van Maanen and Reinharz concepts as a guide to the researcher's role to study feelings, behavior, thoughts, and actions of the elderly. The study is still in process.

The study began by the researcher introducing herself to the elderly residents in both homes as a nursing student interested in studying older persons. They were told that the researcher would be returning weekly to visit with them for a period of one to three years. During the first year of the study, the researcher participated with the elderly in their regular daily activities, observing specific and general lifeways. She was present at festive meals such as Octoberfest, which involved some of the German residents preparing *spaetzle* (noodles), for everyone in the residence to enjoy.

The participant-observation method of anthropology is being used to study and be responsive to the daily activities of the elderly. The researcher visits with and observes the administrators of the residences as well as the families of the elderly. At present, the researcher is viewed as a guest in the residences and is open to whatever the elderly which to share with her. The researcher is interested in what concerns the elderly on a daily basis as well as what makes a day or event special, and how this event is defined by them collectively and individually.

To date, the researcher has been received in an accepting and cordial manner, and only on a few occasions has she encountered an elderly person who prefers not to talk with her. On one occasion, an elderly resident returned to the researcher after she had initially declined to talk with her and expressed interest in visiting with her. She remarked, "You seem to be easy to talk with and I believe I do have some thoughts on aging and some books to share with you." It appears that the researcher's ongoing presence in the residence, the time spent at each residence (two to three days a week), and to be with them for one to three years helps to build a trusting and accepting relationship with the elderly and with the administrators.

As a researcher using qualitative methods, I am keenly desirous of maintaining open communication with the elderly and of being responsive to them. The elderly and the researchers are immersed in an environment of knowing living together which contrasts with the traditional scientific method to which the researcher is not involved with her informants in a participant way, and may often impose his or her ideas as specific questions are asked of the students. Moreover, the scientific method is considered a "controlled experiment," and there is a conscious effort to manage or control the research setting. In contrast, this study, using a qualitative research focus, is not controlled and accepts changes on the part of the researcher and the subjects under study. During the next two years of this field study, the researcher will undoubtedly continue to be shaped by the elderly's thinking and this will both sharpen the focus of the study and reaffirm the findings.

To date, the elderly in the private paying residence have seemed to provide candid information and reflections on their living patterns and beliefs. The researcher's relationship with the elderly in these two settings involves, as Reinharz puts it, a "sense of commitment, participation and sharing of the fate of others." Thus, the researcher role is a person and nurse who appears quite meaningful to the elderly. This role contrasts with that of the scientific researcher, who takes a noninvolved and detached role (Reinharz, 1979, p. 14).

Findings

Shortly after this study was initiated and an ongoing trust relationship established with the elderly in both residences, several features became apparent. Most obvious was the difference in levels of energy and activity between the elderly in the two residences. Elderly residents in the private paying residence (PP) appeared passive and less involved in ongoing community and in-house activities than did the residents of the federally subsidized housing (FH) area. The researcher's observations were substantiated by reviewing some of my findings with the administrators, staff, and residents at both places. The co-director at the federally subsidized housing area, for example, said:

> There always seems to be a lot going on here. For example, many residents gather several times a week to help with different community projects in the dining room upstairs. Many individuals walk to town on a daily basis or take their car to the shopping centers. At mealtime, there's such a level of activity and noise in the dining room, it's difficult to hear others in conversation. (Bailey, 1982–1983, p. 42)

The residents at FH also appeared to be more physically actively engaged with each other. One resident of FH said:

> There is always something to do here. I like to walk to town early—I meet my joggers along the way and I love to see the sunrise. Then I come back for breakfast and take part in activities at FH. Then I'll go to town with one of my neighbors or help out with whatever needs to be done here. In the evening a group of us men have our own table. We discuss sports or news from the newspaper. We really enjoy each other; this is a good place. (Bailey, 1982–1983, p. 56)

There seemed to be frequent preparation and delivering of soups, breads, and homemade sweets to the elderly in residence at FH. A concern for maintaining the elderly's ability to stay well and remain at FH seemed to be a topic that came up in frequent conversations I had with residents. It's interesting to note that some of the residents at FH were involved in maintaining the building and that some residents took evening and weekend duty, being on call in the event of any emergency involving the residents or the building.

The researcher's observations at the private paying (PP) residence have been almost opposite to what were observed at the federally subsidized residence. Although the philosophy of both residences involves elderly individuals in independent living situations, there is a nursing home facility attached to PP. This nursing facility offers nursing consultation in the independent living area, if clients need such care. The residents at PP were different in that, in general, they were more passive. They ventured outside the home to community-sponsored concerts or church meetings and services less often, and were more content to remain in their rooms viewing television, reading, or sleeping. The freedom or desire to visit each other in their own rooms also appeared less at PP than at FH. My interviews with the administrator at PP appear to substantiate some of my observations. He said:

I wish that there was more that I might do to promote greater activity on the part of the residents. For many years we have had the minibus to take residents on color tours of the area, even stopping with a box lunch at a "mystery spot" and returning in the afternoon. There just seem to be fewer "takers" for any of the outside activities here. I know it would do them good to get out, breathe new air, see something different, but with individuals paying their own way, it's difficult to say you should do this, this would do you good. (Bailey, 1982–1983, p. 30)

The administrator seemed concerned, wanting to find ways to offer the elderly residents more involvement with each other. The ability of the residents to pay their own way, in this case, seemed to enter into their patterns of behavior concerning activity and passivity.

One of the residents at PP shared with me some of her thoughts about other residents with this comment:

Why, some of these people I would like to prick with a pin—there isn't much life to them. They go out of their rooms for each of their three meals and then return to their rooms. A few have some afternoon bridge games, but most of them seem content to just sit and let the world go by. I don't know what it would take to get them more involved, more alive. I wonder if they feel good. (Bailey, 1982–1983, p. 17)

During this first year of the three-year study, the researcher also observed and documented a decrease of activity and mobility on the part of some of the residents at PP compared to the activity and mobility level I observed at FH residence. It appears the less the residents do, the less they are able to do. This finding has nursing care implications for health and fitness in the future care of the elderly. One elderly person even stated a positive relationship between being alive, level of activity, and feelings of health.

SUMMARY

To date, the researcher has used a qualitative method with the anthropological participant-observation and interview method and with a focus on the use of the field diary and an open-ended questionnaire. These qualitative methods were selected to study the lifeways (patterns and themes) of the elderly in two residences. This qualitative method is providing a documentary account and description of what is occurring within a given context of place and time.

From the questionnaire, both qualitative and quantitative data, will be compared responses between the two residences and with a national sample of individuals surveyed through the Institute of Social Research at the University of Michigan. An in-depth content analysis of the field diary will be performed, as will a content analysis of the data from the participant-observation and informal interviews. As a participant-observer, the researcher is learning much about herself, and how to enter and leave a field study daily. Knowing how to become as natural a participant in the environment as possible so that the researcher is not a "foreigner" or threatening stranger is important. Comparative responses of the elderly to the research tools being used in this study will also be analyzed.

IMPLICATIONS

This type of study seems important to nursing in discovering the role that social support plays in wellness and health with the elderly. With the increased number of elderly in our society, data from the viewpoint of the elderly (emic data) are needed to develop policies that are sensitive to the needs of the elderly for suitable, humane housing, an active life style, and quality health care. What research is available to nurses in order to deal with this need? What is the best way to use tax monies to maintain a functional level of health in our older population? These are the concerns of the researcher and of many nurses.

Fortunately, most Americans value and respect diversity. However, the concept of diversity of health care among the elderly and their diverse support systems remain virtually unexplored. The author hopes this study will contribute knowledge to these areas so that both nursing and the elderly will benefit.

Nursing is now at a crossroads in its exploration of methods to advance nursing knowledge. Qualitative research methods are essential to provide in-depth understandings and new knowledge about health care and healing. Through the use of qualitative research methods, nursing can understand the world of the elderly and how they know health and illness conditions. Quantitative methods of precise measurements and of fitting variables into a static structure must be joined with qualitative research, to obtain meanings, understandings, and holistic life experience insights. Both methods would appear to offer unique but different approaches in viewing the reality of the elderly.

REFERENCES

Bailey, M. P., Field notes: The elderly at two residences in Ann Arbor, Michigan, 1982–1983.

Berkman, L. F., & Syme, S. L., Social networks, host resistance, and mortality: A nine-year follow-up study of Alameda County residents. *American Journal of Epidemiology*, 1979, *109*(2), 186–204.

Conner, K. A., Powers, E. A., & Bultena, G.

L., Social interaction and life satisfaction: An empirical assessment of late-life patterns. *Journal of Gerontology*, 1979, *34*(1), 116–121.

Gardner, K., & Wheeler, E. C. Nurses' perception of the meaning of support in nursing. *Issues in Mental Health Nursing*, 1981, *3*, 13–28.

Gore, S., The effect of social support in moderating the health consequences of unemployment. *Journal of Health and Social Behavior*, 1978, *19*(2), 157–165.

Kottak, C. (Ed.). *Researching American culture*. Ann Arbor: University of Michigan Press, 1982.

Kuypers, J. A., & Bengston, V. L., Social breakdown and competence: A model of normal aging. *Human Development*, 1973, *14*(3), 181–201.

Leininger, M. Field study notes and reports in New Guinea. Personal data from field studies, 1960–1962.

Leininger, M. *Nursing and anthropology: Two worlds to blend*. New York: John Wiley & Sons, 1970.

Leininger, M. *Transcultural nursing: Concepts, theories and practices*. New York: John Wiley & Sons, 1978.

Leininger, M. Caring: A central focus of nursing and health care services. *Nursing and Health Care*, 1980, *1*(3), 135–143, 176.

Leininger, M. *Care: the essence of nursing and health*. Thorofare, New Jersey: Slack and Company, 1984.

Lowenthal, M. F., & Haven, C., Interaction and adaptation: Intimacy as a critical variable. *American Sociological Review*, 1968, *33*, 20–30.

Moore, D., American neglected elderly. *New York Times Magazine*, January 30, 1983.

Norbeck, J., Social support: A model for clinical research and application. *Advances in Nursing Science*, 1981, 43–59.

Philisuk, M., & Minkler, M., Supportive networks: Life ties for the elderly. *Journal of Social Issues*, 1980, *36*(2), 95–116.

Reinharz, S. *On becoming a social scientist*. San Francisco: Jossey-Bass, 1979.

Spradley, J. P. *The ethnographic interview*. New York: Macmillan, 1979.

Van Maanen, J., Sabbs, J., & Faulkner, R. *Varieties of qualitative research*. Beverly Hills, Calif.: Sage Publications, 1982.

Vernoff, J., Kulka, R., & Douvan, E. *Mental health in America*. New York: Basic Books, 1981.

20

Audiovisual Methods in Nursing Research

Madeleine Leininger

Perhaps one of the greatest and most promising breakthroughs to know and understand human health conditions rests with the use of audiovisual media in nursing and health care research. It is always amazing that some of the most obvious research techniques and methods may not be used until brought to attention in the literature, and audiovisual methods are a case in point. Audiovisual media refers to various messages communicated to humans and others in different ways through sight, hearing, or expressive modes. In this chapter, the purposes, uses, and importance of audiovisual media will be briefly presented and discussed with the goal of helping the reader become aware of the use of photography, drawings, television, productions, symbols, tape recordings, and the use of projective tests for nursing and health care research.

There is a growing variety of audiovisual media available commercially, and these materials and equipment have relevance to health personnel as new ways to document, analyze, and interpret health care behavior and practices. Nurses will be involved in the audiovisual research revolution and need to begin now to consider changes in their modes of studying people. Although most nurses are aware of the values of audiovisual materials for teaching purposes, the research purposes remain meagerly used and valued. Using audiovisual media for research may be viewed as difficult, questionable, and nonscientific, as the data cannot be measured. Considerably more emphasis and usage are needed to make audiovisual materials an important and integral part of qualitative and quantitative types of nursing research methods.

Audiovisual media have been used for research purposes for a number of decades by social scientists, communication specialists (including telecommunication specialists), and other scientists. Bateson and Mead were two anthropologists who began using photography in the late 1920s and 1930s for research purposes with their study of the Balinese people (Bateson & Mead, 1942). Their work caught the interest of other social scientists in discovering the multiple purposes and values of photography to study human cultures. Later, Mead worked with MacGregor (1951) to photograph and study Balinese childhood and socialization practices. Collier (1967) was also an early and strong advocate of the use of photography, as reflected in his perceptive and early book on the subject of photography, which is still utilized by serious scholars interested in the use of still photography.

Since the mid-1960s, Sorenson and Gajdusek (1966), Leininger (1960–1983), and others have used audiovisual media for anthropological research and consultation, and for teaching, and informational purposes. Hall (1966), in his work on proxemics and nonverbal communication has also made major contributions in demonstrating the values of audiovisual media for documentary research. Birdwhistell (1970) has been another pioneer in the use of photography to study systematically kinesic morphology as forms of nonverbal communication. These leaders and others have been outstanding to advance the use of audiovisual media in research.

More recently, a number of telecommunication and photography specialists have been active in the use of a great variety of modern audiovisual materials and equipment to study different ways to document and communicate human expressions and actions. Television and many other kinds of modern audiophotographic media are being used to communicate and historically document international events. Such direct and primary evidence provides important research data to assess historical facts, territorial rights, and legal matters. Many other uses of modern audiovisual media for research purposes can be found in practically every country in the world. The use of audiovisual media intrigues people and is becoming a more frequent means to know, learn, and document human behavior and events.

PURPOSES OF AUDIOVISUAL MEDIA IN RESEARCH

Audiovisual media can provide an invaluable way to document and study health care and nursing phenomena. The purposes and uses are many, and some can be highlighted next.

First, audiovisual media can be used to *document detailed information* about specific phenomena under investigation, such as child and adult caring practices, ritual healing, health promotion activities, nurse-client interactions, living environments, family communication, feeding methods and many other daily and familiar activities of interest to nurses. Documenting exactly how things are performed is extremely important to obtain accurate and reliable data.

Second, audiovisual media may be used to *analyze health and caring behaviors in a variety of human contexts and with reference to space, time and interactional factors.* For example, how the nurse moves toward or away from clients in the hospital or home can be documented by portable television to assess detailed themes and patterns of behavior. The actual sequence of verbal and nonverbal communication as nurses care for infants, disturbed clients, or people in any common or critical nursing context can be studied with time and place factors through audiovisual means for health care implications. Prescise and detailed accounts of human care behavior can be obtained by audiovisual media, and kept for historical changes in behavior over time periods.

Third, audiovisual media can be used to provide *comparative studies about spontaneous or recurrent action held to be of interest to nursing.* Once such raw audiovisual data have been carefully documented by modern methods, the findings can be *compared for historical and replication purposes.* The data can be studied by different researchers prepared in analyzing audiovisual materials against some explicit criteria. Accordingly, nurses need to be taught to analyze such documentary data in formal and systematic ways for replication purposes so that maximal use of the data can be made. *Comparative analysis* of several films on the care of people from Western and non-Western cultures can quickly bring into relief differences and similarities about particular health and care phenomena under study. Studying the totality of human actions in detail and in natural contexts often provides many insights not available by any other type of research method. And seeing cross-cultural or cross-institutional differences related to health and care practices is an added value of photography and audiorecordings. Comparative analysis by researchers of nurse-client, client-physician, and client-social worker by audiovisual media can lead to documenting and understanding precise care behavior and human expressions. Many other types of comparative analysis are needed in nursing to document intranursing and interdisciplinary patterns of helping people.

Fourth, audiovisual media is valuable to *identify and plan for historical, cultural, social, and environmental changes.* Photography *before* and *after* making changes in a situation (or a crisis) can be an invaluable guide to current and future changes in nursing and health systems. Photographic documentation by still or motion pictures of specific places, people, and situations in their natural setting can be extremely valuable in instituting changes in nursing policies or administrative practices. Before and after changes documented by audiovisual means can serve legal and cultural change purposes. Healthy and less healthy environments can be studied by audiovisual media for desired kinds of work environments for health personnel and for clients and families. Actual evidence of the past situation and proposed improvements provide a sound basis for making and evaluating changes. Photographs, recordings, and use of drawings by the people are useful to assess current and anticipated health care changes in communities.

Fifth, audiovisual media can be used *to document and analyze human expressions, feelings, symbols, icons, and rituals in nursing* and of nurse's daily activities over time, in homes, clinics, hospitals, or wherever people use nursing services. Documenting maturation and growth changes of infants, adolescents, and adults by periodically taking pictures and collecting life scripts of individuals and groups is another use of audiovisuals. Photographic study of care and health patterns through the life cycle is an important way to generate theory and research studies. Audiovisual media are also most valuable to establish longitudinal studies of children playing, eating, and interacting with others. Documenting role behavior by audiovisual means of clients in stressful and less stressful contexts can lead to new insights and theories about nursing phenemena.

Sixth, anything recorded by audiovisual methods can become *archival data and can serve as a "data bank" of raw research data available* for current and future study purposes. These materials must, however, be carefully dated and put in protective storage environments. In order to use such archival or any audiovisual data, such as photographs, tapes, or drawings, the researcher needs to obtain permission from the people being studied; consent forms should be signed. Such permission is important to protect people's rights. Thoughtful consideration must also be given to ethical, moral, or other risk concerns of participating informants. It is important to make clear that informants understand the use of the data (films, tapes, scripts, drawings etc.) for research purposes so that no problems or misunderstandings will occur later. Full explanations should be provided about the audiovisual research methods being used to gain the clients cooperation or to prevent law suits. It has been the author's practice to provide a copy of the audiovisual material such as audiocassettes and video films, if the informants so desire such data. This can be considered part of the costs of the research, or the informant may want to pay for the materials because he or she also values and wants to use them. If it is not possible for the informants to have a copy, let them know where they can obtain or see a copy of the audiovisual scripts or films.

Seventh, and most importantly audiovisual media can be used to *document and study teaching, consultation, and clinical field work from a research perspective.* Careful documentation of any of these practices as micro or macro filming can be essential to make improvements in these areas. The methods, techniques, and processes of teaching, clinical interactions, and consultation can be documented by sequences photographed over time to reveal patterns or special foci under study. To achieve such research purposes, nurse researchers need to be prepared in the proper and potential uses of audiovisual equipment, their costs and desired effects of the media. The nurse researcher can move from an amateur photographer to one of a skilled professional person and gain many rewards and satisfactions in the use of audiovisuals.

Today a great variety of audiovisual media are available and may be used for research purposes. Some of the most common types are listed in Table 20-1.

GUIDELINES FOR USE OF AUDIOVISUAL MEDIA FOR RESEARCH PURPOSES

Each of the above different types of audiovisual media should be studied as ways to use effectively the different types for research. Only a few thoughts on the major types will be highlighted below as guides to use the media in research.

Photographic and Auditory Types and Guidelines

Today, television, audiotapes, and a large variety of computer videos are extremely popular and being used in research studies. Human beings remain intrigued with all types of new and old forms of photographic and auditory media, and the market is almost flooded with such equipment. The rapid evolution of television and electronic computers means that many new kinds of equipment will soon transform both research methods and the analysis and presentation of the data to the public. Nurse researchers must be visionary and begin to take seriously the use of audiovisual media for different research purposes. Moreover, some types of research will require that the nurse work closely with photographic and other specialists, espe-

Table 20-1   Types of Audiovisual Materials for Health Care Research

Photographic and Auditory Types

1. Photography (still and motion). This includes the study of icons, symbols, rituals and normal (or strange) interactions
2. Television (videocassettes and regular forms)
3. Computer reproduction (or stimulations): This includes many new kinds of software media now available on the market such as health choices, health marketing and others as games or programs. Display screens with reproductions and graphs are also available with computers.

Artistic or Expressive (Verbal and non-verbal) Types

1. Freehand drawings or sketches (with or without explanations; with or without stories) from the artists or clients
2. Music (includes all types and forms of musical expressions)
3. Pictures as expressive art forms
4. Symbols (material and nonmaterial)
5. Dance forms (natural or free and stylized)
6. Games and play expressions (children, adolescents, and adults)
7. Role playing (real and fictive or simulated)
8. Folk and professional oral and written expressive stories
9. Jokes, humor and related oral expressions
10. Life history oral and written accounts
11. Kinegraphs as study of body motions (Birdwhistell, 1970, pp. 257–282)

Testing Materials: (Projective and Other Types)

1. Thematic Apperception Test (TAT), Holtzman, Rorschach and other projective tests
2. Reflective tests, e.g., games, mosaic test, objects, etc.

cially electronic computer specialists. Many nursing schools and research centers have modern computers, television, and related audiovisual equipment today. Accordingly, the nurse researcher will be expected to work with such equipment and to help other researchers and students use the equipment and work with technical specialists to study nursing phenomena.

During the past two decades, I have been involved in developing videotapes of cultural groups to study cultural lifestyles and care phenomena of people representing different cultures. I have also done some institutional film studies and made films on special topics, such as transcultural nursing, cultural care, and culturological health care assessment modes (Leininger, 1984, pp. 32–33). These experiences have helped to demonstrate the use of audiovisual media for research purposes and the role of the nurse in conducting documentary films. As a producer of the films, I used *naturalistic* and *familiaristic* types of research in order to document spontaneous human feelings, cultural care patterns, and typical living conditions important to nurse researchers. With naturalistic and familiaristic filming, the informants were encouraged to be as spontaneous and natural as possible, and to do things that were familiar or routine to them in their environment. Efforts were taken to avoid unnatural or artificial posing or talking for the audiovisual production. The natural environment and support of known cultural norms were used as a means to obtain reliable and accurate data. In order to obtain naturalistic photographic data, the researcher makes a preliminary visit to the individual in his/her familiar environment and tries to learn about the person, his/her family, community, and environment before taking any documentary pictures or using audiovisual tapes. Permitting the people who are being filmed to know the researcher to build some degree of trust and acceptance (as well as obtaining permission) are essential for effective outcomes with audiovisual research.

Even today, the norms of nursing tend to choose highly structured, artificially contrived, and nearly perfect written scripts with specific time techniques to videotape nursing materials for teaching and commercial publication purposes. The author has watched many nurse educators spend hours getting the subject posed properly and the script written in advance so that the photography and sound fit together perfectly, but often in an unnatural and unfamiliar way to the person being filmed. Thus, the author uses a different approach to obtain naturalistic and spontaneous-like human audiovisual productions.

With transcultural filming, differences in thoughts and actions exist among cultures. For example, Americans and Japanese are generally camera lovers and comfortable in being photographed. There are people in other cultures, however, who are terrified to have their pictures taken or voices recorded. Such actions or thoughts are believed to lead to "soul loss," weakening of the person, potential illness, and many other unfavorable consequences. The nurse researcher must anticipate differential responses to filming due to cultural differences in beliefs, and to deal sensitively to their fears, anxieties, and concerns. Respect and ethical considerations are essential in any transcultural audiovisual nursing research pursuits. The author vividly recalls while doing field research in New Guinea (around 1960 to 1962) that the people were eager to have me use the Polaroid camera, but they were stunned to find that they were "flattened" in the resulting picture. They asked, "How did you flatten us so quickly and completely by the camera?" The author had not thought about that kind of perceptual and general response to the picture-taking. Thus, the researcher should anticipate differential cultural responses and emotional feelings towards audiovisual methods and know as much about the culture or situation as possible. Prior knowledge about the people's world view, values, and environment are extremely helpful to prevent unfavorable consequence.

It is also important for the audiovisual researcher to be knowledgeable about one's camera and other equipment being used for research. Some stationary and mobile televising equipment is complex and requires knowledge of its purposes and potential usage. Cost factors must also be considered as such equipment is often expensive. The researcher must be ready to pay for filming often before doing the production. Such factors need to be considered. The author has tried to limit excessive film editing in order to retain naturalistic and accurate accounts of the people for research purposes. In contrast, many commercial producers often want "perfect" or desired public image productions. Such productions may not yield an accurate documentary film or audio account for research. Furthermore, heavily audited scripts with "cut-outs and add-ins" markedly increase the cost of the production. Most importantly, the nurse researcher should review the production to be sure it reflects her or his intended production.

The following guidelines may be useful for the beginning nurse researcher who wants to use photographic and other types of audiovisual materials for research:

1. Be clear about your purposes and goals for audiovisual research.
2. Consult with an audiovisual professional health resource person and equipment expert well in advance before buying and filming a production.
3. Select your informants carefully for audiovisual research to ensure they are representative of the community and if they meet the criteria related to the purposes of your research.
4. Check to see that your tapes (or films) are fresh and that all equipment is in good running condition before starting your film-researching.
5. To obtain naturalistic qualitative data, use portable taping equipment rather than the stationary equipment found in commercial studios. Sometimes studios can, however, create or restructure the environment for a simulated production of a near similar condition or situation, which is being done more today. Because of the subtleties of human behavior, and for a documentary or historical production, one needs to film where the people naturally live, or where the action or event normally occurs. Prevention of contextual-stripping in audiovisual research must be watched to obtain qualitative types of research data.
6. Spend time with informants *prior* to initiating the audiovisual activities to answer their questions and make them reasonably comfortable with you, the equipment, and your research plans.
7. After taping pictures or voices, review the tape immediately to be sure the recording and filming equipment were working properly. If problems have occurred, the audiovisual production can generally be redone at that time if the production staff has time.
8. All videotape reels, cassettes, and other types of film should be labeled *immediately* after the filming with date, place, producers, directors, length of film, color or non-color, and subject matter. The original videotape is the master copy and should be carefully guarded. At least one copy or dub should be made from the master copy immediately as a backup film in case the master copy is accidentally lost or damaged.
9. Analysis of the videotape or films is done according to the purposes of the researcher. Often contextual, textual, structural, and general content analysis are done according to recorded time segments or phases of the film. The author recommends that other prepared professional film specialists analyze the data independently in light of the researcher's purposes to increase validity and reliability aspects. Using trained and knowledgeable observers as film content specialists (such as those who know about child rearing or folk practices of a culture) is important in order to reaffirm accurate and recurrent patterns of qualitative research with the audiovisual production.
10. The research report can take a variety of forms, e.g., oral (tapes), written, etc. Because of this, creativity can be used in reporting audiovisual findings.
11. All films and audio tapes should be stored in rooms with moderate temperature and a low humidity. (Seek advice from film experts on storage of films in different geographical areas in the world.) Before storing, recheck that the title and author of the film are clearly marked. The researcher should also have clear access to the audiovisual data for research and archival purposes, and the matter should be checked ahead of time with administrative personnel. Most importantly, the master copy should always be retained in a safe storage area;

duplicate copies from the master tape or film are appropriate for checkouts depending on the author's wishes and user's needs.

ADVANTAGES OF AUDIOVISUAL MEDIA

"Seeing and hearing is believing" and "One picture is worth a thousand words" are old Chinese sayings that make one realize the value of audiovisual media. Some of the major advantages of audiovisual media can be summarized as follows:

1. Audiovisual media can provide highly accurate documentation of subject matter under study, e.g., biophysical, emotional, and sociocultural.
2. Audiovisual media can provide insights about detailed, complex, and recurrent human behaviors and sociocultural interactions.
3. Audiovisual media gives contextual reality of multiple factors that influence human responses and expressions in different environments.
4. Audiovisual media provides information about different sequences, patterns and lifestyles of humans to guide nursing interventions.
5. Holistic documentation of real-life situations with *emic* detailed attributes of life events, such as rituals, ceremonies, and daily routines of life can be obtained through audiovisual media.
6. Audiovisual media captures unknown or anticipated human expressions, such as anger, touching people, offering support, feeding humans, and dealing with unexpected life situations.
7. Realistic or naturalistic action patterns and color responses of people can be detailed with the use of films and audio equipment.
8. Audiovisual media can open the doors to new areas of study because of new or different factors seen or heard.
9. Audiovisual media serves as a valuable historical document.

LIMITATIONS IN USE OF AUDIOVISUAL MEDIA

Some of the *limitations* to consider in using audiovisual media for research purposes are the following:

1. The cost of making photographic or televised reproductions (tapes, films, editing, dubbing, reproduction) continues to increase.
2. A film director and team are often necessary to employ to ensure quality documentary production.
3. Protecting the privacy of informants is difficult when audiovisual materials are used for public research publications.
4. Knowledge and skill of the nurse researcher about audiovisual media is usually limited and poses problems for them to use the equipment and develop research media without often considerable help.
5. In some institutions quick access to research films producers and equipment may be difficult or impossible.
6. If the nurse researcher does not speak the informant's language, it is difficult to obtain an accurate interpretation or analysis of the data.

7. Dealing with fear, distrust, and concerns of informants about the use of the film may pose problems for the researcher, especially related to their cultural beliefs, values, and practices.
8. Obtaining informants and scenes that are representative of the culture may be a problem.
9. The researcher may have difficulty in analyzing films owing to lack of preparation in film and audio modes of analysis.

Despite the foregoing limitations (many related to lack of knowledge and skills by the researcher about the use of methods), audiovisual media remain one of the most accurate and reliable qualitative tools to document attributes and characteristics of phenomena under investigation. However, it is essential that nurse researchers be prepared through research method courses on the use of videotaping and other pictorial methods. With the marked increase in electronic audiovisual technology, new forms of computer recording will be available commercially, and nurse researchers will need to be ready to use audiovisual media for study research.

Artistic or Expressive (Verbal and nonverbal) Types

A great variety of expressive art forms can be used to study health, nursing, and care features. Examples of these methods include music, dancing, role taking, acting, body motions, game playing, freehand drawings, gestures (with and without explanations), and telling of folk and professional myths or stories. Jokes and other forms of oral literature along with oral life history accounts are expressive human modes that merit much study for their health care implications. The use of icons, symbols, and rituals is frequent in nursing and needs to be studied by audiovisual means. Much could be written about the use of each of these different methods for explicit audiovisual research purposes; however, the reader can seek other available sources on each method elsewhere (Pelto, 1970; Findahl & Hoijer, 1981). Most assuredly, the study of fine and modern art, music, and other expressive forms should be tapped and analyzed to identify human care and health meanings. The role of esthetics in the discovery of and knowing nursing phenomena is just beginning to be taken seriously. Such new approaches will require focused study to explicate and analysis expressive art forms with and without audiovisual media.

Testing by Projective and Related Tests

Since the 1920s, anthropologists and psychologists have used a variety of projective tests to study human behavior within and across cultures. Debate continues regarding the purposes of different Westernized "projective" tests, and their interpretation of findings of different cultures in the world. The term "projection" implies an assumption that humans will project their needs, behaviors, and other inclinations in an accurate verbal manner when presented with ambiguous stimuli. This assumption does not tend to be upheld cross-culturally. However, Rorschach tests and Thematic Apperception Tests (TAT) continue to be administered to informants of different cultures. The psychoanalytical viewpoint is often used for the analysis of data, with questionable findings and debates between psychologists and anthropologists regarding their validity and cross-cultural comparability. The culture-bound forms and interpretations of the Rorschach, Holtzman, and other Western tests poses problems in cross-cultural research investigations. The author used Rorschach, TAT, and Holtzman tests, with informants of Western and two non-Western cultures and has found problems in the interpretation of responses to scoring criteria. Moreover, when non-Western informants took the tests, the Western color, size, shape, and contextual interpretations did not fit with nor "make sense" to the informant as the cultural signs and meanings were different. When the modified TAT cognitive picture tests were developed and used by the author with specific cultures, the informant's responses could be understood and were accurate, reliable, and productive to the people. The "emotionally sick or neurotic" Western scoring responses tend to make some cultures appear sick when they really are not. Moreover, the scores and interpretations were at great variance with the New Guinean's responses. For example, the New Guinea people saw an elongated object with a tail on the Rorschach as a sweet potato rather than giving it a sexual connotation. The sweet potato response was an accurate, realistic, and cognitive response, and the sexual perception simply was not there. To remedy the accuracy problem, the author used real or near-life pictures to study people and found that they were readily (and gratefully) able to express their feelings, behaviors, responses, and other life experiences in a meaningful and realistic way to the investigator. Developing a trusting and genuinely interested attitude with informants was important for participation and accurate response to the tests. Moreover, introspective, intuitive, or subjective experience were equally as important as the "projective" responses. Phenomenological, philosophical, and *emic* ethnographic data are also important to consider as clients relate their experiences to the nurse researcher on a variety of different audiovisual media. It appears that different audiovisual material are needed to obtain confluent corroborative findings.

In general, there are many books, articles, and rebuttals regarding the ongoing cross-cultural projective testing methods, modes of analysis, and interpretations. The reader will find much interesting data on the subject in psychological anthropology and elsewhere in the literature, Festinger & Katz, 1953; Henry, 1947; Kaplan, 1955; Klopfer et al., 1970; Lindzey, 1961; Minturn & Lambert, 1965; Pelto, 1967, 1970; Spindler, 1955; Winter, 1964. Health-oriented researchers need to be aware of the tendencies with projective and introjective tests in analyzing and interpreting audiovisual data from an outsider or stranger to get an accurate account of the individual or group. A slanted focus on other subjective or objective responses may limit knowing the people fully. In qualitative research the discovery of meanings, language usage, intuition, feelings, and artistic expressions may come from subjective and intuitive data. Combine subjective and objective methodolical approaches often is wisest to grasp humanistic and holistic life patterns and knowledge of people in our multicultural world.

This overview of the purposes and potential uses of audiovisual media to study nursing and health care phenomena is a brief introduction to what will be a much larger field of research for the future. Nurse researchers and authors have barely tapped the potentials of audiovisual media in discovering care, health, and illness behaviors and other phenomena of nursing. Audiovisual methods appear to have many advantages in providing accurate documentation of qualitative and quantitative research findings and to increase high validity and reliability factors. The use of several different kinds of audiovisual and expressive media should be considered to advance, perfect, and verify nursing knowledge. Unquestionably, documentary audiovisual research is much needed in nursing to explicate the hidden attributes of nursing and to know nursing phenomena more precisely and broadly. Most importantly, audiovisual methods and expressive human modes can help us learn patterned behavior, and patterned behavior related to health and care is the heart of nursing. The nurse of tomorrow must be prepared through graduate education in nursing to know, value, and use photography, games, drawings, television productions, and esthetic expressions as new modes of community and research endeavors. The eyes, ears, and bodily movements of humans are the entreé to knowing the human intellect, motivation, and goals of human beings.

REFERENCES

Birdwhistell, Roy L. *Kinesics and content: Essays on body motion communication.* Philadelphia: University of Pennsylvania Press, 1970.

Bateson, G., & Mead, M. *Balinese charter: A photographic analysis.* New York: New York Academy of Sciences Special Publications, 1942.

Collier, J. Jr. *Visual anthropology: Photography as a research method.* New York: Holt, Rinehart and Winston, 1967.

Findahl, O., and Hoijer, B. Media content and human comprehension. In Rosengren (Ed.), *Advances in content analysis.* Beverly Hills, Calif.: Sage Publications, 1981, pp. 111–131.

Festinger, L., and Katz, D. *Research methods in the behavioral sciences.* New York: Holt, Rinehart and Winston, 1953.

Hall, E. T. *The hidden dimension.* Garden City, N.Y.: Doubleday, 1966.

Henry, W. E. *The thematic apperception technique in the study of culture-personality relations.* Genetic Psychological Monographs, 35, 1947.

Kaplan, B. *A study of Rorschach responses in four cultures.* Cambridge: Peabody Museum of Harvard University Papers, *42*(2), 1955.

Klopfer, B., et al. *Developments in the Rorschach technique.* Vol. 2. *Fields of application.* New York: Harcourt, Brace and World, 1970.

Leininger, M. Personal notes: Audiovisual documentary and teaching films (20) done at University of Washington, Seattle; University of Utah, Salt Lake City; and Wayne State University, Detroit, Michigan, 1960–1983.

Leininger, M. *Reference sources for transcultural health and nursing.* Thorofare, N.J.: Charles B. Slack, 1984.

Lindzey, G. *Projective techniques and cross-cultural research.* New York: Appleton-Century-Crofts, 1961.

Mead, M., and MacGregor, F. C. *Growth and culture: A photographic study of Balinese childhood.* (Based upon photographs by Gregory Bateson.) New York: Putnam, 1951.

Minturn, L., and Lambert, W. W. *Mothers in six cultures.* New York: John Wiley and Sons, 1965.

Pelto, P. J. Psychological anthropology. In B. J. Siegel & A. R. Beals (Eds.), *Biennial Review of Anthropology.* Stanford, Conn.: Stanford University Press, 1967, pp. 140–208.

Pelto, P. J. *Anthropological research: The structure of inquiry.* New York: Harper & Row Publishers, 1970, pp. 98–150.

Sorenson, E. R. and D. C. Gajdusek. The Study of child behavior and development in primitive cultures. Supplement to *Pediatrics.* 37, (No. 1, Part II), 1966.

Spindler, G. *Socio-cultural and psychological processes in Menominee acculturation.* Berkeley, Calif.: University of California Publications in Cultural Sociology 5, 1955.

Winter, W. Recent findings from the application of psychological tests to Bushman. *Psychogram, 6:*42–55, 1964.

21

Reflections on Different Methodologies for the Future of Nursing

Jean Watson

In spite of nursing's tradition of human care and a care stance that is reflected in images and ideals of nursing in the literature, and in spite of nursing's spoken or unspoken values and philosophies of human care, we have yet (as a discipline or a profession) to actualize the care component in our theories, our practice, our science, or our research methodologies (Leininger, 1976; Watson, 1981). Nursing today is in somewhat of a dilemma with respect to where it goes from here in the development, study, and improvement of its knowledge.

Perhaps more than ever before, the nursing profession has some new choices to make, both in practice and in research. Both the professional and scientific communities are beginning to openly acknowledge that an anomaly exists—and has existed for some time—between the values, philosophies, and ideals of nursing and nursing practice; and between nursing theories and discovering the nature of nursing. Consequently there is a disjunction between nursing's subject matter of human care and the methodologies nurses have adopted from the traditional natural sciences and medicine.

A version of this chapter was presented as the keynote address at the Sixth National Caring Conference, University of Texas, Tyler, April 6, 1983.

QUALITATIVE RESEARCH METHODS IN NURSING
ISBN 0-8089-1676-9

343

WHICH PATH TO FOLLOW?

In trying to be "scientific" and advance as a profession and a discipline, nurses have suddenly reached a dilemma in knowledge discovery about nursing phenomena. Two different pathways or directions appear evident: One path is the *continuation path;* the other path will be referred to as an *alternative path* for the future.

The traditional way of nursing has been the *continuation path* which takes the concepts, viewpoints, and techniques of natural sciences and medicine and applies them to the phenomena of nursing and the lived world of human health-illness experiences. This pathway makes certain assumptions about human life and the human nursing care process that are nonhuman. The continuation path has these features: (1) a distinctive epistemology based in empirics (sensual, objective data); (2) a philosophy of human determinism; (3) a biology and psychology of organismic-mechanistic physicalism; (4) an ontology of space versus time; (5) a context of parts with mind, body, and spirit splits; (6) a scientific world view that is closed; (7) a methodology of analysis and validation of repetitive facts (Johnson, 1975).

The continuation path is one in which nurses accept the position that the fundamental world view is "scientific," definitive and settled, and so the major responsibility of contemporary nurse scholars and researchers is to simply add to the increasingly complex store of objective knowledge, using the past "scientific method" of empirics research. This path of continuation is limited by the restricted thinking of the scientific and medical paradigm that labels, categorizes, manipulates, controls, and treats disease; or, if not disease, "patients," and if not patients, "variables." This continuation path for nursing as a profession is marred by medical values, goals, and interventions that are ladden with paternalistic notions which are inconsistent with the nursing care ideology. The continuation path for nursing as discipline is further marred by the ethic of "empirical science" that nursing seemingly adopted in its quest to be scientific (Watson, 1981). The ethic of "science" is recognized by nursing's adherence to a research tradition that is so trapped in the world of objectivity, facts, measurement of smaller and smaller parts, and issues of instrumentality, reliability, validity, and operationality that nursing is in danger of exhausting the meaning, relevance, and understanding of the very values, goals, and actions that support its heritage and ideals. Indeed, if nursing continues along this path, it is in danger of losing its very soul, and in turn losing both its scientific and social contribution to humanity. The continuation path is a path of limited thinking, yielding a limited view of human life, person, nature, and health. This path disengages nursing's ultimate meanings and intuitions from its esthetics, ethics, science, and practice. It can only lead to more and more of less and less. The continuation point is limited by its starting point and by the fundamental scientific and philosophical restrictions it places on human life.

If, on the other hand, we stop at this crossroads and consider anew our direction for the future, we have available to us another path. This *alternative path* is one that can combine and integrate the "science" with the beauty, art, ethics, and esthetics of human-to-human care in nursing. Rather than taking concepts, viewpoints, techniques, and methods from natural sciences and applying them to the phenomenon of caring and the world of human health-illness experience, there is another option. The researcher can go directly to nursing phenomena, i.e., human caring and the lived world of human health-illness experience, and discover what concepts, viewpoints, techniques, and methods emerge as a direct result of investigations (Pickering, 1980). This second alternative opens up new pathways, new visions, and new possibilities about ultimate meanings, intuitions, and values of humans in relation to actual or potential health problems.

This second option is based upon an epistemology that includes metaphysics as well as esthetics and empirics. Such pathfinding is based upon the following features: (1) a philosophy of human freedom, choice, responsibility; a belief in human and cultural spirituality; (2) a biology and psychology of wholism (a nonreducible, nondivisible person interconnected with others and with nature (a mind, body, spirit gestalt); (3) an ontology of time and space; (4) a context of interhuman events, processes, and relationships; (5) a scientific world view that is open; and (6) a method that allows for esthetics, empirics, human values, and process discovery (Johnson, 1975). Such an alternative path can be seen as a return to our "roots" to establish knowledge and practice for the future.

So, rather than choosing the continuation path, wherein human life is depersonalized, defined, objectified, measured, and predicted, nursing can choose to see human life as a gift to be cherished. The latter is a process of wonder, awe, and mystery. Nurses can choose methods that allow for the subjective, inner world of personal meanings to be revealed. Nurse researchers can choose to study the inner world of experiences rather than relying totally on an outer world of observation. Nurses can choose to pursue the private, intimate world of human care, rather than concentrating on the public world of nonhuman cure techniques and outer behavior.

The alternative pathway can expand nurses' thinking, to allow them to become true professionals and scholars and develop new views of what it means to be human, to be a nurse, to be ill, to be healed, and to give and receive human care. Whether nurses see human life one way or the other is the result of different intentional acts; morever, the method that is chosen leads to quite different paths and has different consequences for the practice and science of nursing. The choice has consequences for nursing's contribution to society in the preservation of humanity. For example, I can choose to see another person as a person like myself; however, I could also choose to see him or her as a complex physical-chemical system in which case the person becomes an organism, capable of being reduced, manipulated, measured, and controlled (Laing, 1965).

Whether nurses see another as person or organism will have different consequences for these reasons:

1. A nurse's values, goals, and actions toward an organism are different from a nurse's values, goals, and actions toward a person.
2. Likewise, a nurse's relationship to an organism is different from a nurse's relationship to a person.
3. A nurse's description of organism is different from a nurse's description of person.
4. A nurse's theory of practice with an organism is different from a nurse's theory of practice with person.
5. A nurse's science of an organism is different from a nurse's science of a person.
6. A nurse's method for studying an organism is different from the method for studying a person.

If nurses view the human being as a complex organism or machine, then one loses the human as a person and conversely. Nursing's choice at this crossroads can help decide its future.

Nursing has to choose seriously which path it wants to take for its future, i.e., the continuation path or the alternative path. Nursing's view of science and its view of person are two fundamental issues with different directions that can have a major impact on both past and future.

The continuation path (organism-machine perspective), is in conflict with nurses wanting human experiencing. As the existentialists say, it is like trying to make ice by boiling water (Laing, 1965). A person is not simply an organism or material physical being. A person is a spiritual being, but person is neither purely physical-mental, nor purely spirit. A person is whole body, whole mind, and whole spirit. A person's existence is embodied in experience, in nature, and in the physical world, but a person can also transcend the physical world and nature by controlling it, subduing it, changing it, or living in harmony with it. Nursing's early tradition of human care calls upon us to take the alternative path for our study of human care and other aspects of nursing.

New Methodologies for Nursing Research

In considering new nursing methodologies for study of human caring and other phenomena, the following points merit serious attention:

1. Nurse researchers must continue to openly acknowledge that an anomaly exists between our human subject matter and phenomena of interest, and the traditional natural sciences and medicine. Furthermore, nurses must acknowledge that nursing knowledge and experience are more than the empirics of science. Ethical knowledge (morality concerns); esthetics (art); intuition (personal-subjective, tacit knowledge); and a lived world that is not confined to space, physicalism, or materialism must also be considered. Nursing practice incorporates an inner world of spirituality where the physical may be transcended through human caring and healing.

2. Nursing researchers must object to being dependent upon the concept of causality from natural sciences. Instead, nurses must acknowledge through its methods that there are no clear cause-and-effect relationships to human existence and living.

3. Nurses need to reject the positivism, determinism, and materialism that dominate the practice and science of nursing and adopt an epistemology that expands ways of knowing and incorporates metaphysical concerns of humans and human cultures.

It is the author's position and that of others that nursing is the science and practice of human caring (Leininger, 1976, 1980, 1981, 1984; Watson, 1979, 1981, 1983). Human care is the heart of nursing, and it is different from the practice of other health professionals. Human science is not like the science of other disciplines, and therefore it should not be modeled like other natural science fields.

A focus on the experiencing world of human care in health and illness, as a base for integrating knowledge and theory is a distinctive feature for considering new methodologies for nursing care. There are various ways in which nurses can grasp conceptions of reality in order to see concrete human caring in different situations; that is one goal. Methods that can tap human expressions and symbols and their meaning, and then reflect it, would also be an important goal. Nurses need to consider methodologies that help develop new ways of seeing, of understanding, and of knowing. New ideas and conceptions of reality of caring are needed in order to recognize and facilitate concrete acts of the human care experience along with nonconcretistic behavioral expressions. The author believes that nurse researchers of human care should adopt a methodological perspective that incorporates the following features:

1. A beginning approach using conceptualizations of human care that include scholarly and creative exploration before jumping to definitive definitions and measurement.
2. Clarity about nursing's philosophy of human care and underlying values in order to establish a context for human care studies.
3. Knowledge and application of both general and specific methods to discern the differences and similarities of human care cross-culturally.
4. Critical study of health-illness experiences and human responses to care in order to discern their properties.
5. Identification of descriptive properties and categories of everyday common nurse care activities and human health-illness experiences.
6. Exploration of the human experience of caring within context.

The alternative path methods require an interface between the qualitative and quantitative aspects of the art and science of nursing care; they also link the empirics of science with the esthetics of art, literature, humanities, history, and philosophy, and link the controlled observational world of science to the inner lived world of human experiences. There are at least three general methodological approaches that warrant further consideration by nurse scholars: (1) systematic use of existing "scientific" methods of a qualitative-naturalistic distinction; (2) reconsideration of familiar standard "nursing data" through the application of established qualitative and quantitative analysis techniques; and (3) exploration of paradigms that transcend methodologies. Table 21-1 includes examples of the three methodological approaches that meet the general conditions proposed for the study of human care.

These new foundations for nursing are grounded in a professional human care process that connects with and becomes a part of the lived world of human experiences associated with health and illness.

If the human care process and the person with health-illness experiences are taken as the origin and focus of nursing, researchers can identify their views of "care," "person" and "human experience" with theoretical perspectives and research methodologies. Such perspectives cannot be considered to be qualitatively continuous with the natural science or medical science of the continuation path.

What is at issue is considering methodologies for nursing phenomena, and here, human care is new path wherein nursing acknowledges, in the first and last instance, that nursing cannot accept wholesale the world view of natural sciences and imitate the beliefs, style, procedures, and methods of natural science. Nursing must question the position that the fundamental world view is settled and help to create a new

Table 21-1   *Categories and Examples of Three Methodological Approaches for Nursing Knowledge*

Systematic Use of Existing and New Qualitative Methods:

Phenomenological studies
Ethnomethodological studies
Descriptive studies
Philosophical studies
Existential case studies
Combination qualitative-quantitative studies
Historical research
Participant-observation studies (ethnographic etc.)
Clinical individual studies

Exploration of Paradigm Transcending Methods:

Holographic methods
Literary descriptions
Reflections on original art and its meaning
Photographic documentaries
Literary analysis from literature, e.g., medical, nursing, lay publication, poetry, short stories, fiction, drama, journal reports
Use of music-dance, performing arts, other creative works

Reconsideration of Nursing Data Through Application of Qualitative Analysis Methods and Techniques:

Concept analysis techniques (applied to inductive clinical data)
Content analysis of nursing care plans, process recordings, etc.
Phenomenological analysis of self-report data
Identification of descriptive categories of data

---

world view of subject matter, a new science, and new methods that are credible, meaningful, and valid for knowing human care phenomena.

These proposed methodological considerations are limited only by each nurse researcher's creative thinking and abilities. Nurses can develop "new ways of seeing," new ways of generating theories, and they can direct a wide range of creative research for the future.

Perhaps nursing can learn from the wisdom and experience of Koch (1959), an eminent theoretical scholar in psychology and author. After a 30-year career that was devoted to the exploration of the conditions required for psychology to become a scientific enterprise, he concluded; "Psychology cannot be a coherent science and the end result of the enterprise has been nothing more than a proliferation of pseudo-knowledge." Koch further concluded that "after 100 years of experience, psychology has failed and is lost and it must be discovered anew wherein it is established on a more meaningful philosophical foundation." (Koch, 1959, pp. 64, 66).

Nursing is in danger of similarly becoming lost if nurses do not seriously question the path currently being taken. The status of nursing today has room for more optimism if nurses proceed with caution in emulating the research approach of the natural sciences. Most of all, there is time to discover anew our commitments to human care and establish a more meaningful philosophical foundation from which to proceed. Let us consider seriously our path and make the important choices for the future—lest we fail and lose ourself.

REFERENCES

Johnson, R. *In quest of a new psychology.* New York: Human Science Press, 1975.

Koch, S. Psychology cannot be a coherent science. *Psychology Today,* 1969, *3*(4), 64–66.

Koch, S. (Ed.). *Psychology: a study of science.* New York: McGraw-Hill Book Company, 1959.

Laing, R. *The divided self.* Baltimore: Penguin Book, 1965.

Leininger, M. Caring: The essence and central focus of nursing, *American Nurses' Foundation* (Nursing Research Report), February 1976, *12*(1), 2, 14.

Leininger, M. Caring: A central focus for Nursing and Health Care Services, *Nursing and Health Care,* 1980, *1*(3), 135–143, 176.

Leininger, M. (Ed.) *Caring: An essential human need.* Thorofare, N.J.: Charles B. Slack, 1981.

Leininger, M. *Care: The essence of nursing and health.* Thorofare, N.J.: Charles B. Slack, 1984.

Pickering, M. Introduction to qualitative research methodology. Paper presented at American Speech-Language Hearing Association, Detroit; November, 1980.

Watson, J. *Nursing: The philosophy and science of caring.* Boston: Little, Brown and Company, 1979.

Watson, J. Nursing's scientific quest. *Nursing Outlook,* 1981, *29*(7), 413–416.

Watson, J. Considering new methodologies in study of human caring in nursing. Keynote Address, 6th National Caring Conference, University of Texas, Tyler, April 6, 1983.

Index

360

INDEX